Teaching the Chinese Language Remotely

"What do you do when there is not enough knowledge available to solve the problems you face in challenging educational situations? This book provides an overview of efforts by colleagues around the world to meet the challenges of teaching Chinese remotely during the pandemic, to learn from the experience and to pass this knowledge on to others. Real educational engineers in the truest sense of the word."

—-Dr. Jozef Colpaert, *University of Antwerp, Belgium;*
Editor-in-chief of Computer Assisted Language
Learning (Taylor & Francis) since 2002

Shijuan Liu
Editor

Teaching the Chinese Language Remotely

Global Cases and Perspectives

Editor
Shijuan Liu
Indiana University of Pennsylvania
Indiana, PA, USA

ISBN 978-3-030-87054-6   ISBN 978-3-030-87055-3 (eBook)
https://doi.org/10.1007/978-3-030-87055-3

© The Editor(s) (if applicable) and The Author(s), under exclusive licence to Springer Nature Switzerland AG 2022
This work is subject to copyright. All rights are solely and exclusively licensed by the Publisher, whether the whole or part of the material is concerned, specifically the rights of translation, reprinting, reuse of illustrations, recitation, broadcasting, reproduction on microfilms or in any other physical way, and transmission or information storage and retrieval, electronic adaptation, computer software, or by similar or dissimilar methodology now known or hereafter developed.
The use of general descriptive names, registered names, trademarks, service marks, etc. in this publication does not imply, even in the absence of a specific statement, that such names are exempt from the relevant protective laws and regulations and therefore free for general use.
The publisher, the authors and the editors are safe to assume that the advice and information in this book are believed to be true and accurate at the date of publication. Neither the publisher nor the authors or the editors give a warranty, expressed or implied, with respect to the material contained herein or for any errors or omissions that may have been made. The publisher remains neutral with regard to jurisdictional claims in published maps and institutional affiliations.

Cover illustration: Panther Media GmbH / Alamy Stock Photo

This Palgrave Macmillan imprint is published by the registered company Springer Nature Switzerland AG.
The registered company address is: Gewerbestrasse 11, 6330 Cham, Switzerland

Preface

The Chinese word 危機[1] (*wēi jī*, crisis) was made famous by John F. Kennedy in a speech he gave in 1959 prior to becoming a US president. Kennedy stated that the word "crisis" in written Chinese is composed of two characters—"one represents danger and one represents opportunity." Zimmer (2007) pointed out that this interpretation should also be credited to an unsigned editorial of the *Chinese Recorder*, a long-standing English-language journal for missionaries in China. In its January 1938 issue, it says, "The Chinese term for crisis is 'danger-opportunity' (危機). Without the danger there cannot arise the opportunity" (Vol. LXIX, No. 1, p. 2). Mair (2009) provided a comprehensive explanation of this word from the linguistic perspective and claimed that the above interpretation was a misconception. As a native speaker with over two decades of professional experience teaching the Chinese language and with two academic degrees related to Chinese language, linguistics, and literature in China, I agree with most of Mair's explanations and applaud that he made a convincing argument. However, I still believe that the interpretation of the word by President Kennedy and others (including Dorothy Thompson, a noted journalist, 1940, cited in Zimmer, 2007) is acceptable based on the following considerations. First, while it is true that the meaning of the second character 機 in 危機 is

---

[1] The character 機 was officially simplified as "机" in Mainland China in 1964.

similar to its usage in the word "時機" (meaning *time, occasion*), yet 機 is the same character as used in the words "機會" and "機遇," which do mean *Opportunity*. Besides literal meaning and linguistic explanation, we should allow literary interpretation and creative usage of some words in certain contexts. Second, the paradoxical interpretation of this word has also been acknowledged in Chinese-speaking society and often seen in speeches and texts. For instance, Cao (2017) includes this word in an article title to indicate that opportunities for business lie in crises.

While the interpretation of the Chinese word 危機 may remain controversial, people across different cultures continue to find similar encouragement from a related quote "in every crisis lies an opportunity" (often credited to Albert Einstein). Although one can doubt whether this quote is originally from Einstein, it is unquestionable that the Chinese idiom 祸福相倚[2] (*huò fú xiāng yǐ*, misfortune and fortune interdepend) derives from the verse 祸兮福之所倚, 福兮祸之所伏 (*huò xī fú zhī suǒ yǐ, fú xī huò zhī suǒ fú*) in the sacred ancient Chinese book 道德经 (*Dao De Jing*, also spelled as *Tao-Te Ching*).[3] This expression can be roughly translated into English as *Misfortune is where fortune leans, fortune is where misfortune hides*. Langan-Riekhof and coauthors wrote an article titled "Sometimes the World Needs a Crisis: Turning Challenges Into Opportunities" in 2017. While the contents of their article are insightful, its title might be subjected to criticism in 2020 for indifference to the pain and loss that millions of people suffered in the crisis caused by the COVID-19 pandemic. For those over three-million people who lost their lives during the pandemic,[4] it is a cold fact that they no longer have any chances left for themselves in turning challenges into opportunities in the world they have now left behind. For those of us who remain and who have survived this crisis, it is imperative for us to find fortune from misfortune, if not only for ourselves but for our fellow human beings who no longer have the opportunity to do so. To a certain extent, this book's

---

[2] 祸 (huò, misfortune, disaster) 福 (fú, fortune, blessing) 相 (xiāng, mutually, each other) 倚 (yǐ, lean on, depend).
[3] Many sources can be easily found online on this influential book, such as https://www.britannica.com/topic/Tao-te-Ching.
[4] According to the website of World Health Organization at https://covid19.who.int, as of May 21, 2021, there were more than 3.4 million deaths among more than 164 million confirmed cases.

existence is one type of "fortune" fashioned out of the misfortunes caused by the COVID-19 pandemic, and a silver lining amid the dark clouds that had been hanging over the globe since the beginning of 2020.

Before the pandemic, only a limited number of programs offered Chinese language courses fully online and there was scant research on online Chinese teaching and learning. To help prevent the spread of the COVID-19, educational institutions worldwide, one after another, urgently switched instruction to the remote mode primarily to maintain social distancing, beginning with China in February 2020. Remote teaching and learning via the Internet have therefore become a hot topic in education across many countries. Unsurprisingly, teaching and learning of the Chinese language remotely has also received unprecedented attention from related stakeholders worldwide since the outbreak of COVID-19 as a global health emergency. Zimmerman (2020) suggests turning the challenges caused by the coronavirus into opportunities for doing online-learning experiments. Hodges et al. (2020) insightfully pointed out the differences between "emergency remote teaching (ERT)" and "online learning." Nonetheless, Chinese language instructors and students worldwide have gained valuable experiences in fully online teaching and learning through the emergency caused by the pandemic. Documenting and studying what they did and perceived in managing remote teaching and learning in different countries in 2020 is beneficial not only for practice and research in Chinese language education but also for education in general including online education.

Except for the overview, the first drafts of the 14 other chapters in this book were completed in 2020. These chapters recorded the fresh and first-hand experiences of Chinese language instructors and students from five continents in the early stages of the prolonged pandemic, which makes the book unique and important. To learn lessons from this moment and to put those lessons into practice is not only forward thinking but can serve as a measure of respect to all those that have been lost. Additionally, while the perceptions and practices of the instructors and students being studied probably may have changed since then or possibly may differ in the future, what is reported in these chapters remains valuable for research and practical purposes. In a sense, the book itself is also meaningful as part of our historical human record.

I was thankful that my educational background and experiences led me to this book project. My research interest in online teaching and learning began in the fall semester of 2003 when I took the course, *Online Learning Pedagogy and Evaluation*, taught by Dr. Curtis Bonk for my doctorate in Instructional Systems Technology in the School of Education at Indiana University Bloomington (IUB). During my study and part-time employment at IUB, I completed several research projects and published articles individually (e.g., Liu, 2005) or collaboratively (e.g., Kim et al. 2005) related to online education. I would like to especially thank Dr. Bonk and Dr. Barbara Bichelmeyer for their mentoring and guidance, and thank Dr. Xiaojing Liu for her friendship and support. Most of the empirical studies I conducted during that period were not specifically related to Chinese language teaching and learning, partly because fully online courses and programs were mainly offered at the graduate level concerning professional training (e.g., MBA, nursing, and teacher licensure) at that time. Prior to pursuing my doctorate in the US, I was a full-time faculty member of Renmin University of China, Beijing, for five years (1996–2001), teaching Chinese as an international language to students from all over the world. I owe a debt of gratitude to the four-year Chancellor Fellowship from IUB that supported me to systematically study how to apply instructional technology in Chinese language education and to conduct interdisciplinary research.

Liu (2004) was one of my early endeavors in exploring the use of the Internet in teaching Chinese as a foreign language, in which I used *the ten-level web integration continuum for higher education* as the framework. The first and lowest level was to put the syllabi online; the sixth level was to include substantial and graded activities online. The eighth level was to use the web as an alternate delivery system for residential students, which was comparable to the hybrid/blended mode (some class meetings onsite and some online). The ninth level was to put the entire course on the web for students located anywhere. And the tenth level, the highest level, was at the program level, which is to put series of courses and the entire degree program online. I resumed my full-time teaching of the Chinese language in 2008, and my instructional practice concerning technology integration was mainly at or below the eighth level on this ten-level web integration continuum prior to the pandemic. While many colleagues were anxious about the challenges in needing to switch courses from onsite to online due to the pandemic in March 2020, I was excited to some degree for the unexpected opportunity to practice teaching Chinese fully online. Additionally, in Liu (2018) I intended to provide a comprehensive overview regarding online Chinese teaching and learning based on an invited speech I gave in 2016 at the 2nd Online Chinese Teaching Forum and Workshop (OCTFW2) held by the Michigan State University. In that paper, however, I was unable to include the case of teaching and learning online caused by emergent reasons such as the unforeseen pandemic. To some extent this book can be considered an expansion to what was discussed in that paper.

As another Chinese idiom "独木难成林" (*Dú mù nán chéng lín*) states, one tree (木 *mù*) does not make a forest (林 *lín*). I could not have completed this edited book alone. I have received valuable assistance from so many colleagues. I feel particularly honored in having been able to work closely with 20 outstanding scholar-teachers from 10 countries whose chapters are included in this book. Below are only brief acknowledgments to some people who have contributed to the birth and growth of this book.

My sincere appreciation first goes to Drs. Tianwei Xie, Debao Xu, and Jun Da, who welcomed me to the family of Technology and Chinese Language Teaching (TCLT http://www.tclt.us/) in 2010. Dr. Xu, the founding chair of TCLT, further invited me to serve as the editor for the column of the *Journal of TCLT* since its inaugural issue in December 2010. I have been working closely with Dr. Da, the executive editor of the biannual journal (http://www.tclt.us/journal/), over the past 10 years. The experience I gained from editing journal articles benefited me greatly in this book editing process. I am also thankful for their encouragement when I told them of the book project idea and for further assistance from Dr. Da.

In preparing for the Call for Papers (CFP), I also received suggestions and encouragement from many other colleagues, including Drs. Curtis Bonk, Chengzhi Chu, Shih-chang Hsin, Xinsheng Zhang, Hong Zhan, Chin-Hsi Lin, Rui Zhou, and Mei Huang, and Professors Xia Liang and Weibing Ye. Dr. Jue Wang Szilas further helped distribute the CFP in

Europe. A special thank-you note goes to Dr. Zhengsheng Zhang who always is generous in sharing his professional editing skills when needed.

The chapters included in this book only account for approximately one-quarter of the total articles received. Numerous colleagues were involved in the double-blinded review process. The following list only includes some of them who helped review articles published in this book but not as contributing authors: Drs. Helena Casas Tost, Lijing Shi, Ka Ho Tse, Jun Xu, Chin-Hsi Lin, Chuan Lin, Chenqing Song, and Zilu Jiang, and Professors Jingjing Ji, Xiao Zeng, and Chen Gao. In addition, I would like to thank the following colleagues for their support to this project in various ways: Drs. Yea-Fen Chen, Wayne Wenchao He, Cecilia Chang, Sue-Mei Wu, Gang Liu, Avijit Banerjee, Diane Neubauer, Naraindra Kistamah, Chun Zhang, Jiahang Li, Hsin-hsin Liang, Ninghui Liang, Jianhua Bai, Yi Xu, Yang Zhao, Mairead Harris, and Mr. David Surtasky.

I owe heart-felt gratitude to each of the chapter contributors for their collaboration and dedication in the process, who responded with great patience to multiple requests from me. Each article went through at least two rounds of review and edits for highest possible quality. To make the book a coherent volume, some authors were even asked to rewrite and shift the focus of their original articles. Additionally, nearly each author helped review articles in the book anonymously, and many of them helped read more than one. I would like to specially thank the following colleagues for their tremendous help in the review process: Drs. Shenglan Zhang, Michaela Zahradnikova, Siu-lun Lee, Yue Ma, Ching-Hsuan Wu, Ye Tian, and Michael Li. Dr. Zahradnikova further allowed use of her article as a sample chapter for formatting and indexing.

Of course publication is not possible without a publisher. Ms. Cathy Scott, Senior Editor of Language and Linguistics of Palgrave Macmillan, has patiently answered numerous questions I had, and always in a detailed and timely fashion. Her professional assistance proves that I have found a good home for this book. I am also thankful for the help from Mr. Steven Fassioms and the meticulous work of the production team led by Ms. Divya Anish.

Last, but not least, I want to thank my family members in both China and the United States for their unconditional love and unwavering support. I am especially indebted to my husband, Jian, for taking care of everything else, and to our two boys, Alvin and Kevin, for taking care of themselves, while I have been occupied with my professional work including this book. I would like to conclude the preface with a commemorative note to those who have unfortunately left this world during the pandemic, including my beloved 98-year-old maternal grandmother (though her departure was not due to the coronavirus). I will continue to look for opportunities from crises together with others who remain alive on earth, and this book is just one of our products.

Indiana, PA Shijuan Liu

References

Cao, C. (2017). Crisis? Opportunities! Weiji (Crisis) is the business opportunity found from danger. *The Fortune Business, 6*, 6–8. [曹纯纯(2017). 危机?机遇!---危机就是危险中的商机.《智富时代》第6期, 6–8页].

Hodges, C., Moore, S., Lockee, B., Trust, T., & Bond, A. (2020, March 27). The difference between emergency remote teaching and online learning. *Educause Review*. https://er.educause.edu/articles/2020/3/the-difference-between-emergency-remote-teaching-and-online-learning

Kennedy, J. (1959, April 12). *Remarks of Senator John F. Kennedy, Convocation of the United Negro College Fund*. Indianapolis, IN. https://www.jfklibrary.org/archives/other-resources/john-f-kennedy-speeches/indianapolis-in-19590412

Kim, K. J., Liu, S., & Bonk, C. J. (2005). Online MBA students' perceptions of online learning: Benefits, challenges and suggestions. *Internet and Higher Education, 8*(4), 335–344.

Langan-Riekhof, M., Avanni, A. and Janetti, A. (2017, April 10). *Sometimes the world needs a crisis: Turning challenges into opportunities*. https://www.brookings.edu/research/sometimes-the-world-needs-a-crisis-turning-challenges-into-opportunities/

Liu, S. (2004). Ten levels of integrating the Internet in teaching Chinese as a foreign language. In P. Zhang, T., Xie & J. Xu (Eds.). *The studies on the theory and methodology of the digitalized Chinese teaching to foreigners* (pp. 81–86). Tsinghua University Press.

Liu, S. (2005). Faculty use of technology in online courses. *International Journal of Instructional Technology and Distance Learning, 2*(8). http://www.itdl.org/Journal/Aug_05/article03.htm

Liu, S. (2018). Teaching and learning Chinese language online: What and why? *International Chinese Language Education, 3*(2), 11–26.

Mair, V. (2009). *Danger + opportunity ≠ crisis: How a misunderstanding about Chinese characters has led many astray.* http://pinyin.info/chinese/crisis.html

Zimmer, B. (2007). *Crisis = Danger + Opportunity: The plot thickens.* http://itre.cis.upenn.edu/~myl/languagelog/archives/004343.html

Zimmerman, J. (2020, March 10). Coronavirus and the great online-learning experiment. *Chronicle of Higher Education.* https://www.chronicle.com/article/coronavirus-and-the-great-online-learning-experiment/

Contents

1 An Overview   1
Shijuan Liu

2 Behind the Screen: Lessons Learnt from a Chinese Emergency Remote Teaching Experience in Czech Republic   23
Michaela Zahradnikova

3 Emergency Remote Chinese Language Learning at a German University: Student Perceptions   57
Chin-hui Lin

4 Learning Chinese Online in the Age of COVID-19: The Cases of Two Italian Universities   85
Chiara Romagnoli and Valentina Ornaghi

5 A Blessing in Disguise: The Emergency Remote Teaching of Chinese in University of Cape Town in South Africa   111
Yue Ma

Contents

6 Online Mandarin Language Teaching and Learning During COVID-19 Pandemic at University of Mauritius in Africa 135
   Sharon Too

7 Remote Chinese Language Teaching at the University of Queensland During the COVID-19 Pandemic: A Reflection from Australia 167
   Wenying Jiang

8 Online Chinese Teaching and Learning at Massey University in New Zealand 181
   Michael Li

9 Remote Chinese Teaching and Learning at Japanese Universities During the COVID-19 Pandemic 203
   Kazuko Sunaoka and Satoko Sugie

10 Synchronous Online Language Teaching: A Reflection from Hong Kong 235
   Siu-lun Lee

11 Applying Empathy Theory in Online Chinese Language Education: Examples from a Chinese University 253
   Chunxiang Song

12 From Flipped/Blended to Fully Online: Lessons Learned and Strategies for the Future 269
   Shenglan Zhang

13 Instructors' Social, Cognitive, and Teaching Presences in Emergency Remote Teaching of Chinese Language in the United States: A Qualitative Study   295
Ching-Hsuan Wu and Lizeng Huang

14 Reconfiguration of L2 Chinese Learners' Ecologies of Resources During the COVID-19 Pandemic in China and the US   325
Bing Mu, Chunyan Ma, and Ye Tian

15 Perspectives of Instructors and Students on Online Chinese Teaching and Learning in 2020: Preliminary Findings   349
Shijuan Liu, Yanlin Wang, and Hong Zhan

Index   373

Notes on Contributors

Lizeng Huang (黄力增) is a doctoral student in the Learning Technologies program at The Ohio State University, USA. He also serves as a research associate in the Research Laboratory for Digital Learning. He used to work as a Chinese instructor in the following US institutions: the Department of East Asian Languages, Literatures and Cultures at University of Virginia; the Chinese Flagship Program at Western Kentucky University; and the Chinese Program at Brandeis University. He received his dual Master's Degrees in Teaching Chinese to Speakers of Other Languages from Brandeis University and Minzu University of China. Huang has designed and developed online Chinese courses for multiple language levels at University of Virginia. His current academic interests include technology-enhanced language teaching and learning, student's motivation and engagement in a digital learning environment, and teachers' engagement strategies.

Wenying Jiang (姜文英) is Senior Lecturer in Chinese and the Chinese program coordinator at The University of Queensland, Australia. She has previously taught at the University of Alberta, Canada, and The University of Western Australia, Perth. She is a specialist in applied linguistics, a graduate from Qufu Normal University (B.A. 1988, M.A. 1998), China; University of Luton (M.A. 2001), UK; and The University of Queensland

(Ph.D. 2006), Australia. She taught English at Taishan Medical University in China for more than ten years before switching to teaching Chinese as a foreign language in English-speaking countries such as the UK, Canada, and Australia. She has been writing regularly in the fields of second-language acquisition, language teaching and learning, and computer-assisted language learning (CALL) since 1992. Her monograph *Acquisition of Word Order in Chinese as a Foreign Language* was published in 2009.

Siu-lun Lee (李兆麟) is a senior lecturer in the Yale-China Chinese Language Centre at the Chinese University of Hong Kong, Hong Kong. He is the Head of Cantonese Program Division at the university. He received his M. Phil. in Linguistics from the Chinese University of Hong Kong and his Doctorate in Applied Linguistics from the University of Leicester, UK. He is an experienced curriculum designer and administrator for Chinese language programs at the Chinese University of Hong Kong. He is a trained linguist and has been actively involved in linguistic research and pedagogical research. He has publications, including book chapters and articles in refereed journals, published by international publishers. He also serves as a reviewer and an editorial board member of international journals. His research interests include applied linguistics, Cantonese studies, Chinese linguistics, sociolinguistics, and language teaching pedagogy.

Michael Li (李守纪) is Senior Lecturer in Chinese and the coordinator of the Chinese program in the Chinese program of Massey University, New Zealand. Li received his Master's Degree in Teaching Chinese as a Foreign Language from Nankai University, China, and his Doctorate in Applied Linguistics from University of Waikato, New Zealand. He has gained extensive experience in teaching Chinese as a foreign language since 1999. Before coming to New Zealand, he was a full-time teacher of Teaching Chinese as a Foreign Language at Jinan University, Guangzhou, China. His research output has appeared in publications of a number of peer-reviewed international journals. He is the co-author of one of the best Chinese grammar reference books for L2 learners of Chinese (in its 19th edition). He has been a member of the editorial board of the *Journal of Educational Technology Development and Exchange*.

Chin-hui Lin (林钦惠) is Lecturer in Chinese at the Institute of Asian and African Studies, Humboldt University of Berlin, Germany. She taught Mandarin at Leiden University, Netherlands (2001–2012), and Göttingen University, Germany (2013–2015). She received a Ph.D. in Chinese Linguistics from Leiden University in 2014 and an M.A. in Teaching Chinese as a Foreign Language from National Taiwan Normal University (2003). Her research interests include course design and practice, teacher development, and textbook compilation.

Shijuan Liu (刘士娟) has over two decades of experience in teaching Chinese as a foreign/second language in both China and the USA, and currently works as an associate professor in the Department of Foreign Languages at Indiana University of Pennsylvania, USA. She holds a B.A. in Chinese language and Literature from Hebei Normal University and an M.A. in Modern Chinese from Renmin University of China. She received her Doctorate in Instructional Systems Technology from School of Education, Indiana University Bloomington. Liu has written more than 30 peer-reviewed articles and provided numerous presentations and workshops nationally and internationally on language education, technology integration, and online education. She has been serving as an editor for the *Journal of Technology and Chinese Language Teaching* (JTCLT) since 2010 and is the editor of the JTCLT monograph of *Online Chinese Teaching and Learning in 2020*.

Chunyan Ma (马春燕) is Associate Professor of Linguistics and Applied Linguistics at Zhejiang Sci-Tech University, China. Ma holds a Bachelor's Degree in Teaching Chinese as a Foreign Language and a Master's Degree in Language Testing from Beijing Language and Culture University, and a Ph.D. Degree in Linguistics and Applied Linguistics from Zhejiang University. Ma has over 15 years of experience teaching Chinese as a Foreign Language and has written widely in this field, including a monograph, a volume in a book series, and several peer-reviewed journal articles. She has received over a dozen national grants.

Yue Ma (马跃) is the head and senior lecturer of Chinese Section at School of Languages and Literatures, University of Cape Town, South Africa. He received his Doctorate in Linguistics and Applied Linguistics from Guangdong University of Foreign Studies. He has been involved in teaching Chinese as a foreign/second language since 2000. He served as the deputy dean and an associate professor at the College of Chinese Language and Culture, Jinan University, Guangzhou, where he also served as the deputy director of the International Chinese Programs. He was appointed as the Head and Professor of Chinese at Rhodes University from 2009, before joining University of Cape Town in 2015. His publications include a monograph and book chapters in several other books or co-edited ones, as well as nearly 30 journal publications and a number of peer-reviewed conference presentations.

Bing Mu (慕冰) is Assistant Professor of Chinese and the Intercultural Communicative Competence (ICC) Coordinator in the Department of Modern and Classical Languages and Literatures at the University of Rhode Island, USA. Mu received her Ph.D. in Chinese Language Pedagogy from The Ohio State University in 2018 and worked as a Chinese lecturer at the University of Pennsylvania from 2018 to 2019. Mu's research foci include Chinese language pedagogy, intercultural communication and competence, study abroad, and pedagogical material development. She has written peer-reviewed journal articles and book chapters and is the co-author of *Action! China: A Field Guide to Using Chinese in the Community*, a task-based field guide designed specifically to connect classroom learning with real-life communication in the local community in Chinese study abroad contexts.

Valentina Ornaghi (欧华兰) is a doctoral student at the Italian Institute of Oriental Studies (ISO), Sapienza University of Rome, Italy. She graduated in 2009 with a Master's Degree in Chinese Language from the University of Milan. During her studies, she attended two semesters of Chinese language courses at the National Taiwan Normal University. Since graduation, she has been teaching Chinese language at different levels and in different institutions, such as the Master Degree Course in Languages and Cultures for International Communication and Cooperation at the University of Milan and Milan University's Confucius Institute. She has written two Chinese language teaching materials and a book chapter on the situation of Chinese language teaching in Italy.

Chiara Romagnoli (罗齐亚) is Associate Professor of Chinese in the Department of Foreign Languages, Literatures, and Cultures at Roma Tre University, Italy. She received her doctorate from Sapienza University of Rome in 2007. She regularly attends international conferences and has worked as member of scientific committees for a number of conferences in the past 15 years. She has written widely and her work has appeared in *International Journal of Lexicography*, *Histoire Épistémologie Language*, and *Chinese as a Second Language*.

Chunxiang Song (宋春香) is an associate professor in the School of International Education at China University of Political Science and Law, China. Song received her Doctorate in Literature from Renmin University of China and has nearly ten years of teaching experience in language education. She is a visiting scholar at the School of Chinese as a Second Language, Peking University. She has written more than 30 papers and 4 academic monographs, in which 1 monograph and 2 papers were awarded Beijing Municipal Research Achievement Award. In addition, she has created more than 1500 poems. She is a member of the World Chinese Language Teaching Society and a member of the Chinese Poetry Society.

Satoko Sugie (杉江聡子) is an associate professor in the Tourism Department at Sapporo International University, Japan, where she is in charge of the Chinese language program. She received her Ph.D. in International Media and Communication from Hokkaido University. Her research interests include educational engineering (such as ICT utilization in Chinese language education and instructional design) and applied linguistics (such as intercultural cooperative/collaborative learning, and plurilingualism).

Kazuko Sunaoka (砂岡和子) is Professor Emeritus of Waseda University, Japan, where she worked as Faculty of Political Science and Economics from 1998 to 2017. She is the Advisory Director of the Association for Modernization of Chinese Language Education. She has been conducting various research projects related to distance learning, Chinese computer-assisted language learning (CALL), and was awarded as the top winner of WASEDA e-Teaching Award in 2014.

Ye Tian (田野) is Interim Chinese Program Director and Lecturer in Foreign Languages at the University of Pennsylvania, USA. Previously, he taught Chinese at various institutes, including Harvard University, Middlebury College, and Bucknell University. Tian received his Bachelor's Degree in Teaching Chinese as a Foreign Language and a Master's Degree in Chinese Philology from Beijing Language and Culture University. With a Ph.D. in Education, Society, and Culture from University of California, Riverside, his research is centered on Chinese language education, with an interest in register pedagogy, and a focus on investigating Chinese language education through sociocultural and historical frameworks and methodologies. He has co-authored two textbooks and written multiple articles in peer-reviewed journals.

Sharon Too (杜喜云) is a local Mandarin teacher at Confucius Institute, University of Mauritius, Mauritius, since 2019, responsible for teaching Hanyu Shuiping Kaoshi (HSK) courses level one to level three. She received a Master's Degree in Teaching Chinese to Speakers of Other Languages from East China Normal University under the Confucius Institute Scholarship.

Yanlin Wang (王彦琳) is Assistant Professor of Practice of Chinese, and the director and coordinator of the Chinese Language Program at Texas Tech University, USA. She has 20 years of Chinese language teaching experience at universities in both China and the USA. She created *Chinese Language and Area Studies*, a concentration option for a bachelor's degree, at Texas Tech University. Her research and publications address various issues of computer-assisted foreign language learning, especially Chinese language acquisition and pedagogy.

Ching-Hsuan Wu (吴青璇) is Associate Professor of Applied Linguistics and the Chinese Studies Program Director in the Department of World Languages, Literatures, and Linguistics at West Virginia University, USA. Wu holds Master's Degrees in TESOL and Japanese Pedagogy and a Doctorate Degree in Foreign and Second Language Education from The Ohio State University. Wu has extensive experience directing language programs and teaching teacher education courses at the graduate level and Chinese language courses at the K–16 level across institutions both in the USA and in Taiwan. Wu's research interests include teacher education, second language acquisition, and Chinese pedagogy.

Michaela Zahradnikova (叶爱莲) is an assistant professor in the Department of Asian Studies at Palacký University Olomouc, Czech Republic, where she also organized Summer Schools of Chinese Linguistics. She received her Ph.D. in Teaching Chinese as a Second Language from the National Taiwan Normal University. Her research interests include Chinese character instruction, learning strategies, and educational effectiveness in teaching Chinese as a foreign language.

Hong Zhan (战红) is Professor of Chinese at Embry-Riddle Aeronautical University, Prescott, Arizona, USA. Zhan's research interests include technology applications in teaching and learning foreign languages, teacher training, and foreign language proficiency development via virtual environments. Zhan is serving on the editorial boards for the SITE (Society of Information Technology and Teacher Education) Year Book and Technology and the *Journal of Chinese Language Teaching* (TCLT).

Shenglan Zhang (张胜兰) is an associate professor in the Department of World Languages and Cultures at Iowa State University, USA, where she is the coordinator for the Multi-Section Lower Division Courses in the Chinese Studies Program. She received her Ph.D. in Educational Psychology and Educational Technology from Michigan State University. Her research interests include computer-assisted language learning (CALL), designing for online learning, language teaching pedagogy, and self-regulated learning.

List of Figures

Fig. 1.1	Visualization of class types	5
Fig. 2.1	Challenges of distance learning	41
Fig. 2.2	Positive aspects of distance learning	41
Fig. 3.1	Students' preferences in different teaching modes with regard to future course adjustments	74
Fig. 4.1	Platform and course delivery. (a: strongly agree, b: agree, c: neither agree nor disagree, d: disagree, e: strongly disagree)	100
Fig. 4.2	Possibility to practice speaking and writing	101
Fig. 4.3	Difficulties, advantages, and suggestions	102
Fig. 5.1	Part of the front page of one of our Chinese courses	115
Fig. 5.2	Examples of the types of test and examination questions	116
Fig. 5.3	Humanities students' answers to part of the experience survey questions	119
Fig. 5.4	Humanities students' answers to preparedness for ERT	120
Fig. 5.5	Average scores of Chinese characters dictation by different first-year students	129
Fig. 5.6	Semester scores of 2019 and 2020 classes compared	130
Fig. 6.1	Reasons for absence in online classes	143
Fig. 6.2	Reasons for liking online classes	143
Fig. 6.3	Reasons for disliking online classes	144
Fig. 6.4	Degree of technical skill at the start of online classes and after three months	145
Fig. 6.5	Popularity of different class activities	148

List of Figures

Fig. 6.6	Type of homework assigned	149
Fig. 6.7	Reasons for not submitting homework	149
Fig. 6.8	Students' opinion towards homework	150
Fig. 6.9	Satisfaction towards face-to-face and online class	150
Fig. 7.1	Students' satisfaction level on online teaching during Semester One, 2020	175
Fig. 7.2	Students' preferences to CHIN3000 assessment items	176
Fig. 8.1	Visualization of the new online environments	189
Fig. 8.2	Adaptive Vocabulary Study activity design principle	192
Fig. 9.1	Types of distance teaching mode and temporal development	214
Fig. 11.1	Mind map for Chinese word formation during online lessons	257
Fig. 11.2	An empathic model of online Chinese language education	266
Fig. 12.1	A screen capture of a video for the beginning-level course (left) and one for the intermediate-level course (right)	272
Fig. 14.1	Learners' ecology of resources	328

List of Tables

Table 2.1	Chinese 2 course schedule	29
Table 2.2	Activities—statistically significant correlations ($p < 0.01$)	37
Table 2.3	Anxiety 1—statistically significant correlations ($p < 0.01$)	37
Table 2.4	Anxiety 2—statistically significant correlations ($p < 0.01$)	38
Table 2.5	Attention 1—statistically significant correlations ($p < 0.01$)	38
Table 2.6	Attention 2—statistically significant correlations ($p < 0.01$)	39
Table 2.7	Communication 1—statistically significant correlations ($p < 0.01$)	39
Table 2.8	Communication 2—statistically significant correlations ($p < 0.01$)	40
Table 3.1	Students' opinions on the practicability of different learning components in online/in-class modes	72
Table 5.1	Features of conventional classroom and ERT teaching space compared	122
Table 5.2	Pros and cons of on campus teaching and ERT teaching compared	124
Table 5.3	Semester mean scores of 2019 and 2020 classes compared	129
Table 5.4	T-test result for the grouping comparison	131
Table 6.1	Education system in Mauritius	136
Table 6.2	Demographic information of students surveyed	142
Table 6.3	Students' opinion towards class management, atmosphere and teaching pace	144
Table 6.4	Use of online platforms for different purposes	146

List of Tables

Table 6.5	Use of different Zoom features	147
Table 6.6	Student access and satisfaction towards PowerPoint slides	147
Table 7.1	Core Chinese language acquisition courses at UQ	170
Table 10.1	Language activities used in synchronous online teaching	243
Table 11.1	Language "Re-reporting" models for Chinese language learners	260
Table 11.2	Summary of the "Fun-Language Salon" activities	262
Table 12.1	Distribution of work online and FTF	271
Table 12.2	Comparison in course format before and after transition	282
Table 15.1	Student learning outcomes online versus onsite	356
Table 15.2	Faculty preference(s) for instructional modes	357
Table 15.3	Types of classes taken before the transition	360
Table 15.4	Student's perceptions on comparison of learning online versus onsite	360
Table 15.5	Student's preference(s) for instructional modes	361

1

An Overview

Shijuan Liu

1   Overview of Terms and Definitions

Master Kong (also known as Confucius) said "名不正, 则言不顺" (*if the title is not proper, the speech then will not be smooth*), which was recorded by his students in the book *the Analects* (论语) about 2500 years ago. The expression later generated the idiom 名 (*míng*, name/title) 正 (*zhèng*, proper) 言 (*yán*, speech) 顺 (*shùn*, smooth), which was used to stress the importance of matching the name/title with that to which it actually refers to.[1] The first section of the first chapter of the book begins with explaining the key terms used in the title of the book and chapters in the book.

---

[1] See more on "Rectification of Names" (正名) from Key Concepts in Chinese Thought and Culture (中华思想文化术语) by Foreign Language Teaching and Research Press, https://www.chinesethought.cn/EN/shuyu_show.aspx?shuyu_id=3526.

S. Liu (✉)
Indiana University of Pennsylvania, Indiana, PA, USA
e-mail: sliu@iup.edu

© The Author(s), under exclusive license to Springer Nature Switzerland AG 2022
S. Liu (ed.), *Teaching the Chinese Language Remotely*,
https://doi.org/10.1007/978-3-030-87055-3_1

This book includes "remotely" in its title rather than "distance" or "online" based on the following considerations. Distance Education, as described by Dr. Michael Moore (2003) in the Preface of *Handbook of Distance Education*, "encompasses all forms of learning and teaching in which those who learn and those who teach are for all or most of the time in different locations," and "the idea of using communications technologies to deliver instruction at a distance is at least as old as the invention of universal postal systems at the end of the nineteenth century" (p. ix). The communication technologies used for distance education have evolved from phonograph technology, radio broadcasting, television broadcasting, and now to Internet technology. This book focuses on discussions of teaching and learning with Internet technology in recent years (particularly in 2020). While the contents covered in these chapters fall under the umbrella of distance education, the title of the book does not use the term "distance" because the book does not address much other forms of distance education using older communications technologies.

Another reason to not use *distance* but instead *remote/remotely* is that the word "distance" might lead to an impression that instructors and students were far from each other. In the early stages of distance education when students and instructors relied on a slow postal system to communicate with each other, the distance between them was indeed distant in every sense. The distance between students and instructors remained such even after the development of phone technology in the last century, because the communications and interactions between them were still limited due to the comparatively high cost of phone service and low ownership of phones, including mobile phones. With the emergence and advancement of Internet technology, especially the popularity of recent video conferencing tools represented by Zoom, instructors and students can communicate at any time and see each other easily. While the physical distance between them is still the same as in the past, they now can be connected and see each other virtually within seconds. Hence, in some ways the distance between them is not completely distant. Additional consideration for choosing *remote* is that its collocation in terms like "remote control" alludes to connections between devices or entities that are not physically connected.

Liu (2018) discusses the relationships between "online learning" and "distance learning," and defines online learning as one type of distance learning. Several chapters in this book include "online" in their titles, such as Chaps. 6, 8, 12, and 15. The contents discussed in other chapters also belong to the domain of online teaching and learning. The title of the book uses *remotely* instead of *online* by taking into consideration the argument made by Hodges et al. (2020) about emergency remote teaching (ERT). According to them, ERT "is a temporary shift of instructional delivery to an alternate delivery mode due to crisis circumstances," which is in contrast to "experiences that are planned from the beginning and designed to be online." Some chapters in this book, such as Chaps. 2 and 5, use ERT in their titles based on this very consideration.

While it is true that there are differences between ERT and the regular online teaching, it is still reasonable to consider ERT as part of online teaching and learning in a broad sense, because the communications technologies used for ERT during the COVID-19 pandemic are mainly Internet (online) based technologies. Even though some people may disagree with putting ERT under the umbrella of online teaching and learning, all should agree that ERT belongs to remote teaching and learning. It is worth noting that ERT does not have to be always related to the pandemic but includes other emergency situations. In this book, in addition to discussing the ERT caused by the COVID-19 pandemic, Ma in Chap. 5 mentions the emergency blended teaching in the University of Cape Town in 2015–2017, when onsite instruction was interrupted by unexpected protesters and related radical activities in South Africa. Similarly, Lee in Chap. 10 also describes the urgent shift to synchronous online teaching due to the social incidents in Hong Kong during November 2019.

2 Overview of Remote Chinese Teaching and Learning

The origin of remote Chinese teaching and learning can be traced back to 1900. According to one report published in the May issue of *Phonoscope* in 1900, Dr. John Enicott Gardner of the Chinese Bureau of San Francisco taught two Chinese language classes: one at the University of California and the other at the University of Pennsylvania. He did not travel between San Francisco and Philadelphia but rather lectured by voice alone via phonograph cylinders sent to the students in Philadelphia. Students enrolled in the class at University of Pennsylvania reported they had no difficulty with the phonographic lectures.

Dr. Yuen Ren Chao (赵元任) published the book *A Phonoscope Course in the Chinese National Language* through the Commercial Press of Shanghai in 1925. Bruce (1926) stated that the book accompanied with gramophone records supported students in being able to study with or without a Chinese teacher. Although it is true that students can use a book for learning remotely without the aid of an instructor, these types of learning materials alone are not considered as part of remote teaching because there is no reciprocal instructional activity or feedback from the instructor.

China Radio International (CRI) started to include Chinese language learning programs in its English and Japanese channels in 1962. Xu (1989) noted that from 1973 to 1989, the CRI's Japanese channel offered a series of broadcasts of Chinese language learning for the beginner and intermediate level, which were well received in Japan. Similarly, according to Zheng (2012), Japan's public broadcaster, NHK, started to offer programs on Chinese language learning from the 1980s through both radio and television broadcasting. China Central Television (CCTV) also started to produce a series of programs on Chinese language teaching and learning from the 1990s. Although the hosts of the broadcast language programs can be considered instructors and the listeners as learners, this type of remote teaching and learning is informal and the communication is still mainly one directional, from the instructor to learners.

The wide adoption of the Internet supported by the HTTP and W3 (https://www.w3.org/) opened new and unlimited possibilities for human society since the middle-1990s. The Internet allows humans to teach and learn in various instructional modes. Liu (2018) grouped the instructional modes into three categories: (1) Face to Face (F2F), onsite, (2) Fully online, and (3) Hybrid/blended. These three categories with examples and explanation are visualized by Liu (2020a) in Fig. 1.1, which also includes the continuum of online elements from none to 100% fully online in the three modes.

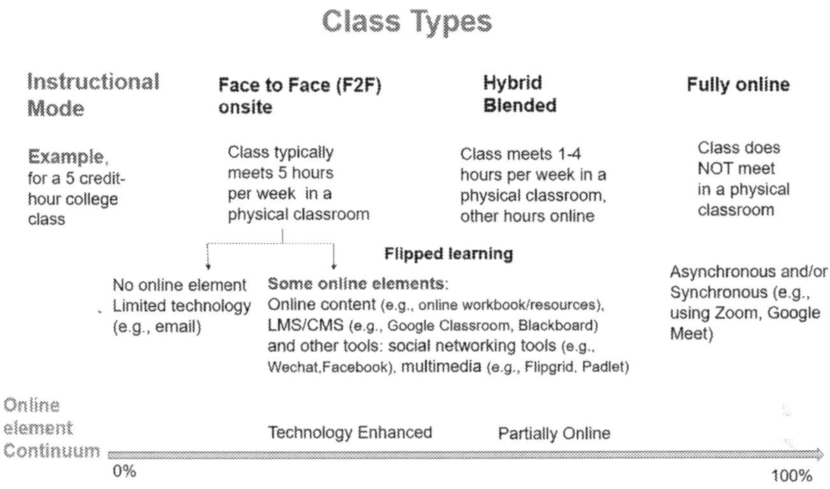

Class Types

Instructional Mode	Face to Face (F2F) onsite	Hybrid Blended	Fully online
Example, for a 5 credit-hour college class	Class typically meets 5 hours per week in a physical classroom	Class meets 1-4 hours per week in a physical classroom, other hours online	Class does NOT meet in a physical classroom

Flipped learning

No online element. Limited technology (e.g., email)

Some online elements: Online content (e.g., online workbook/resources), LMS/CMS (e.g., Google Classroom, Blackboard) and other tools: social networking tools (e.g., Wechat, Facebook), multimedia (e.g., Flipgrid, Padlet)

Asynchronous and/or Synchronous (e.g., using Zoom, Google Meet)

Online element Continuum — Technology Enhanced — Partially Online

0% — 100%

Fig. 1.1 Visualization of class types

In the above three modes, all students studied under the same modality, which means that they all studied onsite, or all fully online, or all in the hybrid/blended mode. There was another mode, as Liu (2016) described, in which most students were taking the class onsite with a subgroup of students participating remotely, typically in a specially equipped classroom with Interactive Television (ITV) technology (see more discussions on the ITV mode from Royal and Bradley (2005)). In the fall of 2020, many institutions in the United States allowed students to choose to take classes onsite and/or online. Such a mode is similar to ITV, but it is more convenient for students on the remote side in that they can take the class through Zoom anywhere with an Internet connection without having to be together in an ITV-equipped classroom. Some called this mode hybrid or blended. Because the term hybrid/blended has also been used to refer to the mode where some sessions of the course are taught in the physical classrooms and some sessions online for all students, Liu (2020b) suggested caution in using the term. Liu (2020c) further elaborated the mode of Hybrid Flexible (HyFlex) coined by Beatty (2019), where students are given flexibility in participating the whole course or part of the course onsite or online.

Before the COVID-19 pandemic, Liu (2016, 2018) summarized the following four categories (with real-life cases for each category) regarding why students chose to take Chinese language classes online: (1) K-12 students taking Chinese online due to lack of teachers in their local schools; (2) traditional college students studying online for convenience; (3) adult (non-traditional) students taking courses online to stay with their daily jobs and families; and (4) others studying online for informal learning due to interest, not as a requirement or for academic credit. Overall, there were a very limited number of students who took Chinese language classes fully online and instructors who taught Chinese entirely online before the pandemic, as confirmed in the findings of the survey study by Liu, Wang, and Zhan (Chap. 15 in this book). Chap. 8 is the only chapter reporting on entirely online Chinese courses offered regularly before the pandemic. Due to the pandemic, schools across the globe moved their instruction online one after another to follow social distancing guidelines in order to mitigate the spread of the virus in their regions in 2020. Chapters in this book all discuss this urgent transition though from various perspectives.

3 Overview of Chapters in the Book

In addition to this Overview chapter, this book includes 14 chapters contributed by 21 authors from 10 countries in 5 continents, which are detailed below.

The order of the 14 chapters is based on the locations of the institutions where the authors work and the topics that the articles addressed. Specifically:

- Three (3) chapters from three countries in **Europe**: Czech Republic, Germany, and Italy;
- Two (2) chapters from two countries in **Africa**: South Africa and Mauritius;
- Two (2) chapters from two countries in **Oceania**: Australia and New Zealand;

- Three (3) chapters from two countries in **Asia**: Japan and China (one from Mainland China and another from Hong Kong);
- Two (2) chapters from United States of **America**: one on practice, and the other on research;
- Two (2) chapters across countries: one across two countries (China and U.S.), and the other across the globe.

The first three chapters are written by (1) Dr. Michaela Zahradnikova from Palacky University in Olomouc, Czech Republic, (2) Dr. Chin-hui Lin from Humboldt-Universität zu Berlin, Germany, and (3) Dr. Chiara Romagnoli from Roma Tre University together with Ms. Valentina Ornaghi from Sapienza University (Rome), Italy. The authors all introduce how Chinese language courses were taught before the pandemic and the subsequent transition to online due to the pandemic. They all surveyed students regarding their experiences and perceptions of taking Chinese language courses remotely. Specifically, Zahradnikova reports findings from surveying 34 students enrolled in a required Chinese language course of the Chinese degree major program; Lin reports findings from responses from 39 students in 3 different Chinese language courses; Romagnoli and Ornaghi report survey responses from students from 2 universities: Roma Tre University (52 students in the first-year Chinese course, 26 students in the second year, and 19 students in the third year) and University of Milan (33 students in the first-year Chinese course and 26 students in the second-year course). In addition to student responses, Zahradnikova reports the results of interviews with three instructors who taught the examined courses.

The next two chapters are from Africa: (1) by Dr. Yue Ma from the University of Cape Town, South Africa, and (2) by Ms. Sharon Too from the Confucius Institute at University of Mauritius (CI-UoM), Mauritius. Ma reports that the Chinese courses were moved online in the middle of the semester after teaching five weeks onsite at the University of Cape Town; he compares the features as well as the pros and cons of teaching onsite and online; he also compares the overall learning outcomes of the first-year Chinese language students and their Chinese character learning in the ERT semester in 2020 with that of regular semester in 2019. Too introduces Chinese language education in Mauritius and the urgent switch of Chinese language courses offered at CI-UoM to remote teaching from March 20, 2020; she reports findings from surveying 125 students and 7 instructors of CI-UoM regarding their experiences, practices, and perspectives.

Chapters 7 and 8 are from Oceania: (1) by Dr. Wenying Jiang from the University of Queensland (UQ), Australia, and (2) by Dr. Michael Li from Massey University, New Zealand. Jiang introduces the Chinese program and the core Chinese language courses offered at UQ, and reports that after teaching three weeks onsite, the Chinese language courses all were transferred to online from week 5 due to the pandemic; she shares the results of student evaluations of the courses and her informal interviews with 35 students enrolled in one of her Chinese language courses. Li introduces the history of Chinese program at the Massey University from 1989 and its distance education option beginning from the early 1990s; he describes the needs for developing new online language learning environments that can be used both for residential and remote students, and details the five components of the new environments and student responses. He also reports the adjustments that the Chinese program made to cope with the COVID-19 pandemic and the plans ahead.

The next three chapters are from Asia: (1) by Professor Kazuko Sunaoka from Waseda University together with Dr. Satoko Sugie from Sapporo International University, Japan, (2) by Dr. Siu-lun Lee from the Chinese University of Hong Kong, and (3) by Dr. Chunxiang Song from the China University of Political Science and Law (CUPSL). The chapter by Sunaoka and Sugie overviews Chinese language education, including review of technology-mediated Chinese language teaching in Japan before the pandemic, and describes how Japanese universities responded to the pandemic and adopted the emergency remote teaching. They also share the major findings summarized from eight surveys (four for instructors and four for students) regarding instructor and student experience and responses to the ERT in 2020, and discuss challenges and strategies for remote teaching and learning in Japan. Lee introduces Chinese language education in Hong Kong before the pandemic including the contingency plan in response to the interruption caused by the social movements in 2019, and shares the voices from students and instructors to a blended learning course developed at the University before the pandemic; he then describes the implementation of changing courses to synchronous remote teaching from February 17, 2020, due to the COVID-19 pandemic. He summarizes activities used for remote synchronous teaching and reported feedback from 52 students and 23 instructors regarding their experiences and expectations. Song introduces the empathy theory and its applications in Chinese language education, and discusses how to apply the theory in online Chinese language education with real examples that she implemented with colleagues in teaching international students majoring in Chinese at CUPSL.

Chapters 12 and 13 are both from the United States of America: (1) by Dr. Shenglan Zhang from Iowa State University and (2) by Dr. Ching-Hsuan Wu from West Virginia University and Mr. Lizeng Huang from the Ohio State University. Zhang describes her design and organization of the original flipped blended courses before the pandemic and how she changed the courses to fully online due to the pandemic in the middle of spring semester of 2020; she also reports feedback from students taking these courses and provides seven suggested strategies for the future. Wu and Huang interviewed five purposively selected instructors teaching the Chinese language at five different colleges/universities to investigate the engagement strategies used by these instructors in their emergency remote teaching; their chapter adopts the Community of Inquiry theory by Garrison and Vaughn (2008) as the framework in analyzing the findings from the following three aspects: social presence, cognitive presence, and teaching presence.

The last two chapters are across countries. Chapter 14 is by Dr. Bing Mu from University of Rhode Island and Dr. Ye Tian from the University of Pennsylvania, U.S.A, together with Dr. Chunyan Ma from Zhejiang Sci-Tech University, China. The three authors examined two Chinese language courses taught at two American universities and one Chinese language course taught at a Chinese university by using the framework they developed on learners' ecology of resources, which includes four key components: Environment, Technological tools, People, and Knowledge and skills. The last chapter, Chap. 15, is by Drs. Shijuan Liu, Yanlin Wang, and Hong Zhan. While these three authors all work in the United States, the two surveys they developed and distributed were targeted to instructors and students across countries regarding their online teaching and learning experiences, practices, and perceptions. Their chapter reports preliminary findings from analysis of responses from 78 instructors teaching in eight countries and 133 students studying in nine countries in 2020 (before June 1).

4 Overview of Key Findings

The 14 chapters address remote Chinese teaching and learning in different countries and continents, and each makes unique contributions to the book. In the meantime, several common themes/findings are found across the chapters. Since readers can read specific findings from individual chapters, this section only highlights four common themes.

(1) *The transition from onsite to online was urgent but not found to be too difficult.*

Each school had to change its instructional mode to the online remote mode urgently due to the unexpected COVID-19 pandemic in 2020. Different schools in different regions made the switch based on the time when the pandemic hit the region. Lin in Chap. 3 mentioned that the outbreak took place in Germany during the month-long break between two semesters and hence the instructors and students had a few weeks to get ready for the transition to begin in April. In the United States, the switch in most schools was made in late March of 2020, which was the middle of the Spring semester (typically from January to early May). Many schools gave the instructors and students a week to prepare for the transition. Jiang in Chap. 7 mentioned the similar arrangement in her university in Australia, that is, instructors and students were given the week (March 16–20, 2020) to prepare for the switch. Zahradnikova in Chap. 2 reported that instructors in her university in Czech Republic only had one weekend to make the transition after three weeks of residential instruction in March.

Although there was time pressure for the transition, many of the Chinese language instructors did not find it too difficult to make the switch. As reported by Wu and Huang (Chap. 13), the five interviewees all stated that their preparation for the ERT was not difficult, and three of them further used "easy and breezy" to describe their experience in making the transition. Several factors are identified below that contributed to the smooth transition.

First, there were already some online elements in onsite Chinese language courses before the pandemic. As illustrated in Fig. 1.1, while the online elements in fully online courses are considered 100%, the online elements in onsite courses are not necessarily zero. There is a continuum on the percentage of online elements that the instructor has integrated into a course. Ma (Chap. 5) describes that before the transition, the Learning/Course Management System (LMS, or CMS) tool was already being adopted, though only some of the features were in practical use (such as for sharing additional resources and making announcements) since the instruction was mainly delivered in physical classrooms. Similarly, Zahradnikova (Chap. 2) states that the Moodle platform (another LMS/CMS) had been used in the Chinese language courses even before the pandemic. Mu, Ma, and Tian (Chap. 14) report similar findings that technological tools were already widely applied to the three Chinese language courses, though mainly as teaching aids before the pandemic. Lin (Chap. 3) mentions that 73.8% of the 42 Chinese language instructors she surveyed from three countries (Austria, Germany, Switzerland) always or often used digital tools in their classroom teaching prior to the pandemic. Jiang (Chap. 7) further details the blended/online activities integrated into different levels of the Chinese language courses that were taught onsite before the pandemic. In Zhang's case (Chap. 12), one-quarter of the course was already online before the transition of the entire course to fully online. The pedagogical and technical skills that the instructors had in integrating those online elements were reported as helpful for them in switching the courses to fully online especially during the emergency.

Second, many instructors received prior training in online teaching from various sources, which also helped with the transition. Liu, Wang, and Zhan (Chap. 15) reported the percentages of different sources from which the instructors received their training, for example, about 30% of the instructor participants received training from the institutions where they work, and another 30% benefited from external workshops/

symposiums/conferences. Lee (Chap. 10) provides detailed information on the trainings that instructors and students received on remote teaching and learning at the university level as well as at the departmental and program levels.

Third, different from designing a completely new online course, many instructors intentionally maintained continuity and minimized the changes during the transition for the ERT in 2020. Wu and Huang (Chap. 13) report that the five interviewed instructors kept comparable course structures when teaching remotely as they had in teaching onsite for students. They also explained that the instructor-student rapport developed before the transition helped them maintain and further built social presence after switching to remote teaching. Zhang (Chap. 12) shares that for the transition she did not change the asynchronous components but only moved in-person meeting sessions of the original blended course to synchronous virtual meetings. Mu et al. (Chap. 14) mention that at the two American universities instructors were advised to make their instruction readily and reliably available to all students in order to keep the online transition as simple as possible for them. This continuity helped make the transition smoother and less interruptive.

(2) *Despite some problems encountered, instructors and students identified several benefits of the remote mode and indicated overall satisfaction.*

Instructors and students encountered some problems when teaching and learning in the remote mode. Technical issues (e.g., the Internet connection) are frequently mentioned across chapters in the book. Another problem identified in some chapters (such as Chaps. 3 and 4) was the reduced interaction reported by some student participants. Lin in Chap. 3 further categorizes student responses into reduced in-class interaction and reduced outside class interaction. It is worth mentioning that according to Jiang in Chap. 7, it is possible to make online teaching and learning interactive and engaging. Similarly, Li in Chap. 8 focuses on developing interactive learning environments online for students.

Concerns about handwriting of Chinese characters in remote environment are discussed in some chapters (e.g., Chaps. 2, 3, and 4). Zahradnikova (Chap. 2) points out that there has been an ongoing discussion about the role of handwriting in learning Chinese in the digital era. Notably, according to Ma (Chap. 5), student mastery of Chinese characters including their handwriting was found better in the ERT semester in 2020 compared to the test results of those students taking the course during regular semester in 2019. According to him, one reason might be because students spent time that would have been dedicated to group work and activities in a more typical F2F semester on learning of the characters during the ERT semester online.

Other identified problems for student online learning include fatigue and loss of attention from sitting in front of the computer the whole day, distraction caused by other electronic devices, and no quiet place at home to connect to online classes.

On the other hand, some benefits are identified for teaching and learning Chinese remotely in some chapters, such as saving commuting time, the comfort of staying home, easy access from anywhere, and the convenience of searching for information during class. According to Lin (Chap. 3), some students further mentioned that the relaxing setting at home had helped them to become more active in online sessions. Similarly, according to Zahradnikova (Chap. 2), the three interviewed instructors reported that they felt even more focused in remote teaching, as they were not distracted in virtual classrooms unlike in physical classrooms by movements and noises of some students.

Chapters in the book report overall satisfaction (at varying degrees) of majorities of students and instructors with their ERT experience and their acknowledgement of the value of the online delivery mode. Liu et al. (Chap. 15) report that more than 60% of student participants were either somewhat satisfied or extremely satisfied with their online Chinese learning experience, with approximately 20% remaining in the middle (neither satisfied nor dissatisfied). Sunaoka and Sugie (Chap. 9) find from four surveys of students in Japan (not limited to Chinese language students) that about 70% of them expressed satisfaction with their remote learning experience in 2020 during the pandemic. Ma (Chap. 5) shares that he and his colleagues of University of Cape Town found that ERT in 2020 did not result in a disaster to the Chinese language courses but rather turned out to be a success story. Similarly, the 23 instructors who participated in the focus group conducted by Lee (Chap. 10) indicated that their synchronous remote teaching experience was positive overall.

(3) *While many instructors and students still like onsite instruction, blended/hybrid instruction is gaining popularity, and fully online is being more accepted.*

Liu et al. (Chap. 15) report that if given a choice, about 59% of the surveyed students would choose face-to-face instruction, about 29% of the students would choose hybrid/blended, and about 10% would choose fully online. Lin (Chap. 3) also finds that more than 50% of the surveyed students supported a blended instructional mode in the future. Too (Chap. 6) reports similar findings. Specifically, 54% of the students advocated blended, 21% preferred mainly face-to-face except during emergencies such as natural disasters or pandemics. While the percentages of students favoring blended/hybrid or fully online may vary in different surveys, it seems clear that after experiencing the fully online instruction during the pandemic, not all students would choose to return to the traditional onsite mode, the only option offered by most of Chinese language programs worldwide prior to the pandemic.

If given a choice, many instructors also would choose other instructional modes. Liu et al. (Chap. 15) find that whereas 38.9% of the surveyed instructors still would choose the face-to-face classroom instruction, 38.2% would choose hybrid/blended and 21.3% for fully online. Additionally, more than 90% of the instructors in their study indicated that they were moderately confident (41.03%), somewhat confident (30.77%), or very confident (19.23%) in teaching courses fully online in the future. Similarly, both Lin (Chap. 3) and Lee (Chap. 10) suggest adopting the hybrid/blended mode for more flexibility for future instruction.

A common tendency between instructors and students is also found in their willingness to teach/take fully online courses in the future. According to Liu et al. (Chap. 15), 74.2% of the surveyed instructors and 68.6% of the surveyed students reported that they were somewhat willing (28.2% vs 25.4%), moderately willing (26.9% vs 27.1%), or very willing (19.2% vs 16.1%) to teach/take future Chinese language courses fully online.

Another notable finding is that students at different levels may have different preferences. For example, Romagnoli and Ornaghi (Chap. 4) find that students with higher Chinese language proficiency level reacted more positively to taking future online courses. Similarly, Sunaoka and Sugie (Chap. 9) note from the four student surveys they analyzed that freshmen (not limited to Chinese language students) showed more negative attitudes toward remote teaching (not limited to Chinese language courses).

(4) *The ERT experience of instructors and students in 2020 is found to have had a positive impact on their Chinese language teaching and learning overall.*

According to Liu et al. (Chap. 15), more than 40% of the surveyed instructors (47.2%) and students (41.2%) chose "use more technology" as one of the impacts on their future Chinese teaching and learning; "better time management" received votes from 22.4% of instructors and 30.9% of students, and "more organized" from 25.6% and 20.6% of instructors and students respectively. Similarly, according to Lin (Chap. 3), 81% of the Chinese language instructors she surveyed from three countries (Austria, Germany, and Switzerland) confirmed that they would consider integrating more digital tools into their future class teaching.

Zahradnikova (Chap. 2) identified several positive aspects from instructors and students' ERT experiences that are transferable, such as submitting assignments online and providing feedback electronically; she also found that both instructors and students would like to continue online consultation (virtual office hours), which provide both groups with more time flexibility and accessibility. Lee (Chap. 10) notes from his analysis of 52 student responses that students were more willing to practice speaking skills online after experiencing synchronous online teaching.

5 Summary and Concluding Remarks

This chapter begins with overviews of the key terms used in the book. Clear definition of terms becomes more important in our present moment when same terms (such as hybrid) are often used to refer to different things. In addition, it is always advisable to be aware that courses under the same instructional mode can be designed and taught in dramatically different ways. For example, after the transition of onsite instruction to online caused by the pandemic in 2020, some instructors used synchronous remote teaching and held the sessions regularly during the regular time slots that the course was originally assigned. At the same institution, there were also instructors who only offered very limited synchronous sessions and students were basically just finishing readings independently and turning in their assignments asynchronously. Student responses to these two different approaches would likely be very different. Jiang (Chap. 7) reports that her students appreciated the synchronous remote sessions provided in the Chinese language courses compared to other courses where they mainly just watched recorded lectures asynchronously. Thus, discussions on instructional modes and related issues (e.g., effectiveness) should always take into consideration the specific contexts and the actual design and delivery of the courses.

The chapter then briefly reviews the history of remote Chinese teaching and learning. Its origin can be dated back to the year 1900 (more than 120 years ago). However, the legacy of remote Chinese teaching and learning in formal settings, where there was an instructor with a group of students, was not much discussed until the late 1990s or early 2000s when Internet technology became increasingly pervasive. In the first two decades of the twenty-first century, there was some practice and research on fully online Chinese language courses at the K-12 level, such as the fully online Chinese courses offered through Michigan Virtual for middle and high school students, and sample research papers published by Li (2019); and at the college level, such as the Chinese courses offered by Open University in the U.K. and empirical studies by Stickler and Shi (2013, 2015). Nonetheless, discussions concerning online Chinese language teaching and learning had received little attention and the number of related studies was also limited prior to the COVID-19 outbreak. The need for ERT during the pandemic made online teaching and learning a "hot topic" and attracted interest from all stakeholders (e.g., instructors, students, administrators, parents, researchers) universally in different regions/countries across the globe throughout 2020.

The 14 chapters in this book altogether provide a comprehensive view of how courses were switched to fully online during the early stages of the pandemic in 2020, and how instructors and students in different parts of the world perceived their experience and related issues based on their still recent memory. The book covers both practice and research. Apart from Chap. 8 (based on eight surveys in Japan), Chap. 13 (based on interviews with five instructors in the United States), and Chap. 15 (based on two surveys of students and instructors from any country/region), the other chapters discuss the specific cases of Chinese language courses taught at 14 universities on 5 continents.

This Overview chapter further outlines each of the following 14 chapters in the book and highlights four themes found across the chapters. Because many of the instructors had integrated various digital technologies into their courses before the pandemic, moving their courses to fully online was found not to be too difficult, though pushed by urgency. After experiencing fully online teaching and learning, instructors, students, and other stakeholders have a better understanding of the advantages and disadvantages of different instructional modes. While many of them still like the F2F mode, majority of instructors and students are now found to be open to fully online instruction and to show their preferences for the blended/hybrid mode, which combines the advantages of both the online and F2F modes. For students who prefer the fully online mode or have to take some or all sessions of courses remotely, the program should consider providing them with such an option. Institutions should also consider providing instructors with more options and flexibility in the design of their courses, such as including some asynchronous or synchronous remote sessions in a F2F course.

In addition to the four findings across chapters, each chapter in the book has made unique contributions. For instance, Jiang (Chap. 7) summarizes six points (such as responding to student emails promptly) from her reflection on her success in teaching courses remotely; Li (Chap. 8) details five components (including community building) for building interactive online environments; Lee (Chap. 10) lists specific activities (such as role playing) for synchronous online teaching; Song (Chap. 11) describes how to apply the empathy theory into online Chinese education with real-world examples from curricular and extracurricular activities; Zhang (Chap. 12) shares seven suggestions for developing flipped online courses.

Aside from helping with the advancement of practice and research in online teaching and learning, the remote teaching and learning experience that instructors and students gained during the ERT is perceived to have had impacts on their future teaching and learning. One impact, as mentioned in the previous section, is that instructors would likely integrate more digital tools in their future teaching. Notably, the importance of instructional technology has received unprecedented attention from all stakeholders, especially in the first half of 2020 when schools all urgently needed to change the mode of instruction from onsite to online. As Liu (2021) points out, in face-to-face classroom settings, technology can be regarded by some traditional instructors as *icing on the cake* (锦上添花), because they can communicate with students face to face and collect homework from students in the physical classroom; Additionally, the instruction and the assessment (quizzes and exams) can also be completed onsite. But during the pandemic the instructor and students were required to maintain social distancing. When the campus is closed, all communications and activities rely on technology out of necessity, from inside and outside classroom instructions, communications between the instructor and the learner, and interactions among learners, to assignment submission and exam administration. Furthermore, for regular online courses, students and instructors usually had a choice. But for ERT due to the pandemic, instructors and students had no other options, and they had to make the technology work, otherwise there would have been no classes. Hence, the role of the technology is so critical that can be described as do-or-die (生死攸关).

In addition to rising to the challenges brought about by the pandemic, educators including Chinese language instructors also found many new opportunities from the crisis. For example, after experiencing teaching fully online, nearly every active Chinese language instructor knows how to attend virtual conferences and use Zoom or other video conferencing technologies. Additionally, thanks to WeChat, the most popular and versatile social networking tool in Chinese society worldwide, Chinese language instructors are able to connect with colleagues in different regions/countries more than ever and to share resources and exchange ideas widely and quickly. Chinese language students also become more familiar with using video conferencing tools, which allow them to practice Chinese with other Chinese speakers more conveniently across campuses, regions and across countries. Chen (2021) shares that because classes were taught online due to the pandemic and the format of online guest lectures has become subsequently widely accepted, she was able to invite more guest speakers with more diverse backgrounds to come to her classes for intercultural exchange to improve student intercultural competence and language proficiency.

Furthermore, due to the pandemic, Chinese language courses for K-12 students in formal and informal settings (e.g., weekend Chinese schools run by parents of heritage learners) are also moving online. Additionally, before the pandemic, nearly all of summer Chinese language programs and camps provided by organizations or individuals were held onsite. In the summer of 2020, these residential programs (including the Middlebury Language School,[2] and the Project Go program[3]) were all offered online. Many of them continued to be online only or provided the online option in the summer of 2021, which allowed them to reach more learners from more regions. Similarly, before the pandemic, only a handful of professional workshops and conferences (such as the Online Chinese Teaching Forum and Workshop (OCTFW)[4] held by Michigan State University) supported presenters and participants in remote attendance. However, since March of 2020, professional conferences were either canceled or switched to fully online. By May 2021, nearly all conferences worldwide have allowed participants to attend remotely. Many regional conferences and workshops that were at usually only open to or

---

[2] Before the pandemic, Middlebury Language School is known for its immersive, intensive, and residential summer instruction. https://www.middlebury.edu/language-schools/languages/chinese.
[3] Project Go, which stands for Global Officer, is a U.S. Department of Defense initiative aimed at "improving the language skills, regional expertise, and intercultural communication skills of future military officers." https://www.rotcprojectgo.org/about-project-go.
[4] The annual OCTFW has been organized by Dr. Jiahang Li and his colleagues at the Confucius Institute of Michigan State University since 2015, which allow presenters and participants to attend the presentations and workshops onsite or online. The first five conferences were held as a mixture (some presenters/participants onsite, some online), Due to the pandemic, the sixth OCFW (OCTFW6) in 2020 was held fully online, https://education.msu.edu/cimsu/conference/6th-forum/.

solely attracted participants from certain geographic regions have become open to anyone interested from anywhere. Additionally, some conferences waived registration fees and were free of charge to everyone, such as the 11th International Conference and Workshops on Technology and Chinese Language Teaching (TCLT11, http://www.tclt.us/tclt11/). The now abundant and convenient professional development opportunities help increase Chinese language instructors' knowledge and skills greatly.

Deusen-Scholl (2021) states that teaching remotely during the pandemic has fundamentally challenged some of our beliefs and assumptions about language teaching with respect to the roles of the textbook, classroom, and assessment. She points out that it would be a "shame" to forget what we have learned from these experiences and to return to the old "normal" after the campus has re-opened. Several chapters of this book also state that the global crisis has actually helped speed up the renovation and innovation of language education including Chinese language education. Finally, as also advocated in the Preface of this book, it is the collective obligation of everyone who has lived through and survived this global crisis to make the best use of what we have experienced and to continually strive for improvement in all aspects of our shared human society including Chinese language education.

References

Beatty, B. J. (2019). Beginnings: Where does hybrid-flexible come from? In B. J. Beatty (Ed.), *Hybrid-Flexible course design*. EdTech Books. https://edtechbooks.org/hyflex/book_intro

Bruce, J. P. (1926). A phonograph course in the Chinese national language. By Yuen Ren Chao, Ph.D. Commercial Press, Shanghai, China. *Bulletin of the School of Oriental and African Studies, 4*(1), 197–200. https://doi.org/10.1017/S0041977X00102836

Chen, X. (2021). *Computer-mediated communication: Strategies and tools to enhance intercultural exchange in online Chinese classrooms*. Presentation given at the at the 11th International Conference and Workshops on Technology and Chinese Language Teaching, hosted by Yale University, via Zoom, May 28–30.

Deusen-Scholl, N. (2021). *Language teaching in a post-communicative and post-pandemic world*. Invited speech given at the 11th International Conference and Workshops on Technology and Chinese Language Teaching, hosted by Yale University, via Zoom, May 28–30.

Garrison, D. R., & Vaughn, N. D. (2008). *Blended learning in higher education: Framework, principles, and guidelines*. Jossey-Bass Publishers.

Hodges, C., Moore, S., Lockee, B., Trust, T., & Bond, A. (2020, March 27). The difference between emergency remote teaching and online learning. *Educause Review*. https://er.educause.edu/articles/2020/3/the-difference-between-emergency-remote-teaching-and-online-learning

Li, J. (2019). Online Chinese program evaluation and quality control. *International Chinese Language Education, 4*(3), 62–70.

Liu, S. (2016). *Teaching Chinese language online: What, when, why, how?* Invited presentation given at the 2nd Online Chinese Teaching Forum and Workshop (OCTFW). Organized by the Confucius Institute of Michigan State University, East Lansing, MI, November 11–12.

Liu, S. (2018). Teaching and learning Chinese language online: What and why? *International Chinese Language Education, 3*(2), 11–26.

Liu, S. (2020a). *Similarities and differences between teaching and learning of the Chinese language online and onsite: Opportunities and challenges*. Invited presentation given at the "A Series of Zoom Presentations on Remote Chinese Teaching", organized by DoIE Chinese Language & Exchange Programs, San Francisco State University, May 29.

Liu, S. (2020b). *Online, remote, hybrid/blended, hyflex: A brief discussion on teaching in different delivery modes*. Invited talk given for the 6th Online Chinese Teaching Forum and Workshop (OCTFW) and Chinese Teachers Association of Michigan Conference. Organized by the Confucius Institute of Michigan State University, via Zoom, November 14.

Liu, S. (2020c). *Hybrid flexible (HyFlex) teaching and learning in the United States*. Invited by Waseda University (Tokyo, Japan) for interested language teachers in Japan, Via Zoom, December 16.

Liu, S. (2021). *Technology and Chinese language teaching since 1900: History and Trends*. Invited speech given at the 11th International Conference and Workshops on Technology and Chinese Language Teaching, hosted by Yale University, via Zoom, May 28–30.

Moore, M. (2003). Preface. In M. Moore & W. Anderson (Eds.), *Handbook of distance education* (pp. ix–xii). Lawrence Erlbaum Associates.

Royal, K., & Bradley, K. (2005). *Interactive Television (ITV) courses and students' satisfaction.* http://citeseerx.ist.psu.edu/viewdoc/download?doi=10.1.1.499.2652&rep=rep1&type=pdf

Stickler, U., & Shi, L. (2013). Supporting Chinese speaking skills online. *System, 41*(1), 50–69.

Stickler, U., & Shi, L. (2015). Eye movements of online Chinese learners. *CALICO, 32*(1), 52–81.

Xu, Y. (1989). The Chinese broadcasting of teaching Chinese as a foreign language. *Shijie Hanyu Jiaoxue, 4*, 225–230. [徐永秀 中国的对外广播汉语教学, 世界汉语教学, 1989 年第四期 (总第10期) 225–230].

Zheng, Y. (2012). *Introduction to educational technologies for teaching Chinese as a foreign language.* The Commercial Press. [郑艳群 (2012). 对外汉语教育技术概论. 北京: 商务印书馆].

2

Behind the Screen: Lessons Learnt from a Chinese Emergency Remote Teaching Experience in Czech Republic

Michaela Zahradnikova

1 Introduction

In March 2020, all schools were closed in the Czech Republic due to the COVID-19 pandemic. Education in the country was delivered using distance learning technology: either synchronous or asynchronous. The aim of this study is to describe the "emergency remote teaching (ERT)" experience with one Chinese language class as it changed to an online delivery format. This study was conducted in June 2020, when little evaluative research had been published about the ERT experiences. It does not intend to provide an in-depth empirical analysis, but rather to identify the challenges and outcomes of ERT, with the hope of understanding what conditions and strategies could improve the education process in case of repeated school closures.

M. Zahradnikova (✉)
Palacky University, Olomouc, Czech Republic
e-mail: michaela.zahradnikova@upol.cz

© The Author(s), under exclusive license to Springer Nature Switzerland AG 2022
S. Liu (ed.), *Teaching the Chinese Language Remotely*,
https://doi.org/10.1007/978-3-030-87055-3_2

2 Literature Review

2.1 Distance Language Learning

Distance language learning (DLL) has been gradually developing for the past thirty years with significant expansion over the last decade (White, 2006). Distance education was defined by Keegan (1996) as education in which technical media is used to provide two-way communication between a teacher and learner who are separated in space or time, and where the educational organization maintains an influence on learning materials as well as student support services, but learning groups are mostly absent. Technological development has contributed to a continuously growing body of terminology for delivery formats, including synchronous and asynchronous online learning, computer assisted learning, distributed learning, hybrid or blended learning, mobile learning, virtual learning, multimodal learning, teleconferencing, etc. While face-to-face (F2F) education is classroom-based and mostly teacher-orchestrated, DLL is promoted as flexible, convenient, and self-paced, with personalized learning facilitating learner autonomy and automated feedback (Jaggars, 2014; Gacs et al., 2020). On the negative side, research results reported several frequently occurring problems, such as feelings of social isolation due to the lack of contact with teachers and peers (Harker & Koutsantoni, 2005; Hurd, 2005), a lack of immediate feedback (Kan & McCormick, 2012), a lack of interaction and speaking opportunities (Kan & McCormick, 2012), stress from using new technologies (Ushida, 2005), and insufficient instructor training (Wang et al., 2010). In addition, issues of language anxiety (Conrad, 2002; Hurd, 2005; Russell, 2020) and maintaining attention during online lectures (Hollis & Was, 2016; Szpunar et al., 2013) were also discussed in the literature.

The COVID-19 pandemic of 2020 introduced a new extension in the field of distance education called "emergency remote teaching." This term was proposed by Hodges et al. (2020) and defined as "a temporary shift of instructional delivery to an alternate delivery mode" which "involves the use of fully remote teaching solutions for instruction or education that would otherwise be delivered face-to-face or as blended or hybrid courses and that will return to that format once the crisis or emergency has abated" (para.13). Gacs et al. (2020) pointed out that, while courses switched to remote teaching were primarily designed as F2F courses, "planned online education has an intentional commitment and buy-in from most stakeholders, carefully vetted resources, faculty training and collaborations between subject matter experts and instructional designers and technology specialists from the beginning" (p. 382). Therefore, online courses delivered under emergency situations should be approached differently than planned online teaching, both in terms of research and evaluation (Gacs et al., 2020; Hodges et al., 2020).

2.2 Chinese Distance Learning

Foreign language classes at the university level have been gradually shifting from fully F2F classes to technology-facilitated instruction over the last decade, with courses of Chinese language being no exception (Liu, 2018). Among the three types of interaction defined by Moore (1989), learner-content online interaction is considered crucial in distance learning (Xiao, 2017). PowerPoint Presentations (PPTs) or interactive boards are used in class, and course materials, presentations, and supplementary multimedia materials are shared through online course management systems (e.g. Moodle, Blackboard, Canvas). Students are asked to complete online tests, to record their speech and submit assignments online. Out-of-class learning activities include using mobile apps with flashcards, digital dictionaries, podcasts, games, and videos. In learner-learner interaction and learner-instructor interaction, email, chat, discussion boards, or social media are used to share information, negotiate, and provide feedback (Sher, 2009). Language education has become interconnected with the online world.

The last decade has brought countless studies on Chinese distance learning, including general guides based on meta-analysis (Zhang, 2014), case studies (e.g. Cheng, 2011; Da, 2011), as well as studies on specific aspects of distance education. These aspects include, for example, online forums (Kan & McCormick, 2012), mobile phone-assisted learning of Chinese Characters (Kan et al., 2018), course material development

(Kubler, 2017), teacher training (Hsin et al., 2017; Tseng, 2017), and blended learning (Hughes et al., 2017). Experiments with using Moodle (Chen, 2013; Hon, 2013), videoconferencing (Wang, 2004), and chats in language instruction (Jin, 2018; Qi & Wang, 2018; Sunaoka, 2012) have also been studied. For further details, see the overviews by Bourgerie (2003), Yao (2009), or Zhang (2019).

Apart from the general challenges of learning a foreign language regarding the aspects of pronunciation, vocabulary, grammar, and culture, Western learners of Chinese struggle most with the tonal phonetic system and the logographic script (Shen, 2004; Xing, 2006; Hu, 2010). While mastering the phonetic system is usually the objective of the beginners' course, memorizing new Chinese characters remains a lifelong challenge. In an online learning environment, Chinese character instruction is a widely discussed topic (Kan, 2013), as it not only requires students to foster a new skill, but it also demands computer-competency. One study by Sun (2011) compared a campus-based group with an online learning group. While the learning progress of the online group depended on individual conscientiousness in order to follow the teaching materials, the campus-based group had "the benefit of observing how characters are written on the "blackboard" stroke-by-stroke on a daily basis" (Sun, 2011, p. 434). Data showed that the online group showed lower performance in both Chinese character reading and writing. There has been an ongoing discussion about the necessity of handwriting itself. Some researchers have argued in favor of typing (Allen, 2008), while other studies emphasized the importance of handwriting (e.g. Longcamp et al., 2006; Tan et al., 2005). Typing Chinese can be demanding also in terms of IT competency—installing Chinese fonts, setting up Chinese input, converting between Pinyin and characters, and so on. (Kan & McCormick, 2012). Stickler and Shi (2013) also noticed that for online multimodal programs for beginners the online environment can be challenging for less computer-competent learners, because "task density can be overwhelming, as can the shifting between different modes and media" (p. 65). In any case, "teaching Chinese characters online adds another level of difficulties and requires extra technology and digital tools to facilitate" (Wang & East, 2020, p. 11).

2.3 DLL and ERT Research

DLL has been under persistent pressure to deliver evidence of its efficacy. Comparison studies have shown no statistically significant differences between learning outcomes of online courses and F2F courses (e.g. Blake et al., 2008; Goertler & Gacs, 2018; Green & Youngs, 2001), or have been slightly in favor of online courses (e.g. Means et al., 2009). However, as Blake (2013) remarked, to a significant degree the success of a class "owe(s) more to the individual instructor talents and limitations and the quality of the learning materials they use, rather than the format itself" (p. 139).

In Chinese ERT research, little data was available by June 2020, when this research was conducted. Wang and East (2020) described changes in one large-scale F2F beginner Chinese class curriculum which was transferred to a hybrid course format during the COVID-19 pandemic in New Zealand. Technical issues, the need for an equity-minded approach, as well as vital changes in assessment were reported and discussed. Regarding Chinese-specific issues, they observed that handwriting activities in character-based curriculums are technically challenging when implemented online and called for "more effective teaching approaches and technologies" (p. 12). The lack of communication with teachers and peers was identified as another shortcoming.

Although ongoing research has provided valuable data about Chinese distance learning, there have been several reasons why ERT teachers were not able to exploit its full potential during the COVID-19 pandemic. First, time pressure forced teachers to run Chinese classes in a remote format with very little time for preparation or training. Instead of receiving training or education in online teaching, teachers were overloaded with the task of transferring their class content online. The abrupt school closure favored quick and effective solutions. As Gacs et al. (2020) remarked, "short term perspective and sacrifices have to be made to guarantee a rapid response with realistically achievable, but modified, outcomes" (p. 383). Second, the curricula of the interrupted classes were limited by study program requirements and could not be changed due to the new temporally sensitive format. Adjustments were therefore limited to activity types rather than content. Third, access to technological resources hindered the process. As neither students nor teachers joined online learning voluntarily, many of them struggled with technical issues, such as Internet connection or inadequate equipment (Wang & East, 2020). Fourth, delivery formats were selected in haste, and temporary solutions were taken to create a connection with minimum resources. For synchronous courses, Zoom, WeChat, Blackboard, Skype, Canvas, Google Hangouts, or similar platforms were used (Liu et al., 2020). In addition, the influence of affective factors on learning should be considered (Russell, 2020). The contextual factors of the pandemic—such as abrupt curfews, enormous stress, and an uncertain future—called for a "less is more" approach. All these factors put limits on the direct application of prior DLL research outcomes and the call for a global evaluation of the ERT experience.

Since the development of the pandemic situation might require repeated transfers of regular university courses to distance delivery, primary experience with ERT situations provides language instructors with a unique opportunity to evaluate the experience and adjust their course settings according to scientific findings.

3 Methods

A mixed-methods approach was employed in this study, including interviews with course instructors and an online survey for the students. Research was conducted from June to July 2020. Participants included all three Chinese language group instructors of a *Chinese 2* course and forty participants of a *Chinese 2* course, first-year students of the Chinese degree program at Palacky University, in the Czech Republic. All student participants had successfully completed the first comprehensive Chinese course *Chinese 1* in the fall semester 2019/2020.

The following research questions were explored:

1. How did students perceive online instruction during the ERT period?
2. What challenges did instructors and students face?
3. Are there any positive outcomes of ERT? Are there any techniques transferable to F2F teaching?

3.1 Context

For the purposes of this study, the Chinese language course with the largest and most homogenous group of students was selected—a compulsory comprehensive course: *Chinese 2* for students in the Chinese degree major program. The *Chinese 2* course was transferred to emergency remote teaching after three weeks of residential instruction in March 2020 for the remaining nine weeks of the semester and the final examinations. The student participants were advanced beginners in the second semester of their studies. At the beginning of the semester, forty students were divided into three groups. Classes were conducted daily. On Monday and Wednesday, there was a 45-minute class with a Czech instructor (Chinese language teacher, a native speaker of Czech) focused on vocabulary, grammar, and Chinese characters. On Tuesday and Thursday, the content of the previous day was practiced during a 90-minute conversation class with Chinese instructor (Chinese language teacher from Taiwan, a native speaker of Chinese). On Friday, students spent 45 minutes with the Czech instructor doing a weekly review followed by a weekly quiz. During the week, students also attended a 30-minute two-to-one conversational tutorial with a Chinese tutor (native speaker of Chinese) to practice conversational topics in a more intensive manner (Table 2.1).

The sudden transformation forced instructors to switch to distance teaching over the course of one weekend. Since the university was not prepared for the transition, instructors were not provided with any immediate IT support or videoconferencing platform subscriptions.

All in-class instruction was transferred to a synchronous online format. The content of the class curriculum was not changed, as it was crucial to reach the learning goals of the original F2F course so the students could

Table 2.1 Chinese 2 course schedule

Monday, Wednesday	45 minutes	Czech instructor	Vocabulary, grammar, characters
Tuesday, Thursday	90 minutes	Chinese instructor	Conversation
Friday	45 minutes	Czech instructor	Review, weekly quiz
Unspecified	30 minutes	Chinese tutor	Two-to-one conversation

smoothly enter the second-year language course in the following semester. Synchronous Chinese instruction began running through free Skype call sessions, which at that time was the only provider assuring free access for the entire class. Due to unstable Internet connections and low-quality transmission reported by students during videoconferences, the instructors and the students had to rely on audio conferencing only. Despite technical limitations, instructors were determined to continue synchronous sessions rather than transferring fully to asynchronous teaching for the following reasons. Firstly, students had only completed one semester of Chinese instruction and their pronunciation still required immediate correction. Secondly, the comprehensive language classes were designed to be communicative rather than descriptive, requiring daily practice of the target language. Thirdly, monitoring students' progress without live interaction would be more challenging for teachers.

Students had been using the Moodle course management system as the university's main course management tool even before the COVID-19 pandemic. During distance teaching, in addition to their usual access to teaching materials, students were also asked to submit daily handwritten assignments and review corrected homework later through Moodle. Weekly quizzes were also transferred to the Moodle. Since students had not been trained in typing Chinese, for the first six weeks of the ERT weekly quizzes focused on vocabulary, grammar, and Chinese character recognition skills. Based on student feedback, timed, handwritten tests were adopted later.

3.2 Data Collection

Teacher Interviews

All *Chinese 2* course group instructors, including the two Czech instructors and one Chinese instructor, participated in this study with a semi-structured interview. None of the instructors had any previous experience with online teaching. Interviews were conducted online at the end of the semester. Each interview lasted for an hour and was recorded with the instructors' consent. Each interview consisted of fourteen open-ended questions (see Appendix 1), which were drawn from the literature and included both general online learning challenges and Chinese-specific online learning issues: Chinese character instruction, pronunciation, attention, anxiety, in-class activities, assessment, communication, and technical issues. Recordings were reviewed and key ideas for each question were noted to identify common themes across the data sets.

Student Online Survey

Hurd (2000) pointed out that students' voices should be also heard, and evaluators should "endeavour to find out as much as we can about our learners in order to be in a position to target their needs and respond appropriately" (p. 78). After finishing the full semester, as well as final exams, students were asked to complete an anonymous and voluntary online survey. Out of the forty students enrolled in the course, thirty-four valid responses were collected, which represents an 85% response rate. Students were surveyed with thirty-six Likert-type questions covering the following topics: learning pronunciation, learning Chinese characters, language practice, attention, communication, and assessment. Several course-specific topics, which emerged during the teacher interview analysis, were added to the survey. These included questions about online consultations through Skype, online quizzes, and the online submissions of assignments. Each of the topics was followed by an open-ended descriptive question. Three general open-ended questions were asked about the challenges and positive aspects of remote learning. For the survey questions, see Appendix 2.

4   Results

4.1   Teacher Interviews

The interviews explored challenges faced by the instructors during the ERT period, the decisions they had to make, and both the expected and unexpected outcomes of the courses. There were no distinctive differences between the responses of instructors, which might be due to very intensive communication between the teachers throughout the semester. To maintain identical learning conditions for all groups of the course, all decisions on assessment and course requirements were made collectively. The following topics are listed alphabetically:

Activities: Instructors did not feel limited in terms of teaching activities. The only activities which could not be implemented were pair work, group work, and games. Although some of the instructors tried to make instruction more interactive, after several trials they decided not to integrate extra digital resources or online games into synchronous sessions. Most of these activities required students to open external websites, reconnect, or install supplementary software, resulting in more time spent on explanations and troubleshooting than the activity itself. The Chinese instructor reported using more animations and pictures on PowerPoint presentations (PPTs) to help students understand new vocabulary without translating the meaning to the Czech language.

Anxiety: The instructors did not report any feelings of anxiety. Teaching remotely was considered more relaxed in terms of saving time spent on commuting, enjoying the comfort of "being home," and "staying in pajamas" with a cup of coffee.

Assessment: The curriculum of *Chinese 2* was character-based and required students to develop Chinese handwriting skills, which were then demonstrated in both assignments and quizzes. Since the beginning of their studies, students had been accustomed to weekly quizzes, including short dictations in characters. As scores on weekly quizzes were an important part of the final score, during the ERT period dictations were not included, to avoid technical issues which would have a negative impact on students' final scores. Students continued with handwritten assignments, but the quizzes only tested character recognition and reading skills. After several weeks of ERT, instructors received feedback from students calling for handwritten quizzes. Students complained that online testing did not require them to foster an active knowledge of characters and they felt they were falling behind. For the last three weeks, students were therefore asked to complete weekly quizzes by hand. The contents of the quizzes were posted in the course management system (Moodle) with time restricted access. Students were asked to complete the quiz on a separate piece of paper, take a picture of the quiz via mobile phone, and upload it into Moodle within a given time limit.

The final assessment included two steps. Firstly, students took a handwritten test focused on grammar and vocabulary. The format of the written test was identical with the last three handwritten quizzes. Secondly, after the successful completion of the test, each student took an individual oral exam via Skype videoconferencing focusing on conversational skills. The content of the oral exam is identical with the in-person exam.

Attention: Instructors themselves did not experience trouble with maintaining attention. They even felt more focused, as they were not distracted by classroom noises and movements around the classroom. They assumed, however, that maintaining attention might be difficult for some students, since they felt students were tired and responding slowly toward the end of the class. On the other hand, one of the teachers noticed that "the fact that students could not see who I was looking at (as in the classroom), kept them more alert."

Chinese character instruction: Stroke order instruction was replaced by Chinese character animations in PPTs, and additional information on character components was explained orally. For the notes and demonstration, instructors used PPTs instead of a blackboard. Typing characters was relatively new to most of the students. Practicing handwriting skills became a fully homebound activity. The instructors were initially inclined to give more homework assignments to the students than usual, but once other courses which the student participants were taking began to compensate for the lack of instruction with homework assignments (reports, readings, etc.), they found students were overloaded and thus reduced the amount of homework.

Communication with students: Instructors described students as generally shy, quiet, and tending to avoid eye contact in F2F classes, which also remained the case during remote teaching. Instructors experienced, however, more intensive out-of-class communication with students through Skype chat than usual. This aspect was attributed to online chat being less official than email, as well as more comfortable and less stressful than meeting in person. One of the teachers commented:

Students felt more comfortable reaching us through Skype. It is also not as official as writing an email which is structured, you need to start with a salutation and some introductory sentence ... I would like to keep it in the future, it is undoubtedly the greatest long-term contribution (of teaching online). Some might think that this type communication could become intrusive, but it definitely did not.

Communication was initiated by both sides. Apart from mistakes in assignments and quizzes, topics of learning strategies and students' well-being were discussed. The unpredictable pandemic situation created a wave of empathy on both sides, which was often an incentive for communication—instructors expressed more intensive interest about students, for example, in case of absence or an unexpected drop in performance; students expressed more gratitude and appreciation. Topics related to Chinese-specific learning strategies were also discussed: how to memorize characters, and how to review more effectively.

Corrective feedback: Instructors did not feel a need to adjust most of their corrective feedback during synchronous online sessions. The only exception was feedback based on body language, which could not be used without video transmission. They also felt that it was easier to identify and correct mistakes which would have been otherwise lost in the hum of the classroom. They described their corrective feedback as more frequent and more individualized. Being behind the screen, listening to students one by one, and not seeing the whole group felt more like one-on-one instruction to them. As for homework correction, assignments were submitted as .pdf or .jpg files into Moodle and corrected through editing programs, which was rather time demanding.

Teaching challenges and outcomes: Instructors identified the following two challenges of ERT: student-student interaction (e.g. pair work, group work) was limited. The teachers' control over the class was limited while conducting the course without videoconferencing, which affected the teachers' ability to help students maintain attention. At the beginning of the teaching period, instructors had to establish rules for maintaining class discipline (such as reminding students to connect on time and react promptly). On the positive side, staying behind the screen allowed instructors to call on students more evenly, as they could keep notes according to the course attendance sheet. It was also easier to make notes on students' mistakes and prepare more individualized follow-up interventions.

Technical issues: Over the entire ERT period, instructors felt that students were experiencing anxiety related to unstable Internet connections and technical issues with microphones and headphones. To eliminate these problems, instructors were forced to switch from videoconferencing to audio conferencing. Losing visual contact brought new challenges: it was difficult to correct the pronunciation of beginning learners without students being able to see the instructor's mouth. Also, visual feedback had helped instructors notice when students did not understand or had difficulties maintaining attention. Switching to videoconferencing would therefore be preferred by instructors, in order to maintain better control of the class. On the positive side, instructors appreciated the possibility to quickly and easily type into PPTs, which would have otherwise been time demanding.

Time management: Instructors had the feeling that online sessions were more intensive and timesaving. In comparison to regular classes, they did not experience the same time pressure as there were no time delays caused by late arriving students, moving around the classroom, giving out handouts, etc. One of the teachers noted: "I think we used the time more effectively. In F2F class, we had a hard time finishing on time. We also saved time by not writing on the blackboard, but I don't think students missed it all that much."

In general, instructors felt positive about their ERT experience and mentioned that the following techniques might be transferable to F2F education:

* online submission and correction of handwritten assignments
* maintaining an informal digital communication channel or chat group with students

The following issues were marked, however, as drawbacks calling for adjustment:

* lack of pressure to foster handwriting skills

- preference of videoconferencing
- need for instruction on learning strategies

4.2 Student Online Survey

The aim of the online survey was to understand students' perspectives on the ERT experience. Kendall's tau, a correlation measure for ordinal data, was computed to identify statistically significant correlations between pairs of data sets. All the presented correlations are significant under 99% confidence level ($p < 0.01$); only moderate ($r_\tau > 0.3$) and strong ($r_\tau > 0.5$) correlations are discussed (Kraska-Miller, 2014). Given the relatively small number of participants (n = 34), results should be interpreted with caution, as will be mentioned in study limitations. The topics are listed alphabetically, and percentage figures in brackets refer to the number of received positive responses to the question in general, not in relation to other questions.

Activities: In-class activities, which are non-transferable to the online mode, included pair work (Q13) and group work (Q14). Thirty-two percent and 50% of students respectively indicated they were missing these activities in the online instruction. The data indicate a moderate positive correlation between missing pair/group work and better attention in class than online (Q17, 62%), missing personal contact with the instructor (Q23, 79%) and peers (Q24, 56%), and missing the chance to watch the instructor's mouth for pronunciation cues (Q3, 59%) (Table 2.2).

Anxiety: For 26% of students, learning online was more stressful than in class (Q26). These students were more likely to struggle with attention (Q17, 62%), the impossibility of practicing handwriting on the blackboard (Q6, 59%; Q7, 38%; Q10, 50%), and the lack of personal contact with the teacher and peers (Q23, 56%; Q24, 79%) (Table 2.3).

Students who felt more comfortable behind the screen than in the classroom (Q27, 24%) were more likely to feel they made adequate progress in pronunciation (Q5, 50%), to have less problems with attention (Q16, 71%), and find the amount of speaking opportunities sufficient (Q20, 79%). They were also more likely to appreciate online

2 Behind the Screen: Lessons Learnt from a Chinese Emergency… 37

Table 2.2 Activities—statistically significant correlations (p < 0.01)

r_τ value	Q3	Q17	Q23	Q24
Q13	0.394	0.383	0.412	0.485
Q14	0.445	0.389	0.490	0.568

Table 2.3 Anxiety 1—statistically significant correlations (p < 0.01)

r_τ value	Q6	Q7	Q10	Q17	Q23	Q24
Q26	0.499	0.423	0.366	0.453	0.439	0.564

consultations (Q28, 65%; Q29, 21%) and feel more comfortable contacting teacher with questions online (Q30, 32%) (Table 2.4).

Assessment: Since the interviews pointed out students' call for handwriting in weekly quizzes, several questions focusing on this issue also appeared in the survey. The results showed that 79% of students found online quizzes to be easier (Q31), and 74% thought they fulfilled the objective of comprehensive review of the lesson (Q33). Students who admitted to using a textbook and notes during testing (Q34, 21%) were more likely to find online learning more time demanding than in-class learning (Q36, 41%, r_τ = 0.422). Additionally, 91% of students expressed missing handwriting in quizzes (Q35), which was in positive correlation with missing dictations in class (Q12, 82%, r_τ = 0.509). In an open-ended question on what students missed in the assessment, handwriting occurred with the highest frequency. One of the students noted: "I really loved writing tests in hand and sending it to the teachers in the last few weeks, that was perfect!"[1]

Attention: Seventy-one percent of students did not experience trouble with maintaining attention during online classes (Q16), yet 62% felt maintaining attention in class is easier than online (Q17). High attention online was in moderate positive correlation with having sufficient speaking opportunities (Q20, 79%), active participation in class (Q25, 50%), preference of distance learning (Q27, 24%), and finding online consultations to be more pleasant than consultations in person (Q29, 21%). The data also indicated a strong correlation with an appreciation of Skype

---

[1] Answers to open-ended descriptive questions were translated from the original Czech or Slovak language.

Table 2.4 Anxiety 2—statistically significant correlations (p < 0.01)

r_τ value	Q5	Q16	Q20	Q28	Q29	Q30
Q27	0.403	0.485	0.479	0.485	0.519	0.424

Table 2.5 Attention 1—statistically significant correlations (p < 0.01)

r_τ value	Q20	Q25	Q27	Q28	Q29
Q16	0.498	0.420	0.485	0.610	0.464

consultations (Q28, 65%). In an open-ended question, some students mentioned fatigue from being online all day long (Table 2.5).

Maintaining better attention in class than online (Q17, 62%) was, in contrast, in strong correlation with missing personal contact with teachers and peers (Q23, 56%; Q24, 79%), and in moderate correlation with missing pair work and group work (Q13, 32% Q14, 50%) and perceiving online learning to be more stressful than F2F learning (Q26, 26%). One of the students added the following comment: "I felt in-class instruction to be more intensive, but it was in all probability also due to my problems with maintaining attention during online classes." (Table 2.6).

Chinese character instruction: In terms of Chinese character explanation, the majority of the students did not miss the instruction of stroke order (Q8, 88%) or components (Q9, 79%). Replacing a blackboard, which is a tool useful for handwriting characters in-class, is technically challenging in an online environment. Although 32% of students indicated they did not like practicing characters on a blackboard in front of the class (Q11), those who missed this activity (Q6, 59%) were more likely to miss seeing others write on the blackboard (Q7, 38%, $r_\tau = 0.483$) and having teacher correct their mistakes in characters (Q10, 50%, $r_\tau = 0.503$). Eighty-two percent of students missed dictations (Q12), which was also the most frequently mentioned disadvantage in the open-ended question about practicing characters. One of the students noted: "I totally missed writing characters; I think this is the best way to find out what mistakes you make."

Communication: Apart from synchronous classes over Skype calls, students also used Skype chat to contact their instructors with questions or other issues. This contact method was appreciated by instructors as

Table 2.6 Attention 2—statistically significant correlations (p < 0.01)

r_r value	Q13	Q14	Q23	Q24	Q26
Q17	0.383	0.389	0.527	0.618	0.453

Table 2.7 Communication 1—statistically significant correlations (p < 0.01)

r_r value	Q5	Q16	Q27	Q28	Q29	Q30
Q28	0.618	0.610	0.485		0.564	0.449
Q29	0.412	0.464	0.519	0.564		0.451

well as 65% of students (Q28). Eighty-two percent of students wished to keep this communication channel open in the future, with Skype being preferred to other messengers (WhatsApp, Microsoft Teams, Facebook, Google Hangouts, etc.). Data indicate that satisfaction with chat consultations (Q28, 65%; Q29, 21%) was in positive correlation with making adequate progress in pronunciation (Q5, 50%), maintaining attention in online sessions (Q16, 71%), perceiving online learning as more comfortable than regular class (Q27, 24%), and having less constraints contacting the teacher with questions online (Q30, 32%) (Table 2.7).

The results show that 56% of students missed contact with their peers (Q23), and 79% of students missed personal contact with their instructors (Q24). Missing personal contact (Q23, Q24) had a positive correlation with perceiving online instruction as more stressful (Q26, 26%), instructors' pronunciation as not clear enough (Q4, 21%), and missing in-class interaction (Q13, 32%; Q14, 50%). There was a strong correlation between missing personal contact (Q23, Q24) and maintaining better attention in F2F class than online (Q17, 62%). One of the students added the following comment: "Although communication was different than in normal class, distance learning did not deprive me of communication with the teacher and some of my peers. It was great to hear each other during our classes." (Table 2.8).

Corrective feedback: Two questions asked about students' perception of corrective feedback during online classes: 79% of students agreed that their pronunciation was corrected sufficiently (Q2). Twenty-nine percent of students indicated that the teacher was not able to correct all of their mistakes, while 41% of students disagreed (Q19).

Pronunciation: Seventy-nine percent of students stated that the teacher paid enough attention to their pronunciation (Q2), and the teacher's attention was also in moderate positive correlation with the feeling of making adequate progress in pronunciation (Q5, 50%, r_τ = *0.449*). Being unable to see the instructor's mouth (Q3, 59%) was in moderate positive correlation with the feeling of the teacher's pronunciation being not clear enough (Q4, 21%, r_τ = *0.455*). One of the students noted: "In general, I think being unable to see the teacher's mouth during pronunciation was a disadvantage, however it was good listening practice, since distance education made me focus more on tones."

Technical issues: Technical issues were the most frequently mentioned negative factors of distance learning. As already mentioned above, an unstable connection prevented students from using the camera, but also caused stress and problems with understanding (mainly native speakers).

Learning challenges and outcomes: Open-ended questions were asked about students' perception of challenges and the positive aspects of distance learning. The most frequent challenges were technical issues, lack of pressure to practice handwriting, attention, memorizing new characters and words, motivation, contact with the teacher and peers, as well as finding a quiet place to study (Fig. 2.1).

Among the positive aspects of distance learning, students mostly mentioned the comfort of staying home, saving time on commuting to school or moving between classrooms, online submissions of homework, etc. (Fig. 2.2).

In general, students appreciated all the effort invested into online teaching by instructors and added numerous thankful notes. One of the students summarized his opinion in the following words:

> I am happy we had a chance to continue with classes. Classes were well organized; however, I hope we will not be forced to switch to online learn-

Table 2.8 Communication 2—statistically significant correlations ($p < 0.01$)

r_τ value	Q4	Q13	Q14	Q17	Q26
Q23	0.401	0.412	0.490	0.527	0.439
Q24	0.434	0.485	0.568	0.618	0.564

2 Behind the Screen: Lessons Learnt from a Chinese Emergency...

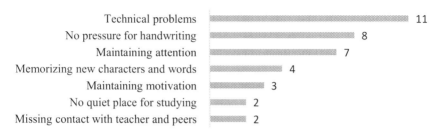

Fig. 2.1 Challenges of distance learning

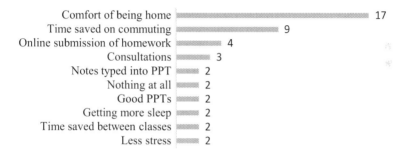

Fig. 2.2 Positive aspects of distance learning

ing again. Nevertheless, it helped us appreciate the quality of F2F instruction which is in my opinion the only way to learn (Chinese) properly.

5 Discussion, Implications, and Limitations

Data analysis of interviews and surveys was aimed at providing answers to the following research questions:

1. How did students perceive online instruction during the ERT period?

Statistical analysis pointed out the varying perceptions of online instruction among learners. In general, most students missed handwriting in quizzes, Chinese character dictations in class, and the personal contact with the teacher. Most students also felt they were provided with enough opportunities to speak and their pronunciation was corrected sufficiently. They did not miss detailed character instruction (stroke order, component analysis) and appreciated the online submission of home assignments.

A quarter of students found online learning more pleasant than F2F learning: these students were less likely to experience problems with attention, and more likely to participated actively in class. They were also more likely to be satisfied with the amount of speaking opportunities and take advantage of online consultations. While some students felt comfortable behind the screen, which protected them from personal contact, the lack of F2F interaction in language learning appeared to be challenging for certain learners. These students were more inclined to feel deprived of communicative activities, which includes practicing Chinese characters on blackboard and generally learning from others.

The data also indicated a correlation between stress, attention, and contentment with distance learning. High attention was in correlation with having enough speaking opportunities and active participation in class. Creating more engaging tasks which would require students to actively participate in dialogues, taking short breaks, or including fun activities (McCabe et al., 2017) to increase attention can be considered. Students who struggled with attention online were more likely to find online learning stressful. The connection between stress and attention has already been described in numerous research projects since the "Affective filter theory" was introduced (Krashen, 1985). First, to help students lower the level of anxiety and stress, technical issues need to be tackled, such as unstable Internet connections, the unclear transmission of voices resulting in difficulties with understanding, or access to videoconferencing tools. Second, during the ERT period, since they were caught unprepared, teachers moved from the classroom to being behind the screen without changing much of their teaching. For the next wave of COVID-19, more blended learning methods (Müller, 2012) can be considered. Teachers should carefully analyze their teaching plans to distinguish between activities that require interaction (such as conversational practice and drills) from those that can be substituted for with pre-recorded sessions (explanation of grammar, vocabulary, characters, etc.). Self-paced, asynchronous learning preceding the synchronous session, should be supported with online exercises with keys, practice quizzes, and chat consultations. Reducing the time of synchronous sessions and providing practice activities prior to synchronous interaction could consequently help with both attention and stress control (Russell, 2020); at the same time, it would not deprive students of interaction or the opportunity to resolve misunderstandings.

2. What challenges did instructors and students face?

Both instructors and students indicated that technical issues were among the most disturbing problems. Providing educators with adequate IT support on the institutional level would solve part of the problem. For students with a poor connection or lacking a private, quiet workspace at home, however, distance learning will always be challenging, as "the pivot to online will hit disadvantaged students hardest" (Nordmann et al., 2020, para. 5). The influence of technical equipment and the study environment on student equity was also mentioned by Wang and East (2020). Instructors' preparedness for online teaching should be prioritized on an institutional level, including training new teaching skills, digital skills, and digital tools. Wang and East (2020) also warn about technology exhaustion among teachers caused by both prolonged working hours and experimenting with new digital tools, as "teachers found they are spending far too much time in low-return-on-investment efforts with online teaching" (p. 15). One-quarter of students described online learning as more stressful than in-class learning, and stress was in positive correlation with maintaining attention. Trained lecturers could be more likely to address attention issues more strategically, as attention seems to have significant impact on the success in distance learning (Robal et al., 2018). Videoconferencing instead of audio conferencing might also help instructors better address attention and pronunciation issues.

The Chinese-specific issue of handwriting Chinese characters appeared to permeate through the entire research study. In regular classes, handwriting practice was incorporated into in-class activities, blackboard instruction, weekly quizzes, and home assignments. Dictations were used in both practice and assessment, as they were perceived to be one of the most complex of the handwritten tasks, because they consist of listening, writing, and understanding. During the distance learning period, active handwriting was only maintained through assignments. Weekly quizzes, as well as synchronous meetings operated with a passive knowledge only, meant that both teachers and students were not actively writing characters during the sessions, apart from several exceptional cases when teachers used a brush in PowerPoint to write a character into PPT. Without adequate hardware, handwriting instruction cannot be easily compensated for in online lectures. While instructors decided to simplify the weekly assessment to testing passive knowledge only, students called for a return to handwritten quizzes and dictations. Eighty-two percent of students missed dictations in class, and 91% of students missed handwriting in quizzes, even though quiz results influenced their final marks. The test design appeared to have a direct effect on their learning. The impact of the testing on learning behavior is known as "the washback effect." In their study, McKinley and Thompson (2018) noticed that "negative washback occurs when there may be a mismatch between the stated goals of instruction and the focus of assessment; it may lead to the abandonment of instructional goals in favor of test preparation" (p. 1). In this case, original quizzes required students to foster an active knowledge of characters which also helped them memorize characters. Without the assessment pressure, feelings of losing motivation and having trouble memorizing new characters were reported, as the handwriting practice in daily assignments provided the practice but not the pressure. To help students maintain pressure, dictations can be included as part of both assignments and quizzes in an online environment.

There has been an ongoing discussion about the role of handwriting in learning Chinese in the digital era. Many researchers argue that learning to write characters is no longer necessary. Zhang (2019) provided a list of benefits of typing Chinese and suggested learning to type along with handwriting or introducing typing "only after students have acquired sufficient knowledge of the structure of characters through handwriting" (p. 501). The definition of "sufficient knowledge" is, however, disputable. Based on the results of this study, the author believes that switching to typing during the first year of an intensive language course toward a Chinese degree for university students might not be desirable. Student participants of this study called for more attention to the character production, which is fostered by handwriting, while typing fosters character recognition only.

3. Are there any positive outcomes of ERT? Are there any techniques transferable to F2F teaching?

Numerous challenges aside, the ERT experience also brought some unexpected positive outcomes. First, both instructors and students reported that the comfort of staying home and saving time on commuting as the biggest advantage of ERT. This finding was also observed by Jaggars (2014): "Most respondents also alluded to the comfort of working at home, with several specifically noting that they enjoyed the ability to take breaks, have snacks, work in your pajamas" (p. 7). Some students, however, also reported having no quiet place to connect to online classes, or general fatigue from sitting by the computer for the whole day. It is, therefore, important to keep less privileged students in mind, as well as the fact that students can be easily overloaded by assignments from other courses. An unexpected wave of empathy between instructors and learners was observed. This finding is identical to Wang and East (2020) who described empathy in communication between teachers and students of a Chinese class during the COVID-19 pandemic. They noticed that "the overall discourse in teacher-student interactions were [sic] highly empathetic, including word choice, heart-warming slogans and multimodal symbols used to make students feel warm and close" (p. 14), and they also called for more research attention to the role of empathy in Chinese language teaching. Third, although in-class instruction would be preferred by the majority of participants, several positive aspects appeared transferable to regular classes. The online submission and correction of homework assignments proved to be practical for both instructors and students. It provided both sides with more time flexibility and accessibility. Last, communication on the teacher-student level did not suffer. Data from this study indicated that communication between instructors and students was even more vigorous than before, and both sides wished to continue online consultations. Online consultations may also solve the issue of frustrations resulting from the lack of immediate feedback, or they may function as an anxiety alleviation tool to support students' learning needs and provide them with words of encouragement (Russell, 2020). The online submission of assignments and online consultations are easily transferable to regular instruction, thus fulfilling predictions by Kim (2020) that the COVID-19 pandemic will also have positive outcomes for student learning: blended learning will increase and "the biggest future benefits of virtual instruction will come after our professors and students return to their physical classrooms" (para. 7).

The small sample size and the selection of participants are likely the largest limitations of the study. This study focused on first-year learners at one university only, in order to avoid the interference of proficiency level or curriculum design. The curriculums of advanced Chinese classes, as well as Chinese curriculums at other institutions of higher education within the country, are too different from each other to be evaluated as one data cluster. Therefore, although the size and the scope of the group places limitations on the interpretation of the results, it eliminates variables such as language level, teaching material, and teaching style. A larger sample size would be needed to confirm the findings.

6   Conclusion

The aim of the study was to describe the ERT experience from both the instructors' and students' point of view. The data indicated varying perceptions of online learning by students; while the online environment was more pleasant than F2F learning for some students, there was another group for whom distance learning was more stressful than the F2F class. Stress was related to poor attention as well as a lack of personal contact with the teacher and peers. Technical issues were also repeatedly mentioned among the greatest challenges of distance learning. While handling technical issues may not be within the capacity of the course instructor, the application of more blended teaching methods was suggested. In addition, finding key contributors to stress, attention, and satisfaction through follow-up qualitative research would help instructors further adjust their teaching techniques to fit the needs of the struggling students. It is important to keep in mind that no student should be left behind in involuntary distance learning—students with a lack of a quiet workspace at home, poor attention, or feelings of anxiety may require additional attention.

On the positive side, teachers were, in general, positive about their experience, discovered several online techniques transferable to F2F learning and observed a large wave of empathy between students and teachers. As for Chinese-specific issues, handwriting appeared to be a largely discussed topic among first-year learners. Although handwriting was required in assignments during the ERT period, learners identified the missing pressure of handwritten quizzes to have significant influence on their motivation and success in memorizing characters. More research on the role of handwritten quizzes in learning Chinese characters is needed.

Appendix 1: Interview Questions

1. Can you describe the teaching process before COVID-19 (in terms of activities, class design, time spent on activities) and what had to be adjusted to the online scheme?
2. What was the biggest challenge of online teaching?
3. Was there any benefit of online education when compared to face-to-face?
4. Are there any activities which could not be done online? How did you substitute them?
5. How did your corrective feedback change?
6. How did you feel about attending to the individual needs of the students?
7. How did you check the general understanding of the class (without seeing the class)?
8. How did you maintain students' attention? Did students have troubles maintaining attention?
9. How did you substitute games/moving around classroom activities?
10. Were you able to run activities in pairs or groups?
11. How did the testing method change?

12. How did you handle: having no blackboard; stroke order correction; calling on students; giving open public questions; testing active Chinese character knowledge?
13. Is there anything that you would like to transfer from online teaching back to face-to-face teaching?
14. If you had a choice, what type of education would you prefer: online, in-class, combination?

Appendix 2: Online Survey

Pronunciation

(Select: disagree—mostly disagree—do not know—mostly agree—agree)
1. Online learning did not pay adequate attention to pronunciation.
2. Course instructor corrected my pronunciation sufficiently.
3. I missed watching the instructor's mouth for pronunciation cues.
4. Instructor's pronunciation was not clear enough.
5. I feel I made adequate progress in pronunciation.

Did you miss anything in the instruction of pronunciation?

Chinese characters

(Select: disagree—mostly disagree—do not know—mostly agree—agree)
6. I missed writing characters on the blackboard.
7. I missed watching the teacher or classmates write characters on the blackboard.
8. I missed the explanation on stroke order.
9. I missed the explanation of character components.
10. I missed having my mistakes corrected when writing characters on the blackboard.
11. I do not like writing characters on the blackboard.
12. I missed Chinese character dictations.

Did you miss anything in the instruction of Chinese characters?

Activities and Attention

(Select: disagree—mostly disagree—do not know—mostly agree—agree)
13. I missed activities in pairs.
14. I missed group activities.
15. I missed games in class.
16. I was able to maintain attention during an online class.
17. Maintaining attention in regular class is easier than online.
18. The teacher paid more attention to me than in regular class.
19. The teacher was not able to correct all my mistakes.
20. I was provided with enough opportunities to speak.
21. Online learning was more intensive than in regular class.
22. Online submission and correction of home assignments work better for me than submitting them in class.

Did you miss anything in terms of language practice?

Communication

(Select: disagree—mostly disagree—do not know—mostly agree—agree)
23. I missed personal contact with my classmates.
24. I missed personal contact with my teacher.
25. My participation was more proactive than in regular class.
26. Learning online was more stressful than in regular class.
27. Online learning was more comfortable for me than in regular class.
28. I appreciated online consultations through Skype.
29. Skype consultations were more pleasant for me than consultations in person.
30. I felt less constraints asking questions online.

Did you miss anything in the terms of communication?

Assessment

(select: disagree—mostly disagree—do not know—mostly agree—agree)
31. Online quizzes were easier than in-class quizzes.

32. Online quizzes did not cover the full contents of the lesson.
33. Online quizzes fulfilled the objective of a comprehensive review of the lesson.
34. I used my notes and textbook during the online assessment.
35. I missed handwriting in the online quizzes.
36. Online learning was more time demanding in preparation.

Did you miss anything in the reviewing and assessment?

What was the biggest challenge in online learning for you?
What did you like about online learning?
Is there anything in online learning that you would like to transfer to regular class?
Would you like to maintain online consultations via (multiple choice):
Skype
Microsoft Teams
Facebook
WhatsApp
Google hangouts
Google classroom
I do not need online consultations
Other:

References

Allen, J. R. (2008). Why learning to write Chinese is a waste of time: A modest proposal. *Foreign Language Annals, 41*(2), 237–251. https://doi.org/10.1111/j.1944-9720.2008.tb03291.x

Blake, R. J. (2013). *Brave new digital classroom* (2nd ed.). Amsterdam University Press.

Blake, R., Wilson, N. L., Cetto, M., & Pardo-Ballester, C. (2008). Measuring oral proficiency in distance, face-to-face, and blended classrooms. *Language Learning & Technology, 12*(3), 114–127.

Bourgerie, D. S. (2003). Computer assisted language learning for Chinese: A survey and annotated bibliography. *Journal of Chinese Language Teachers Association, 38*(2), 17–47.

Chen, H. (2013). Moodle as a learning aid: An example of Chinese extra-curriculum activity design. *Journal of Technology and Chinese Language Teaching, 4*(2), 35–54.

Cheng, Z. (2011). Online Chinese teaching and learning: A case study. *Journal of Technology and Chinese Language Teaching, 2*(2), 50–68.

Conrad, D. L. (2002). Engagement, excitement, anxiety, and fear: Learners' experiences of starting an online course. *American Journal of Distance Education, 16*(4), 205–226. https://doi.org/10.1207/s15389286ajde1604_2

Da, J. (2011). Issues in the development of online CFL learning and resource systems: A case study of Great Wall Chinese and Confucius Institute Online. *Journal of Technology and Chinese Language Teaching, 2*(1), 23–35.

Gacs, A., Goertler, S., & Spasova, S. (2020). Planned online language education versus crisis-prompted online language teaching: Lessons for the future. *Foreign Language Annals, 53*, 380–392. https://doi.org/10.1111/flan.12460

Goertler, S., & Gacs, A. (2018). Assessment in online German: Assessment methods and results. *Die Unterrichtspraxis/Teaching German, 51*(2), 156–174. https://doi.org/10.1111/tger.12071

Green, A., & Youngs, B. (2001). Using the web in elementary French and German courses: Quantitative and qualitative study results. *CALICO Journal, 19*(1), 89–123.

Harker, M., & Koutsantoni, D. (2005). Can it be as effective? Distance versus blended learning in a web-based EAP programme. *ReCALL, 17*(2), 197–216. https://doi.org/10.1017/s095834400500042x

Hodges, C., Moore, S., Lockee, B., Trust, T., & Bond, A. (2020). The difference between emergency remote teaching and online learning. *Educause Review, 27*.

Hollis, R. B., & Was, C. A. (2016). Mind wandering, control failures, and social media distractions in online learning. *Learning and Instruction, 42*, 104–112.

Hon, T. (2013). The application and effectiveness of Moodle—An e-learning platform for intermediate Chinese speaking and listening course. *Journal of Technology and Chinese Language Teaching, 4*(2), 25–34.

Hsin, S. C., Hsieh, C. L., & Chang-Blust, L. (2017). Preservice teacher training for online Chinese teaching: A case of distance courses for high school learners. *Journal of Technology and Chinese Language Teaching, 8*(1), 86–103.

Hu, B. (2010). The challenges of Chinese: A preliminary study of UK Learners' perceptions of difficulty. *Language Learning Journal, 38*(1), 99–118.

Hughes, N., Lo, L., & Xu, S. (2017). Blended Chinese language learning design: An integrative review and synthesis of the literature. *The Language Learning Journal, 47*(3), 313–331. https://doi.org/10.1080/09571736.2017.1280526

Hurd, S. (2000). Distance language learners and learner support: beliefs, difficulties and use of strategies. *Links and Letters 7: Autonomy in Language Learning, 7*, 61–80. http://oro.open.ac.uk/21782/

Hurd, S. (2005). Autonomy and the distance language learner. In M. Shelley, C. White, & H. Boerje (Eds.), *Distance education and languages: evolution and change (pp. 1–19)*. Multilingual Matters.

Jaggars, S. S. (2014). Choosing between online and face-to-face courses: Community college student voices. *American Journal of Distance Education, 28*(1), 27–38.

Jin, L. (2018). Digital affordances on WeChat: Learning Chinese as a second language. *Computer Assisted Language Learning, 31*(1–2), 27–52.

Kan, Q. (2013). The use of ICT in supporting distance Chinese language learning-review of The Open University's beginners' Chinese course. *Technology and Chinese Language Teaching, 4*(1), 1–13.

Kan, Q., & McCormick, R. (2012). Building course cohesion: The use of online forums in distance Chinese language learning. *Computer Assisted Language Learning, 27*(1), 44–69. https://doi.org/10.1080/09588221.2012.695739

Kan, Q., Owen, N., & Bax, S. (2018). Researching mobile-assisted Chinese-character learning strategies among adult distance learners. *Innovation in Language Learning and Teaching, 12*(1), 56–71. https://doi.org/10.1080/17501229.2018.1418633

Keegan, D. (1996). *Foundations of distance education (Routledge studies in distance education)* (3rd ed.). Routledge.

Kim, J. (2020, April 1). *Teaching and learning after COVID-19*. Inside Higher Ed. https://www.insidehighered.com/digital-learning/blogs/learninginnovation/teaching-and-learning-after-covid-19

Krashen, S. (1985). *The input hypothesis: Issues and implications*. Longman.

Kraska-Miller, M. (2014). *Nonparametric statistics for social and behavioral sciences*. CRC Press/Taylor & Francis Group.

Kubler, C. C. (2017). Developing course materials for technology-mediated Chinese language learning. *Innovation in Language Learning and Teaching, 12*(1), 47–55. https://doi.org/10.1080/17501229.2018.1418626

Liu, S. (2018). Teaching and learning Chinese language online: What and why? *International Chinese Language Education, 3*(2), 11–26.

Liu, S., Wang, Y., & Zhan, H. (2020, July 11). *A survey of student perspectives on learning Chinese online: Preliminary results* [Online conference presentation]. The International Forum of Textbook Development and Virtual Conference on Teaching Chinese as an International Language, Hong Kong.

Longcamp, M., Boucard, C., Gilhodes, J. C., & Velay, J. L. (2006). Remembering the orientation of newly learned characters depends on the associated writing knowledge: A comparison between handwriting and typing. *Human Movement Science, 25*(4–5), 646–656.

McCabe, C., Sprute, K., & Underdown, K. (2017). Laughter to learning: How humor can build relationships and increase learning in the online classroom. *Journal of Instructional Research, 6*, 4–7.

McKinley, J., & Thompson, G. (2018). Washback effect in teaching English as an international language. In J. I. Liontas, M. DelliCarpini, & S. Abrar-ul-Hassan (Eds.), *The TESOL encyclopedia of English language teaching* (pp. 1–12). Wiley.

Means, B., Toyama, Y., Murphy, R., Bakia, M., & Jones, K.F. (2009). *Evaluation of evidence-based practices in online learning: A meta-analysis and review of online learning studies*. U.S. Department of Education. https://repository.alt.ac.uk/629/1/US_DepEdu_Final_report_2009.pdf

Moore, M. G. (1989). Three types of interaction. *American Journal of Distance Education, 3*(2), 1–7.

Müller, C. (2012). Experiences and evaluation of a blended learning concept for learning Chinese in higher education. *Procedia-Social and Behavioral Sciences, 34*, 158–163.

Nordmann, E., Horlin, C., Hutchison, J., Murray, J.-A., Robson, L., Seery, M. K., & MacKay, J. R. D. (2020). Ten simple rules for supporting a temporary online pivot in higher education. *PLoS Comput Biol, 16*(10). https://doi.org/10.1371/journal.pcbi.1008242

Qi, G. Y., & Wang, Y. (2018). Investigating the building of a WeChat-based community of practice for language teachers' professional development. *Innovation in Language Learning and Teaching, 12*(1), 72–88.

Robal, T., Zhao, Y., Lofi, C., & Hauff, C. (2018). IntelliEye: Enhancing MOOC learners' video watching experience with real-time attention tracking. In *HT' 18: Proceedings of the 29th on hypertext and social media* (pp. 106–114). Association for Computing Machinery (ACM). https://doi.org/10.1145/3209542.3209547

Russell, V. (2020). Language anxiety and the online learner. *Foreign Language Annals, 53*, 338–352. https://doi.org/10.1111/flan.12461

Shen, H. H. (2004). Level of cognitive processing: Effects on character learning among non-native learners of Chinese as a foreign language. *Language and Education, 18*(2), 167–182. https://doi.org/10.1080/09500780408666873

Sher, A. (2009). Assessing the relationship of student-instructor and student-student interaction to student learning and satisfaction in web-based online learning environment. *Journal of Interactive Online Learning, 8*(2), 102–120.

Stickler, U., & Shi, L. (2013). Supporting Chinese speaking skills online. *System, 41*(1), 50–69. https://doi.org/10.1016/j.system.2012.12.001

Sun, S. Y. H. (2011). Online language teaching: The pedagogical challenges. *Knowledge Management & E-Learning: An International Journal, 3*(3), 428–447.

Sunaoka, K. (2012). Effects of multilingual chatting in Chinese distance learning. *Journal of Technology and Chinese Language Teaching, 3*(1), 1–12.

Szpunar, K. K., Khan, N. Y., & Schacter, D. L. (2013). Interpolated memory tests reduce mind wandering and improve learning of online lectures. *Proceedings of the National Academy of Sciences, 110*(16), 6313–6317.

Tan, L. H., Spinks, J. A., Eden, G. F., Perfetti, C. A., & Siok, W. T. (2005). Reading depends on writing, in Chinese. *Proceedings of the National Academy of Sciences, 102*(24), 8781–8785.

Tseng, M. (2017). The development of skills required for online Chinese language teaching. *Journal of Technology and Chinese Language Teaching, 8*(1), 36–55.

Ushida, E. (2005). The role of students' attitudes and motivation in second language learning in online language courses. *CALICO Journal, 23*(1), 49–78. https://doi.org/10.1558/cj.v23i1.49-78

Wang, D., & East, M. (2020). Constructing an Emergency Chinese Curriculum during the Pandemic: A New Zealand Experience. *International Journal of Chinese Language Teaching, 1*(1), 1–19.

Wang, Y. (2004). Supporting synchronous distance language learning with desktop videoconferencing. *Language Learning & Technology, 8*(3), 90–121.

Wang, Y., Chen, N.-S., & Levy, M. (2010). Teacher training in a synchronous cyber face-to-face classroom: characterizing and supporting the online teachers' learning process. *Computer Assisted Language Learning, 23*(4), 277–293.

White, C. (2006). Distance learning of foreign languages. *Language Teaching, 39*(4), 247–264. https://doi.org/10.1017/S0261444806003727

Xiao, J. (2017). Learner-content interaction in distance education: The weakest link in interaction research. *Distance Education, 38*(1), 123–135. https://doi.org/10.1080/01587919.2017.1298982

Xing, J. Z. (2006). *Teaching and learning Chinese as a foreign language: A pedagogical grammar.* Hong Kong University Press.

Yao, T. (2009). The current status of Chinese CALL in the United States. *Journal of the Chinese Language Teachers Association, 44*(1), 1–23.

Zhang, S. (2014). An evidence-based practical guide to designing and developing Chinese-as-a-foreign-language (CFL) courses online. *International Journal of Technology in Teaching and Learning, 10*(1), 52–71.

Zhang, Z. S. (2019). The current status of CALL for Chinese in the United States. In C. Shei, M. E. McLellan Zikpi, & D. Chao (Eds.), *The Routledge handbook of Chinese language teaching* (1st ed., pp. 493–508). Routledge.

3

Emergency Remote Chinese Language Learning at a German University: Student Perceptions

Chin-hui Lin

1 Introduction

As is the case with many universities worldwide, Chinese language teaching at most German universities in recent years has usually been assisted by online learning management systems (e.g., *Moodle, Blackboard*) and/or digital tools (e.g., *PowerPoint, MS Word*, mobile apps) in course management, presentations, file sharing, assignments, or exercises. However, teacher-student interactions have generally taken place face-to-face in the classroom (Lin, 2021). Since early 2020 the COVID-19 pandemic has had a huge impact on global education and brought unprecedented challenges with it, including the sudden advent of emergency online teaching (or emergency remote teaching (ERT), see Hodges et al., 2020), which is different from traditional distance teaching and regarded as a "temporary" solution for the crisis (Golden, 2020). As Russell (2020) describes, most of the teachers were unprepared and "did not have sufficient time to

---

C.-h. Lin (✉)
Humboldt-Universität zu Berlin, Berlin, Germany
e-mail: chin-hui.lin@hu-berlin.de

© The Author(s), under exclusive license to Springer Nature Switzerland AG 2022
S. Liu (ed.), *Teaching the Chinese Language Remotely*,
https://doi.org/10.1007/978-3-030-87055-3_3

transition to online or remote teaching" (p. 339). While educators endeavored to convert the original in-class face-to-face teaching mode to a workable, fully online mode using the available resources and supports, students were forced to cope in this unusual and difficult new situation with: novel forms of interaction with teachers and fellow students in virtual classrooms, problems with internet connections or insufficient facilities, and so on.

In the field of Chinese language teaching at university level, the outcomes and effects of the first emergency online semester in 2020 have been researched by a number of scholars worldwide with a diverse range of focal points, for example, Gao (2020) on Australian students' perceptions of the challenges of Chinese character learning, Liu et al. (2020a, 2020b) on instructors' and students' perspectives on online teaching and learning worldwide (mainly in the U.S.), Wang and East (2020) on curriculum construction at a New Zealand university, Zhang (2020a) on teachers' beliefs about digital teaching competences in Denmark. Comparable studies which refer to German higher education during the pandemic are still lacking.

Looking at the situation of Chinese language teaching during the emergency online semester in the German context, this article first gives a brief overview of digital tools used in Chinese language classes at tertiary level in three German-speaking countries (Austria, Germany, and Switzerland) before the pandemic.[1] Subsequently, the Chinese language program at Humboldt University of Berlin (Humboldt-Universität zu Berlin, hereafter: HU) will be taken as an example to illuminate students' experiences during the first emergency online semester from April to the end of July 2020, including their perceptions of the online teaching mode, their opinions on the practicability of the online mode with regard to different learning components, and their preferences for future course adjustments.

---

[1] The analysis is based on an online survey among 42 university language teachers from 19 higher educational institutions in these three countries conducted in November 2020 (Lin, 2021).

2 Context

In Austria, Germany, and Switzerland, there are currently around 30 universities and colleges offering Chinese language courses as part of BA and/or MA degrees in China-related studies (e.g., Chinese/Sinology/East Asian studies) (FaCh, 2020). According to the latest comprehensive survey of 25 Chinese degree programs conducted by Klöter (2016), the number of enrolled students was approximately 3800. With very few exceptions, the average number of contact hours of Chinese language course(s) in these programs is eight to ten hours per week during the first four semesters.[2]

While the degree and scope of digital tool use in university Chinese language education in these countries was rarely discussed in previous studies, first insights into the topic are available in Lin's (2016) investigation of the working experiences of 20 Taiwanese pre-service Chinese language teachers at 6 German universities. In this study, 65% of the respondents reported that compared to the class teaching in Taiwan, multimedia was used less frequently. One respondent remarked that "most teachers do not use PowerPoint very often but paper handouts." A few respondents brought up the issue of inadequate facilities in the classroom: no multimedia classrooms, not all the classrooms were equipped with a projector, etc. Four years later, in the author's recent research involving 42 Chinese university language teachers from 19 degree programs in the countries mentioned above, 73.8% of the teachers *always* or *often* used digital tools during classes (Lin, 2021). *MS Word/Pages* and *MS PowerPoint/Keynote* were the most favored digital tools before the pandemic. Furthermore, the preliminary findings of this study show that 61.9% of the teachers were *not at all* or *not very* familiar with online teaching. This low level of familiarity with online teaching may result from the fact that teaching almost always took place in a face-to-face mode before the pandemic. On the other hand, the fact that the same group reported a comparatively high level of digital tool use in class points to the fundamental difference between the simple application of

---

[2] At German universities, a normal contact hour is 45 minutes.

digital tools for the classroom and the more complex digitalization processes involved in fully online teaching modes.

At HU, Chinese language is taught at the Department of Asian and African Studies (Institut für Asien- und Afrikawissenschaften), under the BA program "Area Studies Asia/Africa." The winter term (October to February) and the summer term (April to July) consist of 15 and 14 weeks respectively. The new academic year usually starts in October. Three courses are offered each year: BA1 (Modern Chinese 1 and 2), BA2 (Modern Chinese 3 and 4), and BA3 (Modern Chinese 5 and 6). The BA1 and BA2 courses are mandatory, whereas the BA3 courses are electives. Each BA1 and BA2 course is composed of five 90-minute sessions per week, including *grammar, vocabulary and text* (two sessions), *conversation*, and *homework discussion*. Each BA3 course takes place once a week for 90 minutes. The program currently has four teachers: two German-natives and two Mandarin-natives. The BA1 and BA2 courses are co-taught by teachers with different mother-tongue backgrounds, whereas the BA3 courses are solely taught by one teacher. Due to the limited capacity of teaching staff, a student number control has been implemented. At the beginning of the summer term 2020, the total enrollments for BA1–3 courses, that is, Modern Chinese 2/4/6, were around 50.

During the ERT in the summer term 2020, efforts were made to maintain continuity between courses; no sessions were canceled so as to ensure that students could have a smooth transition to the next course and maintain a reasonable level. Extended online office hours were offered to help individual students who needed additional assistance. All the language courses at HU were required to be taught remotely using Zoom. This video conferencing software, with features such as screen sharing, annotations, breakout rooms, polls, chat, and participation controls (waiting room, participant lists, the "raise hand" function, and so on), offered a great help to educators. For instance, during a homework discussion session students were usually requested to share their handwritten assignments on screen one after another. The teachers discussed the homework with the help of the "annotation" function. Furthermore, in order to achieve a better effect from language learning, all the students agreed to turn on the camera during the session. Only when their home internet was unstable were they allowed to turn it off. As for the course management, all course documents, announcements, homework exchange (hand-in and corrections) for BA1 and BA2 courses were uploaded on *Moodle*, an educational platform offered by the university. The BA3 course used *Google Classroom* for course management instead (for details, see Lin, forthcoming).

Like many other German universities, before the COVID-19 outbreak Chinese language courses at HU were exclusively face-to-face with the aid of a whiteboard, paper handouts, worksheets, audio/video recordings, and digital tools such as *PowerPoint*, *Google Docs*, and *Google Forms*. During the emergency online semester, a large amount of the aforementioned course materials and class activities had to be modified or redesigned in order to meet the specificities of online teaching and ensure efficacy. To foster online interaction and cooperation, various digital tools were applied experimentally. For BA1 and BA2 courses, *Classkick* was employed for giving instant individual feedback for in-class and outside-class exercises; *Google Docs* was used as a class whiteboard and also for written assignment discussions; *Whiteboard.fi* was employed for testing character writing in class. For BA3 students, *Google Tools* (*Google Docs, Google Forms, Google Slides*) were applied for course assignments, discussions, student presentations, and essay corrections. The teachers also offered a myriad of supplementary studying materials and exercises on *Quizlet* and *Wordwall* for BA1 and BA2 students for self-study.

The format of the final exam was the most problematic issue during the online semester. Although the university strongly recommended conducting the final exam online via Moodle, this platform is not ideal for a language test. As on-campus exams were still allowed under strict safety and hygiene controls, it was decided that handwritten on-campus exams for the BA1 and BA2 students would be held, with the addition of an online oral exam via Zoom, in order to avoid the risk of "academic dishonesty" (Olt, 2002; Wang & East, 2020).

3 Research Questions

Hurd (2007a) argues that "knowledge of the process of learning a language at a distance is crucial if we are to design courses that truly meet the needs of our students, and we can achieve this best by listening to their stories" (p. 256). In light of the fact that emergency online teaching was experimentally implemented and that it may be continued in the following semesters, it is vital to have feedback from students of all levels in order to prepare for future teaching. Three research questions were thus asked:

1. What were students' personal experiences during this emergency online semester? How did they perceive online learning?
2. Which course component(s) or what kind of skill training did the students find better when implemented online? Which ones not?
3. What are student preferences with regard to future course adjustments?

4 Methodology

4.1 Research Design and Procedure

With the goal of answering the three research questions and of gathering general feedback from students on the courses they took part in, two anonymous[3] questionnaires were prepared and distributed to the BA1/BA2 group and the BA3 group respectively. Both questionnaires consisted of a general survey of the online learning experience followed by questions relating to the individual course. In this study only the general survey will be discussed.

All the surveyed students had experienced at least one semester of face-to-face teaching and were therefore able to compare this experience with the online teaching mode at the same university. In the survey, the

---

[3] For the BA3 survey the participants could choose to write in their own names at the end if they were willing to be contacted for further questions.

participants were asked about their personal experiences during the online semester, their opinions on the practicability of the online teaching mode compared to traditional in-class teaching with respect to different learning components, and their preferences with respect to future course planning in the form of Likert-scale questions, multiple-choice questions and open-ended questions. In order to better understand their opinions, students were also encouraged to provide explanations and concrete examples with regard to their choices. The survey was formulated in English. Participants could answer in English or in German. The content of the survey is appended at the end of this article.

4.2 Data Collection and Analysis

Due to practical restrictions caused by the pandemic, the data collection was carried out through Google Forms. Students were invited to complete the online questionnaire at the end of the online semester (July 2020). They were made aware that the data would be used for research purposes and the responses were voluntary. Altogether, 39 responses were collected, including 15 from BA1 students, 13 BA2 students, and 11 BA3 students.

A mixed-approach of qualitative and quantitative data analysis was then adopted. To provide a better understanding of what students actually perceived during this online semester, a conventional approach of content analysis (Hsieh & Shannon, 2005) was taken. All the written feedback from individual learners was first read repeatedly in order to get a holistic impression of the data. To capture the key concepts, the meaning units were sought and coded. The key concepts and relevant texts were then categorized and thematized. In the sections that follow, the student feedback will be presented thematically. It should be noted that students' written feedback quoted in this paper was given in English and has not been modified.

5 Findings and Discussions

The following discussions of the findings focus on three themes: personal experiences, perception of practicability of online learning, and preferences with regard to future course adjustments.

5.1 Personal Experiences

As mentioned previously, all the participants of this survey had studied in a face-to-face context at least for one semester. When asked whether they felt more comfortable with online learning, 61.5% of the 39 participants disagreed or strongly disagreed. These responses are in line with the results of an investigation by Zhao et al. (2020), stating that many students who received face-to-face teaching in the first block and then transitioned to online mode in the second block regarded the online mode as an "ultimately inferior replacement" (p. 97). Two students who strongly opposed online teaching stated that if one prefers online learning, one should apply for an online course, such as MOOC, which implies that these students perceive face-to-face learning as being an essential part of a university language course.

On the other hand, 17.9% of the participants found learning online more comfortable. Answers from two students who were positive about online learning illustrated the importance of the ability to self-regulate and self-motivate: "*you only have to invest more initiative of your own […]; if you stay motivated and manage your time well, you can handle it,*" "*it just requires even more independent and disciplined learning at home,*" which suggests that students who have the ability to self-regulate may adapt better to the online learning. This also ties in with the findings in Holcomb et al. (2004): "self-regulation has been demonstrated as a critical component of distance education success." (p. 11).

Positive Aspects of Online Learning

Saving Commuting Time and Easy Access

Covering an area eight times bigger than that of Paris, Berlin is a large metropolis in terms of urban surface. Before the pandemic, long commuting times were a ubiquitous feature of everyday life. Consequently, saving time and easy access are the major merits of online learning from a student's perspective. Many participants indicated that online learning had given them the opportunity to study anywhere (71.8%) and had saved a great deal of time otherwise lost through commuting (64.1%). A number of students reported that the disproportionate commuting time for a single 90-min class was particularly stressful.

One BA3 student also brought up the convenience of easy access to the online course for one's time management: "*it was very convenient and gave me the chance to sometimes join the class between work tasks, which would not have been possible otherwise.*" The relatively "effortless" access seemed to improve attendance, as another student confessed: "*to be honest, I would likely have missed more sessions in a regular semester; even if I don't feel well, didn't sleep well etc. it's much easier to still take part in class.*" Some students emphasized the fairness of offering remote classes during the pandemic, as they could still attend the class in a time where their personal situation restricted their mobility. They could also spend more time with their family.

Increased Flexibility and Reduced Stress

Increased flexibility and reduced stress were also perceived as advantages of the online format, as students highlighted the freedom of studying at one's own pace (30.8%) and of searching for information on one's own electronic device during the class (53.8%). Before the pandemic, the use of electronic devices was usually not permitted in the classroom. However, during this semester it was practically impossible to monitor students' use of electronic devices alongside Zoom meetings, and many students reported that they took advantage of this freedom to use, for example, online dictionaries. Although some students appreciated the opportunity to look up unfamiliar words and save them directly to their mobile phone or computer in class, this "convenience" could negatively affect learning: a few students confessed that they spent less time previewing because they knew that they would have the chance to look up words during the online class session.

One-fifth of students (20.5%) ultimately felt more relaxed while not attending the on-campus classes. Some of them enjoyed the comfortable surroundings at home and thought the relaxing setting had helped them to be more active in class: *"I can listen to the teacher just fine through Zoom from the comfort of my home, even better in fact (with tea and in comfy clothes),"* *"I usually get very anxious around new people so this was actually kind of a relief and I think I spoke more than usual."* This finding is in agreement with previous studies that argue that the distant setting is helpful for some learners in reducing anxiety (Hampel et al., 2005; Hauck & Hurd, 2005; Hurd, 2007b).

Negative Aspects of Online Learning

Reduced In-Class Interaction and Technical Problems

Picciano (2002) states that the "social and communicative interactions" between the course participants is common in the context of learning in a traditional classroom (p. 21). However, distant learning has an "inherently non-social nature" (Hurd, 2005, p. 143). Indeed, reduced interaction was the main criticism of the online course from the students' side. 84.6% of the participants indicated that the online course had led to fewer direct teacher-student as well as student-student interactions. For many students, online education is simply "cold," "awkward," or "unnatural" compared to on-campus education. Two students pointed out the different nature of interactions in online versus traditional learning:

> In the classroom you can easily talk to some classmates, but online you cannot because you would interrupt the lesson, just learning online feels like there is a barrier between teacher/student or student/student.

It is easier for me to take part in a discussion in the classroom and describe/paraphrase what I would like to say, and spontaneously ask a question, whereas the online discussion is sometimes more about making one statement after each other and not as relaxed.

Compared to learning on campus, the students encountered more difficulties in speaking online, even though they could always use the "raise hand" function during times when the teacher or another student was talking. The limited space for spontaneous interjections often resulted in a more passive participation. Naturally, muting and unmuting participants also took up valuable time for interaction in every class. In a remote context, it was harder for teachers to keep track of which students had not yet had a chance to participate or order to include them because teachers' attention was often distracted by screen- or tool-switching and technical problem-solving.

During the online semester, around 41% of the students were confronted with technical problems such as slow internet speeds or computer problems. This does not come as a surprise, as Germany is notorious for its waiting-to-be-improved internet infrastructure, especially in rural areas (Carrel, 2018; Wamsley, 2019). This is also illustrated by the remarks of two students: *"internet in Germany is often not sufficient for online teaching," "I live in a small village and the internet is not really fast, so there are often problems."*[4] This is not a one-sided problem. In Lin (2021), the most frequently encountered problem from the teacher side was *"unstable internet,"* which is consistent with the earlier findings of Liebau-Liu (2020) on university Chinese language teachers in Germany, stating that 90% of her respondents suffered from technical problems. Deficiencies in technical support available to teachers and students have further contributed to unfavorable outcomes in an online language course, especially with regard to listening/speaking training. Due to the restrictions of internet speeds and the functionality of video conferencing

---

[4] These remarks confirm what Beblavý et al. (2019) have criticized: *"Germany has come under scrutiny for under-investment in digital infrastructure, low internet connection speeds, and a lack of broadband access throughout its territory"* (p. 23). They ultimately conclude that *"Germany has a lot of ground to make up in digital learning."* These criticisms are also echoed in Carrel (2018) and Kerres (2020).

tools, it is hard to facilitate a natural flow between participants who have to speak in an orderly fashion one after another. Bad internet connections in Germany can thus be detrimental to the efficacy of online teaching, which is especially problematic when offline alternatives are unavailable.

Reduced Outside-Class interaction and Loss of Motivation

Aside from in-class interactions, the reduction in face-to-face encounters with other students that are associated with on-site attendance was acknowledged by the respondents. One student shared: "*I miss the minutes before and after the class, when you can chat with your classmates, also about Chinese. Last semester, for example, after a grammar lesson we chatted about it afterwards which helped my understanding really a lot. I think it is really important for students to really have a student life, seeing the people interested in the same topics every day, and being able to go to the library to study.*" These remarks reflect the dissatisfaction and frustration felt by students during the pandemic. I also observed that the frustration was not only due to the online learning, but also resulted from the general lack of real social contact during the lockdown.

There are indications that the limitation of social interaction led to a loss of motivation. One student described one strategy to remain motivated: "*for me personally direct contact is really important for motivation. I started meeting a tandem partner one week ago now and immediately I had more motivation.*" In line with what White (2010) observes in distant learning—that the loss or decline of motivation is usually related to "*loneliness, isolation, competing commitments, absence of the structuring aspects of face-to-face classes, and difficulty of adjusting to a distant language learning context*" (p. 115), the survey found that more than half of the participants (51.3%) felt less motivated when not sitting in the classroom, and they found the atmosphere of face-to-face learning was "*just so much better*" or "*just more fun.*"

Several students mentioned that home was simply not a motivating setting for studying and even led to distraction. They found that being home was "*too relaxed*" and became lazier while learning at home, as one student pointed out: "*I think being comfortable is actually the problem of online classes. Everyone is in their home and, speaking for myself, at home it is sometimes difficult to focus in the way you can in a classroom.*" Some students could not find a quiet place at home to join the online class due to their living circumstances: "*it is hard if you live with a partner in a one-bedroom apartment and you both have online classes so for me it was sometimes inconvenient to have a quiet place to focus.*" The loss of concentration may also be caused by the exhaustion resulting from the excessive use of electronic devices: "*I think looking at a screen is more tiring than looking in peoples' real faces,*" "*for me it is hard to stay focused sometimes because you only stare in a screen for 90 minutes without interacting a lot with the students and the teachers.*"

Moreover, students' feedback confirmed the negative impacts brought by the social-distancing policy on their psychological state. As Gao (2020) points out, the mental health and wellbeing of learners is one of the major challenges during the emergency online semester. Stress due to feeling alone or helpless, personal or family issues, unemployment, and overall workload of the semester would certainly reduce the motivation or disturb the concentration of a learner. Two students reported:

> I felt a little bit uncomfortable being just on my own in my room alone in front of the camera […]. Sometimes I just wanted to cry, because I felt lots of pressure in not managing everything that was asked.
>
> I felt like I couldn't make much progress in this semester in terms of learning Chinese […] because the current situation was stressful and especially because the libraries were closed, it was very difficult to concentrate. […] I think my frustration led to a blockage in my head.

These reflections corroborate the findings of current studies on the correlation between students' worsening mental health and the pandemic situation (Elmer et al., 2020; Son et al., 2020). Previous studies state that affective factors are crucial for learning (Ehrman, 1996; Hurd, 2007a; White, 2010). In remote language learning, the affective factors play a more vital role, as Hurd (2007a) argues: "*[a]ffective factors have an impact on all learning, but may be particularly significant for language learning at a distance because of mismatch between an inherently social discipline such as languages and a learning context which is characterized by remoteness, and because of the specific features of languages which make them more difficult to learn at a distance than other disciplines*" (p. 244). It is obvious that the mental isolation on account of remote learning combined with the wider social-distancing policy during the pandemic hinders effective learning.

Less Time for Handwriting Practice

Another noteworthy issue is handwriting. 56.4% of participants revealed that they had spent less time practicing handwriting. This was predictable as, aside from the regular weekly character writing assignments, handwritten skills were tested more often in class through short dictation tests or informal quizzes before the pandemic. The results were checked directly by the teachers or shared with fellow students on the blackboard for further discussion in class. Yet teaching and testing Chinese character writing online "*requires extra technology and digital tools*" (Wang & East, 2020, p. 11), such as writing pads, touch pens, tablets, and so on. At the beginning of the semester, an interactive website *whiteboard.fi* was trialed for the testing of character writing during the class. The students could use the touch screen of their own smartphone, which worked at least for single character writing. However, it is ill-suited to testing writing in full sentences because the screen on a phone is too small. As most of the students did not have adequate equipment for alternative methods, this kind of character writing test was hard to adapt for implementation in online classes. Therefore, students were asked to practice handwriting on their own in order to prepare for the final exam. The character writing assignments of each lesson and after-class writing exercises were still offered and corrected on Moodle and discussed during the "homework discussion" session on a weekly basis. During the class, activities related to character writing were mostly accomplished by typing in order to save class time for other activities.

When it comes to remote learning, students are required to be more autonomous and responsible for their own study (Hurd, 2000; White, 1995), yet many students are ill-prepared for this style of learning (Russell & Murphy-Judy, 2020; Wang & East, 2020; White, 2010). Two students admitted that they needed to be pushed: "*I found it harder to motivate myself to write Chinese characters during this semester. When you don't need to write them in class, there's no pressure to learn them," "I feel that nobody 'controls' me during an online course and I don't feel motivated to prepare for the next lesson."* Some students expressed concerns about the final exam, which must be written by hand, and hoped that more handwriting exercises could be given in the coming semester to help them prepare.

Interestingly, although 51.3% of the students had lower motivation when not sitting in the classroom, the motivation to complete homework assignments during this semester did not drop accordingly: only 20.5% of the students felt less motivated to do their homework. This was not referenced directly by participants in any of the open-ended questions; however, in light of the worries they expressed about the final exam and loss of writing skills, we may speculate that exam pressure could have been a factor. Practicing writing through homework tasks is the most effective way to prepare for the final written exam. Furthermore, a student who completed the homework would receive feedback from the teacher and other students during the "homework discussion" session as well as additional individual feedback from the teacher via Moodle, increasing their opportunities for interaction. In this way they may feel more connected and noticed, which carries greater significance during the pandemic.

5.2 Perception of Practicability of Online Learning

In order to find out whether the participants consider certain learning components to be better suited to online rather than offline teaching, they were asked to compare online and traditional teaching modes with regard to a few skills and learning components and then to decide which would lead to a better outcome in their view. Table 3.1 provides a summary of students' opinions about practicability of learning components in these two modes.

The three learning components for which most students found that the face-to-face classroom mode was superior were speaking (76.9%), pronunciation (71.8%), and handwriting (66.7%). Not a single student considered the online mode for speaking and pronunciation better than

Table 3.1 Students' opinions on the practicability of different learning components in online/in-class modes

In your view, which learning mode would lead to a better outcome for the respective components?	Online	In-class	No difference
Speaking	0 (0%)	30 (76.9%)	9 (23.1%)
Pronunciation	0 (0%)	28 (71.8%)	11 (28.2%)
Handwriting	2 (5.1%)	26 (66.7%)	11 (28.2%)
Listening	7 (17.9%)	17 (43.6%)	15 (38.5%)
Grammar	8 (20.5%)	12 (30.8%)	19 (48.7%)
Vocabulary and text	8 (20.5%)	11 (28.2%)	20 (51.3%)
Homework discussion	6 (15.4%)	11 (28.2%)	22 (56.4%)

the traditional way. These results are in accord with what Lin (2021) reports about the teachers' opinions; "character writing," "pronunciation," and "speaking" were considered the three least favorable components for online teaching.

These results are very understandable. Firstly, the quality of speaking and pronunciation training may be impaired greatly when technical problems are encountered during online teaching. Secondly, due to its complex nature and considerable differences compared to alphabetic writing, Chinese character learning is always regarded as one of the biggest challenges of Chinese language learning. It is not only time consuming, but also requires a high degree of self-regulation. At Germany universities, character writing is usually one of the central curricular components influencing exam results. Before the pandemic, teachers could easily demonstrate the characters on the blackboard, check students' writing, or give dictation tests in class. Online learning, as Zhang (2020b) states, "*minimizes the opportunity for handwriting*" (p. 22). Thus, teaching character writing online requires substantial technical support. One BA2 student who preferred learning handwriting online remarked: "*I would have liked to engage more in online handwriting sessions, so as to enhance my*

3 Emergency Remote Chinese Language Learning at a German... 73

writing and practice it efficiently, maybe using whiteboard.fi; I have an iPad so it is really convenient for me, but I understand that this might be a challenge for almost everyone else." From the remarks of this student it is evident that if handwriting training is supported by adequate equipment such as writing pads, the problems could be mitigated to some extent. Unfortunately, the reality is that not all students can afford to purchase the necessary equipment, as Russell (2020) points out, *"the economically disadvantaged students and students in rural areas without access to hardware and/or the internet are at a greater disadvantage during the 2020 school closures"* (p. 340). This issue needs to be resolved if we plan to continue with online teaching.

Interestingly, more than half of the students believed that it was not necessary for listening training to take place in the face-to-face classroom: 38.5% of students thought there was no difference between online and traditional mode, and 17.9% of students preferred the online mode. Those who preferred the online mode indicated that listening with one's headphones is clearer and louder. In terms of "grammar," "vocabulary and text" and "homework discussion," around half of the participants did not see the difference between teaching online and teaching in a traditional classroom (48.7%, 51.3%, 56.4% respectively). There was also a minority of participants who were more supportive of these components being taught online rather than in the classroom. These findings suggest that if adequate technical support can be provided, these areas have greater potential to be taught online or at least that students do not find the format to be relevant.

5.3 Preferences with Regard to Future Course Adjustments

Despite the high satisfaction with the overall course organization during this online semester (43.6% strongly agree, 51.3% agree), it is interesting to note that the number of students who supported fully online teaching in the future is low. As we can see in Fig. 3.1, 20 out of 39 students (51.3%) supported a blended mode that combines online and offline

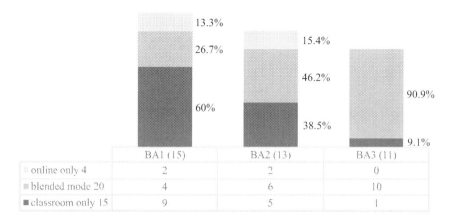

Fig. 3.1 Students' preferences in different teaching modes with regard to future course adjustments

teaching, whereas 15 students (38.5%) preferred the classroom only mode. Those who supported the fully online mode only made up 10.3%.

This result may reflect the fact that, through this new experience, some students recognized the benefits online teaching had brought and believed that this new way of teaching could be an asset to language learning, but that the prospect of solely online learning is not acceptable to the majority of students. One student commented: "*the quality of the course depends a lot on the teachers' dedication. Online courses can be a total disaster.*" Indeed, compared to class teaching successful online teaching depends much more on adequate technical support, as well as on the interplay of teachers' *digital pedagogical competence* (Zhang, 2020a) and dedication, which are much more complex and sometimes hard to ensure. Students' negative experiences with various online courses during this semester may have led to a loss of confidence or trust in fully online teaching.

Notably, the support ratio of a blended mode correlates with the learning level of students (BA1: 26.7%; BA2: 46.2%; BA3: 90.9%). This tendency may be a reflection of certain learning anxieties if we consider the following remarks of two respondents. A BA1 student reported: "*in the second semester I still feel insecure in using the language so it is hard to feel more comfortable with the language [...], but luckily we already learned all the first-semester basics. Without those basics it would have been a lot harder.*"

On the other hand, a BA2 student expressed less anxiety regarding online learning: "*I am in Chinese 4 so I know the basics which makes it in general easier to understand new grammar, vocabulary, etc. I think it's way harder for the Chinese 2 students to continue studying Chinese.*" This is consistent with Pichette (2009)'s claim: "*as students gain language learning experience and increased language competence, their language anxiety tends to go down*" (p. 79). He further indicates that more experienced learners showed less anxiety than beginners in an online setting.

When asked what they would recommend for future course adjustments, many students who supported the blended mode proposed that the conversation class should definitely be carried out in person, whereas grammar lectures and homework discussions could be online. Some students also suggested continuing with the digital tools, such as *Classkick* or *Quizlet*, in the coming semesters. This suggestion fits with the results of the investigation into satisfaction with digital tools used in BA1 and BA2 courses, which was also included in this end of term survey: more than 70% of respondents were satisfied with *Classkick* (75%) and *Quizlet* (72.2%*)*.

6 Concluding Remarks

This paper takes the Chinese language program at HU as a case study to illuminate Chinese language teaching during the first emergency online semester in 2020 in Germany and discusses the results obtained from a student end of term survey. The findings show that, firstly, more than half of the students felt less comfortable in the online setting. This is understandable because they were involuntarily transitioned to this learning mode during the pandemic, and their anxiety levels are likely to have been heightened (Russell, 2020). Nonetheless, online education certainly has unique advantages which cannot be realized in traditional in-class education. Most students still perceive that online learning has the following benefits: saving commuting time, easy access from anywhere, flexibility of studying pace and the comfort of searching for information during class. As regards the disadvantages of online learning, the lack of authentic social interaction was widely identified as a significant issue and one that caused a decline in motivation. Excessive use of electronic devices has resulted in distraction and exhaustion, both mentally and physically. In addition, technical problems related to their own devices, and unreliable internet connections, were often a source of stress for students. Students also expressed feelings of apprehension about final exams as they had less opportunities to practice handwriting.

Secondly, the training of skills related to oral communication and character writing was regarded by the majority of respondents as having a better effect in the face-to-face classroom. On the other hand, around half of the participants did not see a difference between online and on-campus settings when it comes to learning components that related more to knowledge transfer (e.g., grammar) or homework discussion. Thirdly, more than 50% of respondents supported a blended teaching mode in the future. The support rate of BA3 students was the highest. In general the lower the respondent's language competence level was, the greater their support was for the fully in-class teaching mode. Among the digital tools used during this semester, the employment of *Classkick* and *Quizlet* was valued and requested to be continued. This study also found that student motivation for completing assignments was not as heavily impacted as motivation for online learning in general, which could arguably be attributed to the pressure of exams and otherwise reduced opportunity to practice characters making students perceive assignments as more vital, and to the desire of students to be more actively involved in feedback rounds.

One of the limitations of this study is that the sample size is small. Another limitation is that it solely relies on the students' self-reported data, whereas their teachers' voice is not documented in this study. It is also worth considering that during the pandemic students have had numerous and diverse other experiences with online courses, which were not limited to the Chinese language course discussed here. The overall experience of online learning may also have had an influence on their judgment of the Chinese language course: some students may become more appreciative of small successes, whereas others may become more pessimistic about online learning regardless of quality. The broader contextualization of online teaching is not examined in this study.

Many educators agree that, despite the challenges, the COVID-19 pandemic has brought new opportunities, and they envision a wide range of possibilities for the application of more digital tools. In Lin (2021), more than 85% of the teachers surveyed agreed that the online semester had enhanced their competence with digital tools. A majority of teachers (81%) confirmed that they will consider integrating more digital tools into future class teaching. It is also no longer unimaginable that our curriculum will remain partially online, even after the return to the "real" classroom, in order to enable more flexible and effective teaching. Like many universities worldwide, from the autumn of 2020 to the summer of 2021 most German universities still followed a "maximally digital" or "fully digital" approach (DPA, 2020; Warnecke & Burchard, 2020). In light of the possible extension of the online semester and of the fact that (partially) online education may become the "new normal," this article is hoped to help feed the discussion on related pedagogical challenges and be of assistance to teaching design by providing a sample of university Chinese language teaching in Germany during the pandemic and by reflecting on common problems and issues Chinese language teachers worldwide may have confronted.

Appendix: Online Survey

Personal experiences

1. I feel more comfortable to learn the Chinese language online instead of learning in the classroom.
    (select: *strongly agree—agree—disagree—strongly disagree—I don't know*)
2. Please provide the reasons for supporting your opinion (as detailed as better).
    (open-end)
3. According to your personal experience during this term, compared to learning in the classroom, what is/are the advantage(s) when you learn the language online?
    (multiple answers are allowed)

Options:

- *I don't need to spend time on commuting.*
- *I feel more relaxed outside the classroom.*
- *I feel more motivated outside the classroom.*
- *I can easily search for information on my computer or mobile phone during the class.*
- *I can learn at my own pace.*
- *I can study anywhere.*
- *I am more motivated when doing my homework.*
- *Other:*

4. In your view, compared to learning in the classroom, what is/are the disadvantage(s) of learning the language online? (multiple answers are allowed)
    Options:

- *I spend less time on practicing handwriting.*
- *I feel less motivated when I don't sit in the classroom.*
- *My computer (sometimes) has problems.*
- *My internet speed is (sometimes) insufficient.*
- *It is difficult to find a quiet place to take the online courses.*
- *There is less direct interaction between teacher/student and student/student.*
- *I don't feel motivated to do my homework.*
- *Other:*

5. Please explain your choices made above (it would be nice if you could provide some examples of your personal experiences).
(open-end)

Perception of practicability of online learning

6. In your view, which learning mode would lead to a better outcome for the respective components? (multiple answers are allowed)

Options: *pronunciation /grammar /vocabulary and text /listening /speaking /handwriting /discussing the homework*
7. Any comments?
(open-end)

Preferences with regard to future course adjustments

8. If you could decide on the teaching mode for your current course, what would you prefer?
   (select: *online mode only /classroom only /blended mode-partially online, partially classroom*)
9. Please provide explanations for supporting your opinion. If you prefer the "blended mode," please also suggest how this could be implemented.
   (open-end)
10. In general, I am satisfied with the overall organization of the current course.
    (select: *strongly agree—agree—disagree—strongly disagree—I don't know*)
11. Please provide your comments and suggestions on the course you have taken this term.
(open-end)

References

Beblavý, M., Baiocco, S., Kilhoffer, Z., Akgüç, M., & Jacquot, M. (2019). *Index of readiness for digital lifelong learning changing how Europeans upgrade their skills*. Final Report November 2019. Centre for European Policy Studies.

Carrel, P. (2018, June 25). Where Europe's most powerful economy is falling behind. *Reuters Investigates*. Retrieved April 20, 2021, from https://www.reuters.com/investigates/special-report/germany-digital-gap/

DPA (= Deutsche Presse-Agentur). (2020, June 8). Uni-Präsidentin: 'Corona-Krise ist ein großer Katalysator' [University president: 'Corona crisis is a big catalyst']. *Süddeutsche Zeitung*. Retrieved April 20, 2021, from https://www.sueddeutsche.de/bildung/hochschulen-frankfurt-am-main-uni-praesidentincorona-krise-ist-ein-grosser-katalysator-dpa.urn-newsml-dpa-com-20090101-200608-99-344273

Ehrman, M. E. (1996). *Understanding second language learning difficulties*. Sage Publications.

Elmer, T., Mepham, K., & Stadtfeld, C. (2020). Students under lockdown: Comparisons of students' social networks and mental health before and during the COVID-19 crisis in Switzerland. *PLoS ONE, 15*(7), Article e0236337. https://doi.org/10.1371/journal.pone.0236337

FaCh (=Fachverband Chinesisch [Chinese Language Teacher Association in German-speaking area]). (2020). Chinesisch an Hochschulen [Chinese at universities and colleges]. Retrieved April 20, 2021, from https://www.fachverband-chinesisch.de/chinesisch-als-fremdsprache/hochschulen

Gao, X. (2020). Australian students' perceptions of the challenges and strategies for learning Chinese characters in emergency online teaching. *International Journal of Chinese Language Teaching, 1*(1), 83–98.

Golden, C. (2020, March 23). Remote teaching: The glass half-full. *EDUCAUSE Review*. Retrieved April 20, 2021, from https://er.educause.edu/blogs/2020/3/remote-teaching-the-glass-half-full

Hampel, R., Felix, U., Hauck, M., & Coleman, J. (2005). Complexities of learning and teaching languages in a real-time audiographic environment. *GFL: German as a Foreign Language, 3*, 1–30.

Hauck, M., & Hurd, S. (2005). Exploring the link between language anxiety and learner self-management in face-to-face and virtual language learning contexts. *European Journal of Open, Distance and E-Learning, 2*.

Hodges, C., Moore, S., Lockee, B., Trust, T., & Bond, A. (2020, March 27). The difference between emergency remote teaching and online learning. *Educause Review*. https://er.educause.edu/articles/2020/3/the-difference-between-emergency-remote-teaching-and-online-learning

Holcomb, L. B., King, F. B., & Brown, S. W. (2004). Student traits and attributes contributing to success in online courses: Evaluation of university online courses. *The Journal of Interactive Online Learning, 2*(3), 1–17.

Hsieh, H. F., & Shannon, S. E. (2005). Three approaches to qualitative content analysis. *Qualitative Health Research, 15*(9), 1277–1288.

Hurd, S. (2000). Distance language learners and learner support: beliefs, difficulties and use of strategies. *Links and Letters 7: Autonomy in Language Learning, 7*, 61–80.

Hurd, S. (2005). Distance learning in modern languages. In J. Coleman & J. Klapper (Eds.), *Effective learning and teaching in modern languages*. Routledge.

Hurd, S. (2007a). Distant voices: Learners' stories about the affective side of learning a language at a distance. *International Journal of Innovation in Language Learning and Teaching, 1*(2), 242–259.

Hurd, S. (2007b). Anxiety and non-anxiety in a distance language learning environment: The distance factor as a modifying influence. *System, 35*, 487–508.

Kerres, M. (2020). Against all odds: Education in Germany coping with Covid-19. *Postdigital Science and Education, 2*, 690–694.

Klöter, H. (2016). Chinesisch-Sprachkurse in BA-Studiengängen an Hochschulen in Deutschland, Österreich und der Schweiz: Ergebnisse einer Erhebung. [Chinese language courses in BA programs at universities in Germany, Austria and Switzerland: Results of a survey]. *CHUN-Chinesischunterricht, 31*, 51–62.

Liebau-Liu, X. (2020, November 13). 2020年夏季学期德语区高校中文课网课调查 [A survey of online Chinese language courses at universities in Germany, Austria and Switzerland during the summer term 2020] [Online conference presentation]. The 3rd workshop for Chinese language education within China-related BA/MA programs in Germen-speaking countries. Bonn University, Germany.

Lin, C. (2016). 德國中文教學概況—海外視角下的師資培育 [Chinese language teaching in Germany: Looking at pre-service Chinese language teacher education from outside Taiwan]. 臺灣華語教學研究 [*Taiwan Journal of Chinese as a Second Language*], *12*, 67–98.

Lin, C. (2021). *Emergency online Chinese language teaching at the tertiary level: Results of a survey of teachers in Austria, Germany, and Switzerland*. CHUN-Chinesischunterricht, 36, 40–63.

Lin, C. (forthcoming). Google辅助语言学习—门高年级线上課程之设计与实践 [Google-assisted language learning: An online Chinese course for advanced learners], in S. Liu (Ed.), *Online Chinese teaching and learning in 2020*. National Foreign Language Resource Center, University of Hawaii.

Liu, S., Wang, Y., & Zhan, H. (2020a, July 11). *A survey of student perspectives on learning Chinese online: Preliminary results* [Online conference presentation]. The International Forum of Textbook Development and Virtual Conference on Teaching Chinese as an International Language, Hong Kong.

Liu, S., Wang, Y., & Zhan, H. (2020b, July 11). *A survey of instructors on teaching Chinese online in 2020: Preliminary results* [Online conference presentation]. The International Forum of Textbook Development and Virtual Conference on Teaching Chinese as an International Language, Hong Kong.

Olt, M. R. (2002). Ethics and distance education: Strategies for minimizing academic dishonesty in online assessment. *Online Journal of Distance Learning Administration, 5*(3), 1–7.

Picciano, A. G. (2002). Beyond student perceptions: Issues of interaction, presence, and performance in an online course. *Journal of Asynchronous learning networks, 6*(1), 21–40.

Pichette, F. (2009). Second language anxiety and distance language learning. *Foreign Language Annals, 42*(1), 77–93.

Russell, V. (2020). Language anxiety and the online learner. *Foreign Language Annals, 53*, 338–352.

Russell, V., & Murphy-Judy, K. (2020). *Teaching language online: A guide to designing, developing, and delivering online, blended, and flipped language courses.* Routledge.

Son, C., Hegde, S., Smith, A., Wang, X., & Sasangohar, F. (2020). Effects of COVID-19 on college students' mental health in the United States: Interview survey study. *Journal of Medical Internet Research, 22*(9), Article e21279. https://doi.org/10.2196/21279

Wamsley, L. (2019, August 29). Germany's (dis)connectivity: Can the broadband internet gap be bridged? *The Local.* Retrieved April 20, 2021, from https://www.thelocal.de/20190829/germanys-disconnectivity-can-the-broadband-gap-be-bridged-internet

Wang, D., & East, M. (2020). Constructing an emergency Chinese curriculum during the pandemic: A New Zealand experience. *International Journal of Chinese Language Teaching, 1*(1), 1–19.

Warnecke, T., & Burchard, A. (2020, October 20). Präsenzlehre der Unis noch mehr eingeschränkt: Auch das Wintersemester in Berlin wird digital [On-campus teaching at universities restrictions extended: Berlin's winter semester will also be taught online]. Der Tagesspiegel. Retrieved April 20, 2021, from https://www.tagesspiegel.de/wissen/praesenzlehre-der-unis-noch-mehr-eingeschraenkt-auch-das-wintersemester-in-berlin-wird-digital/26290782.html

White, C. (1995). Autonomy and strategy use in distance foreign language learning: Research findings. *System, 23*(2), 207–221.

White, C. (2010). *Language learning in distance education.* Cambridge University Press.

Zhang, C. (2020a). From face-to-face to screen-to-screen: CFL Teachers' beliefs about digital teaching competence during the pandemic. *International Journal of Chinese Language Teaching, 1*(1), 35–52.

Zhang, Q. (2020b). Narrative inquiry into online teaching of Chinese characters during the pandemic. *International Journal of Chinese Language Teaching, 1*(1), 20–34.

Zhao, L. X., Blankinship, B., Duan, Z., Huang, H., Sun, J., & Bak, T. H. (2020). Comparing face-to-face and online teaching of written and spoken Chinese to adult learners: An Edinburgh-Sheffield case study. *International Journal of Chinese Language Teaching, 1*(1), 83–98.

4

Learning Chinese Online in the Age of COVID-19: The Cases of Two Italian Universities

Chiara Romagnoli and Valentina Ornaghi

1 Introduction

One of the consequences of the COVID-19 outbreak was the nearly worldwide closure of schools and universities. Instruction at all levels has undergone a huge change, and this sudden and unplanned shift has found the main actors, that is, teachers and students, unprepared. The challenge faced by all instructors has been particularly hard for language teachers; while many of them were most certainly familiar with the usage of platforms and digital resources already, the prevalent form of teaching at the university level has always been face-to-face with an ever-increasing attention to learners' needs and questions. In this respect, Italy boasts a long tradition of in-class lectures, and university-level instruction is

C. Romagnoli (✉)
Roma Tre University, Rome, Italy
e-mail: chiara.romagnoli@uniroma3.it

V. Ornaghi
Sapienza University, Rome, Italy
e-mail: valentina.ornaghi@uniroma1.it

generally linked with face-to-face lessons. Online training, and online universities, is a relatively young phenomenon in Italy, started and officially recognized less than 20 years ago[1].

Providing didactic material online and moving all didactic activities onto a platform are obviously different things. As shown by the few official reports available, the evaluation of this experiment has been overall positive but problems and weaknesses were impossible to avoid.

The aim of this chapter is to describe the situation of online Chinese teaching at the university level in Italy during the COVID-19 period. In order to do so, we first provide some reference on online teaching and we then describe the main research results on Chinese language online teaching. These paragraphs are followed by the illustration of the figures related to Italian universities courses, with particular attention to two very different public institutions, one in Rome and the other in Milan. The last two sections are focused on the data collected in these two universities in order to verify how learners perceived online teaching and which are the main critical issues. Data have been collected by an online questionnaire, completed by 156 participants belonging to 5 different language levels.

2 Literature Review

2.1 Online Teaching

Many researchers (Braun et al., 2013; Schwienhorst, 2002; Weerasinghe et al., 2009) state that designing an online course means investing time and money. Generally speaking, behind an online course there are different professional figures: not only teachers but also other professionals such as instructional designers, curricula planners, content designers, and art directors. An online course therefore should be carefully planned in advance (Piras et al., 2020). Weerasinghe et al. (2009) provide the following suggestions in design of an online course: display the learning

---

[1] Italian Ministry of Education recognized online universities in 2003 and in the following year, the first Italian public online university was officially founded, the Università Telematica Guglielmo Marconi.

outcomes at the beginning of the course and display the related learning objectives at the beginning of section; order the learning content according to the syllabus; add activities to each unit of the learning content; add at least one quiz to the end of each section of a course to let students evaluate their learning achievements after completing a section of the course; add discussion forums and chatrooms. As for the contents and materials, the content should be built with different types of media such as text, graphics, audio, video, and animations. Similarly, some scholars (e.g., Chen, 2018; Hua, 2018) advise to provide mini-lectures for self-study through a series of videos followed by specific and targeted exercises to guarantee understanding.

Concerning the courses presented in this paper, they had been carried out as face-to-face courses during the first semester and the syllabus, which students could find on the institutional website, had been planned accordingly. The emergency situation did not allow extra time for carefully planning out the online course; therefore, the greatest concern was to try and maintain a degree of interaction as high as possible, since students had enrolled to an in-class course and it was our intention to keep the course as close to the in-class mode as possible. The teacher's presence, the social presence, and interaction are among the main concerns about online courses, and a key point in avoiding high drop-out rates (Crews et al., 2015; Goral, 2013; Griffith & Charles, 2009; Hua, 2018; Kaplan & Haenlein, 2016; Panagiotidis, 2019; Weerasinghe et al., 2009). This is even more true in the case of language learning: "In distance language courses input can be easily provided but not output. Learners must have the opportunity to interact in the target language to negotiate meaning, make input more comprehensible, get feedback, and recognize the need to change their language to achieve successful communication" (Perifanou & Economides, 2014, p. 3563). Also Panagiotidis (2019) states that "learning a language is not comparable to learning other subjects, as it demands a high level of interaction with other speakers and the use of higher order thinking skills" (p. 286).

Sun (2011) suggests one-to-one synchronous online meetings with the instructor or sometimes with small groups. Due to the large class size and the difficulty to manage individual meetings, unless the universities employ a higher number of tutors, one-to-one synchronous online meetings cannot be the case for our university courses. Many other scholars (Kaplan & Haenlein, 2016; Means et al., 2014; Moreira Teixeira & Mota, 2014), therefore, suggest a mix of synchronous and asynchronous teaching to ensure student-teacher and student-student interaction. According to Burgerova and Cimermanova (2014), a way to increase social presence is to organize activities focused on critical review, expressing opinions, reflections and idea sharing, small groups to collaborate, and problem solving to make activities more authentic. As Vygotsky (1986) states, humans learn through interaction. In an asynchronous course, such interaction can be achieved through discussion threads and wikis, which require cooperation and mutual work, being a shared space in which participants can write and edit at the same time. It is also possible to resort to tools for synchronous online chat and discussion or online conversations such as role-playing, virtual office hours, or inviting an online guest lecturer to name but a few. The final suggestion is a mix of synchronous and asynchronous, uploading texts in PDF and PPT to present theoretical material, animated presentations, wiki and thread discussion for asynchronous discussion and chat for synchronous communication (Burgerova & Cimermanova, 2014). Jolliffe et al. (2001) suggest different tools for various interactions, such as using quizzes and forums for asynchronous interaction on a topic, and using videoconferences and face-to-face tutoring for synchronous interaction. Such interactions help reduce sense of isolation for students. Other scholars underline the importance of using synchronous tools such as both videoconferences and computer mediated communication to enhance interaction (McVay Lynch, 2002; Salmon, 2000). A commonly appreciated tool for written synchronous interaction is chatrooms, through which students can receive immediate feedback. Chatrooms also facilitate those students who tend to be shy and do not participate actively in face-to-face classes (Balboni, 2006; Chini & Bosisio, 2014; Payne & Whitney, 2002; Wang & Bellassen, 2017).

Another solution proposed by various scholars (e.g., Means et al., 2014; Picciano, 2017) aiming at overcoming the shortcomings of online courses is blended learning, which is a mix of in-class synchronous teaching and asynchronous online learning. Blended learning involves additional instructional resources and activities that encourage interaction among learners. One type of blended learning is flipped classrooms, which is gaining growing popularity. As described by some scholars (Hua, 2018; Means et al., 2014), in flipped classrooms, learning materials (such as web-based videos to introduce new concepts) are given to students online before the class, during class students engage in practical activities and interaction with the teacher and their peers, based on what they have studied. This method gives more chance to teachers to interact with students individually or in small groups, since the class could be split into two groups rotating, one working in class and one working online from home.

2.2 Online Teaching of Chinese Language

Chinese universities can be considered pioneers in online courses, and especially in MOOCs (Massive open online courses). According to *The New York Times*, 2012 was the year of the MOOC, when different platforms such as Udacity, Coursera, and EdX were launched in the United States (Means et al., 2014). Chinese universities joined right after. In 2013, major universities in China such as Beijing University, Qinghua University, and the University of Hong Kong launched their first MOOCs, some of which including Chinese language courses. One can now find a plethora of free Chinese language courses and resources online. One such example is the possibility to access a wide range of free teaching materials as well as online courses through the *Confucius Institute Online* website[2]. At the same time, there are numerous online tools which both students and teachers can resort to when teaching or practicing oral and written Chinese (Navarre, 2019).

However, one of the main problems is still interaction. In analyzing the use of MOOCs, Lin and Zhang (2014) underline the fact that, due to the high numbers of students enrolled, teachers cannot have individual conversations with each of them; therefore, forums are the main means of interaction and discussion. They point out that in order to solve the problem of teacher-student interaction, some teachers can decide to have

---

[2] https://mooc.chinesecio.com/index.html

a time online to meet students or use synchronous tools such as Google Hangouts to hold online conversations to interact with students and answer their questions. Obviously, this kind of teacher-student interaction is problematic in MOOCs, considering the high number of students enrolled. Other researchers also highlight the fact that the only form of interaction possible with MOOCs is asynchronous written interaction through forums and wikis (Wang & Pei, 2016; Xin, 2019). Some Chinese researchers analyzing Chinese language courses for beginners and intermediate courses offered by Beijing University note that all lessons are teacher centered: the video-lesson is recorded inside a classroom, where the teacher gives explanations but there is no interaction with students. The interaction is left at the end of the video-lesson, where students have to complete some quizzes and exercises (Wang & Pei, 2016; Wei, 2017). This is student-content interaction, but it lacks that kind of social interaction between student and teacher and among students. Some student-student interaction can be achieved through peer-reviewed exercises. For example, students record themselves and upload their recording, which is corrected by other students (Wang & Pei, 2016). The efficacy of peer review at beginner levels is questionable, however, since beginner students are not equipped to provide good feedback in a field in which they themselves are a novice (Means et al., 2014).

Another issue to be considered is writing. Chinese is a morphosyllabic language (DeFrancis, 1984). The phonetic analysis is traditionally based on the syllable, each of which corresponds to a character and to a morpheme. But while each character corresponds to a syllable expressing a certain meaning, the same syllable pronounced in the same tone does not necessarily correspond to a single character and therefore to a single meaning, due to a high presence of homophones. As such, in case of monosyllabic words, the transcription in characters can play an important role in disambiguation. Learning characters is thus fundamental in Chinese language. Some of the above-mentioned online Chinese language courses for beginners include the teaching of characters while others only focus on oral Chinese, while separate courses are offered for learning Chinese characters. However, these courses merely show the selected characters' stroke order and students are required to copy them (Wei, 2017). The challenge posed by writing is also highlighted by Sun

(2011), especially for elementary courses, where students should learn characters' handwriting and recognition: video clips which capture the movements of the writing of characters stroke-by-stroke are not enough, "many students at the end showed poor ability in recognizing and writing characters. Compared with the on-campus students, online students overall character reading and writing abilities were lower" (p. 434). Wang and Bellassen (2017) also agree that writing cannot be excluded from an online Chinese language course. They suggest the following types of exercises for the acquisition of Chinese characters: (1) visual recognition (Chinese character recognition, radicals' combination, Chinese character decomposition); and (2) Chinese character handwriting practice (handwriting Chinese characters with the teacher).

3 Italian Universities During the COVID-19 Pandemic

3.1 General Situation in Italian Universities

Following the outbreak of COVID-19, the Italian government on 4 March 2020 ordered the closure of all schools and universities nationwide. For many universities, that period coincided with the beginning of the second term, and the shift from classroom to distance teaching highlighted both potentialities and critical issues. It is worth mentioning that a number of university courses included e-learning through different platforms well before the global health crisis. Nevertheless, the activities of teaching, assessment, final examinations, boards and committee meetings, students' guidance services, and tutorship in the vast majority of cases took place only in the classroom and within the university public spaces. Even the transcription of the examination result is considered a public act in Italy and has always been done in person with witnesses. The closure of universities has therefore caused a dramatic change and has necessarily found most of the institutions unprepared to face new didactic, technical, and administrative challenges.

According to the data provided by CRUI (Conference of Italian Universities Rectors) at the end of March, 88 out of the 97 universities existing in Italy have transferred the vast majority of instructional activities online with more than half of the universities providing 96% of courses through distance teaching, thus potentially reaching 1,300,000 students[3]. The universities used different platforms such as Microsoft Teams (40%), Google Meet (10%), Webex (5%), and others (Adobe Connect and Zoom).

Another useful, although not unbiased, source to have an idea of the conditions under which this huge change took place is the investigation carried out by the CGIL (Italian General Confederation of Labour), the largest labor union in Italy. The sample included in the CGIL questionnaire comprises less than one thousand participants and is therefore rather small, but nevertheless, the participants come from over 60 Italian universities, mainly public, and include professors, assistant professors, and lecturers, thus representing a variety of different perspectives. The vast majority of participants, 809 out of 914, have provided online teaching, either because they wanted to do it (63%) or because they were strongly encouraged by the university (25%). As for the lesson duration, for more than half of participants (62%) it has not changed after the passage to online courses. The differences reported for this aspect have to be linked to the instructor position and to the geographical areas: for more than 75% of language lecturers, the distance teaching time has not changed compared to that of the classroom lessons, while the percentage for professors is lower (62%). As for the difference related to the geographical area, in the north west of Italy 65% of instructors provided online lessons for the same time as classroom lessons and the percentage decreases to 55% in southern Italy.

Another interesting fact emerging from the CGIL investigation is related to the existence of guidelines and training regarding distance teaching. As for the existence of guidelines, a positive answer has been given by one-third of participants whereas stated that the guidelines they

---

[3] Data provided by the CGIL report are available at http://www.flcgil.it/files/pdf/20200420/l-universita-nell-emergenza-covid-19-report-forum-docenza-universitaria-del-15-aprile-2020.pdf.

were given were not useful enough. In addition to this, only a small proportion of participants have been trained on the pedagogical and technical issues that arise during distance teaching, and the lack of continuous support has caused discontent among instructional personnel.

A more recent and comprehensive picture is the one provided by Ramella and Rostan (2020). The two scholars collected the data drawn from a sample of 3398 professors and researchers in order to (i) know how Italian academics faced the challenge of distance teaching and (ii) highlight critical issues and share experience. According to this research, the evaluation of the instructional activities in the age of COVID-19 is overall positive; less than one week after the order imposing the closure of schools and universities, 72% of instructors activated distance teaching and, as shown by CGIL's report, online lessons duration, in the vast majority of cases, has not reduced from the allotted time of the classroom lessons. Ramella and Rostan (2020)'s report also offers some details on the course content and instructional methods. According to their investigation, 80% of professors completed the objectives listed on syllabi, 11% reduced the amount of content, and 9% added content making it available online.

As for teaching strategies, 67% of instructors partially modified the course's structure and content, only 24% did not change anything, and 9% took this opportunity to considerably modify their teaching practice. One of the issues pointed out in § 2.1 and § 2.2, that is, the tendency of distance teaching to be teacher centered, has also been confirmed by the participants in this investigation; in their view, online teaching marked a backward step in didactic practice. Although Italian universities classes have often been labeled as very traditional, pedantic, and top-down, they actually imply much more interaction than online lessons did.

In this respect, the same report provides some figures on the possibility to interact with teachers during lessons. It emerges that 66% of classes were given live-streaming, and as for student participation, according to 53% of instructors, the number of students during distance teaching has remained the same.

3.2 Chinese Language Courses at Two Italian Universities

In the following paragraphs, we will consider the cases, and data, related to two Italian universities: one in Milan, La Statale (The University of Milan), and the other in Rome, Roma Tre. Although the two institutions are very different in terms of history and number of students, the Chinese programs in both institutions are rather similar and therefore the data drawn from the different samples can be compared.

When the COVID-19 epidemic outbreak spread through Italy at the end of February 2020, Chinese language courses at both universities had just restarted after the winter break, and all classes had to be interrupted and taken online. Therefore, classes which had undergone in-class face-to-face teaching during the first semester had to move to online teaching and learning during the second semester. The shift was sudden and not planned, so it implied taking some quick action and teachers had to re-formulate part of their teaching programs and materials in order to suit the new teaching environment.

Both universities previously had only one asynchronous teaching platform, which was used merely in support of classroom teaching. The platform provided teachers with a space where they could upload some additional materials for students, such as further readings, as well as classroom notices. There was also a forum where students could ask and reply to questions. However, the platform was not powerful enough to support all courses going online, so on the one hand, the universities decided to enhance the existing platform for asynchronous courses, while on the other, they provided all teachers with a Teams account in order to carry on synchronous lessons.

3.3 Chinese Courses at Roma Tre University

Founded in 1992, Roma Tre University is one of the youngest public universities in Rome and has rapidly grown in terms of enrolments as well as in the number of academic courses offered: by the 2019-20 academic year, there were more than 30,000 enrolled students and 101 different courses. Roma Tre University is organized in 12 departments offering Bachelor's and Master's degrees, Postgraduate and Advanced courses, PhDs, and Specialization Schools.

Chinese language and culture courses are taught within the BA degree program in Linguistic and Cultural Mediation (LCM) and the MA degree program in Modern Languages for Communication and International Cooperation (MLCIC). As in most cases in Italian universities, each language course is made of two parts: one delivered by the Italian instructor, the other by the mother-tongue lecturer. The first, who is responsible for the course, provides theoretical explanation on the linguistic aspects taken into account, while the second proposes exercises to master the target language.

The data collected for this study are drawn from the first-, second-, and third-year courses, all of which had already completed one semester of in-class instruction at the time of the COVID-19 outbreak.

The lesson duration has not changed as a result of the transition to online teaching; therefore, first-, second-, and third-year students respectively follow 8, 12, and 12 hours of weekly instruction for these classes. The instructional materials selected for first- and second-year courses are *Il cinese per gli italiani*, volumes 1 and 2, which is a textbook specifically targeted for Italian students learning Chinese (Masini et al., 2006). In addition to this textbook, instructors integrated material selected from other sources in order to help students improve vocabulary size and communicative ability. The content of lessons delivered by Italian and mother-tongue teachers is strictly connected for first- and second- year courses, which are designed to allow students to reach the elementary and pre-intermediate levels respectively. The third-year course content is more challenging since it presents students with authentic material (Chinese press articles illustrated by the Italian teacher) and communicative functions linked to work life (taught by the mother-tongue lecturer who based her exercises on the textbook *Discover China*, vol. 4 edited by Ding et al., 2011).

Since interaction was found to be critical, all teachers decided to primarily rely upon the use of Microsoft Teams to deliver synchronous online classes and to keep them as similar as possible to in-class lessons. Part of the interaction that could not be done orally was carried out via synchronous chat: Microsoft Teams allows participants to interact both orally and through the chatroom. Teachers tried to keep the lesson interactional and active by assigning small tasks to students right after each explanation. One way to do so was to explain a new grammar point and then ask students to build sentences using the newly learnt structure. Many students used the synchronous chat to propose their solutions. The teachers had conducted the same kind of activity previously during in-class face-to-face lessons and did not find students overly willing to participate. As mentioned previously, this may be due to the fact that being at home and "protected" by a computer screen, students feel less shy and more relaxed, and therefore are more confident to give their answer and receive immediate feedback from the teacher. Nevertheless, the feedback on written and oral production was not as effective and regular as that provided during in-class lessons. One reason for this critical aspect is that whereas the instructor feels they have enough time for every learner's question in class, it is harder to properly react online where two channels are simultaneously employed by participants, the oral one used for direct questions and the written one through chat.

3.4   Chinese Courses at the University of Milan

Founded in 1924, the University of Milan counts over 60,000 enrolled students and is organized in 33 departments offering Bachelor's and Master's degrees, Postgraduate and Advanced courses, PhDs, and Specialization Schools. Chinese language and culture courses are taught within the BA degree program in "Language Mediation and Intercultural Communication" (LMIC) and the MA degree program in "Languages and Cultures for International Communication and Cooperation" (LCICC).

The data collected for this study are drawn from the first- and the second- year courses of the MA degree program. Since both courses at the University of Milan had already been carried out in class for one semester, as stated above, instructors decided to continue using the already selected textbooks, adapting them to online teaching. As for course programs, the first-year Chinese language course at the Master degree course in LCICC at the University of Milan focused on the textbook *HSK Standard Course. Level 4* (Jiang, 2016), which included grammar points, conversation, reading, and writing exercises. The second-year course focused on the acquisition of Business Chinese language and the development of writing skills, which included the writing of formal and informal letters, instructions, and business correspondence. Part of the materials were switched to video-lessons which were made with PPT and voice recording for students' self-study.

Also in this case, teachers decided to rely mainly upon the use of Microsoft Teams to deliver synchronous online lessons and facilitate oral interaction as in onsite classes. One finding worth noting was that, due to technical problems, such as poor Internet connection for some students, it was not possible to have the same amount of oral interaction as in class. This was also due to the fact that both classes had quite a high number of students (over 50 and over 30 respectively). Teachers then resorted to a wider use of screen sharing and PPT to explain the lesson in order to offer students a visual aid. Since Chinese is a morphosyllabic language, especially in a situation in which oral interaction is made more difficult by the online tool, which may cause the communication to be at times unclear, having a visual support to read characters on top of listening to the teacher speaking is crucial. Similarly for Roma Tre, teachers for the first-year Master's degree course often used the synchronous chat to carry out written interaction and found students more willing to participate than during onsite lessons. For the second-year Master's degree course, since students were required to write longer assignments, teachers gave coursework at the end of each week, which was sent to the teacher via email for asynchronous feedback.

Finally, all the synchronous videoconferences were recorded and made available among teaching materials on the university platform, in order to help students review, as well as give a chance to catch up with the lesson at their own time and pace to those students who were unable to follow the synchronous lesson. The possibility to review, stop, and play again is one of the main benefits of video-lessons (Griffith & Charles, 2009).

4   Method

The research questions that the present study aims to answer are:

1) How do Chinese language students evaluate online lessons?
2) Given the specific features of Chinese language, is online training on speaking and writing effective?
3) Which are the main challenges encountered?

In order to gather students' opinions on how the emergency remote teaching had been handled, students from Roma Tre University and the University of Milan were asked to fill out an anonymous online questionnaire on a voluntary basis. The questionnaire was divided into two parts.

The first part included the following seven questions. The first six questions were based on a Likert scale (from 1 "strongly disagree" to 5 "strongly agree"), and the last one was a yes/no question.

1) Is the platform practical and simple to use?
2) Can you easily follow the teachers' explanation?
3) Can you interact with the teachers?
4) Can you exercise speaking?
5) Can you practice writing?
6) Are the materials shared by the teachers clearly displayed?
7) Would you take another online course? (Yes/No)

The second part of the questionnaire included three multiple-choice questions on advantages and disadvantages of online teaching and on suggestions for improvement, which are illustrated in detail in the following section.

Thirty-three students out of 50 from the first-year Chinese course (Lin1) and 26 students out of 30 from the second-year Chinese course (Lin2) of the master's degree course in LCICC at the University of Milan filled out the questionnaire during the last day of course.

The questionnaire was also sent to Roma Tre University students at the end of the course: 52 out of 80 students from the first-year Chinese course (Roma1), 26 out of 60 students from the second-year Chinese course (Roma2), and 19 out of 40 students from the third-year Chinese course (Roma3) of the bachelor's degree course in LCM filled out the questionnaire.

Our sample therefore includes 156 participants from 5 different language levels.

5   Results

Our findings showed that the remote online teaching, even carried out in an emergency situation, was appreciated overall, while the main challenge was to guarantee the same type of interaction as in face-to-face lessons. The first seven questions can be grouped into the following three primary aspects: (1) platform and course delivery, (2) willingness to follow another online course, and (3) possibility to practice speaking and writing.

5.1   Platform and Course Delivery

Platform and course delivery refers to questions 1, 2, 3, and 6. In particular, with regard to Teams platform usability and access to materials, which sum up questions 1 and 6. Figure 4.1 below indicates general satisfaction of the students on the emergency remote teaching during the COVID-19 lockdown period.

The dominant answers are (a) "strongly agree" and (b) "agree". This is made evident by grouping together the positive answers, with a+b ranging from 74% to 100% for platform usability and from 79% to 100% for access to materials. It can also be noted that nearly none chose "strongly disagree".

As for the possibility of understanding the teacher's explanations and interacting with them, which refers to questions 2 and 3, there is also positive feedback; in this case, positive answers (a+b) range from 75% to 96% for the teacher's explanations and from 77% to 92% for student-teacher interaction, with the only exception being third-year students at

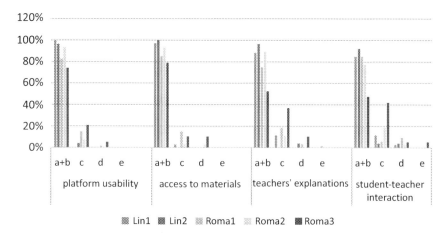

Fig. 4.1 Platform and course delivery. (a: strongly agree, b: agree, c: neither agree nor disagree, d: disagree, e: strongly disagree)

Roma Tre University (a+b around 50% in both cases). Strongly negative answers (e) are almost null as well.

5.2 Willingness of Taking Another Online Course

When participants were asked whether they would take another online course (question 7), the positive answers confirm the substantially positive opinion: about 80% for Lin1 and Lin2, 70% for Roma1 and Roma2, and almost 60% for Roma3.

The answers regarding the possibility to practice speaking and writing (questions 4 and 5) are, however, not as positive compared to the previous questions as can be seen in Fig. 4.2.

5.3 Possibility to Practice Speaking and Writing

As for the possibility to practice speaking, most classes (Lin1, Lin2, Roma1, and Roma2) gave a lower level of positive feedback (a+b) as it ranges from 36% to 54%. The situation is even more critical with Roma3

4 Learning Chinese Online in the Age of COVID-19: The Cases…

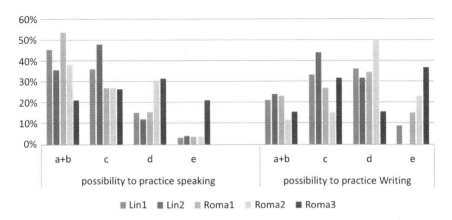

Fig. 4.2 Possibility to practice speaking and writing

students, where positive feedback (a+b) is 21% and strongly negative feedback (e "strongly disagree") is 21% as well.

Regarding the possibility to practice writing, the responses are even more negative. Positive feedback (a+b) is between 12% and 24%, while the percentage of negative responses (d "disagree") is between 32% and 50% compared to speaking exercise (12%-31%). Also in this case, Roma3 students are more critical, giving a higher percentage of e "strongly disagree" (37%).

5.4 Difficulties, Advantages, and Suggestions

This consequently highlights a problem in the two most important activities crucially required in language classes. It can be further confirmed by examining the multiple-choice questions shown in Fig. 4.3, regarding difficulties, advantages, and suggestions. Students were asked to indicate the main difficulties and advantages of online teaching and give suggestions, having the possibility to choose more than one option from the provided choices below:

Main difficulties encountered:
d1   Internet connection problems
d2   little chance to interact with the teacher and other students

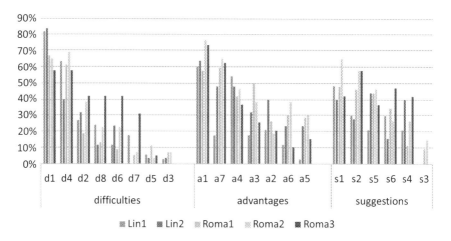

Fig. 4.3 Difficulties, advantages, and suggestions

- d3   materials are not clear
- d4   little opportunity to practice writing
- d5   difficulties in following the teacher's explanation
- d6   little chance of speaking orally
- d7   materials are not suitable for an online course
- d8   little chance of doing exercises in the classroom

Main advantages:
- a1   lesson from home is more comfortable
- a2   I feel less embarrassed and am more willing to take active part in the lesson
- a3   writing exercises are easier at the computer
- a4   it is possible to answer the exercises via chat
- a5   additional materials for self-learning are useful for individual studying
- a6   I can concentrate more and follow the teacher's explanations better
- a7   screen sharing of materials and PPT makes it easier to follow the lesson

Suggestions:
- s1   provide more self-learning materials, such as readings, videos, listening exercises

s2 produce multiple PPTs with recorded voice or video-lessons in support of synchronous lessons
s3 during the lesson, the teacher should devote more time to explanations with PPT
s4 during the lesson, the teacher should devote more time to oral interaction with students
s5 during the lesson, the teacher should dedicate more time to writing exercises, also using chat
s6 assign multiple tasks or intermediate tests to monitor the level of learning

In Fig. 4.3 above, answers have been ordered according to the total of students' choices. By further analyzing the chart, it can be noted that:

Difficulties. The most noted difficulties encountered, after connection problems (d1), were little opportunity to practice writing (d4), ranging from 58% to 69%, with the exception of Lin2 students (40%), and little chance to interact with each other (d2). About the possibility to practice speaking, the situation seems more controversial; little chance of speaking orally (d6) was not considered to be one of the main difficulties overall, with the exception of Roma3 students, since over 40% of them found it difficult to interact orally. The most positive feedback is given by Roma1 students, where only 10% found it difficult to interact orally.

Advantages. The comfort of studying at home (a1), the fact that screen sharing of materials and PPT makes it easier to follow the lesson (a7) and the use of the chat to carry on written exercises (a4) are the most appreciated aspects of online teaching; the comfort of using the computer for writing characters (v3) was more appreciated by Bachelor's degree students, and especially first and second-year students (50% and 38% respectively).

Suggestions. Students mainly required more materials for asynchronous self-study (s1 and s2), with percentages ranging from 40% to 65% and 28% to 58% respectively. During the lesson, the teacher should dedicate more time to the writing exercises, also using chat (s5) shows notable percentages for four out of five classes (37% to 46%), with the lowest percentage being that of Lin1 students (21%). Students also required to assign multiple tasks or intermediate tests to monitor the level of learning (s6), ranging from almost 30% to almost 50%. The only result which is not in line with this is that of Lin2 students (16%). About speaking practice, here the situation seems more controversial too. During the lesson, the teacher should devote more time to oral interaction with students (s4) shows lower percentages. However, also in this case, Roma3 students seem to be more critical, with over 40% of them suggesting to devote more time to oral interaction, as well as almost 40% of Lin2 students. The most optimistic are again Roma1 students, where only 12% felt it was necessary to dedicate more time to oral interaction.

6   Discussions

The answer to the first research question, aimed at asking how students evaluate online lessons, is overall positive with some differences to be connected to the student's level, class size, and to the course-specific content. The highest degree of satisfaction about platform and course delivery has been expressed by higher-level students. It is unsurprising that having already experienced the usage of similar tools, they find it easy to access and participate to online classes whereas BA students were more unprepared. In particular, for platform usability, some problems have emerged due to the high number of participants in BA courses which sometimes caused a poor operation of the platform to share video and audio material. In many cases, students had to turn off the camera so as to improve video meeting quality, thus reducing the interaction opportunities. The low percentage concerning third-year student figures can also be explained by the absolute novelty represented by the content proposed, especially that illustrated by the Italian teacher which certainly required additional explanations, often provided after lessons by email or via Skype. The authentic material presented during the second term was in fact very stimulating for students since it was all connected to the outbreak of COVID-19: students were given official press articles, short videos, and more spontaneous commentary to the health disaster, such as writer Fang Fang's diary. This type of input caused not only linguistic clarification but also stimulated discussion among students, which was not always possible within the limits of online classes. The different approach taken by the students to distance teaching is also confirmed by the intention to follow another online course: as previously shown, higher-level students reacted more positively to the possibility of following other online courses.

The answer to the second research question about the efficacy of online training on speaking and writing was not a positive one. Satisfaction degree toward the possibility to practice speaking and writing was overall lower than satisfaction toward platform usability, with some differences among students of different level. Apart from the highest-level students, all others complained about the lack of opportunity to practice writing, an aspect found to be very critical by second-year students whose program includes a number of new grammatical and lexical items usually the object of written training and assessment. It is not surprising that almost all levels students therefore suggested devoting more time to writing exercises during online lessons, also using the chat function. Interestingly, first-year students find typing characters easier than writing them by hand although at the beginning of the course they were requested to only use pens and pencils and they had been taught *pinyin* just three months prior to the start of online lessons.

As for speaking training, there was a general concern about the insufficient number of occasions to practice speaking, although only a small percentage of first-year students (10%) found it difficult to interact orally. This result can be explained by the fact that this class has been divided into two groups during mother-tongue lecturer's training. Being less numerous, the online oral interaction was more successful than it was for other groups, for instance third-year students, who mostly complained about this issue and therefore suggested to devote more time to oral interaction and add audio material to the PPT provided by the instructor. Dividing the class into smaller groups for more student-student and student-teacher oral interaction is in line with suggestions from Burgerova and Cimermanova (2014) and Sun (2011). It is possible to use tools such as Zoom's Breakout rooms or Teams channels to split students into small groups to facilitate interactivity and group work.

As for the last research question regarding the main issues encountered and suggestions, almost all groups of students had Internet connection problems and reported the diminished opportunity to practice writing. Other problems that have been signaled especially by third-year students have to do with spoken interaction, time devoted to exercise in classroom and quality of instructional material.

By further analyzing answers on difficulties and suggestions, the fact that the most noted difficulty encountered, after connection problems, was the lack of opportunity to practice writing and that the suggestion "during the lesson, the teacher should dedicate more time to the writing exercises, also using chat" (s5) also shows notable percentages, once again demonstrates more need for active writing. The lowest percentage of Lin1 students for s5 was probably due to the fact that teachers resorted to the use of the chat for Lin1 students systematically. This would make the lesson more interactive and would give chance to the students to immediately practice the newly learnt concepts, receiving an immediate feedback by the teachers, which is in line with previous research (Balboni, 2006; Chini & Bosisio, 2014; Payne & Whitney, 2002; Wang & Bellassen, 2017).

Students also proposed the assignment of multiple tasks or intermediate tests to monitor the level of learning. The only result which is not in line with this is that of Lin2 students. In this case, while written interaction was not exercised synchronously during class, since the writing tasks required longer and more elaborated productions, students were given written tasks to carry out autonomously on a weekly basis, which were corrected by the teacher, giving them periodical asynchronous feedback. Therefore, while Lin2 students resented the lack of synchronous written exercise, overall, they felt they had enough intermediate exercises and even though 40% of them still considered little opportunity to practice writing one of the main difficulties, this percentage is relatively smaller compared to other classes. This leads to the suggestion that mixing synchronous and asynchronous exercise and interaction is the best solution, which is in line with previous research.

The fact that, on top of doing more written and oral exercise, students mainly required more materials for asynchronous self-study, together with the comfort of studying at home, is in line with the major literature on the topic. This further highlights the notion that the lack of space and time restrictions is an advantage of online courses (Kaplan & Haenlein, 2016; Piras et al., 2020).

7 Implications and Conclusions

The provisional conclusions that we can draw from the data presented in this work have to be linked to the specific conditions under which online lessons have been delivered. The positive approach expressed both by instructors, willing to engage to a new form of teaching, and by students, willing to participate and try new forms of learning, certainly gives hope to explore the potentialities of online pedagogy. Nevertheless, the unplanned and unexpected shift to remote teaching has also made it difficult, if not impossible, to find the necessary time for instructors to adapt instructional content to a different communication channel. Presenting the same content with the same strategies used for onsite lessons is simply not feasible and could affect crucial factors such as interaction, training of specific skills, and motivation. In order to obtain better results and more satisfaction in e-learning activities, it could be advisable to check instructor and learner familiarity with the resources and tools provided by the platforms and train the instructor to adopt what are most suitable for course content, student level and class size. It could also be recommended to regularly use platforms for self-assessment tasks in order to increase learner awareness of their own learning process and stimulate self-monitoring activities. In general, instructors should be aware of all the potentialities of e-learning in order to conceive it not as a solution to resort to in cases of emergency but as a useful and regular way to integrate both teaching and learning activities. Since e-learning is becoming increasingly popular and there is an ever-increasing number of learners of Chinese, it is of the utmost importance and urgency to share experience and collected data to bring distance teaching closer to students.

Acknowledgments This chapter is the result of the close collaboration between the two authors. Specifically, Chiara Romagnoli takes responsibility for Sections 1, 3, 6, and 7, whereas Valentina Ornaghi takes responsibility for Sections 2, 4, and 5. We wish to thank the anonymous reviewers for their helpful suggestions on earlier versions of this chapter and prof. Giorgio De Marchis for his help in providing some of the references discussed in these pages. All remaining errors are our own.

References

Balboni, P. (2006). *Le sfide di Babele. Insegnare le lingue nelle società complesse*. UTET.

Braun, S., et al. (2013). Interpreting in Virtual Reality: Designing and Developing a 3D Virtual World to Prepare Interpreters and their Clients for Professional Practice. In D. Hansen-Schirra, S. Maksymski, & K. Kiraly (Eds.), *New Prospects and Perspectives for Educating Language Mediators*. Gunter Narr Verlag.

Burgerova, J., & Cimermanova, I. (2014). "Creating a Sense of Presence in Online Learning Environment", *DIVAI 2014: The 10th International Scientific Conference in Distance Learning in Applied Informatics*, 275-284

Chen, K. (2018). "The Contrastive Analysis on MOOCs of Chinese as a Second Language ——Take the Courses on Coursera Platform for Example", Journal of Mudanjiang University, 27 (7), 121-125 [陈肯 (2018). 汉语国际教育慕课平台建设的现状及思考 ——以 Coursera 平台上的课程为例. 牡丹江大学学报27 (7), 121-125]

Chini, M., & Bosisio, C. (2014). *Fondamenti di glottodidattica. Apprendere e insegnare le lingue oggi*. Carocci.

Crews, T. B., Wilkinson, K., & Neill, J. K. (2015). Principles for Good Practice in Undergraduate Education: Effective Online Course Design to Assist Students' Success. *MERLOT Journal of Online Learning and Teaching, 11*(1), 87–103.

DeFrancis, J. (1984). *The Chinese Language: Fact and Fantasy*. University of Hawaii Press.

Ding, A., et al. (2011). *Discover China (volume 4)*. Macmillan.

Goral, T. (2013). "SPOCs May Provide What MOOCs Can't", *University Business*, Retrieved from: https://web.archive.org/web/20160304190607/https://www.universitybusiness.com/article/spocs-may-provide-what-moocs-can%E2%80%99t

Griffith, M. E., & Charles, R. G. (2009). Using Asynchronous Video in Online Classes. Results from a Pilot Study. *International Journal of Instructional Technology and Distance Learning, 6*(3), 65–75.

Hua, L. (2018). Construction of SPOC-based Learning Model and Its Application in Linguistics Teaching. *iJET, 13*(2), 157–169.

Jiang, L. (2016). *HSK Standard Course. Level 4*. Beijing University Press.

Jolliffe, A., Ritter, J., & Stevens, D. (2001). *The Online Learning Handbook: Developing and Using Web-based Learning*. Routledge.

Kaplan, A. M., & Haenlein, M. (2016). Higher Education and the Digital Revolution. About MOOCs, SPOCs, Social Media, and the Cookie Monster. *Business Horizons, 59*, 441–450.

Lin, C., & Zhang, Y. (2014). MOOCs and Chinese Language Education. *Journal of Technology and Chinese Language Teaching, 5*(2), 49–65.

Masini, F., et al. (2006). *Il cinese per gli italiani (volumes 1-2)*. Hoepli.

McVay Lynch, M. (2002). *The Online Educator: A Guide to Creating the Virtual Classroom*. Routledge Farmer.

Means, B., Bakia, M., & Murphy, R. (2014). *Learning Online. What Research Tells Us About Whether, When and How*. Routledge.

Moreira Teixeira, A., & Mota, J. (2014). A Proposal for the Methodological Design of Collaborative Language MOOCs. In E. Martín-Monje & E. Bárcena (Eds.), *Language MOOCs. Providing Learning, Transcending Boundaries* (pp. 33–47). De Gruyter.

Navarre, A. (2019). *Technology-Enhanced Teaching and Learning of Chinese as a Foreign Language*. Routledge.

Panagiotidis, P. (2019). "MOOCs for Language Learning. Reality and Prospects", *SITE 2019*, Las Vegas, 286-292

Payne, J. S., & Whitney, P. (2002). Developing L2 Oral Proficiency through Synchronous CMC: Output, Working Memory, and Interlanguage Development. *CALICO Journal, 20*(1), 7–32.

Perifanou, M., & Economides, A. (2014). "MOOCs for Foreign Language Learning. An Effort to Explore and Evaluate the First Practices", *Proceedings of INTED2014 Conference*, Valencia, 3561-3570

Picciano, A. G. (2017). Theories and frameworks for online education: Seeking an integrated model. *Online Learning, 21*(3), 166–190.

Piras, V., Reyes, M. C., & Trentin, G. (2020). *Come disegnare un corso online. Criteri di progettazione didattica e della comunicazione*. Franco Angeli.

Ramella, F., & Rostan, M. (2020). Universi-Dad. Gli accademici italiani e la didattica a distanza durante l'emergenza Covid-19. *Working papers CLB-CPS, 1*(20), 1–27.

Salmon, G. (2000). *E-moderating. The Key to Teaching and Learning Online*. Kogan Page.

Schwienhorst, K. (2002). Why Virtual, Why Environments? Implementing Virtual Reality Concepts in Computer-assisted Language learning. *Simulation and gaming, 33*, 196–209.

Sun, S. Y. H. (2011). Online Language Teaching. The Pedagogical Challenges. *Knowledge Management & E-Learning: An International Journal, 3*(3), 428–447.

Vygotsky, L. S. (1986). *Thought and Language*. MIT Press.

Wang, J., & Bellassen, J. (2017). "Design, Implementation and Reflection on the Introductory Chinese MOOC Kit de contact en langue chinoise", *Journal of Modernization of Chinese language education*, 6 (1), 31-41 [王珏、白乐桑 (2017). 面向法语母语学习者的中文初阶慕课 Kit de contact en langue chinoise:设计, 实施和发现. 中文教学现代化学报6 (1), 31-41]

Wang, T., & Pei, B. (2016). "A Case Study of MOOC of the Chinese Language", *Journal of Research on Education for Ethnic Minorities*, 2, 128-133 [王添淼、裴伯杰 (2016). 汉语慕课课程个案研究. 民族教育研究2, 128-133]

Weerasinghe, T. A., Ramberg, R., & Hewagamage, K. P. (2009). Designing Online Learning Environments for Distance Learning. *International Journal of Instructional Technology and Distance Learning, 6*(3), 21–42.

Wei, B. (2017). "An Overview of the Construction of MOOC for Teaching Chinese as a Second Language in Peking University", *Journal of Modernization of Chinese language education*, 6 (2), 28-31 [魏宝良 (2017). 北京大学对外汉语教学慕课(MOOC)建设情况概述. 中文教学现代化学报 6 (2), 28-31]

Xin, P. (2019). "Analysis of Teaching Chinese as a Foreign Language from the Perspective of Teaching Philosophy", *Journal of Higher Education*, 16, 6-9 [辛平 (2019). 教学理念视域下的对外汉语教学慕课分析. 高教学刊 16, 6-9]

5

A Blessing in Disguise: The Emergency Remote Teaching of Chinese in University of Cape Town in South Africa

Yue Ma

1 Introduction

To staff and students of the University of Cape Town (UCT) at the beginning of the new academic year starting in February 2020, the news of a frightening epidemic seemed to be merely a problem of Asia. But as the COVID-19 turned out to be a pandemic, it was quickly brought into Cape Town by visiting and returning tourists from Europe. The academic activities at our university were abruptly brought into halt when we barely completed the fifth week of teaching and learning of the 2020 academic year, after a number of cases of were reported on campus. It was one week before the end of the Term 1. Pretty soon the entire nation was locked down due to the quick spread of the disease. The hope that we would be able to return to campus to continue the academic year with simply the loss of a couple of extra weeks apart from a prolonged term

---

Y. Ma (✉)
University of Cape Town, Cape Town, South Africa
e-mail: y.ma@uct.ac.za

© The Author(s), under exclusive license to Springer Nature Switzerland AG 2022
S. Liu (ed.), *Teaching the Chinese Language Remotely*,
https://doi.org/10.1007/978-3-030-87055-3_5

break soon faded away and became an obvious wishful thinking. The national lockdown extended. The plan for a changed academic calendar of the year had to be changed again due to unexpected circumstances. Now the real concern arose as teachers and students began to worry about how the academic activities could continue and in what way the academic year can be completed.

This was an unprecedented situation that we had ever been in, which seemed even to be worse than 2015–2017 turmoil that was brought about by the #RhodesMustFall and #FeesMustFall students protests (see detailed review and discussion on the protests from Czerniewicz et al., 2019; Czerniewicz, 2020). At that time the academic year was managed to be completed with blended teaching and learning as disruptions often interrupted lectures by groups of unexpected visiting protesters who attempted to shut down the campus with their radical activities. In comparison, the pandemic now had forced everyone to legitimately stay off the campus that had been totally shut down. What worried Chinese teachers was that how the students, especially those first-year beginners, would survive the learning of a language that is normally viewed as alien and more difficult than a language with an alphabet writing system. The Emergency Remote Teaching (henceforth ERT) approach was adopted as a solution to continue the second term from early May with an added orientation week of preparation from the end of April.

Would the efficiency of language teaching still be achieved when the change of conventional methods of teaching aided by modern technology? The sudden turn of the adverse situation for teaching and learning accidentally provided us a chance for a bold experiment and opportunity of reforming the strategies of the language teaching and learning. Though a bit unreluctantly, both the students and teachers would have to face the new challenge and adapt to the new virtual campus. Both sides were aware that either we had to explore what we could do to achieve the best results we could expect in our teaching and learning or we simply gave up and would cancel indefinitely the academic activities with an unknown consequence. Fortunately, we had in hands some powerful means to maintain virtual interactive contact with our students through modern technology. The existing online interactive platform for teaching and learning provided by the university had only been used marginally in our daily practice in the past. Would it now prove that it indeed has an indispensable value in facilitating teaching and learning of a foreign language? How well both students and instructors would adapt to the changed environment of cyberspace interaction? With many questions in mind, we trod cautiously into the unknown waters of ERT and were exhilarated to see in the end the bright light of hope around the corner.

2 Changes of Teaching Environment: Major Factors at Work

2.1 Emergency Remote Teaching (ERT)

What is ERT? Suddenly both the teaching staff and students had to take some time to digest the piles of new concepts and ideas. In particular, the teachers would have to understand what they could do in such an unprecedented situation to continue teaching off the campus. Hodges et al. (2020) provide a standard answer:

> *Emergency remote teaching (ERT) is a temporary shift of instructional delivery to an alternate delivery mode due to crisis circumstances. It involves the use of fully remote teaching solutions for instruction or education that would otherwise be delivered face-to-face or as blended or hybrid courses and that will return to that format once the crisis or emergency has abated.*

The definition does not seem to be too difficult to understand, as it seems that ERT is clearly not a well-planned and prepared standard "online teaching" course that may have been recorded and produced in a studio and then published online for students to take as a course like in an open university or a distance education program, or not even comparable with anything like the so-called MOOC. As Hogue (2020) correctly stated, "Online learning isn't something you can throw together in a week." ERT is a cover name for taking advantage of any possible means that is available to handle an emergency educational task in a situation that may be only temporary. What we, as instructors, learned with a relief was that we did not have to become a serious producer of entirely online courses overnight, but might take advantage of the available tools that could bring students and us closer in the cyberspace on an existing platform like Vula at UCT.

To help teachers to cope with the new way of teaching, UCT's Centre for Innovation in Learning and Teaching (CILT) quickly set up the "CILT Teaching Online Portal" (http://www.cilt.uct.ac.za/teaching-online-portal) to help educate the university community to meet the challenge of the newly emerged technologies and strategies that are needed to continue the teaching and learning for the coming terms of the academic year.

2.2 What Is Vula? In What Way It May Help to Achieve ERT?

One of the important factors that paved the way for the success of ERT at UCT was the existence of an online learning platform named as Vula. According to the CILT webpage (http://www.cilt.uct.ac.za/cilt/vula), "Vula" is a Swahili word, meaning "Open." It was jointly developed with other universities worldwide as part of the Sakai Project. It is "UCT's online collaboration and learning environment, used to support UCT courses as well as other UCT-related groups and communities." The platform started to be built from 2006 and undergone a major upgrade in 2017. It "offers a broad spectrum of features, including tools for administration, assessment, communication, resource sharing and collaborative learning."

Vula became a handy tool for us to upload "temporarily" our lessons and turning it partly into a class interaction space for our courses. The following graph shows a glimpse of a Chinese class site on Vula (Fig. 5.1).

At the usual time when we could have contact classes on campus, we almost ignored the Vula site except using it for administrative purposes, like making an announcement, helping students breaking into different tutorial groups and signing up for oral tests and so on. Besides, we had used the "resources" menu to upload additional reference materials for students. Now all of a sudden, we had to start to explore other functions of the platform so that we could carry out our ERT.

5 A Blessing in Disguise: The Emergency Remote Teaching...

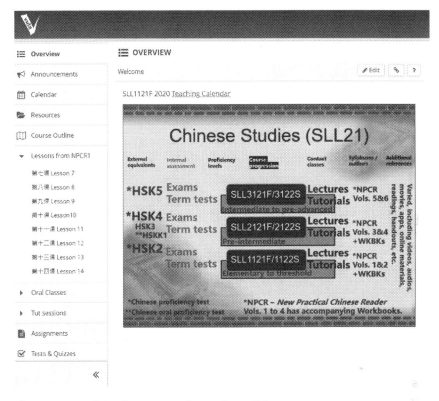

Fig. 5.1 Part of the front page of one of our Chinese courses

Fortunately, we soon became familiarized with the platform and discovered that we could actually turn it into a virtual classroom with almost all the major features that exist in a normal teaching and learning environment. For example, we could create lesson pages that would replace the outline of lectures and content of lessons that we used to present with power point slides and even audio-visual means by embedding video and audio contents directly into the lesson pages. Besides, we found that we could even use the platform for tests and examinations that involve the types of questions essential for language teaching and learning, as indicated in Fig. 5.2.

The availability of these important functions had certainly given us more confidence in the transition from a contact class environment to a

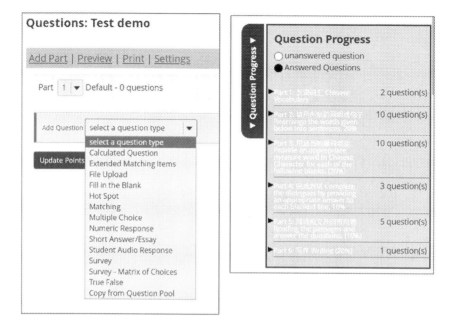

Fig. 5.2 Examples of the types of test and examination questions

virtual class one on the internet, as we were able to fulfill practically all teaching and evaluation activities including lecturing, assignments, tests and examinations.

2.3 External Tools for Class Meetings and Communication

One of the important issues for choosing an external tool for class meetings and teacher-student communication was the cost of data. Even though the university granted students 30 to 40 G of data to use at home, for some students, accessibility of internet and cost of data remained a big concern. Therefore, the university encouraged the staff to use "low-tech" means for ERT and Vula platform as much as possible so that it will reduce the affordability issues for students. However, Vula itself could not provide the convenience for synchronous video communication. For language teaching, a certain amount of synchronous virtual communication would be essential for the effective learning to take place through interaction. Therefore, we would have to take into account of some freely available external tools for class meetings though this might make it a bit difficult for those who could not afford or were unwilling to spare that much amount of data to access the external tools.

Before ERT, we had been using WhatsApp social media software in addition to Vula as a means of communication for class information, questions and answers outside class meeting time. During ERT, WhatsApp remained a channel that linked the students and instructors for administration and announcement purposes.

Vula platform had already integrated a menu for Zoom, though it would still be a link to an external website that wouldn't be counted as a zero-rated site and therefore it would still cost students data to use it. Needless to say, Zoom had become one of the most popular tools for ERT despite of this drawback.

Then the university had also provided the access to Microsoft Teams as a tool for class meeting, though it was not counted as a zero-rated internet access site either. To avoid confusion and complication, we basically sticked to Zoom as our chief channel for class meetings, leaving Microsoft Teams as a backup, in case Zoom failed at the time of class.

2.4 Psychological Preparedness for Both Teachers and Students

Apart from the physical and material conditions that were available for meeting the upcoming challenges of ERT, psychological factors were also important player in the game. For the teachers, anxiety from delivering lectures in an unprecedented way with a lot of unknown and unpredictable possibilities bothered them before the first week of ERT even though preparations had been made carefully and CILT had provided tutorials and guidelines for delivering online lectures under ERT and how to make effective use of menus on Vula.

As to students, we could trace back how they felt at the beginning of ERT from an experience survey made by the university after the Term 2 completed. Mental health challenges seemed to be the biggest category of students' concerns. Although we do not have specific data for students of Chinese, the reactions from the students of Humanities collectively may be of some value to reflect what our students felt about this as well. In the "UCT Emergency Remote Teaching Student Experience Survey" (University of Cape Town, 2020a), questions like the following ones were asked:

> I faced the following challenges studying remotely (check all that apply):

- On average, I spent the following hours a day studying in a typical week, including weekends:
- I typically studied at these times of day (check all that apply):
- Slow or unreliable Internet connection
- Insufficient mobile data or capped ISP connection
- Shared access to a laptop/computer
- Family or caring responsibilities
- Work/job commitments
- Lack of a quiet study space
- Mental health challenges (e.g. anxiety, stress, depression)
- Physical health challenges (e.g. illness, fatigue)
- Food security (insufficient access to healthy food)
- Housing security (uncertainty about having somewhere to live)
- Physical safety and security
- Financial stresses
- Other

The 1076 students from Humanities (who accounted for 20.4% of 5269 undergraduate students at the Faculty of Humanities) gave the following answers (University of Cape Town, 2020b).

Figure 5.3 shows the survey results of major challenges faced by students from the Faculty of Humanities. Our language students were obviously among the Humanities students group. In times of the sudden change of learning environment, students were most likely to have an anxiety or stress issue, especially with our first-year new students. Even during the time of normal contact teaching and learning, we often received students' LOA (leave of absence) due to stress or depression issues. Through interaction with our students during ERT, we also had

5 A Blessing in Disguise: The Emergency Remote Teaching... 119

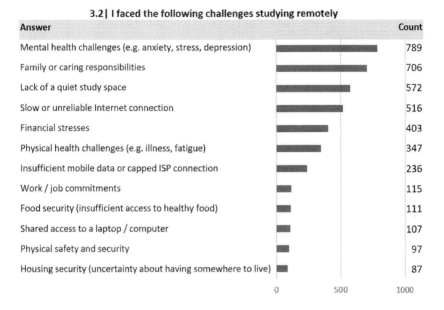

Fig. 5.3 Humanities students' answers to part of the experience survey questions

the impression that anxiety from students in this ERT situation had been a major challenge for many of them, as instructors reflected that they would often need to encourage students by giving them positive feedback from time to time for them to move on. Though we could not identify the exact number of our own students from the survey, our impression of students' behavior conformed to the result of the general pattern shown in the above figure of the 789 responses received from the total of 1076 students' responses, with "Mental health challenge" (e.g., anxiety, stress, or depression), viz. 73% of Humanities students identified this as one of the challenges they faced, being the highest proportion of all categories of challenges (University of Cape Town, 2020c). Besides, "Lack of quiet study space" and "Slow and unreliable internet connection" were also often the reasons we heard from our students when they chose to keep their cameras shut and declined to switch on their microphones.

However, even if most students seemed to have gone through Term 2 under ERT fairly successfully, the proportion of students who claimed that they were not quite well prepared for the Term 2 mostly seem to have remained unprepared for the coming Term 3, as is shown in the answers to the following questions. Figure 5.4 gives us some idea.

In this figure we could see that the majority of the students agreed that instructors had done sufficient to prepare students in their learning, as is shown in 4.6 (there is a 42.4% + 42.3% = 84.7% of students indicating "agree"). The total number of students who claimed not quite well prepared at the beginning of Term 2 seemed to remain feeling roughly the same for the coming Term 3, as we can see in 4.4 the total number of "felt prepared" for Term 2 equals 49.5% (14.3% + 35.2%), while in 4.5 the total number of "felt prepared" for Term 3 is 52.2% (22.5% + 29.7%), a marginal increase by cutting a small proportion out of those "neutral"

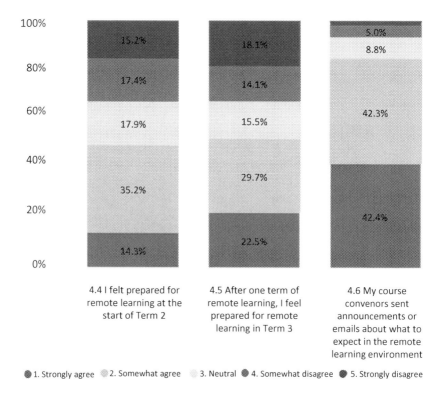

Fig. 5.4 Humanities students' answers to preparedness for ERT

ones. On the other hand, the "not felt prepared" groups remained largely unchanged or even got worse (with a slight increase in the number of "strongly disagree") across the time, being 32.6% (15.2% + 17.4%, for Term 2) and 32.2% (18.1% + 14.1%, for Term 3) respectively. These figures may suggest that once a student was prepared and adapted to the new learning environment, it is likely that they would follow through successfully. On the other hand, if they had a "bad" beginning, the adverse effect could last throughout the whole course of time. Fortunately, above a two-thirds majority indicated that they "felt prepared" at the beginning of the ERT. In our case, the positive trend of achievements did show that our students conformed or even overperformed against this pattern.

3 Chinese Teaching and Learning Under ERT

Given the changes the teaching and learning environment, Chinese teaching under ERT must have to adapt to the new situation as well. The success of language learning depends a lot on interaction between instructors and students, especially those who are beginner learners. As we mentioned earlier, the first-year beginner learners merely had five weeks of contact class learning before the lockdown. Would they survive the ERT as they were much inexperienced as the second- and third-year students who should have much more familiarity with Chinese and should be more likely to make progress by relying largely on their own efforts supported with remote assistance from their instructors? It turned out that the outcome was much better than expected in the end.

3.1 Comparison of Features of a Conventional Classroom and a Virtual One

What are the differences between conventional contact teaching classroom and the online virtual classroom? Would the virtual classroom be equally effective as the conventional classroom? Or if not, in what way the virtual classroom is weaker than a conventional classroom? One big obvious difference is that convenience of teacher-students face-to-face contact and contact via cyberspace. Face-to-face interaction seems to be a desirable and essential requirement for foreign language learning for effective teaching and learning. But would there be any means to compensate for this feature loss in a virtual classroom? Below is a comparison of features in these relevant situations (Table 5.1).

As we mentioned earlier, with ERT, it does not mean that we would start with an entirely new syllabus of well-organized online teaching like MOOC. It was simply a temporary measure of relocating our teaching space with technologically available means due to the emergency situation that forced everyone out of the classroom on campus. Therefore, we would very much like to complete the academic year as we had originally planned despite of the fact that unpredictability lies ahead. The syllabus and learning materials related to curriculum requirements remained in place unchanged, though the way of interactions between teachers and

Table 5.1 Features of conventional classroom and ERT teaching space compared

Conventional classroom	ERT teaching space
• Physical space (classroom)	• Virtual space (cyberspace)
• Textbook (Textbook + Workbook)	• Textbook (Textbook + Workbook)
• Optional network resource utilization	• Mandatory network resource utilization
• Fixed class time	• Fixed real-time meeting + non-real-time browsing
• Face-to-face interaction	• Virtual face-to-face interaction
• Synchronous	• Synchronous + asynchronous
• Tutoring and self-study	• Online tutoring + self-study
• Oral face-to-face tutoring	• Online synchronous and asynchronous counseling + audio and video materials
• Written/oral exam	• Online written/recorded exam
• Relatively fixed learning time	• Relatively fixed + flexible study time
• Off-hour communication via social media	• Off-hour communication via social media
• No additional study fees	• Steep increase in network expenses
• Relatively fixed teaching workload	• Increased teaching workload

students had to adapt to the new way of ERT. However, when we could sit down to make a careful comparison of the features of the conventional classroom and the ERT virtual learning space, we actually found that the major factors that facilitated interactive teaching and learning in a Chinese teaching and learning class at our university did not lose that much than we originally feared, though some changes naturally had to take place due to the limitation of physical space. Some features should exist to a lesser or stronger extent respectively.

3.2 Pros and Cons: Would ERT Actually Be a Blessing in Disguise?

The liberal arts students in a South African university usually have to complete at least two majors to earn a bachelor's degree within three academic years. Apart from a few students who would decide to do a foreign language as a major, many students in the first year usually take a foreign language course merely as an elective so that they will be exposed to a foreign language and some exotic cultural experience. To accommodate varied needs of different categories of students, a foreign language course normally can at best be schedule for one 45 minutes lecture a day, five days a week, with an additional tutorial and a lab session per person per week. Compared with foreigners learning Chinese in a Chinese university, this may possibly be only one fifth of their class hours during a week. With this already comparatively unfavorable conditions for learning Chinese on campus, how could ERT make it even worse than ever? As the ERT scenario unfolded, we actually found that it might as well give us an opportunity to gain a little bit of ground despite of the obvious setbacks that everyone has experienced.

We can list the possible pros and cons of the earlier on campus teaching and the current ERT on the basis of our own situation, though everyone may not agree with these entirely depending on their specific context (Table 5.2).

From the above comparison we may get a feeling that for both on campus teaching and ERT teaching, each actually has its own merits. We cannot just focus on certain aspects of either way of teaching to deny the merits of the other. It is really a matter of how to adapt to a real-life situation to explore the possible merits of an adverse situation so that we can make the best out of it despite of the obvious foes. Attitude of both teachers and students count significantly at this time. When both teachers and students were aware that we were suddenly thrown into an unfavorable situation, both sides decided to put in a bit more efforts to compensate for the lost advantage of studying on campus. The positive working attitude played an important role in saving our academic terms from the adverse situation resulted from the pandemic. We will examine below what unexpected achievements we gained from these unusual circumstances.

3.3 What Has Possibly Made the Difference?

A reflection on the comparison of the features of the contact teaching on campus and the online teaching via virtual campus would help reveal the factors that may have contributed to the positive results that we are going to discuss below.

First of all, the understanding of the new roles in the teaching and learning provided students with stronger motivation in taking initiative in the learning process. Part of the transition from contact teaching to

Table 5.2 Pros and cons of on campus teaching and ERT teaching compared

On campus teaching		ERT teaching	
Cons	45 minutes per day	Pros	45 minutes Zoom meeting per day + Vula (online lesson pages)
	Classroom teaching only		Real-time virtual classroom + asynchronous video recordings
	Limited to textbooks		Textbook + supplementary resources (e.g. YouTube etc.)
	Workbook assignments only		Additional written assignments
Pros	Easy to communicate	Cons	Hard for face-to-face communication
	Group communication possible		Group communication constraints
	No data cost issues		Data constraints for some students
	Easy to urge students to work		Rely on strong self-motivation

ERT involved the mobilization before the online teaching actually started. Students were made to be aware of the fact that they themselves would play a key role in deciding the success or failure of their learning when moving into the virtual space of teaching and learning. The redefining of the role and responsibilities of the instructors and learners helped to change the attitude of students toward learning and responsibilities. As most students would like to complete their learning rather than withdraw from the course, they were ready to adapt to the changed learning environment from Term 2, after a prolonged break following the one week earlier ending of the planned Term 1 of contact teaching by sudden order of lockdown because of the pandemic. We were lucky to have completed the Term 1 test ahead of the lockdown, as our test focused mainly on the pronunciation/pinyin phase of teaching and learning. Just as we were starting to switch into a new phase of teaching and learning, we were cut off.

However, this in turn offered us an opportunity to change our assignments requirements from our original plan. Therefore, the second factor that may have contributed to our success story would be the timely addition of written assignments that we had not previously included in our teaching process before. At the beginning of the online teaching in Term 2, we quietly added an additional assignment category of "precis writing" (in handwritten form). As this started with a new phase of teaching, students were not aware that this requirement was not a conventional component of required assignment, and therefore it was not felt as some "extra work" that was newly added to their curriculum. This assignment type has not been part of the assignments in either the textbook or workbook, thus it has never been included in students' assignment before. We were worried about the absence of contact teaching would offer students less exposure to the use of Chinese characters in instructor and students interaction and therefore had decided to use this innovative way of keeping students practicing Chinese character writing in addition to the usual workbook assignments. Besides we announced that this assignment accounted for 20% of the continuous assessment marks. Students were asked to handwrite the precis of each lesson they had learned by answering a number of questions in full. Then they would submit their work as an image or pdf file via online assignment submission system. We then mark the students writing and gave students feedback through the Gradebook function on Vula platform.

This weekly practice was fairly demanding and kept students busy all the time. But it did help students check their thorough understanding of the texts and have an additional channel to practice writing Chinese characters and reinforced their memory of the "Sino-graphs." In the end, we noted not only an unprecedented students' progress in handwriting of Chinese characters but also a remarkable achievement in the mastery of Chinese characters as was reflected in tests and examinations. This outcome was in line with our findings in our earlier continuous research work, summarized in Ma (2019, 2020), on the role of Chinese characters as a key to the efficiency of Chinese learning at the initial stage. The addition of the precis writing in handwritten Chinese characters certainly played a key role in reinforcing the students' practice and understanding of the Chinese characters. The result again confirmed that a proper mastery of Chinese characters would benefit the overall progress in their learning of Chinese.

Apart from these measures, with the use of online lesson pages, we had expanded the learning space by including additional content that we were unable to include in contact teaching situation. Additional resources on characters, words and grammar, as well as cultural background information were kept online with each lesson to help students to get an in-depth understanding of the lessons. There had been no place for such information to be offered to students as contact lesson time were too limited. Now in addition to the synchronous virtual lectures online, students could have access asynchronously the lecture recordings and the additional information and resources available on the lesson pages. Not only students felt the pressure of tons of work and assignments, but also the teachers had added workload to prepare the additional materials and integrated new resources to lesson pages on Vula platform. Undoubtedly this new setting in teaching and learning arrangement has well compensated the loss of the advantages of contact teaching and learning.

4 Unexpected Results from the ERT Experience

4.1 Improved Ability in Mastery of Chinese Characters

Compared with the previous years of learning on campus, the ERT situation encouraged some students to adopt voluntarily a compensatory effort in study at home, thus bringing about some amazingly unexpected results, in particular in the use and mastery of Chinese characters. When teaching on campus, we already gave very prominent emphasis on the learning of Chinese characters from the very first day of class. With the first five weeks of on campus learning, students had already been driven by the idea of focusing on Chinese characters rather than pinyin when learning Chinese. This practice happened before ERT and also in previous years.

However, we were aware that even though we made an effort to cover up all the pinyin text on the presentation slides, the students mostly will be distracted by pinyin text when they review their textbooks at home. When ERT started, some students requested that the author as the instructor put on Vula lesson pages the texts with pinyin removed so that they will have an opportunity to read texts without being distracted by pinyin, as they no longer had the exposure of reading texts of pure Chinese characters from the instructor's presentation slides in class. Obviously on Vula lesson pages they would see these character texts more often than before.

Moreover, to compensate the loss of opportunities of group work and activities during lecture time on campus, students agreed to start with a **precis writing** exercise during ERT for each of the text we learned, as we mentioned earlier. This had to be done in handwritten Chinese characters on a piece of paper. Word processed work on computer would not be accepted. Students were guided by a number of questions on the texts or text related content. Students would answer all these questions in full sentences in Chinese on the basis of facts and information as they would get from the texts in the lesson and then they should string all answers into a coherent paragraph. They were requested to hand in their work or as a photo image or as a scanned pdf file. Students' submissions were marked electronically and returned with a feedback to students online. A grade was given each time and recorded in the Gradebook on Vula. Although this writing exercise of "silent communication" could hardly compensate for the face-to-face oral interaction in group or pair work in class, it did give students additional opportunities in practicing Chinese characters in handwriting. Moreover, this was not only handwritten work, as students would have to read and review the characters in the textbook and possibly also refer to dictionaries to make sure of their meanings. It was actually an additional comprehensive learning activity. And then it seemed that this worked particularly well with their learning of Chinese characters. Their handwriting of characters improved. And in the written examination, their mastery of Chinese characters seemed also have improved dramatically. Of course, this was not the only kind of assignments that required them to handwrite Chinese characters. Handwritten dictation work with the tutor also continued during the ERT, when the tutor offered prerecorded instructions so that students could do the diction from online audio instruction and submit their handwritten result online within the limited time frame. A comparison showed that their efforts certainly had gained. I have compared the section of character test scores between 2020 and 2019 groups using exactly the same test papers and found that the average score of 2020 group under ERT scored much higher than 2019 group, as is shown in Fig. 5.5.

4.2 Significant Improvement for Overall Course Achievements

The result of the semester examination for 2020 also seemed to be significantly improved than the previous year, as both involved the same test items and difficulty level. However, the only difference was that the 2020 semester examination was carried out as a non-invigilated online test rather than a strictly monitored and invigilated examination on campus, though it was carried out in a strictly timed synchronous manner with only one exception of a "Semester Study Abroad" student, who returned

5 A Blessing in Disguise: The Emergency Remote Teaching...

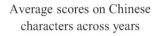

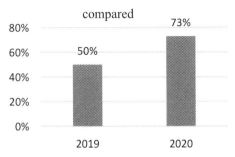

Fig. 5.5 Average scores of Chinese characters dictation by different first-year students

Table 5.3 Semester mean scores of 2019 and 2020 classes compared

Group statistics					
	Grouping	N	Mean	Std. Deviation	Std. Error Mean
Semester	2019	43	63.28	20.085	3.063
	2020	43	74.53	17.320	2.641

to the United States after the lockdown in South Africa but continued to finish the semester online, thus we had to put himself alone in a different time slot due to time differences. It happened that the number of registered students in the first-year class of both 2019 and 2020 was the same (see Table 5.3), though a number of students, who wanted to deregister the course from the second term due to constraints of ERT but did not complete the official procedure, remained in the class list without attending the second term tests, thus leaving some outliers in the record, as is clearly reflected in Fig. 5.6.

However, despite of this imbalance of number of students that contributed unfavorably to the total average scores of the 2020 group, the statistical analysis still seemed to support the assumption that with strengthened measures under ERT, the students actually had performed significantly better than before. Below are some of the statistical results from the comparison.

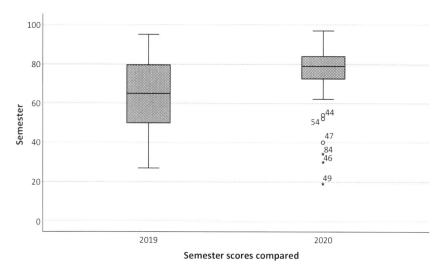

Fig. 5.6 Semester scores of 2019 and 2020 classes compared

Although the difference of the mean scores, as is shown in Table 5.3, was only 11.25 between the 2019 and 2020 groups, the standard deviation also seemed to suggest that 2019 group was a more dispersed one. The *t*-test results for the group comparison seemed to support the assumption that the class under ERT in 2020 (given the fact that they had only a five week of contact class on campus before moving their learning online) performed slightly better than the 2019 class, which completed the first semester entirely on campus, as is shown in Table 5.4.

5 Discussion

Despite of the fact that the semester final examination in 2020 was done online without the usual setting of invigilation, we felt that the results in most cases would be reliable and valid. First of all, students made pledge that they would complete the tests on their own within the designated time frame. Secondly, the tests were administered in a strictly timed manner that students would only be allowed to start the tests at a certain time and submit within the valid test hours, otherwise the system would automatically submit students'

Table 5.4 T-test result for the grouping comparison

Independent sample test		Levene's test for equality of variances		t-test for equality of means					95% confidence interval of the difference	
		F	Sig.	t	df	Sig. (2-tailed)	Mean difference	Std. Error difference	Lower	Upper
Semester	Equal variances assumed	3.909	0.051	-2.783	84	0.007	-11.256	4.044	-19.299	-3.213
	Equal variances not assumed			-2.783	82.222	0.007	-11.256	4.044	-19.301	-3.210

answers. Actually, it did happen to one or two students when they left some items unfinished but the system automatically cut and submitted their answers. Thirdly, though the tests were completed online, the conventional items that required handwritten answers in Chinese characters were done in the same way as it was done on campus in the past with the only difference of submitting their handwritten answers as images or pdf files immediately after they completed their tests. Therefore, on the whole, the validity of the tests on campus and for this online one under ERT should be reasonably comparable and matched.

Perhaps the only "unfair" advantage the students had for online tests was that for those items when the handwriting of Chinese characters were not the focus to be examined, like re-arrange the given characters into a grammatical and sensible sentence, students were allowed to use computer keyboard to input the correct answer by copying and pasting or typing the given characters in the correct order. This was rather mechanical type of using the given characters for completing the test items, unlike those such as dictation, composition, and so on, where knowledge of the Chinese characters was tested independently and handwritten answers were required. In the latter case we did examine the students by looking at their handwritten answers submitted. As we mentioned previously, the average scores for these items involving the Chinese characters did seem to be very well done this year. Actually, the better command of Chinese characters was also reflected in the weekly written assignments, in particular composition exercises submitted in handwritten form.

Given as a concession on the assumption that newly enrolled students in 2020 enjoyed more "privileged" conditions for their online examinations, we might want to reject the claim that the first-year students in 2020 were doing somewhat better than those on campus in 2019. Nevertheless, the final results and comparison would give us sufficient confidence to say that the first-year students in 2020 under ERT were at least doing similarly well as those on campus in 2019. We were relieved to observe that the lockdown and ERT did not result in a disaster to our teaching and learning of such a "hard" language as Chinese like most of us had originally feared. This alone would be viewed as a success story, given the examination results obtained under slightly different conditions might not be strictly comparable.

6 Limitations and Conclusions

The current study obviously has a number of limitations. First, the ERT was still at its preliminary stage at the time of writing. Students might be still enthusiastic about this new way of learning. We cannot yet foresee what the long-term effect will be when fatigue started to be reflected after a prolonged period of ERT. Second, only the first-year students' data were collected and analyzed. Even though the same instructor and same examination formats were maintained, other factors may well be at play, especially when students were aware that they must survive this unexpected situation and the motivation for learning had been boosted by the sudden lockdown and a wish to reunite with the class has been strong. Third, extended data and further observations need to be made to examine the long-term effect so as to consolidate the findings that have been made so far. Also, inter-institutional comparative studies may be needed to see if the generalization can hold or this only represents the situation of a very special group.

Despite the above limitations, we can still possibly draw a number of pedagogical implications from this study on the appropriate reactions and measures that may be implemented to keep Chinese teaching and learning going effectively under the emergency situation. First of all, since language teaching and learning depends heavily on human interaction, both instructors and students keep regular virtual communication and hear each other's voice helps maintain the motivation of learning and communication. Second, a certain measure of *synchronous interaction* with the class is essential to the potential success of effective learning. For example, despite of the data cost, making an effort to get the class meet virtually at the usual fixed class hour would help students maintain the study habit and it helps to maintain a sense of community during the difficult time of the isolation from the lockdown. Finally, a safe and secure online platform, a meeting place other than the commercially available real-time meeting tool, is very important for both instructors and students to have a sense of community. External tools for the technical convenience of class presentation and communication in cyberspace are indispensable, but a platform for internal online communication or via a closed group on social media would increase the feeling of belongingness and a sense of togetherness. All these favorable factors facilitate learning.

As the world has become an increasingly unpredictable place, language teaching and learning has to be ready to embrace new and creative ways of surviving the crisis and emergencies. With collective efforts of language teaching and learning communities, we will see a future with hopes and solutions rather than worries and anxieties.

References

Czerniewicz, L. (2020, March 15). What we learnt from "going online" during university shutdowns in South Africa. *PhilonEdTech*.

Czerniewicz, L., Trotter, H., & Haupt, G. (2019). Online teaching in response to student protests and campus shutdowns: Academics' perspectives. *International Journal of Educational Technology in Higher Education, 16*, 43. https://doi.org/10.1186/s41239-019-0170-1

Hodges, C., Moore, S., Lockee, B., Trust, T., & Bond, M. (2020, March 27). The difference between emergency remote teaching and online learning. *EDUCAUSE Review*.

Hogue, R. J. (2020). Let's stop calling it online learning – It is something different…. https://rjhogue.name/2020/03/16/lets-stop-calling-it-online-learning-it-is-something-different/

Ma, Y. (2019). Giving priority to Chinese characters as a breakthrough to psychological barrier in Chinese learning: practice and observance. In *Proceedings of the 13th international conference on Chinese language teaching* (pp. 242–250). The Commercial Press. [马跃 (2019). 汉字领先作为汉语难学的心理障碍突破点：实践与观察.《第十三届国际汉语教学研讨会论文集》pp. 242–250. 商务印书馆].

Ma, Y. (2020, November 4). Contrastive linguistic approaches as a key to dilute the stereotype of Chinese as a superhard language. *Chinese as a Second Language Research, 9*(2), 313–336. https://doi.org/10.1515/caslar-2020-0012

University of Cape Town. (2020a, July 21). *UCT emergency remote teaching student experience survey*. Unpublished internal report.

University of Cape Town. (2020b, July 24). *ERT student experience survey – HUM UG* [i.e. Humanities undergraduate students]. Unpublished internal report.

University of Cape Town. (2020c, July 24). *Insights from the ERT student experience survey*. Unpublished internal report.

6

Online Mandarin Language Teaching and Learning During COVID-19 Pandemic at University of Mauritius in Africa

Sharon Too

1 Introduction

CI-UoM is engaged in Mandarin language teaching and promotion of academic and cultural exchanges since its establishment on December 14, 2016, and is partnered with Zhejiang Sci-Tech University (ZSTU), Hangzhou, China (Li Ching Hum, 2016). This study investigates the online teaching situation at CI-UoM during the first lockdown period from March 19, 2020, to May 31, 2020 (Ministry of Health and Wellness, 2020). In order to better understand and analyse the emergency remote teaching situation at CI-UoM, an online survey was filled by learners while educators were also invited to record their observations, strategies and reflections. The outcome of the resulting discussion and analysis may help towards better online teaching at CI-UoM.

S. Too (✉)
Confucius Institute at University of Mauritius, Moka, Mauritius
e-mail: s.tooyok@umail.uom.ac.mu

2 Background Information and the Chinese Programme Introduction

2.1 About Mauritius

Mauritius island is located 1130 km east of Madagascar. The island has an area of 2040 square kilometres. Any place is accessible within 80 minutes by car. The capital of Mauritius is Port Louis, and there are also four towns. In 2020, the population of the Republic of Mauritius was estimated at 1.26 million and is of diverse ethnicity, including mostly Indo-Mauritians, Mauritian Creoles and a minority of Sino-Mauritians (mainly descendants of early Hakka immigrants from Guangdong, China) (Statistics Mauritius, 2020a). Citizens of Mauritius enjoy free universal health care, and students have free access to public transport and education up to tertiary level.

2.2 Education and Chinese Teaching in Mauritius

The Mauritian education system is based on the British system, consisting of primary, secondary and tertiary education as shown in Table 6.1. Grade 6 students take part in national examinations for the Primary School Achievement Certificate (PSAC). After the Nine Year Continuous Basic Education (NYCBE) reform, Grade 9 students must sit for national examinations to obtain a National Certificate of Education (NCE). Students have two years to prepare for O-Level/School Certificate (SC) at grade 11. In grade 13, they sit for A-Level/Higher School Certificate

Table 6.1 Education system in Mauritius

Level	Primary	Secondary			Tertiary
Grade	1–6	7–13			–
Age	6–11	12–18			>18
Student population	82 514 (2020)	51 259 (2020)			41 754 (2019)
Examination	PSAC at Grade 6	NCE at Grade 9	SC at Grade 11	HSC at Grade 13	–

(HSC) examinations. SC and HSC examinations are both carried out by the University of Cambridge (Ministry of Education, Tertiary Education, Science and Technology, 2019).

Mandarin language is taught in most primary schools as part of elective classes in Asian languages. The educators are mostly teachers sent from China for a one-year contract, or first-generation Chinese immigrants who settled in Mauritius. At secondary level, Mandarin is offered as an elective in fewer schools. In 2020–2021, there were 2648 Mandarin learners at primary level and there were 409 learners at secondary level up to Grade 9 (Statistics Mauritius, 2020b). Students who wish to continue learning Mandarin up to O-Level and A-Level may do so through private tutoring. Mandarin textbooks and the curriculum for primary and secondary level are designed locally by the Mahatma Gandhi Institute and the Ministry of Education.

In addition to public schools, Mandarin courses are also available during weekends for primary, secondary and public students at private Chinese schools, such as Xinhua Chinese Middle School and Huaxia Chinese School. They both use textbooks designed for heritage students as well as additional materials preparing students for national examinations. The Chinese Cultural Centre (CCC) also provides Mandarin courses to the general public for different HSK levels as well as specialized courses such as Business Mandarin.

There are four public universities in Mauritius: University of Mauritius (UoM), University of Technology Mauritius (UTM), Open University of Mauritius (OU) and Mauritius Institute of Education (MIE). UoM is the largest university with a population of 11,427 students, accounting for 35.2% of students at tertiary level in Mauritius (Higher Education Commission, 2019). The UoM campus is located in Moka village, in the central region. At tertiary level, Mahatma Gandhi Institute in collaboration with UoM, offers Diploma, Bachelor of Arts and Master of Arts in Modern Chinese (Mahatma Gandhi Institute, n.d.) while CI-UoM offers HSK courses and Mandarin for Tourism as elective credit-bearing modules to UoM students.

2.3 Confucius Institute at the University of Mauritius

Since the establishment of CI-UoM in 2016, the number of Mandarin language learners has increased rapidly, with more than 500 students at present (University of Mauritius-Confucius Institute, 2020). There are two directors, the Chinese director is appointed by the partner university, Zhejiang Sci-Tech University (ZSTU, Hangzhou, China), and the local director is a faculty member of UoM. The author of this article is the first and only local instructor, and started to work for CI-UoM as from 2019. Each year, there are six to seven teachers sent from China for a contract period of one to three years. The CI-UoM office is located within the UoM campus and accommodates a library with extensive materials accessible to both teachers and learners. Apart from providing Mandarin language courses, CI-UoM and ZSTU also promote cultural and academic exchanges, fostering mutual understanding between Chinese and Mauritian people through various cultural activities, workshops, academic talks as well as summer and winter camps in China.

Mandarin Courses at CI-UoM are either elective credit-bearing modules for UoM students or as interest classes for students and faculty members of UoM, businesspersons and the general public. Courses are taught face-to-face on a weekly basis at the UoM campus in Moka, except for one class for businesspersons, taught at the Chinese Chamber of Commerce in Port Louis. Courses at CI-UoM usually begin in September and end in July in the following year as per the UoM academic calendar whilst the class for businesspersons continues during winter vacation (June–August). Due to the COVID-19 pandemic in 2020, courses at CI-UoM began later in October and ended in August.

Most CI-UoM teachers refrain from accessing the internet during class, they are free to bring their personal laptop should they wish to use technology or previously downloaded resources to enhance their teaching. WhatsApp is informally used by most teachers as Learning Management System to send notices, videos and learning resources, while some teachers also use email or WeChat to communicate with students. After completing a course, written and oral examinations are held to assess the listening, reading, writing and speaking skills of students.

Students are also encouraged to take part in official HSK examinations, which were previously only held by the Chinese Cultural Center in Bell Village, Port Louis. CI-UoM held its first HSK examinations from HSK level 1 to 4 on October 17, 2020 with a maximum capacity of 80 candidates (Li, 2020).

2.4 Chinese Emergency Remote Teaching

After the first confirmed cases of COVID-19 were announced in Mauritius, all courses at UoM shifted to online classes (University of Mauritius, 2020). The teachers at CI-UoM promptly began exploring and comparing the different platforms available for delivering live online lectures, such as DingTalk, Tencent Meetings, Zoom and QQ Live (Han & Yu, 2020). In the end, all teachers agreed to use Zoom, considering its ease of access and multiple learner-friendly features, namely the Screen Share and Digital Whiteboard.

To guarantee the smooth delivery of the online lectures, and for teachers to familiarize themselves with Zoom settings and functions, CI-UoM teachers conducted a few trial tests before the start of online classes. On March 20, 2020, CI-UoM officially and successfully shifted all classes to online mode. Mandarin learners at CI-UoM, including students stranded abroad since the travel ban, had the opportunity to experience online learning safely at home, thus complying with social distancing measures. The schedules of most online Mandarin classes were unchanged to minimize schedule clash, except for a few classes where all learners agreed to adjust the class time with their new schedules. Due to the 40-minute time limit on the free Zoom version, most classes were divided into three sessions with short breaks.

3 Methodology

In order to better understand the emergency remote Chinese teaching at CI-UoM, a short survey was sent to each of the seven instructors and another survey was also sent to students before the end of the semester in July 2020. The instructors were asked to reflect on their online teaching experience during the pandemic and students were surveyed on several aspects of online learning.

3.1 Student Survey

An online student survey was designed and sent to each class by the instructors, to gather information about students' opinions and online learning experience in an anonymous way. Learners were surveyed through 36 questions, covering five parts: (1) Demographic information; (2) Attendance and satisfaction; (3) Technical aspects of online Mandarin classes; (4) Online teaching methods; and (5) Teaching pace, homework and evaluation. The complete survey is available in the Appendix.

A total of 125 valid survey responses were returned and the data collected was analysed to produce a comprehensive report on the state of online classes during the COVID-19 pandemic at CI-UoM and to develop better teaching strategies for future online Mandarin courses.

3.2 Faculty Survey

The seven instructors were asked to fill out the survey and to email back the completed surveys back to the author. The survey included the following five open-ended questions:

- Which type of online teaching was used and how was your online teaching experience during the pandemic lockdown (synchronous class, asynchronous class, other)?
- How did the transition from face-to-face to online classes affect your teaching?
- Did you assess students during the lockdown? What was the assessment content and method, and how did you supervise students?
- What were the major challenges in online teaching during the pandemic, in terms of technical issues, classroom management, etc.?
- What are your reflections on your online teaching experience and for its future use?

4 Findings

4.1 Major Findings from the Student Survey

Student Demographic Information

Of the 125 valid responses, 79% were female, 48% were aged between 20 and 30, 43% were students, 46% learned Mandarin for less than a year, 42% are studying HSK level 1 (Table 6.2).

Attendance, Satisfaction and Opinion

Concerning student attendance during the lockdown, 50% of the students were always present, 28% were regular, 12% were sometimes absent, 8% were often absent and 2% were present but not on time. Respondents who have been absent selected one or more reasons for absence. Thirty-seven out of 79 respondents for this question stated that it was due to personal matters, accounting for 47%. Other reasons were work or study schedule clash (28%); absence of internet network or internet speed issues (24%); while 11% of students cannot concentrate in their home or work environment, especially in the presence of children, noise or other distractions (Fig. 6.1).

A majority of 66% liked online classes as it allowed them to save time, money and energy. Thirty-seven per cent of students stated that they could clearly see the PowerPoint slides on their device as opposed to face-to-face classes, especially on large screen devices such as tablets or laptops. The sharpness and size of the projected slides in face-to-face classes are not optimum and students sitting in back rows or with a poor eyesight have difficulty to follow lectures. Twenty-eight per cent also have a preference for online learning and 24% students find online classes more flexible (Fig. 6.2).

Students disliked online classes mainly due to a decrease in interaction with the teacher and classmates (58%), slow or unstable internet (38%) and distractions at home or at work (24%). Fourteen per cent of students also felt less motivated and thought that online classes were less

Table 6.2 Demographic information of students surveyed

Question 1. What is your gender?				
79.2% female			20.8% male	
Question 2. What is your age?				
12.8%	48.0%	7.2%	8.8%	15.2%	8.0%
<20 yrs old	20–30 yrs old	31–40 yrs old	41–50 yrs old	51–60 yrs old	>60 yrs old
Question 3. What is your occupation?				
43.2%	39.2%	7.2%	0.8%	5.6%	4.0%
student	full-time worker	work-study mode	part-time worker	retired	housewife/housohusband
Question 5. How many years did you learn mandarin?				
46.4%	36.0%		12.0%	5.6%	
<1 yr	1–2 yrs		3–4 yrs	>5 yrs	
Question 6. Which course are you studying?				
42.4%	33.6%	8.8%	1.6%	8.8%	4.8%
HSK 1	HSK 2	HSK 3	YCT children class	New practical Chinese 1	New practical Chinese 2

6 Online Mandarin Language Teaching and Learning… 143

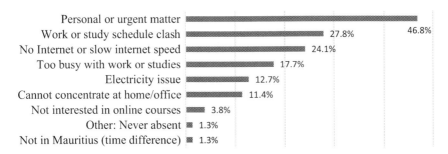

Fig. 6.1 Reasons for absence in online classes

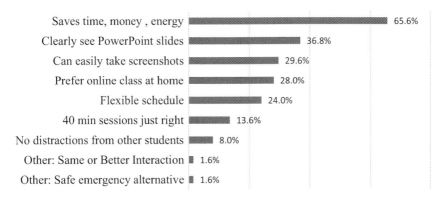

Fig. 6.2 Reasons for liking online classes

interesting. Sixteen per cent thought that joining Zoom every 40 minutes was not convenient but another 14% thought the opposite. Nineteen per cent of responses also stated that their eyes were tired from watching a screen over a prolonged period, and 13% complained that the screen was too small to focus properly (Fig. 6.3).

In terms of class management, 61% of students considered their teacher to be excellent. Class atmosphere was perceived by 45% as fun and lively, 35% stated it was good and 18% found it average. In terms of teaching pace, 82% stated it was just right, while 14% said it was a bit fast and 4% stated it was a bit slow (Table 6.3).

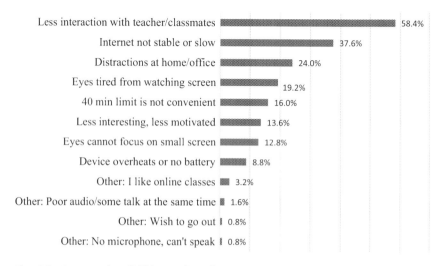

Fig. 6.3 Reasons for disliking online classes

Table 6.3 Students' opinion towards class management, atmosphere and teaching pace

Question 23. How good was your teacher's class management in terms of time, pace, behaviour, etc.?				
60.8% Excellent	36.0% Good	3.2% Average	0% Not good	0% Poor
Question 24. How was class atmosphere online?				
44.8% fun and lively	35.2% good	17.6% average	2.4% A bit dull	0% dull
Question 27. How was the teaching pace/speed for you?				
0% too slow	4.0% A bit slow	82.4% just right	13.6% A bit fast	0% too fast

Technical Aspects

There were two main challenges regarding the technical aspect of online teaching: unfamiliarity with digital devices/Zoom and loss of connectivity due to power cut or internet cut. Before the pandemic, the majority of the learners at CI-UoM had little or no experience in attending online classes, as only 38% stated they were skilful to some degree. After three months of online classes 86% of students thought they were skilful and none stated being not skilful at all, as shown in Fig. 6.4. Respondents chose one or more solutions adopted when a technical problem surfaced. Fifty-eight per cent stated they seek help from their teacher, and 30% seek help from a family member or friend who is more skilful with digital devices, 9% search for a solution on the internet, 5% try to solve the issue on their own, 2% had no technical issue, 1% would inform the teacher if issues persist.

In 2018–2019, 70% of Mauritian households had access to internet, 71% of households had access to smartphones and 51% had access to computer or tablet devices (Statistics Mauritius, 2019). The internet connection in Mauritius was quite stable most of the time, with few internet connection or power supply issues, mostly due to repair work. Twenty-three per cent of students have been absent due to lack of internet facilities or low internet speed issues whilst 38% of students also pointed out internet connection issues as being a deterrent factor to the delivery of online classes. Thirteen per cent of students also acknowledged power supply issues as reason for their absence. Sixty-three per cent of the learners used mobile phones as connecting devices. Nine per cent of respondents agreed that their electronic device heated up or the battery was used up quickly, especially given that online lectures lasted for a total of two hours.

Due to technical issues and online environment limitations, actual length of lectures were often shortened, causing some teachers to feel pressured to complete the curriculum and put additional stress on the learners who had less time to write down class notes. As a solution, some teachers shared the PowerPoint presentations as confirmed by 69% of surveyed students.

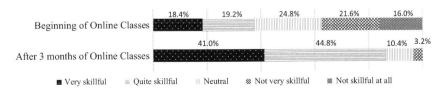

Fig. 6.4 Degree of technical skill at the start of online classes and after three months

Online Learning Platforms and Features

Four main applications were used by instructors during the pandemic: Zoom, WhatsApp, Google Classroom and WeChat, as shown in Table 6.4 below. Respondents chose one or more purposes for each online platform. Ninety-seven per cent of the learners stated their teacher used Zoom as main video conference application for lectures. WhatsApp was used as main Learning Management System, as was the case before lockdown. Seventy-nine per cent used it to communicate with the teacher, and 64% used it for submitting homework.

Respondents also chose one or more Zoom features used by themselves and the teacher. Ninety-eight per cent of students stated that Screen Share was often used by the teacher (to view PowerPoint presentations, PDF documents or other online resources). Students could also see how their teacher used Pinyin input system to type Chinese characters, a very useful skill in today's digital era. Fifty-one per cent stated that Breakout Room was often used for group work. Twenty-six per cent also stated that the Digital Whiteboard was often used by the teacher. Thirty-eight per cent stated that the teacher used the Chat Room and 56% of students use the Chat Room to communicate silently with the teacher or with classmates, publicly or privately, without interrupting the class (Table 6.5).

Concerning the teacher's PowerPoint presentation, 46% of students confirmed that they received the presentations before each lecture, allowing them to preview and 26% of respondents received it after lectures, allowing for review. In general, 56% of students were highly satisfied with regard to the quality of PowerPoint presentations (Table 6.6).

Table 6.4 Use of online platforms for different purposes

Online platform	Lectures (%)	Messages (%)	Homework (%)	Documents (%)
ZOOM	96.8	12.0	27.2	17.6
Google meeting	4.8	3.2	5.6	5.6
Google classroom	5.6	5.6	20.8	7.2
WhatsApp	7.2	79.2	64.0	53.6
WeChat	4.0	16.0	12.8	10.4
Email	12.0	12.8	13.5	16.8

Table 6.5 Use of different Zoom features

	Screen share	Chat Room	Breakout Room	Digital whiteboard	Annotation	Reactions (raise hand, thumb up)
Teacher	97.6%	38.4%	51.2%	26.4%	12.8%	20.0%
Student	24.0%	56.0%	41.6%	0%	0.8%	38.4%

Table 6.6 Student access and satisfaction towards PowerPoint slides

Question 13. Does your teacher usually provide PowerPoint slides since COVID-19?				
45.5% Yes before each chapter	25.6% Yes after each chapter	13.2% Sometimes a few slides	15.7% No, we take screenshots/pictures	
Question 14. How satisfied are you with your teacher's PowerPoint slides and its contents?				
56.0% Excellent	37.6% Good	4.8% Average	0.8% Not satisfied	0.8% Not satisfied at all

Teaching Techniques and Activities

Students chose one or more teaching methods that they liked in online classes, and 80% enjoyed communicative language teaching (interactions with authentic examples and real communication), 78% enjoyed an explanatory approach, 70% preferred discussions (questions and answers), 46% liked grammar-translation approach, 31% liked collaboration (group work), 21% enjoy gamified learning, 19% liked the 'total physical response' method (with objects and gestures) and 11% preferred the direct method (without using mother tongue). Students also chose one or more classroom activities they enjoyed, as shown in Fig. 6.5. The most popular activity (86%) was reading aloud in turns. Fifty-four per cent enjoyed questions and answers and 47% liked creating sentences. Twenty-four per cent enjoyed games while 11% did not like it. Pair or group work through Breakout Rooms was enjoyed by 52%, whereas 11% of students did not like it.

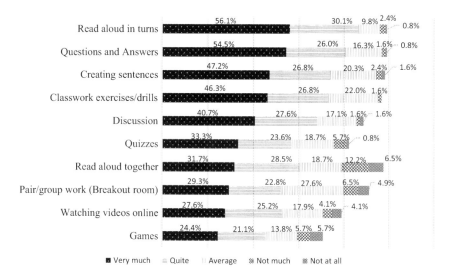

Fig. 6.5 Popularity of different class activities

Homework and Assessment

Students chose one or more types of homework assigned as shown in Fig. 6.6. Eighty per cent of students were assigned basic written homework (dialogues, short essay writing), 76% were assigned workbook exercises, 70% were assigned character writing exercises, 50.4% were given oral homework (reading aloud, short speech), 26% of students were engaged in self-study, and 11% shared learning tips and online resources, an equally important aspect of learning.

79% of students stated they cannot complete homework due to lack of time, 16% usually forget it, 12% stated they lack understanding or skills required to complete the homework, or they did not understand the question, suggesting that questions should be rephrased or accompanied with worked examples. Sixty per cent were satisfied with the correction, 41% stated that the homework was very varied, and 57% thought that the homework was highly useful (Figs. 6.7 and 6.8).

Concerning assessments, the frequency varied a lot. Thirty-five per cent of students were not assessed at all during the lockdown, 9% had

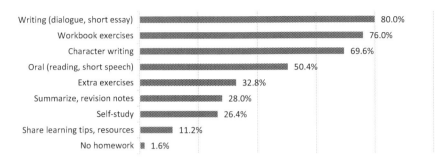

Fig. 6.6 Type of homework assigned

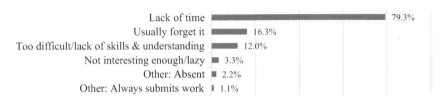

Fig. 6.7 Reasons for not submitting homework

one assessment, 21% had two to three assessments and 35% had more than three assessments. As to the difficulty level, 61% stated that it was just right, 33% believed it was slightly hard, 2% said it was too hard while 4% stated it was slightly easy.

Future of Online Teaching and Learning

A majority of 54% advocated a blended teaching mode (both face-to-face and online). Twenty-one per cent of students preferred mainly face-to-face classes except during cyclones, pandemics, and so on. Twelve per cent wished to attend classes exclusively online, except for examinations. Seven per cent preferred completely online classes for learning while 6% preferred completely face-to-face classes. Twenty-three per cent stated that they have withdrawn from the course or plan to do so. Out of these 23%, reasons were: hard to catch up after absence (35%); work or study schedule clash (31%); too busy (28%); online classes not interesting or

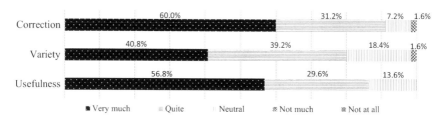

Fig. 6.8 Students' opinion towards homework

Fig. 6.9 Satisfaction towards face-to-face and online class

lost motivation (17%). A decrease in level of satisfaction has also been observed when compared with face-to-face classes; 91% of students stated that they enjoyed offline classes as opposed to 79% who enjoyed online classes (Fig. 6.9).

4.2 Major Findings from the Instructor Survey

Instructor Background and Online Teaching Experience

During the pandemic lockdown in 2020, there were 7 instructors. Three of the educators had 2–15 years of Mandarin teaching experience. The other four educators, including the local educator, were current Master degree internship students or fresh graduates with nearly no previous teaching experience. Since some teachers completed their contractual term before the lockdown and later could not be replaced due to travel restrictions, the remaining seven teachers shared the additional workload. Many teachers also mentioned that the workload was more than usual due to the transition to online lectures. None of the seven teachers at CI-UoM had previous online teaching experience, and no one was familiar with Zoom either.

In terms of workload, the teachers spent a considerable amount of energy and time in preparing lecture notes, designing PowerPoint presentations, delivering online lectures, correcting assignments, completing administrative tasks, organizing online activities, communicating with students online as well as continuing to learn about online teaching. All these tasks were carried out mainly on digital devices. Most of the teachers felt an extra strain on their eyes as a result of prolonged exposure to digital screens and some mentioned physical pain caused by poor sitting postures. Continuing online courses on a long-term basis may have an impact on the occupational health of educators and this concern should be taken seriously.

An online students' meeting was organized in April 2020, with one student invited from each class, to share their online learning experience and give suggestions. During the meeting, students expressed general satisfaction concerning the promptness and quality of online classes at CI-UoM; they highly appreciated the dedication of their teachers. Many liked the immersive approach through authentic daily life examples that they could easily relate to and put in practice. Teachers often included additional vocabulary and sentences that were relevant to the local environment, culture or modern society, such as the beach, online shopping and catchphrases. Many suggestions were also mentioned about online teaching content, techniques, communication skills, and they also hoped for more oral interaction and cultural activities.

Technical Aspects

Different strategies were used to address technical issues such as background noise, loss of connectivity and unfamiliarity with Zoom. Students were advised to mute themselves during classes and unmute only when speaking. Initially, most students were not familiar with Zoom, elderly students in particular needed assistance from teachers to unmute themselves. However, after three months, even elderly students became familiar with Zoom and could unmute themselves without assistance. In the event of a power cut, device malfunction or internet issue at the teacher's house, teachers chose to reschedule the lecture or assign an emergency learning activity to complete via WhatsApp until the aforementioned issues were solved. This was an interesting and engaging alternative when managed with clear guidelines. For example, the teacher would start with a question in Mandarin, students would be required to continue the conversation in turns, either by audio or text message. The teacher would later discuss mistakes made by students during class.

One reason for low student response during class was that the question itself was too difficult or unclear. In face-to-face classes, students often sought help from neighbouring classmates, which was less probable in online classes. Instead, the teacher could rephrase the question or break it down into more simple questions to be answered by different students, and this can lead to answering the difficult question together as a team. Teachers sometimes explicitly chose to ask an open question to all, and the competition to answer first was encouraging for higher achieving students. On the other hand, some students needed more time to think. The teacher would move on with another student and later revert back to the previous student. This strategy was beneficial for slow learners who needed more time, and allowed for differentiated learning. Another reason was microphone/internet connection issues, whereby students were then encouraged to answer in written form in the Chat Room instead.

Chat Rooms were also a way to increase feedback from introvert students and improving their learning experience. If additional sentences were difficult to assimilate orally, the Chat Room was often used as substitute for the physical whiteboard by quickly displaying characters and Pinyin. The Chat history could also be saved by students for review. One teacher did not use a Chinese character-to-Pinyin converter as it could not correctly display Pinyin for characters with multiple pronunciation. Instead the teacher used numbers to represent tones when quickly typing sentences in pinyin in the Chat Room, for example: 'pin1yin1', with students understanding tone marking rules as prerequisite. The teacher later used Pinyinput, a manual pinyin input system which solved the problem of characters with multiple pronunciation and displayed the tones on the correct letters (Pinyinput, n.d.).

Concerning the use of camera, teenage and adult students often felt the need for privacy and in some classes rarely switched their camera on. It was difficult for the teacher to correct the pronunciation of students without looking at their mouth shape. With cameras switched off, teachers could also not observe the students' facial expression, body language and other non-verbal signals that help teachers to adjust their teaching approach. Teachers also tend to forget or neglect students who participate less in the online environment. Teachers should make a conscious effort to divide attention equally so that each student has the opportunity to participate.

The Digital Whiteboard was often used to show the stroke order or to compare specific Chinese characters and radicals while most characters in the curriculum were shown as animated GIF form or in stroke-by-stroke table form in the PowerPoint. Despite having the Digital Whiteboard feature, one teacher felt that physical whiteboards were still easier to use and as a result, she felt the need for her PowerPoint content to be as comprehensive as possible.

Teachers observed that university students, faculty members and full-time workers became considerably more busy during the COVID-19 pandemic. This group of learners shifted their focus to their core degree studies or priorities and were more often absent for Mandarin class. Most teachers did not record their lectures for students to replay afterwards, absent students were encouraged to keep up-to-date by seeking notes from classmates or additional guidance from the teacher. One teacher also provided extra remedial sessions on some occasions.

Teaching Techniques and Activities

Two teachers frequently used realia as pedagogical tools in face-to-face classes to help students associate the vocabulary learned with the object itself. The demonstration method was often used for certain grammar points, such as 把字句, by showing object displacement while explaining how to phrase 'bǎ' in a sentence. In online classes, teachers could still do the same but the choice of objects available was slightly different.

Simultaneously reading texts aloud was common in face-to-face classes but this was difficult to carry out online as the multiple voices could not be synchronized and sounded quite noisy due to sound transmission lag. Most teachers opted for reading aloud in turns, and this proved to be much more efficient. Learners had the opportunity to receive individual feedback from their teacher on pronunciation and tones. Similarly, questions were usually asked individually instead of asking the whole class. However, some students were not used to answering questions on their own and probably experienced some stress to answer as soon as possible.

Breakout Rooms were used for students to put their knowledge into practice within a small group where each group member could clearly be heard. Students had the opportunity to learn from each other and feel less intimidated than when speaking in front of the whole class. The teacher then visited each room to provide further guidance. Some students were willing to participate but could not participate orally due to microphone issues and thus chose to quit the Zoom session. Some simply did not wish to collaborate with others and preferred learning on their own. One teacher also mentioned that a few students did not contribute to a good learning environment in Breakout Rooms, and they might have affected their group members who consequently were no longer willing to work together.

The children class was considerably difficult to manage as the age span was very large, ranging from 7 to 14 years old. Ideally, the age span should be reduced by dividing the class. Moreover, Chinese culture themed activities, such as storytelling and singing, were often organized in face-to-face classes for children to learn about Chinese proverbs, myths and traditions. Students then shared their thoughts or retold the story. However, these did not receive as much popularity online and were less productive. Learners perhaps were less confident to speak online, or had technical issues and distractions at home. Gamified learning was also frequently used with children. The approach was highly popular, effective and sometimes even necessary. However, classroom games requiring physical movements or face-to-face interaction such as Chinese Character Relay Race were difficult to implement online. One teacher made a first attempt at online gamified learning when teaching words indicating directions such as left and right. Students made the corresponding gesture with their thumb on the teacher's command in Mandarin. Most students enjoyed the activity, which was different from the traditional teaching approach, but a few might consider games as childish or a waste of time. The game was easy to carry out without any equipment and the overall effect was satisfactory.

Homework and Assessment

Homework, such as short essay and character writing were mostly handwritten and sent as photos on Google Classroom or WhatsApp. Teachers corrected the work by editing pictures. More proficient students submitted work in Word format, allowing easier correction. Oral homework was mostly submitted as audio files or as voice messages on WhatsApp. This medium was considered user-friendly and convenient for both students and teachers.

For assessments, the Screen Share feature was often used to display questions on PowerPoint. Answers were handwritten and submitted in picture form (as for homework) at the end of the assessment within the time limit imposed. Initially, one teacher requested all students to switch on their camera for supervision, but the internet speed dropped significantly, and affected sound transmission. As a result, supervision by camera was cancelled. Evaluation through online survey platforms was considered by some teachers, but it would require identification. Students would also be able to take screenshots of the survey questions and forward them to their classmates, while elderly students might have more technical difficulties to participate. One anti-cheating strategy was time control. The students who completed all questions on one specific slide were instructed to use the Raise Your Hand feature. When half of the students were done, one minute or more was allocated before moving to the next slide. Questions were also designed so that answers cannot be found directly from learning materials or online. The Chat Room's private message feature was cancelled to prevent communication among classmates. All students were also muted to remove all noise, but they could still communicate publicly or privately with the teacher in the Chat Room to ask questions not related to the assessment content. If several assessment dates were available, designing different versions of the test paper by reshuffling questions and altering the question was an additional precautionary measure.

5 Discussion and Implications

5.1 Technical Aspects and Online Learning Platforms

After three months of using Zoom, students became significantly more at ease with online classes. In the future, students can better participate and interact online. More emergency learning activities could also be designed and used in the event of connection issues. The teachers agreed that Zoom was an ideal video conference tool for live online class, while WhatsApp was an essential communication tool for most teachers outside class hours. PowerPoint slides could be made available, allowing students to catch up on missed classes. Screen Share was a key feature to display PowerPoint slides and other materials. The Chat Room was a highly useful way to display new words and sentences, and a good alternative for students not interacting verbally. Breakout Rooms and Raise Your Hand were also very useful to organize group work and to receive quick feedback.

5.2 Teaching Techniques and Activities

As online resources are readily available during online classes, features of the virtual environment should be used as an advantage by adapting tangible objects or face-to-face situations into animations, videos and other interactive ways through online platforms. Breakout Room was a useful feature for group work, but it was very challenging for the teacher to cater for all the different needs and to address the various issues mentioned earlier. Nonetheless, Breakout Rooms in online language classes remains a highly interesting topic to be explored. For young students, effective and specific class management strategies must be adopted in order to maintain their attention, perhaps through the use of short videos, games or competitive learning.

Concerning online gamified learning, the choice of games depends on the target audience and should be carried out with caution. Online learning games could be designed to be carried out without equipment and within the sitting space. The Annotation feature in Zoom could be an alternative to let students choose a correct Chinese character or a correct answer in a similar fashion to the Fly Swatter game. Choosing suitable classroom games and adapting them to an online setting remains a topic worth exploring in the future.

5.3 Online Assessment

In order to ensure the assessment security, educators should try to minimize risks of cheating through multiple measures (Nguyen et al., 2020). Time control was critical to minimize cheating during assessment. Assessment was especially important during emergency remote teaching to evaluate the teaching effectiveness and the learner's aptitudes. As online assessments are even more challenging to design and implement, assessment guidelines specifically in the pandemic situation were highly useful for educators (Fuad, 2020).

5.4 Online Teaching and Learning Experience

Due to lack of experience in online teaching, not to mention emergency remote teaching, it was a tremendous challenge for educators to adapt to an online environment and to familiarize themselves with Zoom within such a short period of time. The teachers began online classes in 'survival mode' and they prioritized the completion of the curriculum, while trying to maintain the course quality and the students' motivation. Issues and suggestions concerning all aspects of online classes should be promptly communicated between the teacher and students so as to improve the situation. Increasing and optimizing student engagement and interaction online remains a challenge for educators at CI-UoM. Zoom features can be very engaging for students when used properly (Kohnke & Moorhouse, 2020; Mukhopadhyay & Mukhopadhyay, 2020).

5.5 Future of Online Teaching

During the lockdown, educators rapidly acquired basic online teaching skills and familiarized themselves with Zoom. Educators were encouraged to share teaching tips and to continue learning by reading the latest research (Li et al., 2020; Lu, 2020), especially concerning Zoom as a teaching platform (Ramsook & Thomas, 2019). Different online teaching modes for Mandarin language (Wang, 2020), and effective strategies in emergency remote Chinese teaching (Cui, 2020) are also important aspects to learn. Educators also learned about new emergency remote Chinese teaching techniques through articles in WeChat, which were written by teachers across the world. In August 2020, all CI-UoM educators attended online talks organized by the Centre for Language Education and Cooperation (CLEC) and Confucius Institute Online (CIO). Another series of online talks for local teacher training was organized by CIO in October 2020. These talks specifically covered the emergency remote Chinese teaching during the Covid-19 pandemic. After attending the talks, educators learned a lot and felt more confident about online teaching. As the pandemic has not ended yet, it is probable that online courses will become more widespread. Thus, more in-depth research should be carried out to develop better emergency online Chinese courses, especially in areas with limited facilities and internet access. As stated by Hsin et al. (2017), professional training specifically designed for online language teachers is essential for successful online teaching.

6 Conclusion

In this paper, we have collected valuable observations, reflections as well as students' and teachers' perspective towards online learning and teaching. Although every effort was made to ensure that the results obtained are presented objectively, the author acknowledges the possibility of personal biases and limitations in the survey design. The research methodology could also have been improved by increasing the survey sample size. Nonetheless, the author hopes that these findings will be of some reference value to resource persons in the field of Emergency Remote Chinese Teaching research, or those interested in the online Mandarin teaching situation in Mauritius during the pandemic. This study shows a general acceptance and willingness among learners to attend future online Mandarin language classes after attending more than three months of online classes. Learners also acknowledged the considerable efforts made by CI-UoM teachers to address issues throughout the delivery of online classes during COVID-19 pandemic. Emergency remote Chinese teaching has become a viable, acceptable and even necessary alternative in the event of poor weather conditions such as torrential rainfall and cyclones, during pandemics or when face-to-face class is impossible. CI-UoM has indeed made substantial progress in online Mandarin teaching. However, the relatively low response for fully online learning suggests that issues related to online teaching methods, assessment and internet connectivity should be addressed for a more conducive learning environment. As mentioned by Gacs et al. (2020), planned online teaching are not comparable to emergency remote teaching. Therefore, it is an opportunity for CI-UoM educators to better design and prepare for online classes in the future. It is believed that online learning will bring about new possibilities and far-reaching prospects in Mandarin teaching in Mauritius in the future.

Acknowledgements The author thanks the Confucius Institute at University of Mauritius, especially Professor Dr Mingduan Fu and Associate Professor Dr Naraindra Kistamah, the Chinese and local directors, for their support and proofreading. The author thanks Miss Xiaoxia Li, Miss Lanhui He, Miss Xiaoping Wu, Miss Danfang Yang, Professor Dr Kangfu Zhang, Dr Yanmei Zhao for their valuable contribution by sharing their observations concerning online teaching. The author also thanks all students who participated in the online survey.

Appendix: Student Survey

Basic Information (Part 1/5)

Gender:*
- ○ Male 男 nán
- ○ Female 女 nǔ

Age:*
- ○ <20
- ○ 20~30
- ○ 31~40
- ○ 41~50
- ○ 51~60
- ○ >60

Occupation: *
- ○ Student
- ○ Work & Study
- ○ Full-Time Work
- ○ Part-Time Work
- ○ Retired
- ○ Housewife/husband

Teacher's name: * _____.

Attendance and Satisfaction (Part 2/5)

Years learning Mandarin:*
- ○ <1
- ○ 1–2
- ○ 3–4
- ○ >5

Which course have you been studying? Nǐ zài xuéxí nà yī mén kè? 你在学习哪一门课?*
- ○ HSK 1
- ○ HSK 2
- ○ New Practical Chinese Beginner (màn bān)
- ○ HSK 3
- ○ YCT3
- ○ New Practical Chinese Advanced (kuài bān)

Your attendance online since COVID-19 lockdown:*
- ○ Always Present
- ○ Regular
- ○ Sometimes Absent
- ○ Often Absent

Reasons for being absent:*
- ○ Personal/urgent matter
- ○ Work/study time clash
- ○ Not interested in online class
- ○ No Internet/too slow
- ○ Too busy with work/studies
- ○ Other: _____
- ○ Electricity issue
- ○ Can't concentrate at home/office

If you withdrew or are thinking of withdrawing from Mandarin course, why?
- ☐ Work/study schedule clash
- ☐ Online classes not interesting
- ☐ Too busy
- ☐ Content too difficult to learn
- ☐ Not enough oral practice
- ☐ Lost motivation

☐ I don't like the teacher/ ☐ Hard to catch up ☐ Other:_____
teaching style   after absence

How much do you enjoy/are satisfied with Mandarin class? *

	1 (not at all)	2	3	4	5 (very much)
Face-to-face (before lockdown)	○	○	○	○	○
Online (since lockdown)	○	○	○	○	○

Why do you like Online Mandarin class, compared to face-to-face class? *

☐ Saves time, money, energy   ☐ Flexible schedule   ☐ Prefers online learning   ☐ Other: ____
☐ Clearly see PowerPoint   ☐ Easily take screenshots   ☐ No distractions from others

Why do you dislike Online Mandarin classes, compared to face-to-face classes? *

☐ Eyes tired from watching screen   ☐ Less interaction with teacher/classmates   ☐ Other: ____
☐ Less interesting, less motivated   ☐ Internet not stable or slow
☐ Join ZOOM each 40 min not convenient   ☐ Device heats up/no battery

Technical aspect of Online Mandarin Class (Part 3/5)

Does your teacher usually provide PowerPoint slides since COVID-19?*

○ Yes before class   ○ Yes after class   ○ Sometimes   ○ No, we can take pictures   ○ Other:_____

Which device do you use to attend online Mandarin class?*

☐ Desktop Computer   ☐ Laptop   ☐ Mobile Phone   ☐ Tablet or iPad

Which application/programme does your teacher use and for what purpose?*

	Lectures	Messages	Guidance	Homework	Documents
ZOOM	☐	☐	☐	☐	☐
Google Meeting	☐	☐	☐	☐	☐
Google Classroom	☐	☐	☐	☐	☐
WhatsApp	☐	☐	☐	☐	☐
WeChat	☐	☐	☐	☐	☐
Email	☐	☐	☐	☐	☐

Which features do you/your teacher often use in ZOOM?*

	Screen share (Power Point)	Chat Room (messages)	Breakout Room	Digital Whiteboard	Annotation (draw)	Raise your hand	Clap hands/ Thumbs Up
You	☐	☐	☐	☐	☐	☐	☐
Teacher	☐	☐	☐	☐	☐	☐	☐

How skilful are you with digital devices or programmes like ZOOM:*

	1 (not at all)	2	3	4	5 (very much)
When online classes started	○	○	○	○	○
Now (after 3 months of online classes)	○	○	○	○	○

If you are having difficulties with using digital devices or ZOOM, what do you do?*

○ Ask teacher for help   ○ Ask spouse/children for help   ○ Do nothing   ○ Other: _____

During class lectures, most of the time*

	No camera/microphone	Off	On	On except when noisy	On when required to speak
Camera	○	○	○	○	○
Microphone	○	○	○	○	○

If camera/microphone is off, why do you refrain from using them?

	Privacy	Internet too slow	Technical issue	Feeling shy	Questions too difficult
Camera	☐	☐	☐	☐	☐
Microphone	☐	☐	☐	☐	☐

Online Teaching Methods (Part 4/5)

Which activities are you satisfied with in online classes?*

	1 (not at all)	2	3	4	5 (very much)
Vocabulary explanation	○	○	○	○	○
Grammar explanation	○	○	○	○	○
Pronunciation	○	○	○	○	○
Characters	○	○	○	○	○
Reading text aloud together	○	○	○	○	○
Reading text aloud in turns (role play)	○	○	○	○	○
Creating sentences	○	○	○	○	○

	1 (not at all)	2	3	4	5 (very much)
Questions and answers	○	○	○	○	○
Classwork exercises	○	○	○	○	○
Pair/group work (Breakout Room)	○	○	○	○	○
Games	○	○	○	○	○
Watching videos online	○	○	○	○	○

How good was your teacher's class management in terms of time, pace, behaviour, etc.?*

○ Poor ○ Not good ○ Average ○ Good ○ Excellent

How was class atmosphere online?*

○ Dull ○ A bit dull ○ Average ○ Good ○ Fun and lively

How much progress in online teaching did your teacher make until now?*

○ None ○ A little ○ Average ○ Quite much ○ A lot

In the future, which mode of instruction would you prefer?*

○ Face-to-face only	○ Online except for exams	○ Blended: face-to-face & online
○ Face-to-face, except for cyclone, pandemic, etc.	○ Online only	

Teaching pace and homework load (Part 5/5)

How was the teaching pace/speed for you?*

○ Too slow ○ A bit slow ○ Just right ○ A bit fast ○ Too fast

Which type of homework were you assigned since Covid-19*

☐ Workbook exercises	☐ Extra exercises	☐ Share learning tips, resources
☐ Writing (dialogues, short essay)	☐ Character writing	☐ Other: _____
☐ Oral (reading, short speech)	☐ Summarize, revision notes	

How often do you complete homework assigned?*

○ Rarely ○ Sometimes ○ Average ○ Most of the time ○ Always

If homework was seldom submitted, the reasons are:

○ No time. ○ Too hard/ unclear. ○ Not useful. ○ Not interesting. ○ Not important. ○ Often forgets

Was the homework load too heavy or too light for you?*

○ Too heavy   ○ A bit heavy   ○ Just right   ○ A bit light   ○ Too light

How satisfied are you concerning homework?*

	1 (not at all)	2	3	4	5 (very much)
Usefulness	○	○	○	○	○
Variety	○	○	○	○	○
Correction	○	○	○	○	○

Since the start of online classes, how much did you gain in terms of:*

	1 (nothing)	2	3	4	5 (a lot)
Knowledge	○	○	○	○	○
Language skills	○	○	○	○	○
Practice	○	○	○	○	○
Motivation	○	○	○	○	○
Progress	○	○	○	○	○

Any areas your teacher did particularly well, aspects to improve, or other comments:

_____
_____
_____
_____
_____

References

Cui, X. L. (2020). Mandarin teaching during unexpected global public sanitary incidents. [崔希亮 (2020). 全球突发公共卫生事件背景下的汉语教学]. *Shijie Hanyu jiaoxue, 3*, 291–299.

Fuad, A. (2020). Guidelines for online assessment in emergency remote teaching during the COVID-19 pandemic. *Education in Medicine Journal, 12*(2), 59–68. https://doi.org/10.21315/eimj2020.12.2.6

Gacs, A., Goertler, S., & Spasova, S. (2020). Planned online language education versus crisis-prompted online language teaching: Lessons for the future. *Foreign Language Annals, 53*(2), 380–392. https://doi.org/10.1111/flan.12460

Han, X. N., & Yu, L. T. (2020). Brief talk on teaching mandarin online during pandemic. [韩欣楠, 陈佳尔, 于蓝婷 (2020). 浅论疫情期间对外汉语线上教学]. *Wenxue jiaoyu, 1*(8), 164–165. https://doi.org/10.16692/j.cnki.wxjys.2020.08.071

Higher Education Commission. (2019). *Participation in tertiary education, 2019*. Higher Education Commission. Retrieved May 11, 2021, from http://tec.mu/pdf_downloads/Participation_%20in_Tertiary_Education_2019_171220.pdf

Hsin, S. C., Hsieh, C. L., & Chang-Blust, L. (2017). Preservice teacher training for online Chinese teaching: A case of distance courses for high school learners. *Journal of Technology and Chinese Language Teaching, 8*(1), 86–103.

Kohnke, L., & Moorhouse, B. (2020). Facilitating synchronous online language learning through zoom. *RELC Journal, 003368822093723*. https://doi.org/10.1177/0033688220937235

Li, X. X. (2020). Confucius Institute at University of Mauritius held HSK and HSKK tests for the first time. [李晓霞 (2020). 毛里求斯大学孔子学院首次举办HSK和HSKK考试]. *Mauritius China Times*, 4.

Li Ching Hum P. (2016). Confucius Institute in Mauritius: A dream comes true. *Mauritius Times*. Retrieved May 13, 2021, from http://www.mauritiustimes.com/mt/philip-li-ching-hum-11/

Li, Y. M., Li B. Z., Song, H., Bai, L. S., Liu L. N., Wu Y. Y., Li Q., Wen X. H., Chen W., & Ren Y. (2020). Mandarin international teaching challenges and strategies during the covid pandemic. *Experts Talk* (Volume 1). [李宇明, 李秉震, 宋晖, 白乐桑, 刘乐宁, 吴勇毅, 李泉, 温晓虹, 陈闻, 任鹰 (2020). 新冠疫情下的汉语国际教育挑战与对策:大家谈(上)]. *Yuyan jiaoxue yu yanjiu,* (4), 1–11.

Lu, J. M. (2020). Mandarin international teaching challenges and strategies during the covid pandemic. *Experts Talk* (Volume 2). [陆建明 (2020). 新冠疫情下的汉语国际教育挑战与对策:大家谈(下)]. *Yuyan jiaoxue yu yanjiu,* (05), 1–16.

Mahatma Gandhi Institute. (n.d.). Department of Chinese Studies. Retrieved from https://www.mgirti.ac.mu/index.php/component/content/article?id=133

Ministry of Education, Tertiary Education, Science and Technology. (2019). Retrieved from https://education.govmu.org/Documents/downloads/Documents/Statistics/Education%20%20Card%20%202019.pdf

Ministry of Health and Wellness. (2020). Mauritius management and prevention of COVID-19 report. Retrieved from https://www.afro.who.int/publications/mauritius-management-and-prevention-covid-19-report-october-2020

Mukhopadhyay, B. R., & Mukhopadhyay, B. K. (2020). COVID-19 and 'Zoom' for remote teaching: Enhancing student engagement. *The Sentinel*, Post-Editorial.

Nguyen, J., Keuseman, K., & Humston, J. (2020). Minimize online cheating for online assessments during COVID-19 pandemic. *Journal of Chemical Education, 97*(9), 3429–3435. https://doi.org/10.1021/acs.jchemed.0c00790

Pinyinput. (n.d.). Retrieved from https://www.pinyinput.net/

Ramsook, L., & Thomas, M. (2019). Perspectives of prospective teachers on Zoom as a transformative teaching methodology. *International Journal for Innovation Education and Research, 7*(11), 946–957. https://doi.org/10.31686/ijier.vol7.iss11.1955

Statistics Mauritius. (2019). *Information and Communication Technologies (ICT) statistics, 2019*. Statistics Mauritius. Retrieved May 7, 2020, from https://statsmauritius.govmu.org/Documents/Statistics/ESI/2020/EI1530/ICT_Yr19.pdf

Statistics Mauritius. (2020a). Population and vital statistics Republic of Mauritius, year 2020. Statistics Mauritius. Retrieved May 11, 2021, from https://statsmauritius.govmu.org/Documents/Statistics/ESI/2021/EI1572/Pop_Vital_Yr20_150321.pdf

Statistics Mauritius. (2020b). Digest of education statistics 2020. Statistics Mauritius. Retrieved May 11, 2020, from https://statsmauritius.govmu.org/Documents/Statistics/Digests/Education/Digest_Edu_Yr20_290321.xlsx

University of Mauritius. (2020). Covid-19 Communique No. 2. Retrieved from https://www.uom.ac.mu/images/FILES/Events/2020/COVID19/COVIDCommunique2.pdf

University of Mauritius-Confucius Institute. (2020 January 20). The first Chinese director of CI-UoM bid farewell to Mauritius. Retrieved from https://www.uom.ac.mu/confucius/index.php/ci-news

Wang, R. F. (2020).Analysis of teaching mode for mandarin skills class during pandemic crisis. [王瑞烽 (2020). 疫情防控期间汉语技能课线上教学模式分析.世界汉语教学] (3), 300–310.

7

Remote Chinese Language Teaching at the University of Queensland During the COVID-19 Pandemic: A Reflection from Australia

Wenying Jiang

1   Introduction

The emergence of the COVID-19 pandemic has impacted human lives all over the world. Many nations across the world witnessed complete lockdown, with no social, religious, or public gatherings, and people were to adhere to social distancing rules. Individuals were required by their governments to stay away from others as anyone could be infected with coronavirus and proximity increases the chance of spreading the virus. While the spread of COVID-19 has reconfigured the lives of millions of people around the world, it has affected teaching at all levels. Particularly it highlighted the need for educational institutions to be able to respond quickly to unpredictable contexts and environments. Australian universities had no choice but to adapt their courses for online delivery with very short notice. This chapter is a reflection on the strategies and approaches that the author adopted in the rapid response to the change from face to

W. Jiang (✉)
The University of Queensland, Brisbane, QLD, Australia
e-mail: w.jiang2@uq.edu.au

face (F2F) teaching to remote teaching of a Chinese language course at the University of Queensland (UQ) in Australia.

2 Background Information

2.1 Chinese Program Overview

The Chinese program at UQ in Australia consists of nine full time academic faculty members: five teaching undergraduate courses and four teaching postgraduate courses. At the same time there are more than ten additional language instructors who work on an hourly payment basis. The number of undergraduates who take the Chinese language courses at UQ seems stable from year to year until 2020. The enrolment figure for the first semester in 2021 is about 200 (excluding enrolments in courses at Chinese native speaker level), which dropped about 20% due to the pandemic when international students were (and still are) not allowed to travel to Australia.

UQ Chinese offers four undergraduate Major Streams ranging from (A) beginning level, through (B) intermediate and (C) advanced non-native speaker levels, up to (D) native speaker level. Stream A is for students who start learning Chinese from the very beginning. Stream B is for students who have studied Chinese in high school. Stream C is for students who have a Chinese background and those who have studied in other universities and transferred over to UQ and those who have stayed in Chinese-speaking countries or regions for more than a year. Stream D is for native speakers of Chinese. The uniqueness of UQ Chinese lies in the fact that a Stream in Teaching Chinese as a Second Language (TCSL), namely Stream D, has been offered since 2015 while other universities of the Australian Go8[1] group retain a focus on language acquisition and literary studies. The career goal of the graduates from this TCSL Stream is becoming teachers of Chinese in secondary schools.

---

[1] The Group of Eight (Go8) comprises Australia's leading research-intensive universities—the University of Melbourne, the Australian National University, the University of Sydney, the University of Queensland, the University of Western Australia, the University of Adelaide, Monash University and UNSW Sydney.

Spoken and written courses are separated out in the "language acquisition" Streams (A-C), in order to accommodate the student cohort's language competencies in these skills. This separation is important for the UQ student cohort, given the number of students who are from Chinese-speaking households ("heritage" students). They can speak at varying proficiencies, but have poor, if any, reading and writing skills. Students who have lived overseas in Chinese-speaking settings also commonly have higher spoken than written skills, while Japanese native speaking students commonly have higher written than spoken skills. Separating spoken and written courses thus serves the students' skill-based needs and personalizes their learning experience, which is highly emphasized at UQ. The rationale for separation of spoken and written courses is also supported by contemporary Teaching Chinese as a Second Language pedagogical research (Zhao, 2011).

UQ Chinese program leads its counterparts of other Australian universities in that new HSK tests are used in benchmarking the core Chinese language courses (Jiang, 2020). The practice of HSK benchmarking was designed to achieve three purposes: (1) provide students with the opportunity to get familiar to the format and difficulty level of the HSK tests; (2) promote learning by attending HSK tests as students can chart their progresses along their study; and (3) use the test outcome to assist the screening and placement process and support any adjustment when it is needed (Jiang, 2019, 2020).

The academic year at Australian universities, for the majority of undergraduate programs, is divided into two 13-week semesters plus a short Summer semester in which some courses are offered intensively. Located in the southern hemisphere, Semester 1 (S1) in Australian universities usually lasts from February to June while Semester 2 (S2) usually lasts from July to November. During each of the 13-week teaching semesters, there is usually one-week break in between. Each semester is followed by a one-week revision time and a formal examination period of two and half weeks. The standard Bachelor of Arts (BA) program consists of three years of study, so does the BA in Chinese in this university.

2.2 Core Chinese Language Acquisition Courses Taught at UQ

Given that the Chinese BA program consists of Year I, Year II, and Year III studies, Table 7.1 below lists the core Chinese language acquisition courses taught at UQ, which consists of 12 courses, 4 in each year, 2 in each semester.

Before the COVID-19 pandemic, blended learning, and online activities/tasks were integrated in each of the course curricula. These activities and resources are either part of the curricula or are used to consolidate knowledge taught in class. This practice is in line with a key goal of the UQ Student Strategy[2] to prioritize the online delivery of course content in order to complement active learning on campus. Examples of blended learning and on-line activities/tasks and resources are as follows:

* Two software tools developed in-house, the talking pinyin chart and the Mandarin pitch tracker, provided on Blackboard[3] for students to download to assist them in the acquisition of Chinese pronunciation and tones outside classroom hours (CHIN1100 & CHIN2100).
* Listening comprehension and dictation exercises available on Blackboard for students to use on their own as practice (CHIN1100, CHIN2100, CHIN3000, CHIN3010, CHIN3100 & CHIN3110 = Streams A-C).

Table 7.1 Core Chinese language acquisition courses at UQ

	Year I	Year II	Year III
S1 spoken	CHIN1100	CHIN3000	CHIN3100
S1 written	CHIN1200	CHIN3001	CHIN3200
S2 spoken	CHIN2100	CHIN3010	CHIN3110
S2 written	CHIN2200	CHIN3020	CHIN3210

---

[2] In July 2016, UQ launched the Student Strategy: a five-year transformational plan that focuses on working toward four inter-related goals that are fundamental to the realization of its vision (for details see https://student-strategy.uq.edu.au/).

[3] Blackboard is a virtual learning environment and learning management system developed by Blackboard Inc. Each course at UQ has a Blackboard site.

- Links to several internet sites offering animated stroke order of Chinese characters available on Blackboard to assist students in acquiring skills in writing Chinese characters (CHIN1200, CHIN2200, CHIN3001 & CHIN3020 = Streams A & B).
- Links to several online Chinese-English and English-Chinese dictionaries on Blackboard. Some dictionaries also provide audio output (CHIN1200, CHIN2200, CHIN3000, CHIN3001, CHIN3100, CHIN3110, CHIN3200& CHIN3210 = Streams A-C).
- Computer-mediated sound-file exercises incorporated as part of the curriculum for spoken courses. An instructor listens to the learner sound-file replies each week and provides individual feedback through sound-file or e-mail in a timely manner. (CHIN3000 & CHIN3010) (Jiang & Ramsay, 2005; Jiang, 2016).
- WeChat task linking up learners with native speakers of Chinese for weekly sub-tasks involving one to one oral communication based on learners' learning material. The learner-native speaker pair were required to complete weekly assigned communication sub-tasks through WeChat "hold and talk" function. It is a great learning task that makes use of the native speaker resources and mobile assisted language learning technology to achieve the best learning outcome in teaching Chinese as a foreign language (CHIN3010) (Jiang & Li, 2018) .
- A web-diary task on Blackboard. Each class week for a semester, students are required to post a "diary entry" on the class Blackboard site. The diary records a current real event, or an imaginary event (e.g. a world trip or a trip around China; life as a movie star or sports star, or a political prisoner). One theme uniting all the entries is required for their writings to have coherence or continuation between weekly entries (CHIN3001 & CHIN3020) (Jiang, 2012).
- Online Chinese proficiency tests developed in cooperation with the National Taiwan Normal University's Mandarin Training Centre. In the middle of semester 2 each year, students enrolled in CHIN3100 & CHIN3110 are required to complete 40 questions in 45 minutes allocated for each test.

The above technology-enhanced tasks/resources used in residential or F2F teaching before the pandemic turned out to be a very important foundation for the teaching mode change from F2F to entirely online with short notice when the pandemic hit Australia in early March 2020.

2.3 The Chinese Language Acquisition Courses Taught by the Author at UQ

The author has been teaching Year II courses, namely CHIN3000, CHIN3001, CHIN3010, and CHIN3020, as shown in Table 7.1. She firmly believes that strong learner's motivation is critical to efficient and effective language learning, which forms the basis of her teaching philosophy. However, it is challenging to keep language learners' motivation at a high level all the time. Hence a significant proportion of her efforts and time are used in motivating students rather than simply transferring knowledge of the target language. In today's high-tech learning environment, it would be unfair to limit students to traditional teaching and assessment methods. Using computer assisted language learning (CALL) tasks or making use of smart phone technology in language learning are some of the effective ways to increase language learners' external motivation. Through years of teaching, the author has gained skills in developing various CALL tasks in teaching Chinese as a foreign language. For example, the WeChat oral assessment task for CHIN3010 and web diary task for CHIN3001 and CHIN3020, as mentioned above.

3 Emergency Remote Teaching at UQ Due to the Pandemic

Across 20 developed countries, the intra-university responses to COVID-19 have varied considerably from no change to complete online offerings (Crawford et al., 2020). In fact, there has been no consistent move to online teaching internationally; rather, each institution in each country has responded to its immediate enrolment pressures (Crawford et al., 2020). UQ's response was that all teachers be requested to turn to emergency online teaching.

Specifically, in S1, 2020 (February to June) when COVID-19 became a worry, after three weeks' F2F teaching (from February 24 to March 13, 2020), UQ decided to have one-week (March 16–20, 2020) pause with no teaching, during which all teachers were requested to prepare and deliver teaching entirely online via Zoom starting from week five (March 23–27, 2020), cover the content of week four. Many teachers encountered pressure in fast learning in regard to how to use Zoom in delivering online teaching.

As far as Chinese language courses were concerned, the technology enhanced online activities/tasks/resources mentioned in Sect. 2.2 above turned out to be a very important foundation for the teaching mode change from F2F to entirely online with a very short notice for teachers in our Chinese program. Additionally, some of our students mentioned that the teachers of Chinese did an excellent job in converting to synchronous online teaching with very short notice while teachers of other subjects heavily relied on recorded lectures.

4 Student Feedback

4.1 Teaching Evaluation Conducted at UQ

UQ implements a number of quality assurance processes to maintain our commitment to the highest standards of teaching. Student Evaluation of Course and Teacher (SECaT) is one of them being implemented for each course it offers. SECaT evaluations give students the opportunity to provide feedback on their experience of the course and teaching at UQ. Each time a course is offered, students enrolled in that course will be invited to evaluate their course and teacher(s) via an online SECaT evaluation. Students are requested to circle a number between 1 to 5 inclusive indicating whether they agree or disagree to statements such as *I had a clear understanding of the aims and goals of the course*. The final question goes as *Overall, how would you rate this course/this teacher?* 5 = Outstanding,

3 = Satisfactory, 1 = Very poor. The scores achieved for this question are recorded for each teacher in their portfolio and reviewed by his/her supervisor from time to time. When discussing SECaT scores, the default refers to the average scores students rated on the final question. The author's SECaT scores for teaching CHIN3000 in S1, 2020 is 4.0 for the course and 4.36 for the teaching. Her SECaT scores for teaching CHIN3001 in S1, 2020 is 4.07 for the course and 4.4 for the teaching. Such scores indicate that students were satisfied with the course design as well as the delivery of teaching. In addition, the satisfaction level was slightly higher for the teaching than for the course design.

Apart from the Likert scale questions, students also have the opportunity to respond to questions like *What were the best aspects of this course?/What aspects of this teacher's approach best helped your learning?* Most students were very positive informing us that the transition from F2F teaching to entirely online was very smooth. Students were happy that the online delivery was also very engaging and interactive. The online assessment items for both CHIN3000 and CHIN3001 were also well received. Particularly, for CHIN3000, several students wrote that they liked the assessment item named Oral Vocab Study.[4] For CHIN3001, students kept mentioning that writing Chinese by word processing is easier than handwriting. The online exam made writing Chinese characters less challenging.

4.2 Interview with the Chinese Language Students

At the end of semester 1, 2020, this author conducted one-on-one informal interviews with 35 students enrolled in CHIN3000 after their final oral exams. The interview includes five simple questions:

---

[4] Oral Vocabulary Study was designed to replace the usual weekly in-class dictation for online teaching mode. For each new lesson, students are required to read and record each new vocabulary item followed by a phrase or a sentence including the item, namely making a phrase or sentence with the item to show their understanding. It is recommended that they use the reference number listed in the new words lists in the textbook. They can record an audio file beforehand or use the online facility to record on the spot. Then they should upload the file to "Spoken Vocabulary Study" folder under "Assessment" on Blackboard. An example was provided.

7 Remote Chinese Language Teaching at the University... 175

1. *If you have a choice, do you prefer F2F or online teaching?*
2. *How satisfied have you been with teaching online this semester?*
   a. *very dissatisfied, b. dissatisfied, c. neutral, d. satisfied, e. very satisfied.*
3. *Which assessment item do you like the best in this course?*
   a. *Oral Vocab Study, b. Oral Presentation, c. Mid Semester Test. d. Final Oral Exam.*
4. *What is the best aspect of this course?*
5. *What is the most dissatisfactory part of this course?*

Each interview took only two to three minutes, which was audio recorded. Students' responses were calculated and analyzed.

In answering the first question, 30 out of the 35 students (85.7%) preferred F2F teaching while the remaining 5 students (14.3%) preferred online teaching. This result might indicate that online teaching cannot replace F2F teaching in the future.

Figure 7.1 below shows the satisfaction level for the 35 students who responded to the second question.

As Fig. 7.1 shows, the majority of students were generally satisfied with our online teaching during Semester One, 2020. Adding the percentages of "somewhat satisfied" (34.3%) and "very satisfied" (17.1%), those were

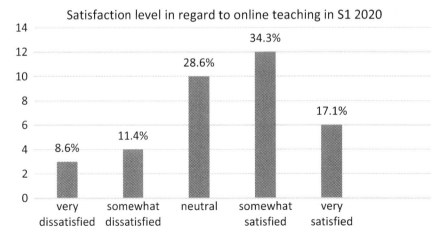

Fig. 7.1 Students' satisfaction level on online teaching during Semester One, 2020

generally satisfied occupy 51.4%. The percentage reaches 80% if those who responded "neutral" (28.6%) are also added. Those who were "very dissatisfied" (8.6%) and "somewhat dissatisfied" (11.4%) are certainly in the minority. The findings may indicate that it is possible to maintain comparatively high levels of student satisfaction even in an emergency fully online delivery mode.

Is it contradictory that for the same cohort of students, the majority preferred F2F teaching and the majority were also generally satisfied with online teaching during Semester One, 2020? The possible explanation might be as follows: During normal circumstances, this cohort of students generally preferred F2F teaching. However, when abnormal circumstances occurred, namely when online teaching became inevitable, students showed their understanding as well as supporting the teaching mode change, which made the transition of our teaching from onsite to online comparatively smooth during the pandemic.

CHIN3000 had four assessment items in Semester One, 2020. They were *Oral Vocab Study, Oral presentation, Mid Semester Test* and *Final Oral exam*. In answering the third question *Which assessment item do you like the best in this course?* Figure 7.2 below shows student preferences among the four assessment items.

As Fig. 7.2 shows, more than half students liked the *Oral Vocab Study* assessment item. The percentage for *Oral Presentation, Mid Semester Test*

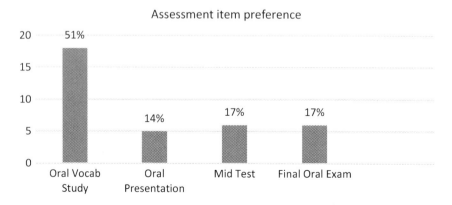

Fig. 7.2 Students' preferences to CHIN3000 assessment items

or *Final Oral Exam* is quite low. Maybe this is because students could use various resources in completing the *Oral Vocab Study* task and there was no time limit either.

In answering the fourth question *What is the best aspect of this course?* 13 out of the 35 students (37%) responded that they appreciated the prompt email replies from the teachers while studying at home. Seven students (20%) responded that they liked the way how class activities were handled such as using breakout rooms frequently for students to do pair or group work. Another six students (17%) said that they really liked the feedback from teachers from time to time.

When asked what they found most dissatisfactory, most students mentioned technical problems such as unstable internet or issues encountered in uploading assignments. This might be one of the reasons why students preferred face-to-face over online teaching.

5   Reflection

During and after Semester One, 2020, teachers at UQ were well supported with a series of workshops helping teaching staff to develop the skills needed for online teaching. After the end of Semester One teaching in 2020, various experience sharing seminars have been organized for teachers to learn from each other for achieving the best practices in virtual classroom. Without physical presence in the classroom, it's vital that teachers establish a virtual presence at the very beginning of the online teaching. Strategies specially targeted for engaging and supporting students right from the start and for the duration of the whole semester teaching are particularly important for managing a class online. For the online delivery of CHIN3000 and CHIN3001 in Semester 1, 2020, the author reflected on her virtual classroom management and believed that the following points are worth mentioning.

1. **Make good use of Blackboard platform**. Given that each course at UQ has a Blackboard site, it is wise to make good use of this learning platform. All learning objectives and specific assessment tasks are clearly set out at Blackboard. Before each assessment item/task is due,

it is always useful to remind students by either sending a bulk email or make an announcement at Blackboard.

2. **Prompt response to students' emails**. Students almost always expect a quick response whenever they send an email to their instructors. The author sets a rule to herself that she replies all students' emails before she goes to bed each day during teaching semester. The quick response conveys teachers' care and rapport to their students. Studies show that the more rapport students have with their instructor, the better they study the course/subject (Wilson et al., 2010; Mardahl-Hansen, 2019). The one-on-one interview the author conducted with CHIN3000 students has shown that this strategy was highly appreciated by students.

3. **Provide opportunities for students to work together**. Teaching via Zoom, the author frequently used breakout rooms allowing students to work in pair or in small groups. Every time when students learn a new lesson, they would be asked to role play the dialogue/text in pair in the breakout rooms. They can work out the meaning of the dialogue through asking each other questions rather than listening to the teacher's lecturing/monologuing/explaining. Sometimes students also use this opportunity to clarify their understandings of relevant assessment tasks/items. Apart from interacting with the teacher, students also appreciate the opportunity to work with their peers/fellow classmates.

4. **Provide timely feedback to students' work**. For every assessment task, students were and are eager to know how well they did. General feedback to the whole class talking about common issues is essential. An opportunity for individual feedback is also vital. Therefore, as a rule in the Chinese discipline, each instructor/teacher needs to provide at least one-hour consultation time per week for each course he/she teaches. During this hour, students can drop in freely without the need to make an appointment. When teaching turned to entirely online in Semester 1, 2020, a weekly one-hour Zoom consultation time was set up by each instructor. The purpose of this one-hour consultation time is to make sure students' individual needs were taken care of.

5. **Consider learning style diversity in designing assessment tasks.** Nowadays students like options. It is recommended to provide task options, due dates options, assignment handing-in options and even options in either handwriting or word processing in writing Chinese characters. Tasks that students can incorporate their life experiences into the learning are usually very popular. For example, the "web-diary task" for second-year Chinese written courses (CHIN3001 and CHIN3020) is such a task as it allows students to choose what they want to write about. Good learning tasks allow students to incorporate their life experience into the learning of the target language (Jiang, 2016).
6. **Establish a sense of comfort and create a relaxing atmosphere.** It is believed that a good teacher is passionate about what he or she is teaching. While being passionate, it is also important for the audience to feel comfortable and keep their anxiety to the minimum. Informal chat while waiting for class to start is a very good opportunity to involve students in sharing anything interesting or just telling a joke. Teachers who are confident enough to laugh at themselves publicly among students often can relax their students. Having some fun in learning is always one of the goals in the author's class.

To conclude, from the author's perspective, teaching principles or strategies for effective learning are universal, no matter the teaching is F2F or entirely online. Successfully motivating and engaging students are constant challenges for every teacher. Yet it is possible to maintain high levels of student satisfaction by ensuring an interactive and engaging teaching style even in a fully online delivery mode. Additionally, those technology-enhanced tasks/resources used in residential or Face to Face (F2F) teaching before the pandemic turned out to be a very important foundation for the teaching mode change from F2F to entirely online with short notice when the pandemic hit Australia in early March 2020.

References

Crawford, J., Butler-Henderson, K., Rudolph, J., Malkawi, B., Glowatz, M., Burton, R., … Lam, S. (2020). COVID-19: 20 countries' higher education intra-period digital pedagogy responses. *Journal of Applied Learning & Teaching, 3*(1), 1–20.

Jiang, W. (2012). Use of a web-diary as a CALL task in teaching Chinese as a foreign language. In J. Hajek, C. Nettelbeck, & A. Woods (Eds.), *The next step: Introducing the languages and cultures network for Australian universities: Selected proceedings of the inaugural LCNAU colloquium*. LCNAU Colloquium 2011, Melbourne, Australia (pp. 263–274). 26–28 September 2011.

Jiang, W. (2016). A Storytelling Sound file CALL task used in a tertiary CFL classroom. *International Journal of Applied Linguistics, 27*(2), 542–554. https://doi.org/10.1111/ijal.12161

Jiang, W. (2019). An empirical study on the graduation standard in BA Chinese proficiency in Australia. *Proceedings of the 13th International Conference on Chinese Language Teaching*, 82–88, Commercial Press.

Jiang, W. (2020). Benchmarking students' attainment in Chinese proficiency in Australian BA programs using the new HSK tests. *Creative Education, 11*(5), 624–638.

Jiang, W., & Li, W. (2018). Linking up learners of Chinese with native speakers through WeChat in an Australian tertiary CFL curriculum. *Asian-Pacific Journal of Second and Foreign Language Education, 3*, 14. https://doi.org/10.1186/s40862-018-0056-0

Jiang, W., & Ramsay, G. (2005). Rapport-building through CALL in teaching Chinese as a foreign language: An exploratory study. *Language Learning & Technology, 9*(2), 47–63.

Mardahl-Hansen, T. (2019). Teaching as a social practice. *Nordic Psychology, 71*(1), 3–16. https://doi.org/10.1080/19012276.2018.1457451

Wilson, J. H., Ryan, R. G., & Pugh, J. L. (2010). Professor-student rapport scale predicts student outcomes. *Teaching of Psychology, 37*, 246–251.

Zhao, J. (2011). An effective approach to elementary Chinese-teaching: The dialectic of 'starting with oral work and character teaching follows'. *Chinese Teaching in the World, 25*(3), 376–387.

8

Online Chinese Teaching and Learning at Massey University in New Zealand

Michael Li

1 Introduction

According to Joksimović et al. (2015), various terms have been used to describe online learning, such as eLearning, Internet-based learning, and web-based learning. Online learning is regarded as one type of distance learning, which is delivered by using multimedia sources including "CDs, DVDs, Internet links, and the use of electronic writing forums" (Blake, 2017, p.159). Nowadays, online learning has evolved significantly as a result of the rapid advancement of educational technologies. This rate of advancement has resulted in online learning management systems (LMS) such as Blackboard, Moodle, and Canvas, which function as synchronous and asynchronous communication tools. These tools have been developed to help learners learn and interact with each other.

Similarly, Chinese online language programs in New Zealand are traditionally referred to as Chinese distance language programs and have a

---

M. Li (✉)
Massey University, Palmerston North, New Zealand
e-mail: s.li.1@massey.ac.nz

© The Author(s), under exclusive license to Springer Nature Switzerland AG 2022
S. Liu (ed.), *Teaching the Chinese Language Remotely*,
https://doi.org/10.1007/978-3-030-87055-3_8

relatively long history. They have largely been developed in response to New Zealanders' increased awareness of China's cultural, economic, and geopolitical influence in the Asia-Pacific region and the world (White & Li, 2016). These online programs were originally set up to meet the needs of students who live in remote areas and consequently could not participate in face-to-face language courses. The programs can be categorized into two levels: secondary school courses (taught through New Zealand Correspondence School) and university courses. Since Massey University is the major provider of distance language programs and has a history of distance language teaching for half a century, this article, therefore, focuses on the development and the current practices of the Chinese online courses at Massey University. The study begins by providing an overview of the Chinese program regarding its history, course offerings, and students' diverse learning needs, and then reports the current teaching practices that adopt a student-centered online learning approach. This study aims to deepen our understanding of the interplay between online teaching pedagogy and instructional design concerning the teaching of the Chinese language.

2 Program Description

2.1 Program Overview

The Chinese program at Massey University was established in 1989 and started offering Chinese language and culture courses in the same year such as *Modern Standard Chinese (Oral and Written)* and *Introduction to Chinese Civilization*. With a steady increase in student enrollment, more courses were gradually added to the Chinese curriculum in the following years. Currently, the Chinese language courses are divided into three levels: elementary, intermediate, and advanced. The courses at each level are further divided into two stages, so there are six courses in total. These courses are: 1A and 1B set at a beginner level, 2A and 2B set at an intermediate level, 3A and 3B at an advanced level. For those who complete these six courses, two more advanced courses are available for them to continue their study-*Contrastive Study of Chinese and English* and

Translation from and into Chinese. Students who are interested in Chinese culture and society also have the option to choose from four culture-related courses: *Chinese Cultural World*, *China under Transformation: Economy, Society and Diplomacy*, *Contemporary Chinese Society in Literature and Film*, and *Chinese Diaspora*. If a student has an interest in studying a topic relating to Chinese language, literature, history, politics, or other cultural aspects, s/he also has the opportunity to enroll in a full year advanced-level course *Individual Research Project in Chinese Studie*s. The student can carry out a research project under a teacher's supervision. For those who have an interest in formalizing their higher education in Chinese studies, they have the opportunity to choose from five degrees: Graduate Certificate in Chinese, Graduate Diploma in Chinese, Diploma in Chinese, Bachelor in Chinese, and PhD in Chinese studies.

2.2 The Dual-Mode Teaching System

Massey University is a dual-mode institution, offering the same courses in face-to-face and distance modes, with the same assessment requirements and learning outcomes. It is worth noting that the distance cohorts are the same as onsite cohorts, studying toward degrees and therefore requiring the same amount of tuition fees. This is unlike many MOOC courses that are "free or at a very low price" (Liu, 2018) and function as a form of informal continued education. Students who enroll in Chinese courses can thereby choose from the two study modes. The two cohorts use the same learning materials and have to complete the same set of assessments through an online learning management system called *Stream* (a platform based on Moodle). The onsite students are required to attend 3 one-hour lectures and 1 one-hour tutorial each week during the scheduled class periods and are expected to spend the same amount of time to consolidate their learning in their spare time. Likewise, the distance cohorts are required to do the same by following a study schedule similar to the onsite cohorts, although they must rely on their own endeavors to make progress in their learning. This includes spending time watching pre-recorded lecture videos, reading study guides, studying prescribed learning content, and completing all learning tasks in addition to the assessments. To compensate the lack of speaking and interaction opportunities in the distance mode, 2 one-hour online synchronous tutorial sessions are offered to distance students each week. The tutorial sessions are held during regular time periods agreed by the students, offering them opportunities to practice their speaking and listening skills with a tutor and interact with their peers. A contact course (two-day face-to-face study session) is also offered for distance students during the study break in the mid of each semester. This is usually held during a weekend on the university campus so they can all make their time to attend. During the two days, apart from attending lectures, students also have the opportunities to participate in a range of language learning activities such as scavenger hunt, experiencing Chinese cuisine at Chinese restaurants, as well as watching Chinese movies. To provide more opportunities for students to practice the language with their peers, onsite students are also encouraged to attend online tutorials, distance students are also welcomed to attend onsite lectures if conditions permit. Online tutorials and lecture recordings are also available online to all students.

2.3 Students' Diverse Learning Needs

There has been a great diversity among students in many aspects such as their background and learning needs. In terms of their language background, the majority of students are New Zealand European, Maori, and some second-generation Chinese immigrants, with a small percentage of international students from countries like Australia, South Korea, Japan, Philippines, and Malaysia. Students' learning motivations range from career development, business, family relationships, tourism to personal interests. Regarding their age, most students who study on campus are relatively young university students, while distance cohorts tend to be comparatively mature students with some being in their fifties and sixties. However, there are also a small number of senior high school students studying through distance. The majority of the mature students are full-time or part-time workers or housewives/househusbands, with a small percentage being retired people. Most students, no matter onsite or distance, study Chinese courses as part of their degree, such as Chinese major, minors, or as electives, with a small number of students taking them as non-degree courses. This student diversity has always been an invaluable advantage in creating social bonds and promoting peer interactions among both onsite and distance students, as it pools a wealth of knowledge and resources from all students which have helped to develop, transform, and enrich their language learning experiences in the blended learning context.

2.4 The Teaching Materials

Initially, the Chinese program used *You Can Speak Mandarin* (Lee, 1993) as the main textbook because it was set in Australia and is thereby relatively close to the social customs of New Zealand. By 2007, with the rapid technological development in the educational context, the teaching resources provided by this textbook gradually became insufficient to meet the needs of teachers and students. Therefore, starting from 2007, *Chinese Link* (Wu et al., 2011) was used instead to provide students with richer multimedia learning resources and more engaging learning content. The textbook has its companion website which provides audio and video materials of the learning content in each lesson. Students can also complete their homework online. The use of this textbook to a great extend enriched students' learning experience and facilitated their learning in particular in their practice of listening and speaking. However, by 2015, some disadvantages relating to the use of the textbook gradually became apparent. For example, since students had to use two separate online systems, the Massey *Stream* and the companion site of *Chinese Link*, they often found it confusing to navigate due to the fact that they had to switch between the two systems when studying. In addition, since the textbook is a US-based text system, it is to a certain extent insufficiently attuned to the specific study needs of New Zealand students. What's more, some students found it costly to purchase both the textbook and access code to its companion website which was independent to the cost of course's tuition fees. In 2015, taking these factors into account, the Chinese program decided to develop its own teaching materials that centered around an enhanced online environment with a coherent pathway for students' Chinese language learning. By 2017, all teaching materials were fully developed, digitalized, and integrated into the dual-teaching environment according to the needs of learners.

3   The Needs for Development of New Learning Environments

The offering of the Chinese distance courses at Massey University was initially resisted by a number of academics "who were not language teachers and who had no experience in distance education", and they claimed that "it would be impossible to teach, and thereby to learn Chinese, except in a conventional classroom setting" (White, 1997, 178-9). The teaching model for Chinese distance language courses during the early stage (early 1990s) was centered on print-based learning materials with additional audio-based resources. When developing course materials, special emphasis was placed on enabling students to hear a clear "teaching voice" by providing students with sufficient explanation, support, and encouragement. To overcome the isolation in distance learning and to compensate for the absence of direct and ongoing mediation of the learning experiences by a teacher and the lack of interaction among peers, ongoing support was identified as one of the most crucial factors for student success. Consequently, timely telephone support and compulsory face-to-face contact courses (usually two days long) in the mid of each semester were provided to students. The defining feature of this model can be summarized as independent learning facilitated by self-instructional materials with access to support, feedback, and face-to-face learning opportunities.

With the rapid development of network technology, two different tools were integrated into the online environment in 2004 and 2010 respectively. In 2004, online tutoring became available to distance students using a voice tool called *Wimba*. The integration of *Wimba* not only enabled students to learn and speak Chinese in asynchronous and real-time modes, but also made it possible for students to easily access pronunciation tools. This allowed students to readily ask for feedback on their pronunciation. This mode of tutoring continued until 2010. In 2010, with more multimodal tools becoming accessible, the Chinese distance courses started to use *Adobe Connect* as the tutoring tool, which was more convenient to use and had more user-friendly teaching functions. For example, students could choose to use either video or audio to communicate with the teacher, and the teacher could explain certain items using a virtual whiteboard. Students could listen to the teacher's or their peers' pronunciation while reading Chinese characters or paragraphs on a screen. Tutoring sessions could also be recorded for those who were unable to attend the live sessions. Students who used the multimodal teaching approach reported that it not only satisfied their different learning styles but also fostered smoother teacher-student and student-student interactions.

With the rapid and ongoing technological innovation in online language education since 2010, the role technology plays has shifted significantly from being ancillary to "become a core source of content" (Otto, 2017, p.21). Consequently, the existing Chinese online learning environment could no longer meet the needs of learners. By 2015, the teachers and tutors in the program felt that there was an urgent need to re-design the online learning environment, in doing so the potential affordances of online learning (such as its ubiquity, multimodality, adaptivity, and interactivity) could be fully utilized to engage students in ways that would support their learning of Chinese. The re-design process began with identifying challenges and issues that teachers and students encountered in their teaching and learning process.

These identified challenges included: (1) Lack of communication opportunities (both synchronous and asynchronous). Since the existing delivery system only provided them with 2 one-hour online tutorials using *Adobe Connect*, it was far less than what they needed to develop their communicative proficiency. (2) The need for more formative and effective assessments. Up to 2015, all courses had been using only formal summative assessments to evaluate students' achievements at the conclusion of certain instructional units and the end of the courses. Students were required to complete three assignments throughout a semester which added up to 40% of their total grade. The final exam weighed 60% and was conducted in the same manner across all language courses. The assignments consisted of various types of questions to evaluate students' mastery of vocabulary and grammar. Although the assignments were effective tools to measure students' language skill acquisition, due to the low frequency of the assessment, they were not able to help students regularly check their learning progress and subsequently adjust their learning strategies according to their teachers' feedback. Regarding the final exam weighting, as previous studies (e.g., Davis, 1993; Franke, 2018) have shown, a heavily weighted final exam was likely to encourage students to adopt a less effective learning strategy-cramming, which is a common massed learning strategy. According to students' feedback, what they need was a more distributed learning condition created by using more frequent, low-stakes formative assessments. Such condition has several advantages, such as increasing students' long-term knowledge retention and learning performance (Holzinger et al., 2009), promoting students' active engagement, and generating timely feedback regarding students' progress (Kuh et al., 2011).

Drawing on the effective design principles and practices in the current literature on online course design, the second step of the re-design process involved consulting teaching and learning specialists at the university, developing a course framework as well as designing various learning activities. By the end of 2017, all Chinese language courses started using the new online learning system which is reported in the next section and is the main focus of this study.

4 Description of the New Online Learning Environment

In this section, we provide a detailed account of how the new learning environment is constructed and how the teaching has been carried out using the new environment. The new online learning environment comprises five basic components and an iterative and ongoing improvement process. The five components are: (1) Community building, (2) Teaching materials, (3) Teaching activities, (4) Formative assessments, and (5) Summative assessments. The five components are detailed below, and the

8 Online Chinese Teaching and Learning at Massey University...

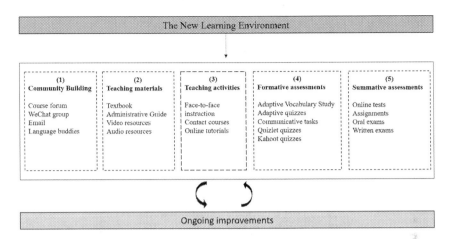

Fig. 8.1 Visualization of the new online environments

relationships among the five components are visualized in Fig. 8.1. It is worth noting that the majority of these components are relevant for both onsite and distance cohorts. However, due to the difference of their study modes, a couple of teaching activities are specifically designed to offer more synchronous practice opportunities to distance students. For example, the contact course and the online tutorials are designed to help distance students, although onsite students are also welcomed to attend these activities.

(1) **Community Building:** the importance and necessity of social presence in online learning environments have been emphasized by a number of scholars in the current online teaching literature (Garrison, 2007, 2016; Garrison et al., 2000; Sun & Chen, 2016). The new online learning environment uses course forum, WeChat group, email, and language buddies to create and maintain an effective and engaging learning community. Once students complete their enrollment process and have access to the online learning system, they are encouraged to use the course forum to introduce themselves and share their prior Chinese learning experiences. Such activities serve as ice-breakers to break down social barriers and to create a relaxed and positive atmosphere, paving the way for a more enjoyable learning experience. The teachers and tutors also use the forum to post important notices and regular reminders, answer students'

questions, and help with solving technical issues. After students start their learning, they are also encouraged to use this space for exchanging learning strategies and seeking help from each other. To create more communication opportunities in a more interactive and convenient way, students are also encouraged to use the Chinese social media tool WeChat. Although joining WeChat group is voluntary, it helps to motivate students to use the target language to communicate more frequently and also encourages mutual peer assistance. At the beginning of the courses, students are also required to form one-on-one language buddies with their teachers' help so they can work collaboratively on assignments as well as study together online or in physical settings. The forming of buddies is primarily dependent on students' proficiency level and whether they are comfortable with each other. Students who live close to each other are also more likely to form buddies. Usually students would nominate their buddies to the teacher for approval. However, there are rare occasions that certain student can't find a partner. In such a case, the teacher would get involved to help the student to join an already-formed pair after a discussion with them. The social presence created through these tools has been evident in students' increased course satisfaction. Thus, their feedback has been mostly positive due to the aforementioned online tools helping them feel less isolated in distance learning resulting in enjoyment; Due to the utilization of WeChat and the forum, the use of emails between students and teachers has diminished. Email thus has been mainly used for students to ask teachers private questions.

(2) **Teaching materials:** these included digitalized textbooks, administrative guides, videos, audio resources. These resources are primarily used to create a prominent teaching presence and therefore lead to student-content interaction in their learning process. The textbooks contain all the learning points with step-by-step, thorough, and clear explanations. The administrative guides provide students with clear guidelines and detailed measurable and specific learning objectives, including suggested study schedules, itemized assessments and completion dates, grade weightings, online tutorial information, library and learning support, and extra resources links. Guided by the explicit guidelines and expectations, students find it easier to have meaningful interactions with the learning content. Taking advantage of the learning analytics offered by

Stream-such as the frequency of viewing and downloading resources, times of attempting quizzes, the timing of posting and replying to messages, teachers and tutors can monitor students' learning progress and check their learning outcomes. This has been very helpful in providing specific support to students who are struggling with their learning.

Video and audio resources are crucial and indispensable to second language learning. During the development of the teaching materials, the teachers and tutors worked together to create mini-lecture videos and audio recordings for each lesson. These videos include grammar videos, character videos and conversation videos. Grammar videos are used to explain the usages of key grammar items in each lesson. Character videos are created to demonstrate the stroke sequences of each character and their radical elements and compounds. Conversation videos are made to help student acquire the speaking skills. Audio recordings include new word pronunciation, conversation pronunciation, and self-assessment exercise-related sound files. All these resources are available online in two formats, one is through web streaming and the other as downloadable files. Students can choose to watch or listen them online or download them to their devices. Students have found these resources very useful in helping them to learn and practice their speaking, listening, and writing skills. In addition, mobile-assisted learning resources like Quizlet and Kahoot quizzes are also utilized to encourage bite-sized learning by helping students to optimize small chunks of time.

(3) **Teaching activities:** these include onsite face-to-face teaching, contact courses, and online tutorials. The details of these activities have been provided in section 2.2. It is worth noting here that although in general, onsite students have more opportunities to interact with their teachers and peers than the distance cohorts, the boundary between the two learning modes seems to have become less clear since the use of the new learning environment. This is particularly true during the COVID-19 lockdown period. Although all onsite teaching activities had to switch to distance mode using ZOOM within a very short time, the impact to onsite students seemed to be minimal because they had already accustomed to the dual-teaching mode at the university.

(4) **Formative assessments:** these are carried out through the use of adaptive vocabulary study, adaptive quizzes, and communicative tasks in

each lesson. Adaptive vocabulary study activity is designed to help students grasp the key vocabulary in each lesson with a personalized approach. Based on a built-in tool "Lesson" in *Stream*, this activity utilizes its branch and cluster functionality to cater to a range of student abilities. Figure 8.2 shows the design principle of its adaptive feature. In each lesson, students are required to use this online activity to study the key vocabulary before accessing other formative assessments such as communicative tasks and quizzes. For each key new word in a lesson, three receptive knowledge questions and three productive knowledge questions are normally presented to students in consecutive order for them to answer. If they answer all of them correctly, they are prompted to go to the next key word. If they answer one of them wrong, they are directed to a study page where the pronunciation, meaning, and the key usage of the word with a few example sentences are provided for study. Once students complete the activity, they are granted access to other formative assessments.

Adaptive quizzes in each lesson are designed for students to self-evaluate their progress in all areas of language learning including

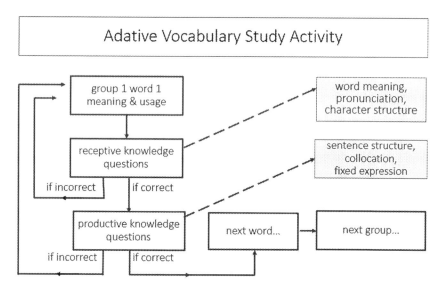

Fig. 8.2 Adaptive Vocabulary Study activity design principle

listening, speaking, reading, and writing. By attempting a quiz several times, students usually can identify the challenges they have and make the appropriate improvements. Each quiz is made up of various types of questions including multiple-choice, true and false, short answer, and "fill in the blanks" type questions. To effectively evaluate students' writing and speaking skills, two special types of questions are also used in these quizzes. For writing, open-ended type questions are used. This gives students the freedom to write sentences or short paragraphs using given words or joining phrases together into sentences using given conjunctions. For speaking, oral questions are particularly useful to help students practice their conversational skills. For example, when answering such questions, students first have to listen to dialogic questions that require oral responses. Then students would be required to construct their answers before recording their speaking using a built-in voice recorder and submitting their answers for grading. Although the last two types of questions require manual grading, they are useful in helping students identify areas they need to improve on and are also helpful for teachers to provide timely feedback. Student feedback indicates that they highly value the digitally mediated oral and written suggestions given by teachers as this allows them to assess their progress and helps them to adjust their learning strategies.

Communicative tasks are designed to be structured, facilitated, and systematic asynchronous discussions, providing students with opportunities to practice their listening and speaking skills. Similar to the use of course forum, at the start of a course, students are also encouraged to post a few icebreaker messages in the form of audio or video format. These can be self-introduction, language learning stories, or responses to other's posts. Through such oral interactions, a warm, friendly, and welcoming atmosphere can usually be created for the class to kick start their online learning. Based on learned content in each lesson, teachers would post six questions for students to listen and answer using an embedded mp3 recorder. In addition, students are required to post two oral questions and to answer two questions posted by other students. This creates a virtual community for students to practice listening and speaking by using specific learned sentence structures and grammatical patterns. The tutor would listen to each student's oral questions and answers and provide timely oral feedback including their pronunciation, tones, use of vocabulary, grammar, and sentence structure. A simple task rubric is also provided to help students to self-evaluate the quality of their posts. The tutor also grades students' posts according to the rubric.

It is worth noting that the rationale for designing and utilizing these forms of evaluation is to create a more distributed learning condition. Through the use of more frequent and low-stakes assessments, learners have more opportunities to identify potential learning gaps and promote student-content interaction. To maximize the benefits of these formative assessments, significant changes to the assessment weighting distribution are also made by putting more weight on the regular activities and by reducing the grade weight of the final exam to 30% which included a 20% written exam and a 10% oral exam.

(5) **Summative assessments:** these are carried out through the use of online tests, assignments, oral and written exams. Online tests are relatively easier summative assessments and are designed to enhance students' engagement from the early stage of their studies. The first online test is usually administered in the third week of the semester and the second in the sixth week of the semester. Although the tests are similar to the quizzes at the end of each lesson in terms of question types and difficulty level, they often give students a sense of success and achievement, which, as a result, helps boost and maintain students' motivation throughout the first half of the semester. In the second half of the semester, students are required to complete two assignments with each being made up of oral and written components. These are more difficult summative assessments as they are designed to assess students' productive language use. For example, the oral component requires students to compose a dialogue with a peer using a given topic related to what they learned in a lesson. Once they are satisfied with their composition, they often meet physically or collaborated by online means to practice and rehearse before recording their conversation for submission. This allows students to practice the language with a peer and also to facilitates their collaborative learning. The written component is a more independent body of work focusing on their writing skills. Using some given words and phrases, they are required to write a few paragraphs on a given topic, which is usually closely related to their real-life experiences. This is designed to develop

the students' abilities in turning their receptive vocabulary into productive vocabulary. In doing so, students grow their productive vocabulary and develop more effective vocabulary and learning strategies. Oral and written exams are also part of the summative assessments, with the purpose to evaluate students' overall performance in language acquisition. Due to the impact of the COVID-19, the way to administer written exams has changed from supervised exams to online exams, and lately to open-book exams. Oral exam remains as face-to-face exam for onsite students and ZOOM exam for distance students.

In addition to the above main components of the online learning environment, the ongoing improvement process is also critical to students' positive learning experience. At the end of each semester, the teachers and tutors would come together to discuss and reflect what works well and what needs to improve. The reflection often leads to some fine-tuning of content delivery and task design. For example, at the end of 2017, based on beginner students' feedback that they found the video dialogues containing onscreen written text with spontaneous pronunciation useful, the team created more similar videos for intermediate and advanced-level courses. In addition, more accurate task instructions are also frequently re-adjusted and updated in response to student feedback.

5 Students' Feedback on the New Online Learning Environment

In this section, we report students' feedback collected from a university-administered course evaluation survey called *Massey Online Survey Tool (MOST)*. The survey is administered at the end of each semester. All students' responses gathered from MOST are anonymous. The survey contained two parts: the first consists of ten questions using a six-point Likert rating scale. Students are also encouraged to write their comments underneath each question. In the second part, students are asked to provide their detailed comments on the course offering in two aspects: the aspects of the course that help their learning, and the areas that need improvement. The following feedback is based on students' comments taken from the 2016 and 2017 *MOST* surveys, and the courses surveyed are Chinese 1A and 1B. Due to the voluntary nature of the survey, the response rates were relatively low (at about 30–40%). Despite the small sample size (n=20), it is still possible to get a sense of what has worked well and what areas need improvements, especially from their written feedback. The following section is thus mainly based on the second part of the surveys.

In general, students enrolled in the 2016 and 2017 beginner courses showed a positive attitude toward the overall quality of the new online learning environment. Analysis of students' feedback showed evidence of the value of creating social presence, teaching presence, and cognitive presence in the new online learning environment.

(1) The value of creating social presence in the new online learning environment

The course tools and activities offered in the new system afforded teachers and students collaboratively to create a secure climate and a purposeful learning environment. The student-student interaction opportunities offered by the course forums, communicative tasks, and contact courses were valued by students because this helped to reduce their feelings of isolation as distance language students. A student highlighted how the communicative tasks, weekly online tutorials, and face-to-face contact course encouraged his/her participation: "*the communicative tasks and weekly tutorials were really good. The language camp was also extremely helpful. It's just encouraging to be able to meet with other people in the same boat as you and to help each other*".

The new system also allowed teachers to cultivate a supportive learning environment by offering students continuous and timely support and feedback. Such effort strengthened the student-teacher social connection and consequently paved the way for an engaging learning experience. A student exemplified this idea: "*the lecturers were very supportive, and always accessible when asking for help. The oral feedback on my weekly posts was amazing, it really helped me stay on track*".

(2) The value of creating teaching presence in the new online learning environment

Students' comments revealed that the tools provided were useful in guiding them to remain engaged and to achieve their learning objectives.

Firstly, from an organizational perspective, students felt that the courses were well-structured based on a well-researched delivery mechanism. This enabled them to make meaning of the manageable content in a progressive manner and through both individual work and collaboration. One student made special mention of this aspect:

> The fact we were constantly required to complete regular online tasks, quizzes, tests and assignments so we had to try and keep on top of the workload. The way of assessing us has been excellent and has forced us to work continuously throughout the course, continually building on our knowledge.

Students also reported that course content was well planned and paced by creating distributed learning conditions. A number of students specified that the practices of chunking (dividing content into smaller pieces for presentation) and delivering paced and sequential content helped them to achieve their desired learning outcomes. A student response in the survey regarding this aspect was: "*It was great having it all in little chunks. The weekly online contribution was a great strategy for learning. The communicative assessments were regular and helpful with putting learned material into practice*".

(3) The value of creating a cognitive presence in the new online learning environment

Quality, purposeful, and systematic discourse has been regarded as essential for creating a strong cognitive presence (Garrison & Cleveland-Innes, 2005). Students reported that the student-content interaction was engaging and meaningful resulting in the achievement of student's desired learning outcomes. For example, a student's cognitive development was seen from him/her in favor of the adaptive vocabulary study activity in each lesson.

> I feel that the vocabulary study activity really adds to the efficiency of my self-study. I really like the fact that the new words/expressions are grouped, with plenty of examples of how they are used in sentences. Another useful point—the recorded pronunciation of the new words. I would certainly like to be able to use this tool for the language papers in the next terms.

Because of the adaptive nature of the given activity, students felt that this not only helped them to digest and master the content but also provided them with a positive learning experience. One student made a special mention of this point: "*I would like all aspects of the course to be taught in this manner. Very interactive and progressive. Unlocking levels of learning like a game add to the joy of learning*".

Secondly, students' academic achievements were seen from their appreciation for the use of diverse formats of content delivery, which was beneficial to make course content easier to digest and retain: "*Well structured content and together with other learning tools such as Quizlet, online video conference tutorial plus video and audio files on each lesson have enable me to achieve my target of writing and speaking Chinese*".

Lastly, students' cognitive development was demonstrated through their higher level of engagement with their peers, which not only enabled them to practice their language skills but also promoted their deep learning processes and knowledge construction. A student explained: "*It was great that we had the opportunities to talk to other students through the communication tasks. It was helpful to hear the questions said by both the tutor and other students. It was a lot of work but really challenging in a good way*".

Despite the positive feedback, some drawbacks and issues were also reported by students. Areas of improvement include: providing more face-to-face time or online synchronous opportunities, better-structured assessment timing, and more technical support. Although the new system offered both synchronous and asynchronous opportunities for students, they felt that more face-to-face time and synchronous online interaction should be provided. They indicated that this would help them practice the language and establish social connections which have proven to be an integral part of learning in today's increasingly digitalized world. The following feedback provides some insights into this aspect: "*I wish there was more face-to-face time to practice conversation skills. Conversation was very helpful, I think speaking is probably the most important part of learning a language*".

Some students indicated that attending face-to-face sessions was not feasible for them due to their work, family commitments, or living in remote areas. In such cases, they strongly suggested that more online synchronous contact should be made available, so they could seek help from their teachers or practice speaking and listening skills with their peers or teachers online. Another aspect that needed improving was the timing of assessments. Due to the number of assessments limited to a 12-week teaching period, some assessments overlapped which increased the workload on students. This led to some students feeling overwhelmed or frustrated with having to complete two or three assessments within a short timeframe. Moreover, as mentioned above, due to the course being conducted online, it was inevitable that technical issues would occur. Occasionally, these issues would hinder student's abilities to complete tasks and assessments. Some of these issues were related to the misunderstandings of the online course design while others were due to some student's difficulties with their devices. Regarding the first issue, a more thorough online orientation could be conducted so that students will not be confused by the course's design. In terms of the second issue mentioned, IT support from the Massey University could be given to assist students who are experiencing technical difficulties.

6 Chinese Courses During the COVID-19 Pandemic

Since the outbreak of the COVID-19 at the beginning of 2020, there were a few national and local lockdown periods in New Zealand. Consequently, the university campus was temporarily closed during these periods, and the normal instructional delivery methods and the course assessments for both onsite distance cohorts had to be changed to meet the needs of students with higher levels of anxiety and increased stress. For example, during the first lockdown in April 2020, all the onsite courses were switched to online teaching using ZOOM. The assessments were also postponed for a few more weeks so students had sufficient time to quickly adapt to a range of new learning experiences. Similarly, the ways to administrate exams were also changed from real-time paper-based examinations to take-home exams, online tests, or other forms of assessments.

Although the above changes inevitably caused some interruption for students who enrolled in Chinese courses, the impact on their learning was relatively low for both onsite and distance cohort and the way they were affected was also slightly different. For onsite students, although they had to switch from a classroom learning environment to online learning via ZOOM, they were able to quickly adapt to the new instructional delivery method because they had already been using the online learning system for studying the content and completing their assessments. During this period, they attended their ZOOM lectures according to the same scheduled times as they would have attended the face-to-face classes. The tutor reported that the attendance rates of the online lectures were relatively lower than that of the face-to-face class, but according to students' feedback, this was mainly caused by students' higher levels of uncertainty, anxiety, and stress related to the pandemic, not the change of the course delivery. For distance cohorts, since they had already been using ZOOM for online tutorials and using the online learning system for studying, the change of teaching delivery almost had no impact on their learning. However, because the majority of distance students were full-time or part-time workers and house-husband or housewives, the way they managed their work and study was greatly affected. In particular for those who had children, when the whole family was staying at home, they found it challenging to manage their workload and study while looking after their children's home learning and welling being during the lockdown time.

7   Looking Ahead

We are planning to make more efforts in developing the blended learning approach and implement the strategy in teaching practices. According to students' feedback, more synchronous opportunities are urgently needed for distance students. Because many of them are unable to attend the onsite classes, one way to accommodate this need is to provide them with access to a real classroom teaching environment via video-linked teaching technology. With this new generation of technology, students who won't be able to attend the face-to-face lecture may join the class via ZOOM and interact with the onsite students in the classroom. The lecture can also be recorded and posted online so those who won't be able to join the class may still have access to the recorded lectures. Currently, Massey University is upgrading the technology so more teaching rooms can have such blended functionalities. When such teaching rooms are available to use, we are planning to integrate this practice into our learning system so distance students can have more synchronous learning opportunities. For onsite students, this will also be a good opportunity to interact with distance students and learn from their rich experiences in life and work.

References

Blake, R. (2017). Distance education for second and foreign language learning. In S. Thorne & S. May (Eds.), *Language, Education and Technology. Encyclopedia of Language and Education* (3rd ed.). Springer. https://doi.org/10.1007/978-3-319-02237-6_13

Davis, B. G. (1993). *Tools for Teaching*. Jossey-Bass.

Franke, M. (2018). Final exam weighting as part of course design. *Teaching & Learning Inquiry, 6*(1), 91–103.

Garrison, D. R. (2007). Online community of inquiry review: Social, cognitive, and teaching presence issues. *Journal of Asynchronous Learning Networks, 11*(1), 61–72.

Garrison, D. R. (2016). *E-learning in the 21st century: A community of inquiry framework for research and practice*. Taylor & Francis.

Garrison, D. R., Anderson, T., & Archer, W. (2000). Critical inquiry in a text-based environment: Computer conferencing in higher education. *The Internet and Higher Education, 2*(2-3), 87–105.

Garrison, D. R., & Cleveland-Innes, M. (2005). Facilitating cognitive presence in online learning: Interaction is not enough. *The American journal of distance education, 19*(3), 133–148.

Holzinger, A., Kickmeier-Rust, M. D., & Ebner, M. (2009). Interactive technology for enhancing distributed learning: a study on weblogs. *People and Computers XXIII Celebrating People and Technology, 1*, 309–312.

Joksimović, S., Kovanović, V., Skrypnyk, O., Gašević, D., Dawson, S., & Siemens, G. (2015). The history and state of online learning. https://www.researchgate.net/publication/313752141.

Kuh, G. D., Kinzie, J., Schuh, J. H., & Whitt, E. J. (2011). *Student success in college: Creating conditions that matter*. John Wiley & Sons.

Lee, P. Y. K. (1993). *You Can Speak Mandarin*. Harcourt Brace.

Liu, S. (2018). Teaching and learning Chinese language online: What and why? *International Chinese Language Education, 3*(2), 11–26.

Otto, S. (2017). From past to present: A hundred years of technology for L2 learning. In C. Chapelle & S. Sauro (Eds.), *The handbook of technology and second language teaching and learning* (pp. 10–25). Wiley Blackwell.

Sun, A., & Chen, X. (2016). Online education and its effective practice: A research review. *Journal of Information Technology Education: Research, 15*, 157–190.

White, C. (1997). Effects of mode of study on foreign language learning. *Distance Education, 18*(1), 178–196.

White, C., & Li, S. (2016). Technology application in distance Chinese teaching in New Zealand and some reflections. *Journal of International Chinese Teaching. 12* (4):15-19. [White, 李守纪 (2016). 新西兰汉语远程教育的技术应用与反思. 国际汉语教学研究, 12(4), 15-19.]

Wu, S., Yu, Y., Zhang, Y., & Tian, W. (2011). *Chinese Link*. Pearson Education.

9

Remote Chinese Teaching and Learning at Japanese Universities During the COVID-19 Pandemic

Kazuko Sunaoka and Satoko Sugie

1 Introduction

As in many other countries, higher education institutions in Japan have been severely affected by COVID-19. Although remote teaching and ICT utilization in education were not widespread in Japan before the COVID-19 pandemic, almost all universities, faculty members, and students were forced to make a hasty shift to remote education as a result of the emergency situation, and have typically been highly appreciative of the technologies that afforded this transition. Based on a large-scale questionnaire survey, this study summarizes the actual conditions of the Emergent Remote Teaching (ERT) and its evaluation by faculty and students. Moreover, we also summarize the achievements and reflections

K. Sunaoka (✉)
Waseda University, Tokyo, Japan
e-mail: ksunaoka@waseda.jp

S. Sugie
Sapporo International University, Sapporo, Japan
e-mail: satoko-sugie@ts.siu.ac.jp

© The Author(s), under exclusive license to Springer Nature Switzerland AG 2022
S. Liu (ed.), *Teaching the Chinese Language Remotely*,
https://doi.org/10.1007/978-3-030-87055-3_9

of ERT at Japanese universities. The purpose of this study is to consider the implications of remote teaching, intended to be a temporary solution carried out during the pandemic, and to contribute to improving the quality of Teaching Chinese as a Foreign Language (TCFL).

In this article, we first review the characteristics of Chinese language education and the realities of ICT use in Japan before the COVID-19 pandemic, before giving a general outline of the ERT implemented as a result of the pandemic, including in Chinese language education; we then introduce the characteristics of ERT in Japan, describe the physical and human resources for online education including network infrastructure, public network resources optimization, instructional support, online teaching skills training; next, we analyze eight questionnaire surveys conducted by Japanese higher education institutions and research associations, followed by three findings related to remote teaching types, degree of satisfaction and attitudes of teachers and students. At last, we discuss the current and potential future challenges concerning physical and human resources, ICT utilization in education, quality of remote teaching, and diversification of the educational environment.

2 Overview of Chinese Language Education in Japan Before the Pandemic

2.1 Characteristics of Chinese Language Education in Japan

Prior to ERT, most Chinese classes in Japan shared the following characteristics: Fixed-time schedules; face-to-face classes; almost all students of Japanese heritage; typically novice learners in large-sized classes; using paper textbooks; students generally enrolled concurrently in many other elective courses in addition to the Chinese language classes; students have little time to engage in self-study; and lack of opportunity for interaction between the teachers and the students.

The majority of students are of Japanese heritage: The diversification and internationalization of Japanese universities had been falling behind other nations, which caused difficulty in adapting to ERT in a timely manner. Although the number of overseas students and foreign-heritage students has gradually increased in recent years, they still account for less than 20% of all students (Sunaoka et al., 2017). Part of the reason for this is the rigid university entrance exam system in Japan, which can discourage foreign and working student applicants.

Large-sized, elective classes and credit-hour overloads: In 2014, 624 universities offered Chinese courses (MEXT, 2016), equivalent to 80% of the total number of universities in Japan, with nearly 500,000 students taking Chinese as an elective course each year (Sunaoka, 2017). The average class sizes of Japanese universities are significantly larger than in Europe and the United States: The number of Chinese classes with 21–30 students represents the largest percentage of classes (48%), followed by 31–40 students (31%). While there are also large-sized classes with more than 41 students, classes with less than 20 students are less common (11%). At the same time, most university students who take Chinese courses do not major in Chinese: Students who specialize in social sciences and humanities comprise about 73% of the learners, for whom Chinese is mostly listed as a required elective course. 75% of the students begin learning Chinese after entering the university, with no prior experience of the language, and the majority do not continue to pursue their study after obtaining the necessary credits, with the result being that average Chinese ability is roughly equivalent to the A2 level of the CEFR (Sunaoka et al., 2017). In addition, as the number of courses taken by Japanese students often reaches more than a dozen per week, the burden of other courses on freshmen is heavy (Sunaoka et al., 2017). All of these factors compound to limit opportunities for teacher-student interaction in the classroom.

Lack of human resources: The Chinese Linguistic Society of Japan (CLSJ) and The Japan Association of Chinese Language Education (JACLE) are the major sources of TCFL teachers in Japan. As of 2018, CLSJ has 1188 registered members (including 75 foreign members), and JACLE boasts 517 as of 2020 (including part-time teachers). The sum of the two organizations' members is less than half of the required number of Chinese language teachers (Sunaoka, 2017), suggesting that there are simply not enough CSL professionals in Japanese universities, and a number of universities employ part-time teachers to solve the shortage of full-time academic staff: Part-time teachers account for nearly two-thirds of CSL teachers, and female teachers represent a high percentage of them. At the same time, CSL teachers have various types of pedagogical beliefs and teaching skills. For the sake of faculty development (FD) for Chinese language teachers, while most institutions also held various regular workshops and seminars before the outbreak of the COVID-19, only half of the full-time faculty have participated in FD (MEXT, 2020a).

Traditional pedagogical methods and classroom activities: Traditionally, TCFL in Japan was mostly conducted in simultaneous classes in the classroom at a fixed time. Classroom activities were often composed of conversation practice, grammar, and vocabulary instruction (43.2% for conversation, 36.6% for grammar and vocabulary); additionally, as most courses were offered for novice learners, they generally focused on simple tasks to train the four basic communication skills (Sunaoka, 2017).

2.2 Technology-Mediated Chinese Language Teaching in Japan Before the Pandemic

The early period of e-learning systems development: Development of online materials for Chinese language learning in Japan began in the 2000s. Since 2013, workshops on online materials began to be held as part of the annual conference of JACLE, which included presentations such as how to share databases and teaching materials (Hino, 2014; Kiyohara, 2014). At the same time, online self-study e-learning systems were developed by several institutions: Examples include the Computer-Assisted Instruction System for learning the Chinese Four Tones (Liu et al., 2010), the Chinese Language Module (the University of Tokyo of Foreign Studies), and the Chinese e-Learning Systems (Yuyama & Takeda, 2009). However, due to the retirement of the initiators of these projects, a number of these sites are unavailable at present. Recently, the utilization of ICT in teaching and learning has been widely expanded, and the digitalization of education has been given greater attention. Over half of higher education institutions have started utilizing ICT for their education (MEXT, 2017). Results of an official investigation by MEXT in 2018 show that 46% of universities in Japan held 'blended' classes in regular courses, incorporating technologies such as clickers, and a great number of teachers have made various attempts to incorporate more ICT (Hino, 2016; Kamiya & Kiyohara, 2016; Sugie et al., 2015; Sugie, 2017, 2019a, 2019b, 2020; Tanabe, 2019; Watanabe, 2019).

Among alternative approaches, the instructional design of the flipped classroom has advantages. However, because of the shortage of digital learning resources and lack of pedagogical skill, only a small number of flipped classrooms for Chinese language education had been conducted before the COVID-19, in such manners as combining classroom learning with LMS and e-learning assignments (Sugie et al., 2015; Zhao, 2015), CAT-style Chinese web tests and on-demand lessons (Murakami et al., 2005). During the COVID-19 pandemic, institutions and teachers who had already experienced the flipped classroom teaching model have successfully conducted asynchronous or hybrid classeses and improved the quality of Chinese language education.

Distance teaching for Chinese language education: As Japan is still largely a monoethnic and monolingual society, the degree of diversification of universities is limited. In addition, because of the lack of robust network connections, facilities, and systems such as LMSs in the 2000s, it had been difficult to actualize synchronous distance education. Under these circumstances, several universities such as Kansai University, Waseda University, and Keio University have conducted long-term video distance teaching for Chinese language courses through specific optional equipment including ISDN lines (Sunaoka et al., 2006). Institutions which have experience in distance teaching account for nearly one-quarter of all institutions nationwide (27% for asynchronous; 25% for synchronous), while the remaining three-quarters of institutions had never implemented distance teaching before the pandemic (MEXT, 2020a).

3 Emergent Remote Teaching (ERT) in Japan Due to the Pandemic

3.1 Timetable During COVID-19

In August 2020, the International Labor Organization (ILO) stated that the impact of COVID-19 had particularly damaging effects on youth, who have globally suffered a loss of over 65% of learning opportunities, and 17%, lost employment (ILO, 2020). Japan has not been immune to these aspects of the pandemic. From April to August 2020, 1069 higher education institutions in Japan were forced to cancel almost all in-person lectures. As a result, each university switched to ERT so as to avoid total cancelation of classes, a shift that was achieved swiftly, with the rate of open courses (including both online and face-to-face classes) reaching 99.7% in June, and 100% in July (MEXT, 2020d). But the rate of remote teaching-only was not high, with only slightly more than half (60.1%) of universities teaching online in June. As the epidemic slowed its pace in July, public opinion shifted toward a negative appraisal of remote learning. In addition, there was pressure to hold semester-end examinations, and thus many universities temporarily halted online teaching at the beginning of August. As a result, 'blended' classes increased from 30.2% in June to 60.1% in July, and face-to-face classes from 9.7% to 16.2% (MEXT, 2020d). However, as the COVID-19 pandemic had not come under control in major cities, both domestically and internationally, it was not known exactly when face-to-face classes would be able to be resumed in full scale in the autumn semester. Thus, most universities (80.1%) opted for a continuation of blended classes, and only 19.3% fully resumed face-to-face classes after September (MEXT, 2020c). Despite pressure from MEXT to resume in-person teaching, a large number of universities took a cautious stance in their implementation in the 2020 autumn semester (MEXT, 2020b).

During this period, roughly 630,000 newly-admitted students had to begin their tertiary education through online courses, including 20,000 international students with restrictions upon entry into Japan (Statistics Bureau of Japan, 2019). Developing appropriate online teaching methods and nurturing a sense of belonging to the universities became priority issues.

3.2 Physical and Human Resources for Online Education

Network infrastructure: The Japanese telecommunication environment is ranked as highly advanced (The Ministry of Internal Affairs and Communications, 2020[1]), with an internet penetration rate of 94%, and the penetration rate of the broadband network (LAN) has reached 32.6 out of 100 persons, with an internet connection speed achieving up to 91.9 Mbps, whereas the cell-phone penetration rate has reached 141%, with a connection speed of 30.9 Mbps. This sufficient condition of network infrastructure has provided physical support for online education during the ERT period.

Optimization of public network resources: Since shifting to remote education, the frequency of visits by teachers and students to LMSs has increased tremendously. For example, at Kyoto University, the number of LMS logins has increased 20 times, and online assignment submission has reached showed a 30-fold increase compared to 2017 (Shibayama et al., 2020). The majority of synchronous classes were conducted during daytime business hours, resulting in access concentration and increased traffic: Even some of the larger institutions such as Kyushu University, Tohoku University, and Waseda University faced network outages and LMS platform server systems going down for two days just after the start of the semester. In May 2020, the Japanese government and the National Institute of Informatics (NII) issued a written statement with provisions to ensure network stability throughout the country by saving network bandwidth. Educational institutions made adjustments and met the requirements with many universities restricting or recommending against synchronous classes with video conferencing systems such as Zoom, promoting asynchronous classes so as not to cause network or system crashes (Matsukawa, 2020).

---

[1] All data are for 2019, except for this point, which is for 2018.

Instructional support: In order to conduct distance teaching smoothly, an effective combination of physical and human resources is indispensable (Garrison, 2017; Moore, 1997). While LMSs are key to the normal and proper operation of online courses, only slightly more than half of the universities (57%) utilized LMSs properly to support the students' learning process prior to COVID-19 (MEXT, 2017). While 66% of Japanese universities have already utilized Teaching Assistants (TAs) (MEXT, 2020a), they are generally involved in required courses, and seldom available for foreign language classes, particularly because part-time lecturers have no right to request TAs. Before 2018, 62% of universities had not established offices for Institutional Research (IR), and as such, most teachers have had to manage teaching/learning data by themselves.

Online teaching skills training and workshops: The sudden onset of the COVID-19 pandemic brought about a paradigm shift in teaching and learning, and education institutions offered FD sessions via various channels such as online courses, mailing lists, and support desk hotlines. The number of FD sessions has thus increased several-fold since the pandemic, and the majority of teachers, including part-time teachers, started to attend proactively to acquire the newly necessary knowledge and skills (Yamazaki, 2020). The Chinese language academic community in Japan has held frequent training workshops on ICT utilization and application, supported front-line teachers to create digital materials with computer software to help them take the first step of online education (JACLE, 2020; Chuken Forum, 2020; Kiyohara, 2020). Japanese copyright law inhibits the development and distribution of digitalization of materials, and traditional paper-based textbooks and handouts are widely used. Due to the uniqueness of the situation, however, the Japanese government implemented a temporary measure to approve the use of copyrighted materials for education.

4 Some Findings from Eight Surveys Related to ERT in Japan

4.1 Data Sources

JACLE (The Japan Association of Chinese Language Education) conducted a survey of its members between May 25 and June 4, 2020. In addition to the small number of participants, the raw data of that survey was undisclosed, and was not analyzed statistically. To help understand a larger picture of remote teaching and learning in Japan during the pandemic, we also selected seven additional surveys: three were on faculty, and four on students. In the early period of the COVID-19 pandemic, specialists in the field of information science led the surveys. Although systematic surveys focusing on foreign language education have not been conducted, including Chinese language teaching and learning, the seven independent surveys have been conducted by different seven education institutions which were officially reported at international conferences of the online symposium to share online learning from universities since April, and these are supplemented here by The National Institute of Informatics (NII-CS), and JACLE survey (results non-disclosed). These are large-scale surveys that reflect the dynamic situation at the time. For this reason, we selected data sources that met the following four conditions in consideration of the balance between university location, type of institution, and the timing of the survey: (1) Apart from JACLE, the sample size ranges between more than one hundred to thousands, which is sufficient for the population; (2) the research method and the data analysis appeared scientific; (3) The questions were detailed enough to reflect the actual situation of respective educational fields; and (4) the raw data was disclosed. The analysis in this paper relies on information from these sources, and as such, it is not possible to refer retroactively to the original data. Nevertheless, being able to grasp the whole context from the large-scale data is advantageous. Below is a summary of the eight surveys. A detailed description of the surveys is shown in the Appendices.

Four surveys of teachers:

- Teacher survey 1 [T1]: Keio University Shonan Fujisawa Campus (Keio SFC), a private university (https://www.sfc.keio.ac.jp/en), conducted a university-wide survey between May 7 and May 13, 2020, with 117 responses received. Based on the information from the university website, there were about 15–20 faculty members associated with Chinese teaching who were responsible for about 50 Chinese classes. The number of part-time teachers is estimated to be three to five times that of faculty members.
- Teacher survey 2 [T2]: The survey of JACLE (http://www.jacle.org/) was conducted between May 25 and June 4, 2020, with 91 responses received. Because the final report was undisclosed to the public, some records were analyzed based on the authors' memory. Based on the information from the association website, there were 507 members associated with Chinese teaching.
- Teacher survey 3 [T3]: Kyoto University, a national university (https://www.kyoto-u.ac.jp/en), conducted a university-wide survey July 22 and August 5, 2020, with 1182 responses received. Based on the information from the university website, there were about 30–35 faculty members and part-time teachers associated with Chinese teaching who were responsible for 204 Chinese classes.
- Teacher survey 4 [T4]: National Institute of Informatics (https://www.nii.ac.jp/en/) conducted a survey between August 21 and September 7, 2020, with 909 responses received. The affiliations and expertise of the survey respondents are unknown.

Four surveys of students:

- Student survey 1 [S1]: In addition to the faculty survey mentioned above, Keio SFC conducted a student survey during the same time period, with 377 responses received. The questions were also written in both Japanese and English. The information about faculty members and Chinese classes is the same as [T1].
- Student survey 2 [S2]: Tohoku University, a national university (https://www.tohoku.ac.jp/en/), conducted a university-wide survey between June 6 and June 25, 2020, with 4063 responses. Based on the information from the university website, there were about 15–20

faculty members associated with Chinese teaching and 156 Chinese language and related classes. It is expected that there were additional part-time teachers but the number is unknown.
- Student survey 3 [S3]: Kyushu University (https://www.kyushu-u.ac.jp/en/), a national university, conducted a university-wide survey between June 22 and August 5, with 4835 responses. Based on the information from the university website, there were about 20–25 faculty members and part-time teachers associated with Chinese teaching and 153 Chinese language and related classes.
- Student survey 4 [S4]: The University of Tokyo (https://www.u-tokyo.ac.jp/en/), another national university, conducted its university-wide survey between July 22 and August 20, with 4822 responses received. Based on the information from the university website, there were about 70 faculty members and part-time teachers associated with Chinese teaching and 113 Chinese language and related classes.

The eight questionnaires vary in implementation time, purpose, and format, but all contained questions about the quality, degree of acceptance, advantages and disadvantages of online teaching, and satisfaction with their implementation. The different institutions have different question item designs, which are not easy to summarize. Simple statistics on the closed-ended questions, arranged in the order of T1–T4 and S1–S4 survey time are displayed on the tables in Appendices 1 and 2. The open-ended questions in the questionnaires about the specific difficulties and challenges faced by teachers and students will be explained in the next section.

In addition, this paper also comprehensively refers to the following two sources: (1) a teacher-student questionnaire of Nagoya University, implemented from May 25 to June 7, 2020, by Akira Fujimaki (2020), published in NII seminar, with a number of valid responses including 412 teachers and 3302 students; (2) the reports of students from the University of Tokyo (Takei, 2020) in order to fully reflect the content of online classes from the perspective of students.

4.2 Findings on Three Aspects

This section reports findings from the eight surveys on the following three aspects: (1) types of remote teaching during the COVID-19 pandemic, (2) degree of satisfaction of faculty and students toward remote teaching and learning, and (3) attitude toward future remote teaching and learning.

1. Types of remote teaching during the pandemic

Remote teaching began synchronously and shifted to blended: Of the results of the eight questionnaires, ERT at Japanese universities can be categorized into six general types: (A) Synchronous; (B) Asynchronous+video materials; (C) Asynchronous+text materials; (D) Blended (Network-Based Language Teaching: NBLT, Kern & Warschauer, 2000); (E) Hybrid-blended; and (F) Hyflex. The six types are visualized in Fig. 9.1.

However, the classification of the six types and the aggregate data is not rigorous, but rather shows general trends, as each institution has its own definition of teaching modes and posed questionnaire items differently.

The time of instructional mode adopted seems to depend on institution-wide decisions. The majority of institutions chose type (A) as a result of respecting the autonomy of faculty members (Taura, 2020; Uehara,

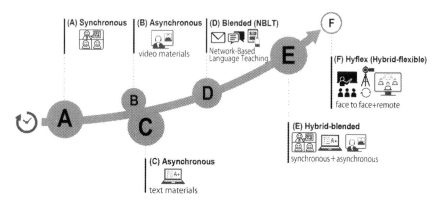

Fig. 9.1 Types of distance teaching mode and temporal development

2020; Yamada, 2020). On the other hand, Tohoku University and Kyushu University selected type (B/C) primarily as a result of concerns regarding the overall network environment (Nose, 2020). Type (D) was used by most participants of NII. Type (F) was almost invisible in the questionnaire, and it only began to be mentioned as a choice of teaching mode after September 2020.

2. Degree of satisfaction

Nearly 70% of students expressed satisfaction with online courses: Most students generally accepted online courses (more detail in Appendix 2). At the University of Tokyo, positive evaluations (6 or above from a maximum of 10 points) account for 72% of responses, while negative evaluations (4 or below with 0 as lowest) accounted for only 20%. At Keio SFC, 61% of students responded positively, and 80% of students at Nagoya University also found online courses valuable (Fujimaki, 2020). If most students find remote teaching advantageous, it is possible for study time to be used more efficiently, and for greater and more precise personalized instruction to be given by teachers. For example, the online setting can ease nervousness and thereby make it easier to practice pronunciation and conversation (results of the open-ended questions in the JACLE and Keio SFC). In particular, synchronous classes conducted using games are simple to conduct and result in greater satisfaction (as reported by Uehara, 2020; Nose, 2020; Takei, 2020). In contrast, at universities that offer only asynchronous classes, students struggle with the burden of large numbers of assignments and report extreme tiredness, both mentally and physically (according to the reports of Keio University, Tohoku University, Kyushu University, and Nagoya University).

Freshmen took a negative attitude toward remote teaching: Freshmen were relatively less satisfied with online courses than Non-First Year Students (Non-FYS). For example, at Tohoku University, 72% of sophomores and higher report positively, compared to only 54% of freshmen. Similarly, at Kyushu University, 53% of Non-FYS thought online classes to be valid substitutes for face-to-face classes, while only 20% of freshmen responded in the same way. It is likely that Non-FYS are, the more learning resources they can use, and the more confident they become about self-regulated learning. On the other hand, freshmen encounter greater difficulties under the new educational model, and thus evaluated remote teaching more negatively than Non-FYS.

The teachers' satisfaction was lower than students': The results of four institutions indicated that a large number of the teachers have accepted distance teaching models (both synchronous and asynchronous) and found more advantages to online classes than traditional pedagogical models, including plentiful teaching/learning resources, and possibilities to create variation in the class operations. For instance, 76% of the teachers at Nagoya University acknowledged the value of online courses (Fujimaki, 2020), a figure lower than the students; 82% of the students recognized online courses as valuable. This may be because around half of the teachers in Japan had no experience of e-learning or distance education before COVID-19. The lower individual ICT skills are, the more frustrations they feel in the process of teaching/learning (Kinoshita, 2020; Kita, 2020; Yamazaki, 2020, results of JACLE), resulting in a lower degree of satisfaction in online courses. Furthermore, such teachers rarely reported gaining a sense of teaching/learning achievements. According to the results of the JACLE survey, 40% of the CFL teachers responded that the remote teaching was ineffective (20% felt online courses were worse than face-to-face; 20% reported negligible differences between teaching modes; 40% unknown; 20% a little better than face-to-face classes).

3. Attitude towards future online classes

The desire of students to continue online courses: Students generally reported looking forward to continuing remote education. For example, at Keio University, 68% of students wished to continue remote education after COVID-19, while 32% of them did not (Appendix 2). The desire for continued online learning was once again higher for Non-FYS than for freshmen. At Kyushu University students from Non-FYS demonstrated a higher rate of desire to continue remote education (73%) than freshmen (48%).

Future anticipation toward online classes by the teachers: Regarding the degree of expectation about hybrid teaching models in the future, the NII results suggested that 48% of the teachers highly anticipated it, 43% 'relatively,' and 20% 'do not anticipate.' In the case of Kyoto University,

32% of the teachers wished to restart face-to-face classes in the autumn semester, 47% desired hybrid classeses (mainly online plus face-to-face: 22%, mainly face-to-face plus online: 25%), and 21% wished for fully online classes (Appendix 2).

Conflicts among stakeholders: Due to the tacit cooperation of universities, teachers, and students, conflicts among stakeholders regarding remote teaching were not prominent in Japan. Both teachers and students responded that the greatest advantages of remote teaching included the ability to take classes anytime, anywhere, the ability to learn at their own pace, the ease of making (using) lecture materials, and of analyzing data. Most students appeared to have attended most of the classes diligently. For example, the attendance rate for the average student at the University of Tokyo for synchronous classes was 80% or more for students across years (87% for first-year students), while freshmen had 17 courses (approximately 25 hours) per week, and freshmen at Tohoku University had 19 courses (approximately 28 hours) per week (Takei, 2020; Taura, 2020).

On the other hand, regarding disadvantages of remote teaching, faculty members responded that classes were 'dependent on the internet connection,' (80% at NII), they 'spend too much time for preparing accounts' (50.9% at Kyoto University), the necessity to 'to update materials and assignments specifically for online classes' (47.4% at Kyoto University). Faculty also reported that it was 'difficult to teach practical skills and experimental training' (74% at NII), a need for 'need more detailed support and mental care for students' (54% at NII) and that it was 'difficult to make classes interactive with students' (60% at NII; 41.3% at Kyoto University). Students also demonstrated concern regarding the poor learning environment and lack of ICT skills. They expressed particular dissatisfaction regarding the following aspects: 'Online classes make it hard to concentrate on learning,' 'freedom increased and learner autonomy is required,' and 'no interactions with other students' (survey from Kyushu University). Many students complained about physical symptoms such as fatigue and back pain (51% of students at Kyushu University).

Many JACLE members are not used to teaching with technology and take a more pessimistic view of the effectiveness of online teaching for interactive instructions (Appendix 1). In the early stages of ERT, many

Chinese teachers needed to deliver synchronous (real-time) courses such as through Zoom, and these classes were more popular among students (synchronous 70.4% positive; asynchronous 22.2% positive: Students of the University of Tokyo, Takei, 2020), however, some universities prohibited their use to optimize public resources. Lack of physical and human resources exacerbates issues of tiredness in teachers, but they nevertheless must complete teaching tasks independently (Results of JACLE open questionnaire).

5 Challenges and Suggested Strategies for Remote Teaching and Learning in Japan

This section discusses the challenges of remote teaching and learning in Japan with some suggested strategies.

5.1 Challenges

Remote teaching highlighted the problems of face-to-face classes: Face-to-face classes have been thought to be the best instructional form, however, through the urgent remote teaching, both teachers and students found it useful to break the old concept of fixed-time classrooms and to promote two-way interaction. As Japanese universities have announced a policy to resume face-to-face classes in the spring semester of 2021, it will no longer be possible to return to outdated teaching and learning styles in classes. The biggest challenge is to summarize the remote teaching experiences of the 2020 year to apply to the remaining challenges in the next phase of education.

Poor quality dialogue in the virtual space remains an issue: Not only in face-to-face classrooms but also in remote education, there is a psychological and communicative space to be crossed, a space of potential misunderstanding between the input of instructor and uptake of the learner, which profoundly affects both teaching and learning (Moore, 1997). Kyushu University reported that when the students took online courses, communication between teachers and students happened at a ratio of 45%, while communication between students sat at 28% (Nose, 2020: Appendix 2). Only approximately 13% of teachers and 13% of students felt that the distance between students and teachers was closer in remote teaching than in face-to-face instruction (Kyoto University). 'Dialogue,' 'structure,' and 'learner autonomy' are the affective factors in establishing sufficient interaction between instructors and learners or among learners in remote spaces (Saba & Rick, 1994). There were some reports of an increase in dialogue in out-of-class activities (Takano, 2020), but few remarked upon instructional structures and learner autonomy in Chinese language teaching. How to promote qualified online digital dialogue and more personalized instruction remains an issue.

Reflection and summary of TCFL are insufficient: In the ERT period, university information science experts played a leading role, including in their reporting of online teaching practice in repositories such as NII-CS. In comparison, the TCFL community focuses on training for ICT uses and applications (see Sect. 3.2), and there have been fewer reports on TCFL itself in Japan. Most Chinese teachers believe that this experience of online teaching will not be wasted, and it will certainly bring about great changes in the future of education (Murakami, 2021). In order not to let the efforts of the 2020 year go to waste, it is necessary to summarize and reflect on the practical experience of Chinese remote teaching and clarify the surrounding issues. We believe that 2020 has been a year of development for TCFL, which will lead the way in the sustainable development of Chinese education for the next generation.

5.2 Suggested Strategies

Informatization/Utilization of ICT in education will continue: This ERT has made the educational community realize that the informatization/utilization of ICT is the way to the future of education (Matsuda, 2020). As stakeholders, universities are rebuilding the next generation of LMSs, mainly developing management systems such as open e-books, visualizations of the learning process, automatic feedback, and examinations (Yang et al., 2021). These functions will likely contribute to alleviating difficulties in the implementation of online teaching and empower students with more individualized choices of learning (Shigeta, 2020; Shimada, 2020; Ogata, 2020). Chinese language teachers, as stakeholders themselves, also need to be actively involved in making suggestions and taking responsibility for ensuring appropriate remote foreign language teaching.

Reducing the gap in the distribution of educational resources: The COVID-19 pandemic has created apparent gaps in the allocation of educational resources, teaching management systems and demonstrated that teachers' knowledge of ICT is insufficient (see Sect. 5.1). Chinese ERT is still typically provided in fixed time, large-sized classes, and most teachers had no experience in remote teaching, and suffered from a lack of support from LMSs and TAs, leading to teacher exhaustion and subsequently reduced effort put into lessons (see Sect. 3.2). In addition, freshmen experiencing a digital divide, as well as part-time teachers, have very few educational resources available to them, and thus often fall into a crisis of lower quality online education. The Japanese government and educational institutions have provided funds and measures to address these issues, and the academic community has actively shared successful online teaching experiences and information to help narrow the gap in the distribution of educational resources (NII-CS). We hope that Chinese language teachers in Japan will publish research papers on remote teaching, and share information regarding overseas contexts, which will contribute to the further narrowing of this gap.

Improving the quality of online teaching: Lack of dialogue and learner autonomy is a characteristic of traditional education in Japan (Wang, 2019). As described in the previous paragraph, two of the three factors (dialogue, structure, and learner autonomy) in the remote space are weakened (Moore, 1997). It is necessary to address the 'structure' factor. Curriculum design is an essential aspect in promoting distance learning systems (Hata, 2020; Kogo, 2005, 2020). Enriching the structure of distance education curriculum design is effective in the early detection of student issues (Saba & Rick, 1994). The unification of the beliefs of teachers and learners, and integration of curriculum design into the syllabus is the key to accepting new teaching models (Gilquin & Granger, 2010). In order to improve the quality of TCFL post-COVID-19, it is necessary to learn more of the theory of distance learning and to develop professional curriculum designers of TCFL.

Shifting toward more diversified universities: Japanese universities have a low ratio of adult learners and overseas students, and the demand for remote teaching is therefore relatively low. As a result, it was difficult to unilaterally adopt ERT promptly, or to apply previous experience from at home or abroad in order to quickly improve teaching practice. As cross-cultural communication education is a meaningful goal of foreign language teaching and learning, we language educators must continue to contribute to shifting toward more diversified universities.

6 Conclusion, Limitation, and Future Research

In this study, we attempted to infer the actual situation of Chinese remote teaching through the analysis of questionnaire survey data which were conducted by the eight higher education and research institutions independently. There were no questionnaires or reports on Chinese remote teaching practices specifically in the early period of ERT. Although the JACLE survey was conducted focusing on TCFL, the main purpose of the survey was to investigate the educational environment, and as the results of the survey were not made public, the use of JACLE survey data source was restricted. However, we strongly believe that the amalgamated surveys reflect the voices of stakeholders, including those involved with TCFL, because the educational resources available and decisions by the

Government and affiliations strongly affected the implementation of foreign language courses during the ERT period.

For these reasons, this study remains the following limitations.

Participants: Only the JACLE survey was designed and conducted focusing on TCFL teachers (members of JACLE), whereas the other seven university surveys reflected the general trends of remote teaching during the ERT period.

Accuracy: Due to the differences in timing and design criteria among the surveys from different institutions, the results in this paper may include some errors. In addition, since these questionnaire surveys were conducted during ERT, the results will not necessarily be the same in the future.

Representativeness: The results in this study may not represent the situation of average Japanese institutions. For example, the ratio of the types of remote teaching at the seven institutions was higher than that of the Japan-wide university survey conducted by MEXT.

The future direction of research: In order to overcome the limitations of survey data in this study, a questionnaire specific to online Chinese courses should be conducted and analyzed. Recently, the number of questionnaire surveys implemented by foreign language departments has been increasing. It is expected that more Chinese-specific surveys will be conducted soon. Furthermore, it is also necessary to reflect more survey resources focusing on the TCFL. Through examination of balanced data which cover entire educational situations, we will be better able to understand the reality of TCFL in the ERT period.

In this study, we attempted to understand the actual situation of ERT and learning in Japanese higher education institutions and the reactions of students and teachers by analyzing reliable, large sample questionnaire data. Based on the results of this study, it is clear that ERT in 2020, a potentially historical turning point in higher education, has achieved a measure of success. Nevertheless, it is difficult for both teachers and students to immediately adapt to or embrace a paradigm shift from traditional educational beliefs. We also reviewed the educational environment of TCFL before the pandemic in Japan: the summarizing of TCFL issues will help provide grounds for developing sustainable achievements in the future. Because of the limitations in data sources, the results analyzed here were not especially focused on TCFL. However, the results of the recent questionnaire surveys, which especially focused on foreign language questionnaires including TCFL (e.g., Sunaoka & Sugie, 2021), are consistent with this report, and as such, we hope that this study will provide meaningful insights for choices of instructional designing TCFL.

Acknowledgments This work was supported by JSPS KAKENHI Grant Number 21K00773. We would like to express our gratitude to Professor Kaori Nishi of Meiji Gakuin University in Japan for her assistance in downloading the internal files. Finally, we would like to thank Daniel Roy Pearce of Kyoto Notre Dame University, for his proofreading of the manuscript.

Appendices

Appendix 1: Survey Results for Japanese Teachers

		T1	T2	T3	T4
Basic information	Institution	Keio University	JACLE	Kyoto University	NII
	Type	Private university	Association	National university	National Institute
Summary of the surveys	Time of the questionnaire (in 2020)	5/7–5/13	5/25–6/4	7/22–8/5	8/21–9/7
	Target	Full-time academic staff	Teachers of members	Teachers (including part-time)	Teachers in Japan (including part-time)
	Numbers responded (n)	117	91	1182	909
	Response rate (%)	32%	N/A	67%	N/A
Types of online classes	(A) Synchronous	39%	40%	61%	26%
	(B) Asynchronous (video materials)	6%	25%	12%	14%
	(C) Asynchronous (text materials)	19%		14%	
	(D) Blended (synchronous +asynchronous)	36%	32%	13%	57%
	(E) Others	N/A	3%	N/A	3%

Views on online classes	Satisfied	49%	Better	20%	Feel effect	20%
			About the same	20%	Some extent	62%
	Unsatisfied	51%	Unknown	40%	Haven't really felt	15%
			Worse	20%	Haven't felt	3%
Expectation	Highly anticipate	N/A	N/A		Online only	21%
	Slightly anticipate				Hybrid online+face-to-face	22%
	Neither				Hybrid face-to-face+online	25%
	Do not anticipate				Return to face-to-face	32%

N/A
48%
43%
7%
20%

Appendix 2: Survey Results for Japanese Students

		S1	S2	S3	S4
Basic information	Institution	Keio University	Tohoku University	Kyushu University	University of Tokyo
	Type	Private university	National university	National university	National university
Summary of surveys	Time of the questionnaire (in 2020)	5/12–5/18	6/11–6/25	7/22–8/5	7/22–8/20
	Target	Undergraduates	Undergraduates	Undergraduates	Undergraduates+Postgraduates
	Numbers responded (N) N	377	4063	4835	4822
	Response rate %	8%	83%	27%	20–30%
Types of online classes	(A) Synchronous	39%	7%	95%	75%
	(B) Asynchronous (video materials)	6%	83%	69%	Few
	(C) Asynchronous (text materials)	19%	10%	73%	Extremely few
	(D) Blended or hybrid (synchronous + asynchronous)	36%	N/A	86%	N/A
	(E) Others	N/A		88%	N/A

		Non-FYS		Non-FYS		Non-FYS	
Satisfaction	Positive	61%		72%		53%	72%
	Negative	39%		54%	FYS	20%	20%
Expectation	Positive	68%	Online Non-	77%	Non-FYS	73%	78%
			classes FYS	53%	FYS	48%	
			FYS	23%			22%
	Negative	32%	Face-to- Non-	47%	FYS		
			face FYS				
			classes FYS				

Note 1: Regarding the survey sources, see [T1] to [T4] and [S1] to [S4] in Sect. 4.

Note 2: On the types of online classes:

* The original survey such as [T1], [T2], [S1], and [S4], (B) and (C), (D) and (E) is not clearly differentiated. In the Appendix, based on the distribution tendencies of each institution, five types of (A) to (E) were classified. Type (F) is not included in the Appendix because it did not appear in the questionnaire items. See Sect. 4.1 for more detailed information. The numbers of [S1] are the same as [T1].

Note 3: The total exceeds 100% because multiple answers were allowed, such as [S3].

Note 4: On the views on online classes and expectations to online classes.

* As the original questionnaire items have many variations between institutions, the Appendix simplified and divided them into two categories, Positive and Negative.
* The total exceeds 100% because multiple answers were allowed, such as [S2].

Note 5: The original data were answered on a 5-point scale (such as [S2]) or a 0–10 point scale (such as[S4]). The results are presented here in %.

References

Chuken Forum. (2020). Looking at post corona—thinking about a new way of teaching, learning, and testing Chinese. Forum of The Society for Testing Chinese Proficiency Japan (http://www.chuken.gr.jp/). October 17, Kansai University. http://www.chuken.gr.jp/association/forum/forum_19.pdf

Fujimaki, A. (2020, June 26). *Review on education using ICT*. The 11th online symposium to share online learning from universities since April. The National Institute of Informatics (NII), Tokyo. https://www.nii.ac.jp/event/upload/20200626-4_Fujimaki.pdf

Garrison, D. (2017). *E-learning in the 21st century: A community of inquiry framework for research and practice* (3rd ed.). Routledge.

Gilquin, G., & Granger, S. (2010). *How can DDL be used in language teaching*. Researchgate. https://www.researchgate.net/publication/228984095_How_can_DDL_be_used_in_language_teaching

Hata, N. (2020, June 5). *Application examples of active learning in distance teaching*. The 10th online symposium to share online learning from universities since April. The National Institute of Informatics (NII), Tokyo. https://www.nii.ac.jp/event/upload/20200605-3_Hata.pdf

Hino, Y. (2014). Accumulation and sharing: Database creation and open education of learning/educational contents. *The Journal of the Japan Association of Chinese Language Education, 12*, 14–21.

Hino, Y. (2016). A study to grasp learned items in Chinese as a foreign language learner. *Studies in e-Learning Language Education, 11*, 35–42.

ILO: International Labour Organization, Survey Report. (2020, August 11). Youth & COVID-19: Impacts on jobs, education, rights and mental well-being. https://www.ilo.org/wcmsp5/groups/public/%2D%2D-ed_emp/documents/publication/wcms_753026.pdf

Kamiya, K., & Kiyohara, F. (2016). A trial product of PinYin quiz generator. *Studies in e-Learning Language Education, 11*, iv.

Kern, R., & Warschauer, M. (2000). *Network-based language teaching: Concepts and practice*. Cambridge University Press.

Kinoshita, Y. (2020, August 21). *Distance remote lesson in the first semester and its problems; Part-time lecturer*. The 14th online symposium to share online learning from universities since April. The National Institute of Informatics (NII), Tokyo. https://www.nii.ac.jp/event/upload/20200821-05_Kinoshita.pdf

Kita, H. (2020, July 31). *Online classroom and part-time teachers*. The 13th online symposium to share online learning from universities since April. The National Institute of Informatics (NII), Tokyo. https://www.nii.ac.jp/event/upload/20200731-07_Kita.pdf

Kiyohara, F. (2014). Enrich your lessons digitally!—Repeat practice: TTS and Chinese voice input, word card Quizlet that can make sounds and play games. *The Journal of the Japan Association of Chinese Language Education, 12*, 30–37.

Kiyohara, F. (2020). Online seminar series for the Chinese Language Teaching with ICT. https://www.kokuchpro.com/group/ZH_ICT/

Kogo, C. (2005). *Foundations of E-learning: Behavioral, cognitive, situated, learning theories and their integration*. The proceedings of the 3rd WebCT Workshop.

Kogo, C. (2020, May 8). *Specific examples of online class design by class size*. The 7th online symposium to share online learning from universities since April. The National Institute of Informatics (NII), Tokyo. https://www.nii.ac.jp/event/upload/20200508-5_Kogo.pdf

Liu, S., Urano, Y., & Hiki, S. (2010). A computer-assisted instruction system for self-teaching of discriminating Chinese four tones. *Japan Society for Educational Technology, 34*(3), 223–233.

Matsuda, N. (2020, May 29). *Distance education practice and the development of the next-generation online education system in North Carolina State University's*. The 11th online symposium to share online learning from universities since April. The National Institute of Informatics (NII), Tokyo. https://www.nii.ac.jp/event/upload/20200626-3_Matsuda.pdf

Matsukawa, H. (2020, June 26). *Tohoku University's questionnaire survey on online classrooms*. The 11th online symposium to share online learning from universities since April. The National Institute of Informatics (NII), Tokyo. https://www.nii.ac.jp/event/upload/20200626-5_Matsukawa.pdf

MEXT. (2016). About the reform status of education in universities. https://www.mext.go.jp/a_menu/koutou/daigaku/04052801/__icsFiles/afieldfile/2017/12/06/1380019_1.pdf

MEXT. (2017). About the reform status of education in university. https://www.mext.go.jp/a_menu/koutou/daigaku/04052801/__icsFiles/afieldfile/2017/12/06/1380019_1.pdf

MEXT (The Ministry of Education, Culture, Sports, Science and Technology). (2020a). About the reform status of education in universities. https://www.mext.go.jp/content/20200428-mxt_daigakuc03-000006853_1.pdf.

MEXT. (2020b, December 23). Survey on the implementation status of late classes at universities. https://www.mext.go.jp/content/20201223-mxt_kouhou01-000004520_01.pdf

MEXT. (2020c, September 15). About the questionnaire survey on the implementation of post-semester courses. https://www.mext.go.jp/content/20200915_mxt_kouhou01-000004520_1.pdf.

MEXT. (2020d, June 1 and July 17). About the teaching status of universities under the influence of the new coronavirus infectious disease. https://www.mext.go.jp/content/20200605-mxt_kouhou01-000004520_6.pdf (June 1) and https://www.mext.go.jp/content/20200717-mxt_kouhou01-000004520_2.pdf (July 17)

MIC (The Ministry of Internal Affairs and Communications). (2020). International comparison data. https://www.soumu.go.jp/johotsusintokei/field/tsuushin08.html]

Moore, M. G. (1997). Theory of transactional distance. In D. Keegan (Ed.), *Theoretical principles of distance education* (pp. 22–38). Routledge.

Murakami, K. (2021). Experiment of multi-class common online learning and online exam, Chuken Forum October 17, Looking at Post Corona—Thinking about a new way of teaching, learning, and testing Chinese.

Murakami, K., Sunaoka, K., & Liu, S. (2005). *Development of computerized adaptive testing (CAT)-based online oral Chinese test.* Proceedings of the 4th Symposium of The International Conference on Internet Chinese Education (ICICE), pp. 471–477.

Nose, K. (2020, July 10). *Kyushu University student online questionnaire.* The 12th online symposium to share online learning from universities since April. The National Institute of Informatics (NII), Tokyo. https://www.nii.ac.jp/event/upload/20200710-08_NoseNaganuma.pdf

Ogata, H. (2020, July 25). Grade evaluation and analysis of learning data in Open eBook format. *The 9th JMOOC (Japan Massive Open Online Courses Promotion Council) Workshop*, Tokyo.

Saba, F. S., & Rick, L. (1994). Verifying key theoretical concepts in a dynamic model of distance education. *The American Journal of Distance Education, 8*(1), 36–59.

Shibayama, E., Sekiya, T., and Okada, K. (2020, October 9). *Online lessons in the first half of this year looking back from log data.* The 18th online symposium to share online learning from universities since April. The National Institute of Informatics (NII), Tokyo. https://www.nii.ac.jp/event/upload/20201009-05_Shibayama.pdf

Shigeta, K. (2020, July 25). *Understanding of learning situation in online classes and multi-faceted performance evaluation.* The 9th JMOOC. Tokyo.

Shimada, T. (2020, August 21). *Analysis of learning activities during online classes.* The 14th online symposium to share online learning from universities since April. The National Institute of Informatics (NII), Tokyo. https://www.nii.ac.jp/event/upload/20200821-10_Shimada.pdf

Sugie, S. (2017). Qualitative values created by cross cultural distance learning between Japan and China. *The Journal of the Japan Association of Chinese Language Education, 15*, 105–123.

Sugie, S. (2019a). The development of guide training VR material based on university campus guide. *The Journal of Modernization of Chinese Language Education, 8*(2), 17–29. http://xuebao.eblcu.com/xuebao/essay/sixteen/03.pdf

Sugie, S. (2019b, December). *The design, implementation and evaluation of active learning with mobile learning system for the Chinese tour guide training*. The 23rd Annual Conference of Japan Association of Foreign Language Education. Tokyo University of Foreign Studies.

Sugie, S. (2020, August 29). *Useful tools and tips of Chinese online course: The introduction of network-based language teaching practice and the workshop*. The 2nd Study Group in 2020. The Japan Association of Chinese Language Education. Zoom online. http://www.jacle.org/meeting-20200829/

Sugie, S., Shimizu, K., & Tanabe, T. (2015). *The challenge of active learning with flipped learning design and movie creation with tablet PC*. The 13th annual conference of Association for e-Learning Language education. Osaka University.

Sunaoka, K. (2017). *Chinese classes and class management—Towards for open educational system*. WINPEC Working Paper Series No. J1610.

Sunaoka, K., Monden, Y., Morishita, Y., & Ikegami, D. (2006). The construction of foreign language learning environment in international distance conference. *Cross cultural distance learning teachers' manual*. Media Mix, Waseda University, pp. 74–95.

Sunaoka, K., & Sugie, S. (2021). *How to upgrade online Chinese language teaching at Japanese universities with after Corona*. Proceedings of the 11th international conference and workshops on Technology and Chinese Language Teaching (TCLT11), May 28–30, Yale University, Zoom online.

Sunaoka, K., Yamaguchi, T., & Hori, S. (2017). Current situation of foreign language education in Japanese universities. In K. Sunaoka & Y. Muroi (Eds.), *The teaching of foreign languages in Japan and International Academic Activities* (pp. 3–20). Asahi Press Inc..

Takano, A. (2020, June 26). *Support for student life in with Corona era—From the student counseling center*. The 11th online symposium to share online learning from universities since April, Tokyo. https://www.nii.ac.jp/event/upload/20200626-9_Takano.pdf

Takei, Y. (2020, May 29). *How students perceive online courses*. The 9th online symposium to share online learning from universities since April. The National Institute of Informatics (NII), Tokyo. https://www.nii.ac.jp/event/upload/20200529-5_Takei.pdf

Tanabe, T. (2019, March). *The new CLIL: Chinese Language Learning through/for Programming Education*. The 17th annual conference of Association for e-Learning Language education. Tokoha University, Shizuoka.

Taura, K. (2020, September 4). *Introduction of questionnaire results regarding online classes*. The 15th online symposium to share online learning from universities since April. The National Institute of Informatics (NII), Tokyo. https://www.nii.ac.jp/event/upload/20200904-06_Taura.pdf

The Japan Association of Chinese Language Education (JACLE). (2020, June 7). *Small material that can be used in distance learning from tomorrow*. The 18th annual conference, after session. Zoom online. http://www.jacle.org/annual18/

The National Institute of Informatics. (2020). Online symposium to share online learning from universities since April (NII-CS). The first round (March 26, 2020) to the 31st (April 23, 2021). https://www.nii.ac.jp/event/other/decs/

The Statistics Bureau of Japan. (2019, December 25). Basic survey data on schools. Higher education students. https://www.e-stat.go.jp/stat-search?page=1&toukei=00400001&bunya_l=12.

Uehara, K. (2020, June). *Distance teaching and survey results in Keio University SFC*. The 10th online symposium to share online learning from universities since April. The National Institute of Informatics (NII), Tokyo. https://www.nii.ac.jp/event/upload/20200605-5_Uehara.pdf

Wang, S. (2019). Influence of English learning self-efficacy on Chinese learning motivation and self-efficacy for Japanese university students: Based on third language acquisition. *The Journal of Modernization of Chinese Language Education, 16*, 69–76.

Watanabe, Y. (2019, March). *The creation of pronunciation test for conquering the weak point with Chinese phonetic searching system*. The 17th annual conference of Association for e-Learning Language education. Tokoha University, Shizuoka.

Yamada, T. (2020, September 25). *How do teachers view online courses—according to a survey of teachers from Kyoto University*. The 17th online symposium to share online learning from universities since April. The National Institute of Informatics (NII), Tokyo. https://www.nii.ac.jp/event/upload/20200925-08_Yamada.pdf

Yamazaki, Y. (2020, November 20). *How do part-time English as a second language lecturers deal with online classes during the corona epidemic (university, high school, junior high school)*. The 21st online symposium to share online learning from universities since April. The National Institute of Informatics (NII), Tokyo. https://www.nii.ac.jp/event/upload/20201120-09_Yamazaki.pdf

Yang, C. Y. C., Chen, L. Y. I., & Ogata, H. (2021). Toward precision education: Educational data mining and learning analytics for identifying students' learning patterns with Ebook systems. *Educational Technology & Society, 24*(1), 152–163.

Yuyama, T., & Takeda, N. (2009). The lesson effect by compound use of Chinese WEB teaching materials. *Journal of Japan e-Learning Association, 9*, 10–17.

Zhao, J. (2015). The flipped classroom in active learning: On the application of flipped classroom methodology in beginning Chinese language education. *Forum of Language Instructors, 9*, 33–39.

10

Synchronous Online Language Teaching: A Reflection from Hong Kong

Siu-lun Lee

1   Introduction

Computer-Assisted Language Teaching (CALL) is a decent academic field developed for decades with achievement on technical side (Butler-Pascoe, 2011) and fruitful development on pedagogical side (Hoopingarner, 2009; Liu, 2018; Stickler & Shi, 2013; Tseng et al., 2019). Both synchronous and asynchronous online language teaching still have room for improvement because of the ever-evolving educational technology and the changing needs of students. With such a sudden need to change from face-to-face plus asynchronous teaching to synchronous plus asynchronous online language teaching because of the pandemic situation, both curriculum planners and frontline teachers, on the one hand, needed to face lots of challenges, and, on the other hand, can see lots of possibilities opened up in language teaching theory and practice.

S.-l. Lee (✉)
The Chinese University of Hong Kong, Hong Kong, China
e-mail: slee@cuhk.edu.hk

© The Author(s), under exclusive license to Springer Nature Switzerland AG 2022
S. Liu (ed.), *Teaching the Chinese Language Remotely*,
https://doi.org/10.1007/978-3-030-87055-3_10

At the beginning of 2020, the world has been threatened by the spread of coronavirus disease 2019 (COVID-19). The virus is primarily spread between people during close contact, through small droplets produced by coughing, sneezing and talking, as well as through touching a contaminated surface and then touching their face. The pandemic has caused disruption of social and economic activities globally. Educational activities in different regions in the world have faced severe challenges because social distance was required to be maintained. Schools and institutions of different levels, from kindergarten to tertiary, were temporarily stopped face-to-face classrooms to avoid close contact among students, teachers and staff. Schools and educational institutions were adopting, according to their scale and available resources, different contingency plans in response to the worldwide pandemic situation. Various forms of online teaching were adopted, including synchronous, asynchronous and blended modes. Language teaching activities throughout the world has also "experimented" different teaching modes to adapt to this pandemic situation. When the World Health Organization (WHO) declared the outbreak of a Public Health Emergency of International Concern on January 30, 2020, the different contingency plans, adopted by different schools, were turned from planning phase to actual implementation phase. Although different schools had different contingency plans due to differences in available resources, one common feature was to turn face-to-face classroom teaching to synchronous online teaching.

This part presents a case study and experience of an international Chinese education program in a tertiary institution in Hong Kong. This study describes actions taken during contingency planning phase and actual implementation phase. Implementation practices as well as teachers' and students' perceptions toward online language teaching are analyzed. This case throws some lights on future development and possibilities in Chinese as a Second Language (CSL) as well as international Chinese education.

2   Background Information

Internationalization has been one of the phenomena as well as "target" for tertiary institutions in Hong Kong in recent decades. The author is currently working in one of the tertiary institutions in Hong Kong. The university caters hundreds of exchange students and international undergraduates every year from all over the world. International students and exchange students selected Hong Kong for their study due to their interest in the socio-economic situations and culture of the region. Chinese language learning is one of the targets of the international undergraduates and exchange students. Apart from Putonghua and Cantonese courses for international undergraduates and exchange students, the university provides Putonghua trainings for undergraduates and Cantonese courses for Mandarin-speaking undergraduates. International undergraduates and non-local undergraduates from different backgrounds constitute about 14% of the university enrolment (The Chinese University of Hong Kong, 2019). University students can take Putonghua or Cantonese courses from beginning level to advanced levels to cater their academic and cultural needs. Each Putonghua/Cantonese course traditionally constitutes 3 credits with 3 contact hours.

In 2009, Hong Kong education had gone through a series of education reform. One of which was to change the university curriculum from 3 years to 4 years. A general belief, in view of this, considered that university needed to cater a lot more students with existing resources. Since then, university senior management encouraged and suggested to implement e-learning in language courses offered to university undergraduates (King, 2016). Because of the implementation of these e-learning projects, language centers and language teachers were very "cooperative", but in fact, nervous about the change. Teachers had to follow the instructions and finish the task on time. Since it was a top-down administrative policy, university administration provided teacher training on computer literacy and on the use of educational technologies on university and on departmental level. Lee (2016) discussed the planning and implementation of asynchronous e-learning components with traditional face-to-face language classroom as well as the normalization process of such implementation. After such implementation, language courses were equipped with face-to-face components and asynchronous e-learning exercises (Lee, 2011, 2018). Asynchronous platforms, such as Moodle and Blackboard Learn, were used. E-learning exercises in Chinese as a second language (CSL) courses consisted of "pronunciation practices", "vocabulary exercises", "listening comprehension", "reading comprehension" and "speaking exercises". Multiple choice questions, short-answer questions and matching were the popular question type for the first 4 exercises, while "speaking exercises" can consist of question-and-answer questions and situational speaking topics.

During 2019–2020, there were large-scale social movements triggered by the introduction of the Fugitive Offenders Amendment Bill by the Hong Kong government. The first wave of social movement against the extradition bill was started on March 15, 2019. Both scale and frequency were escalating till the beginning of 2020. The social movements were intensified with road blocked and public transportation suspended till the end of 2019. There were sieges of universities in Hong Kong in November 2019. Face-to face education mode was affected. Since then, universities, secondary schools, primary schools, as well as kindergartens suspended their face-to-face classes and, at the same time, working on contingency plan. One of the contingency possibilities was the use of synchronous online teaching mode to deliver courses. The challenges faced by schools, of all level, were not only about how to deliver course but also how to do student consultation, assessments and school admission procedures. On the technical side, some synchronous online teaching platform, such as Zoom, Skype, Google Meet, Google Classroom, Microsoft Teams, Blackboard Collaborate, ClassIn and so on, were tested and being explored concerning their capacity in course delivery (Zimmerman, 2019). On the pedagogical side, school administrators, curriculum planners and front-line teachers needed to rethink the educational basics, such as teaching materials, curriculum design, "classroom" teaching and assessment, when dealing with the changing social situations.

3 Before the COVID-19 Pandemic: Voices of Students and Instructors

Before the pandemic period, 3-credit CSL courses were delivered in a blended model with 2 face-to-face sessions (50 minutes per sessions) and 2 asynchronous learning sessions (50 minutes per sessions). In other words, teaching and learning activities were consisted of a total of about 4 hours per week. Asynchronous learning sessions were divided into pre-classroom tasks (a 50-minute session) and post-classroom tasks (a 50-minute session). The blended model started with pre-classroom tasks, which provided semi-authentic language inputs to students. Target language was training through mimicking and analyzing in pre-classroom asynchronous exercises. Face-to-face classroom sessions provided training on vocabulary usage with pragmatic focuses through various language activities, such as role-play (Lee, 2015). Post-classroom asynchronous exercises focused on reinforcement as well as diagnostic assessment. Feedback of the diagnostic assessment was given in face-to-face classroom. To sum up, asynchronous learning sessions in this blended model included both online listening and speaking exercises. Online listening exercises consisted of "recognition of speech sounds" and "listening comprehension". Online speaking exercises comprised "pronunciation drills", "vocabulary exercises" and "situational speaking exercises".

3.1 Voices of Students

On students' side, Lee (2016) studied students' e-learning readiness when learning CSL at the Chinese University of Hong Kong (CUHK). The research was done during the "first wave" started around 2009 of e-learning implementation. It was done before the social incidents and the pandemic situation and CSL students had been exposed to asynchronous teaching but had not yet experienced synchronous teaching. In this students' readiness survey, majority of the CUHK students (63.8%) reported that they spent 1–4 hours every day for using ICT device for various learning activities including web-based learning, blogging, social networking and web-surfing for information. Around 97.1% of the local students indicated that they would use ICT device for learning and all the respondents (100%) in the non-local group indicated a positive answer. About 88.4% of local students indicated that they were willing to use ICT devices in language learning activities. Majority of the non-local students (97.6%) were willing to use ICT in language learning. This was due to the fact that primary and secondary schools in Mainland and other regions in the world already had systematic plans in e-learning. Students from Mainland, in particular, already have got used to this mode of learning (Zheng et al., 2014).

The subjects indicated in the survey that among the different language skills, listening skills were in the highest rank of the list that students were willing to use ICT device to practice. About 73.5% of CUHK students were willing to use ICT devices in practicing listening skills. The second and third in the rank were pronunciation practice (55.5%) and reading comprehension practice (49.7%). The fourth in the rank was speaking skills (25.9%). In terms of e-exercises or e-activities formats, local students liked "multiple choice" and "interactive Q/A" most. Non-local students were in favor of "interactive Q/A". However, "fill in the blanks" and "short answers" were less favorite e-activities types. And 28.7% of local students, while 44% of the non-local students, indicated that e-learning should be linked to classroom activities.

About students' expectation of the e-learning effectiveness, 68.5% of the respondents in the survey thought that the effectiveness was average. When asking what kind of language skills students thought ICT devices/e-learning can help, the highest rank was listening skills. The second was pronunciation improvement. The third was speaking ability. The fourth was reading skills and the lowest was writing skills.

3.2   Voices of the Instructors

During the social incidents and sieges of universities happened in November 2019, a "synchronous online teaching availability survey" has been undertaken within the teaching team of a CSL program at the university in order to alert teachers about the changing teaching environment, to get information concerning the resources available among teachers, as well as to understand teachers' capacity of and perception toward synchronous and asynchronous teaching. The survey was sent via email to teachers (N=21). Eighteen questions were asked in the survey. Although majority of the teachers were equipped with computer hardware (71.5% teachers with normal or high-speed internet connection) and were supportive to both asynchronous and synchronous teaching, there were limitations on the capacity of running synchronous online teaching. Eighty-six percent of the teachers did not have the experience and training in delivering synchronous language teaching before. Forty-three percent of the teachers were willing to deliver language courses in synchronous mode, while 57% of the teachers had reservation. Teachers raised their concerns about physical location of students (stability of internet connection) and time-zone differences. Technological and pedagogical issues were also teachers' concern.

4   Implementation of the Contingency Plan

The COVID-19 pandemic urged educational institutions in the whole world to implement synchronous online teaching in order to minimize the disruption of teaching and learning activities. Both public and private educational institutions in Hong Kong, from kindergarten to universities, did their best to implement synchronous online teaching since the beginning of 2020. The Chinese University of Hong Kong selected Zoom as the primary platform to support synchronous teaching and learning activities during the pandemic period. From the previous discussion, this sudden but unavoidable implementation of synchronous online teaching was challenging for administrators, teachers and students. In view of this, workshops on synchronous teaching were organized on university level, departmental level and program level during the first quarter of 2020. Between January 30 and February 14, 22 online workshops on the use of Zoom for class purposes were offered at university level. The training workshops covered over 9200 students, over 2700 teachers and administrative staff from the academic departments in different faculties. Since the resumption of classes at University on February 17, 2020, an average of over 1100 e-classes had been held every school day, with participants over 70,000. The average attendance rate was close to 90%. Feedback from teachers and students had been collected by surveys conducted by the University. The survey showed that the students were adapting to this mode of learning well (The Chinese University of Hong Kong, 2020).

On departmental level and program level, smaller-scale training workshops (around 10 workshops catering for 10–60 CSL teachers and administrators) were frequently organized to handle technical and pedagogical issues. Training workshops included simulated synchronous teaching, assessment simulations, technical try-outs, question-and-answer sessions and various discussion sessions were organized to prepare teachers for the newly implemented synchronous online teaching.

Since February 17, 2020, synchronous teaching replaced traditional face-to-face teaching. All CSL courses were delivered through synchronous teaching with asynchronous online exercises. There were 14 Cantonese as a second language classes with 302 enrolments and 32 Mandarin as a second language classes with 592 students enrolled during spring term 2019–2020. University allowed late add/drop during the pandemic period, the late drop rate of Cantonese as a second language classes is 1% and the late drop rate of Mandarin as a second language classes is 5%. The average attendance rate of all CSL courses was 95%. The enrolment situation during summer term 2019–2020 was similar to previous academic year. There were 9 classes of Cantonese as a second language with 138 enrolments and 6 classes of Mandarin as a second language with 104 enrolments.

5 Synchronous CSL "Classroom" Activities During the Pandemic

In addition to lectures conveying linguistic knowledge, language activities are important to give CSL students chances to test their hypothesis and practice (Jin, 2006). Most of the face-to-face classroom teaching activities, such as pronunciation drills, pattern drills, question-and-answer sessions and so on, could be carried out in synchronous online teaching mode. Table 10.1 shows different language activities held using synchronous online teaching platform during the pandemic period.

Table 10.1 Language activities used in synchronous online teaching

Language activities	Interaction mode	Skills trained	Functions of Zoom involved
Question-and-answer drills	• Teacher-student • Student-student (both teacher and students are active participants)	• Pronunciation accuracy • Vocabulary usage • Grammatical accuracy	• Basic functions (virtual meeting room) • Share screen (sharing of teachers' slides and internet information)
Interactive sentence-making exercises	• Teacher-student • Student-student (teacher acts as coach, students are active participants)	• Pronunciation accuracy • Vocabulary usage • Grammatical accuracy	• Basic functions • Share screen (sharing of teachers' slides)
Debate and topical presentation	• Student-student • Teacher-student (teacher acts as coach and moderator, students are active participants)	• Pronunciation accuracy • Vocabulary usage • Grammatical accuracy • Appropriate language use	• Basic functions • Breakout room • Share screen (sharing of teachers' slides, tables and charts, students' notes and internet information)
Role-playing	• Student-student • Teacher-student (teacher acts as coach and moderator, students are active participants)	• Pronunciation accuracy • Vocabulary usage • Grammatical accuracy • Appropriate language use	• Basic functions • Breakout room • Polling • Share screen (sharing of teachers' slides, tables and charts, students' notes and internet information)
Language games: Pictionary (猜猜畫畫)	• Student-student • Teacher-student (teacher acts as coach and moderator, students are active participants)	• Pronunciation accuracy • Vocabulary usage	• Basic functions • White board • Share screen (sharing of teachers' slides)

(continued)

Table 10.1 (continued)

Language activities	Interaction mode	Skills trained	Functions of Zoom involved
Language games: Sentence rely (接龍)	* Student-student * Teacher-student (teacher acts as coach and moderator, students are active participants)	* Pronunciation accuracy * Vocabulary usage * Grammatical accuracy	* Basic functions * Share screen (sharing of teachers' slides)

"Question and answer drills" and "interactive sentence making exercises" in face-to-face classrooms could be adopted in synchronous online teaching. Teachers shared their slides and give instructions using the share screen function in Zoom. Both teacher-student and student-student interaction were carried out in the virtual meeting room.

The "breakout room" function in Zoom allowed teachers to group students for small-group activities. Students concentrated with group members in the "breakout room" without being influenced by other groups. Students discussed and worked out their presentation notes, and even presentation slides, collaboratively inside breakout rooms and presented to the whole class during the presentation session. Collaborative language activities, such as small-group role-playing, topical presentation, as well as debates (especially for intermediate- and advanced-level classes), were developed to utilize the "breakout room" function of Zoom. Teachers entered to different breakout rooms in the virtual classroom and acted as coaches to assist students in case of difficulties and answer questions. In addition to teacher's feedback after students' presentation, the polling function of Zoom can be used for simple peer-assessment. Collaborative tasks created interactive peer-learning environment and fostered peer-assistance (Chiu, 2000; Harding-Smith, 1993; Lee & Chen, 2013; Smith & MacGregor, 1992).

Synchronous online teaching platforms also suffice for some kind of language games. Among the interactive games, two language games, "Pictionary (猜猜畫畫)" and "Sentence rely (接龍)", were tested in synchronous online teaching platform. "Pictionary (猜猜畫畫)", as a language activity, developed from the table game "Pictionary". Students were separated into groups. One group was given a lexical item or a sentence by the teacher and they drew related information in the "white board". Other student groups were trying to think and guess the lexical items or sentences.

"Sentence rely (接龍)" works when practicing complex sentence structures, which consist of an independent clause plus a dependent clause. Complex sentence structures include but not limited to 雖然 … 但是 … (…, but …), 因爲 … 所以 … (because …, therefore …), 如果 … 就 … (if …, then), 一面 … 一面 … (… when/while …) and so on. In synchronous online platforms, one student (or group) can start with the independent clause while the next student (or group) continues with the dependent clause to complete the meaning. "Sentence rely (接龍)" also applied to students' collaborative work on language scenarios, such as 旅遊計劃 (travel plan), 我的一天 (my day), 怎樣去 … (how to go to …). Teachers acted as moderators and coaches during the activity. Student or student group continued the narratives or instructions in order to complete the stories or language tasks. These two language games used schemata, which outlined a general conception to be presented to the mind, for students to revise and practice lexical items and sentence structures, especially grammatical patterns showing preceding-succeeding events and cause-effect relationship.

6 A Paradigm Shift: New Perceptions of Students and Instructors

An abridged version survey of Lee (2016) was conducted in April 2020 to examine whether there were changes in students' e-learning habit and expectations after the implementation of synchronous online teaching during the social incident period in 2019 and the pandemic period since January 2020. Due to COVID-19, the survey was run in a smaller scale with online questionnaire sent via email and focus group meeting held via Zoom.

One-hundred questionnaires were sent out to students in CSL courses at the university. The questionnaire survey examined students' learning habit with synchronous online CSL learning and their expectations. Fifty-two valid questionnaires were returned with a return rate of about

52%. Of the 52 questionnaires, 35 were local students from Hong Kong and 17 were non-local undergraduate students who came from different areas, such as America, England, Japan, Korea, Indonesia, India and different parts of Mainland China. At the end of each post-course questionnaire, respondents were invited to focus group discussions. Six students (including three local students and three non-local students) attended the focus group discussion arranged online via Zoom.

The survey shows a paradigm shift of students' expectations of using online technology in CSL learning. Students' expectations about different language skills to be trained in ICT, there were some significant changes when comparing to Lee (2016) survey. Similar to Lee (2016), listening comprehension skills was ranked as the first set of skills that students (92.1%) were willing to use ICT device to practice. However, speaking skills (89.5%) was ranked second, in contrast to its fourth place ranked in the survey of Lee (2016). This shows that students were more willing to practice speaking skills using ICT after the implementation of synchronous online teaching. The language activities and the two language games discussed in last section were tested effective when operated in synchronous online teaching platform. The focus group data showed that students reported to have more opportunities to talk in synchronous online teaching platform.

> *I think we all need this class more. (Student D)*

> *I love this class. This is so so good. Practicing parsing the stories is useful for me, but this is the place in Cantonese where I'm weakest: sentence production and it does nothing but force me to do it for hours. (Student F)*

The focus group data also showed students appreciated the "chat room" (text chat) function of Zoom. A sample is provided in Appendix to demonstrate in-class chat conversation using personal message (PM) function in a Cantonese as a second language class. This in-class text-chat conversation extract contains teacher-student communication in English and in Cantonese (with Yale-Romanization). Teachers can deal with students with different needs, learning pace and questions without interrupting class time.

A focus group discussion session was also organized with 23 CSL teachers via Zoom during the pandemic period. Basically CSL teachers were positive about using synchronous online teaching for CSL. Teachers could handle most of the technical operations for their classes and classes were finished according to the planned curriculum and schedule; however they requested training and discussion on pedagogical issues in order to look for effective communication via synchronous online teaching. In the literature, there were studies focusing on the communication patterns in face-to-face language classrooms (Garton, 2012; Ingram & Elliott, 2014; Seedhouse, 2004) and effective language activities in physical classrooms (Jin, 2006; Lee & Chen, 2013).

7 Final Reflection on Language Teaching and Future Possibilities

UNESCO (2020) pointed out that one and a half billion people are deprived of education due to the COVID-19 pandemic and that traditional education shifted to different versions of online education dramatically. It is observed that some mistakes are inevitable and some teachers, students and even parents are not aware of the pedagogical shift related to distance education. Although it was difficult to predict the outcomes of this pedagogical shift with accuracy, there was a massive demand to use technology in education; it was able to observe teachers' and students' self-discipline and the immediate responses of supportive groups to deal with technological and pedagogical issues.

According to Hodges et al. (2020), what was happening worldwide during the pandemic in education can be known as Emergency Remote Teaching (ERT). The term indicated "a temporary shift to an alternate delivery mode due to critical circumstances". ERT actively restored education in areas challenged by manmade or natural disasters. During the pandemic period, educators saw the needs to build teams of experienced teachers in each country/region to take over in the crisis. ERT provided important solutions in education. ERT not only delivered educational content to students but also support students' learning and development during the time of crisis (Bozkurt & Sharma, 2020). The educational values produced by ERT were far-reaching and positively affected students' motivation and perceptions toward educational principles. Teams of ERT teachers also supported the teaching process in very isolated areas, where the physical presence of an instructor was almost impossible. ERT can not only continue to sustain educational process, but also can create new job opportunities for teachers and supporting teams to improve educational services at regional, national and international levels. ERT should gradually and eventually lead to mature distance education, more blended teaching options in order to fulfill the educational needs beyond the current crisis. ERT experience can be incorporated into e-learning design in the long run. Rethinking and further researching some moderating factors (Means et al., 2014), such as online communication synchrony, pedagogy, modality, pacing, roles of online assessment, sources of feedback, student-teacher ratio, teachers' and students' roles online, can have far-reaching contributions in aspects of language teaching practices, such as curriculum design (for distance language education, blended teaching etc.), teaching materials development, assessment as well as teachers' training.

To conclude, the study presented in this chapter showed that the contingency strategies and experience were important and threw some light on the development of e-learning in language education. It is suggested to focus only on benefits of this pedagogical shift, and retain the best practices to improve our planning and design for the future. This study showed that there are potential strengths of synchronous online language teaching as well as the possibility of adopting blended teaching and learning in the long run. Further systematic research on teacher-student communication patterns as well as different effective language activities to be used in synchronous online teaching platform in CSL and in language education are needed. The global crisis, in fact, speeded up the development of e-learning in language education.

Appendix

A sample to show in-class chat conversations

09:03:15	Teacher to student A (PM)	Hi, just reply your email. See if you need more explanation.
09:10:48	Student A to teacher (PM)	Mgōi
09:41:06	Student B to teacher (PM)	How do you say polite in Cantonese?
10:49:50	Teacher to student B (PM)	yáuh láihmaauh 有禮貌= polite; móuh láihmaauh 冇禮貌 = not polite
11:30:33	Student C to teacher (PM)	Is there any meaning difference between gāmyaht móuh lohk yúh 今日冇落雨 vs gāmyaht móuh yúh lohk 今日冇雨落?
11:31:45	Teacher to student C (PM)	gāmyaht móuh lohk yúh would mean "it didn't rain today"
11:32:18	Teacher to student C (PM)	gāmyaht móuh yúh lohk, I would translate as "there is no rain today"
11:32:26	Teacher to student C (PM)	Good question!
11:33:32	Student C to teacher (PM)	I see. so it's slightly different when in use.
11:34:16	Teacher to student C (PM)	Yes
11:34:41	Student C to teacher (PM)	Thanks, and sorry one more thing. page 135 gam āam dihnwá móuh dihn ā ma! 咁啱電話冇電吖嗎! here gam is still meaning "so"?
11:35:16	Teacher to student C (PM)	gam āam is "by coincident"
11:35:25	Teacher to student C (PM)	Or "just"
11:36:09	Student C to teacher (PM)	So here in this sentence, it's coincident meaning?
11:36:38	Student C to teacher (PM)	If you put just āam āam 啱啱instead, it would mean "just now I had no bettery?"
11:38:19	Teacher to student C (PM)	Yes
11:40:36	Student C to teacher (PM)	I see, yìhgā mìhng la. mgōi saai, Lóuhsī! (now I understand. thank you teacher!)

References

Bozkurt, A., & Sharma, R. C. (2020). Emergency remote teaching in a time of global crisis due to CoronaVirus pandemic. *Asian Journal of Distance Education, 15*(1), 1–6.

Butler-Pascoe, M. E. (2011). The history of CALL: the intertwining paths of technology and second/foreign language teaching. *International Journal of Computer-Assisted Language Learning and Teaching, 1*(1), 16–32.

Chiu, M. M. (2000). Group problem solving processes: Social interactions and individual actions. *Journal for the Theory of Social Behavior, 30*(1), 26–49.

Garton, S. (2012). Speaking out of turn? Taking the initiative in teacher-fronted classroom interaction. *Classroom Discourse, 3*(1), 29–45.

Harding-Smith, T. (1993). *Learning together: An introduction to collaborative learning.* Harper Collins College Publishers.

Hodges, C., Moore, S., Lockee, B., Trust, T., & Bond, A. (2020, March 27). The difference between emergency remote teaching and online learning. *Educause Review.* https://er.educause.edu/articles/2020/3/the-difference-between-emergency-remote-teaching-and-online-learning

Hoopingarner, D. (2009). Best practices in technology and language teaching. *Language and Linguistics Compass, 3*, 222–235. https://doi.org/10.1111/j.1749-818X.2008.00123.x

Ingram, J., & Elliott, V. (2014). Turn taking and 'wait time' in classroom interactions. *Journal of Pragmatics, 62*, 1–12.

Jin, H. (2006). Interaction of group work and investigating teaching mode. In T. Yao (Ed.), *Chinese language instructional materials and pedagogy.* Beijing Language and Culture University Press.

King, I. (2016, July 29). E-learning is the way forward for quality education. *South China Morning Post.*

Lee, S. (2011). Online components for advanced Chinese reading classes 高班閱讀課的網上課件. *Journal of Technology and Chinese Language Teaching, 2*, 1–22.

Lee, S. (2015). Revisit role-playing activities in foreign language teaching and learning: Remodeling learners' cultural identity? *Electronic Journal of Foreign Language Teaching, 12*(1), 346–359.

Lee, S. (2016). E-learning readiness in language learning: students' readiness survey and normalization process. *Journal of Technology and Chinese Language Teaching, 7*(2), 23–37.

Lee, S. (2018). Modular approaches in eLearning design. *Journal of Technology and Chinese Language Teaching, 9*, 48–61.

Lee, S., & Chen, Y. (2013). Effectiveness of collaborative language tasks in language teaching and learning. *Journal of Creative Practices in Language Learning and Teaching, 1*(1), 36–48.

Liu, S. (2018). Teaching and learning Chinese language online: What and why? *International Chinese Language Education, 3*(2), 11–26.

Means, B., Bakia, M., & Murphy, R. (2014). *Learning online: What research tells us about whether, when and how*. Routledge.

Seedhouse, P. (2004). The interactional architecture of the language classroom: A conversation analysis perspective. *Language Learning, 54*, x–300.

Smith, B. L., & MacGregor, J. T. (1992). *What is collaborative learning?*. National Center on Postsecondary Teaching, Learning, and Assessment at Pennsylvania State University.

Stickler, U., & Shi, L. (2013). Supporting Chinese speaking skills online. *System, 41*(1), 50–69. https://doi.org/10.1016/j.system.2012.12.001

The Chinese University of Hong Kong. (2019). *Facts and figures*. http://www.iso.cuhk.edu.hk/images/publication/facts-and-figures/2019/html5/english/24/

The Chinese University of Hong Kong. (2020). Learning's labour's lore. *CUHKUPDates*. http://www.iso.cuhk.edu.hk/english/publications/CUHKUPDates/article.aspx?articleid=2603

Tseng, M., Gao, Y., & Cai, L. (2019). Enhancing interaction through the effective incorporation of technology tools for a virtual Chinese language classroom. *Journal of Technology and Chinese Language Teaching, 10*(1), 91–113.

UNESCO. (2020, March 24). *Handbook on facilitating flexible learning during education disruption*. UNESCO Institute for Information Technologies in Education. https://iite.unesco.org/news/handbook-on-facilitating-flexible-learning-during-educational-disruption/

Zheng, H., Bao, H., & Chen, G. (2014). *E-learning in China*. SAGE.

Zimmerman, E. (2019, February 13). Google Classroom and Microsoft Teams for education: find the blended learning tool that works best. *EdTech*. https://edtechmagazine.com/k12/article/2019/02/google-classroom-and-microsoft-teams-education-find-blended-learning-tool-works-best-perfcon

11

Applying Empathy Theory in Online Chinese Language Education: Examples from a Chinese University

Chunxiang Song

1 Introduction: The Theory of Empathy and Its Applications

Empathy is the ability to feel each other's inner world, to experience each other's emotional experience, and to express one's understanding and appropriately care for each other (Lu, 2019). Empathy is a psychological concept initially proposed in the early 1940s by Carl Rogers (1902–1987), an American psychologist and one of the leading figures of the humanistic approach in psychology. He developed a distinctive point of view about psychotherapy which he presented in counseling and

---

This study is the result of a collaborative project of the Ministry of Education (202101121047). This study is also a phased result of the 2020 school-level education and teaching reform project of China University of Political Science and Law, entitled "Research on 'the Belt and Road Initiative' Legal Talents Training and Chinese Textbooks" (JG2020A014) and a phased result of the research project on the ideological and political work of teachers at China University of Political Science and Law "Research on the ideological status and cross cultural quality of Chinese as a foreign language teachers".

C. Song (✉)
China University of Political Science and Law, Beijing, China

psychotherapy (Zimring, 1994). Since 1941, through his psychological experiences and case studies, his concepts of "client-centered therapy" and "group therapy" have extended from psychotherapy to educational approaches, igniting spirited discussions in the West on "student-centered" educational approaches (Rogers, 1980, p. 7). Dr. Carl Rogers has received wide acclaim from educators for his psychological experiments, which advocated empathy and attention to personal emotions. His works included *A Way of Being* (1980) and *Carl Rogers on Encounter Groups* (2006). Other representatives of humanistic psychology include American psychologists Daniel Goleman, Cyndi Dale, and Arthur Ciaramicoli.

Based on psychological case studies, psychologists have identified several concepts related to the core principle of "empathy", including "sympathy", "empathic attitude", "empathic dialogue" and "empathic cognitive-behavioral therapy" (CBT), a form of therapy used to relieve stress (Ciaramicoli, 2017). These concepts point to the emotional field of the student and play a positive role in paying attention to the emotions of the student. As Ciaramicoli (2017) argues, at a certain level, the process of empathy is a form of virtual reality, where the surrounding world is viewed through the eyes of others. A good learning attitude can encourage students to learn and form a positive learning environment through effective communication. Börje Holmberg (2003) advocates the transition from the traditional didactic teaching method to having conversations between teachers and learners based on empathy in distance education. However, there is still no feasible solution on how to apply empathy theory in distance education, how to design teaching content and form, how to carry out interactive dialogue teaching between teachers and students, and many other issues. Therefore, analysis of the Theory of Empathy can be applied to international Chinese language education to help teachers better address issues that arise during classroom instruction.

The core theories of social emotion cannot be separated from the student or the teachers. Similarly, an analysis of the Theory of Empathy can be applied to international Chinese language education to help teachers more readily address issues that arise during classroom instruction. Technology-assisted education has provided unprecedentedly rich educational resources for teaching Chinese including diverse resources that integrate oral, visual, and verbal functions. On the other hand, there are some common challenges Chinese language learners facing with online classes such as technical issues, distractions and time management, and above all, lack of in-person interaction, which leads to the existence of varying degrees of emotional perception and "fine-tuning" issues with regard to students taking online Chinese lessons.

A case study on the reflection journals of 15 New Zealand students studied a short language immersion program in China has been conducted by Shouji Li (2020). Li used qualitative analysis methods to classify these students' emotions, and at the same time the relevant statistics were compiled to discover factors that lead to different emotional experiences among foreign students, such as the degree of success in using the language, expected learning outcomes, views on new teaching methods, and adaptative capacity. His results showed that the key to the learners' proactivity in learning lies in whether learners have the ability to manage their emotions or select more suitable learning strategies. Honglin Chen (2020) introduced issues regarding how social emotions affect current Chinese teaching, arguing that emphasizing "Empathy Education" not only allows teachers to discover if students need to make further academic improvements but also helps students establish right attitudes regarding learning. Similarly, Qing Xue (2020) explored issues related to the development and conduct of empathic online education and further discussed how emotions can be embedded into teaching and actions from the perspectives of student analysis, teaching activities, and collaborative learning to ultimately achieve the ideal result of transitioning from "empathy" to "joint action". Additionally, Xugang Zhao (2020) explored problems related to empathic education in language classes by introducing the concept of "empathy" and using basic teaching methods such as word formation exercises.

Due to COVID-19 online education has brought different degrees of anxiety and pressure to Chinese teachers and learners from all over the world. Research on methods for relieving these pressures through teaching with empathy and enhanced teaching quality is limited and has become issues that Chinese language educators need address urgently. Inevitably, it has drawn attention to empathy as a teaching theory.

Meanwhile, a key aspect of teaching is how to use the theory of empathy to make empathic education feasible, especially in terms of playing a positive role in student-teacher relationships and innovations to interactive teaching models.

Limited literature has been found on how to implement the empathy theory in online Chinese language teaching and learning. This chapter intends to provide some examples on application of empathy theory in both instructional activities and cocurricular and extracurricular activities in the following section.

2 Example Activities for Applying Empathy in Online Chinese Language Education

The China University of Political Science and Law has 68 international students majoring in Chinese at the undergraduate level. These students participated in a nearly year-long online course from February to December 2020. They are from 17 countries spread across continents including Asia, Africa, South America, and Europe. Time zones differences vary from 1.5 hours (Myanmar) to 13 hours (Ecuador) from these countries. Due to spatiotemporal factors, online Chinese language lessons are mainly carried out via the "Chaoxing" video platform, supported by the Tencent Meeting app, WeChat, and public email groups. Over the course of this period, the university held 36 Chinese online courses totaling 2072 class periods, during which 384 class periods (19%) were spent on "Developing Chinese" coursebooks (including elementary, intermediate, and advanced levels). This chapter focuses only on online Chinese courses, specifically introducing how multidisciplinary theories of empathy are applied to online learning and thus providing a model of reference for existing online Chinese language education.

2.1 Instructional Activities and Techniques

Vocabulary and Textbook-Related Activities

In the first lesson of the textbook titled *Developing Chinese: Elementary Reading and Writing II*, the cultural vocabulary is related to "home". The Chinese character "家 (Jia, home)" is used to form words and sentences. Given the fact that many students were confined to their homes due to the COVID-19 pandemic, cultural sharing activities based on the Chinese character Jia (家) ("home") were conducted primarily online. These activities aimed to help students understand China through Chinese characters and appreciate the humanistic connotations of Chinese characters. During word formation and sharing activities, a series of Chinese words associated with harmony including the character Jia (家) were selected to improve students' understanding of the cultural connotations of Chinese characters. For instance, characters such as Jia (家), An (安), and Hao (好) were used as root linguistic components to help students understand the "family" culture embodied in Chinese characters. This allowed students to deepen their understanding of the cultural connotations of Chinese characters. Figure 11.1 shows a mind map of lesson design and plans.

- "+家[jiā]": 回家 [huí jiā] go home; be home; return home; 在家 [zài jiā] be at home; 爱家 [ài jiā] love home; love family; 人家 [rén jiā] household.
- "家[jiā]+": 家庭 [jiā tíng] family; 家人 [jiā rén] family member; 家园 [jiā yuán] homeland; homestead; hearth and home; 家乡 [jiā xiāng] hometown; homeplace; native place.

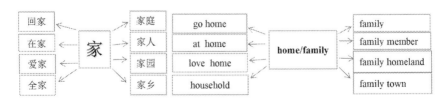

Fig. 11.1 Mind map for Chinese word formation during online lessons

"安[ān]+": 安家[ān jiā] set up a home; settle down; 安全[ān quán]safe; secure; safety; security; 安心[ān xīn] feel at ease; be relieved; set one's mind at rest; 安乐[ān lè] peace and happiness; peaceful and happy

"+安[ān]": 早安[zǎo ān]good morning; 午安[wǔ ān]good afternoon; 晚安[wǎn ān]good night; 平安[píng ān]safe and sound; without mishap; well.

"好[hǎo]+": 好人[hǎo rén]good person; a healthy person; a person who tries to get along with everyone; 好事[hǎo shì]good deed; good turn; 好心[hǎo xīn]good intention; 好话 [hǎo huà]a good word; word of praise.

"+好[ān]": 问好 [wèn hǎo] send one's regards to; say hello to; 祝好 [zhù hǎo] Good luck; 美好 [měi hǎo]fine; happy; 友好 [yǒu hǎo] close friend; friendly.

The lesson in that book, from words, texts to cultural learning, is filled with messages of family culture and good wishes for peace and safety. For example, there is a new word "安心" (*Anxin*, ease of mind) and the cultural phrase of 既来之则安之 (*Ji Laizhi, Ze Anzhi*, [back translation: since one has come, one should find peace of mind]). The content of the first lesson quotes the lyrics of songs and makes a new adaptation, (中文: 送你送到中国来，有几句话要交代: 记住我的情，记住我的爱，记住有我在等待。认真学汉语，安心学汉语，等你回来教汉语。)[1] "*I will send you to China with a few words of advice: Remember my affection, remember my love, and remember that I am waiting. Earnestly learn Chinese, learn Chinese with peace of mind, and I am waiting for you to come back and teach Chinese.*" This content coincided with the online, stay-in learning context at that time, providing the corpus and context for empathy-based online teaching.

Empathetic Language "re-reporting" Techniques

Based on factors such as the number of learners and their available time, the empathic concept of "using language to describe language" can be

---

[1] Note: please refer to the text of the first lesson of primary reading and Writing II, a series of textbooks of developing Chinese published by Beijing Language and Culture University Press.

applied during online courses. During these exercises, emphasis should be on student experience, and teachers should speak at a slower pace and "listen responsively". Online education adopts the reporting model, repeating sentences to achieve memorization and understanding. Based on the theory of empathy, learners can consolidate the linguistic points they learned through Q&A sessions. The dialogue between different learners can form an empathic dialogue chain via Q&A sessions with teachers. These questions and answers are oral. In this case, the oral dialogue of learners can eventually enable them to learn and understand the Chinese language.

Students who learn Chinese as a second language or a foreign langue may "report on other students' reports" under orderly guidance of teachers and in conjunction with their acquired linguistic knowledge during their class. These reports are presented orally in class, from A to B, from B to C, from C to D. Finally, from N to A, repeat any discovered knowledge and understand each other's meaning through a circular relay (Table 11.1).

Techniques on Empathic Listening and Online Interaction

The empathetic communication between learners and teachers is carried out in three ways: (1) reading textual materials provided by teachers, (2) listening to and repeating the audio materials provided by teachers, and (3) watching the visual materials provided by teachers; subsequently learners make evaluations and responses to those teaching resources and submit their reading audios and videos as homework or discussions. In this scenario, teachers and students are listeners or readers to each other. Teachers and students achieve two-way interaction and online empathic education through reading and listening to each other.

In online teaching activities, one way of creating empathy between teachers and students is when the teachers read, and the students listen. By hearing the voice of the teacher, the emotional distance between teacher and student is shortened. This is the ideal goal of empathy education. Requirements for "Students Read while Teachers Listen": Read the text aloud and record it and then upload the file in MP3 or MP4 format

Table 11.1 Language "Re-reporting" models for Chinese language learners[a]

Topic	Sports and exercise	Chinese food
Examples	They enjoy sports.	They enjoy preparing Chinese food.
Empathic utterances After Oral Compositions	He likes all sports. He is a person who loves sports./I enjoy skiing in China and Russia./I can teach you to ski./I was once a professional athlete; now [sports] are a hobby./None of us know how to ski; you can teach us./I enjoyed badminton when I was young; I don't play anymore./He enjoys soccer./I enjoy badminton./I do not like sports./He does not like sports, without any reason whatsoever./I enjoy jogging and wrestling.	I do not know how to prepare Chinese food. But, I enjoy Chinese food./I know how to prepare Chinese food./I also know how to prepare Uzbekistani food./I know how to prepare Turkish food./I know how to prepare Spanish food./I know how to prepare Japanese food: instant noodles./I know how to prepare Chinese food too./Teacher, do you know how to prepare Chinese food?/Teacher, what dishes do you know?/I know a Chinese dish: Kung Pao chicken./Let us all go to Beijing for Chinese food.

[a] These sentences from oral compositions that were generated after reading are compiled from audio recordings of online lessons conducted through live streaming

to the homework area of online Learning Management Systems. Apart from livestreaming videos, teachers need to make sure teaching resources such as included mp3/mp4 videos and PPTs available to learners at all times. During independent learning activities learners in different locations and at different learning levels could see and hear teachers' audio and video recordings, this proved to be a very efficient communicative method, wherein the smiles and voices of teachers in these videos conveyed their emotional greetings. Furthermore, the appropriate addition of facial expressions, music, or a change of clothes would bring new oral and visual experiences to Chinese language learners, to enhance online interactions between teachers and students.

"Empathetic Listening" and Encouraging Feedback

"Empathic listening" is a form of "empathic dialogue", where empathic dialogue originates from the "empathic attitude" of the Chinese language teaches. Teachers need to engage in verbal communication with students to convey emotion, which in return provide them an opportunity to receive verbal feedback from students. Thus, through student task evaluations, teachers can obtain a better understanding of the needs of online learners, design scientific and effective teaching activities in a timely manner, and improve their teaching quality. Empathic dialogue is the attainment of "reciprocity", the process of giving and taking. In the "Comments" section of the online Chinese teaching platform, teachers not only correct errors in Chinese pronunciation but also incorporate positive words and encourage students such as "A great improvement from the last time!", "Awesome!" and "Looking forward to reading aloud next time." Therefore, this achieves instant text-based interaction and in-depth communication. In consideration of individual students who struggle from personal issues, individual visits, and online contact should be conducted to carry out further one-on-one teaching and after-school counseling activities, in order to achieve a more efficient communication and increase student motivation and engagement.

2.2 Cocurricular and Extracurricular Activities

It is understandable that the COVID-19 pandemic resulted in various negative emotions such as anxiety and tension of learners and special consideration and support should be provided to students. Therefore, the author together with other four Chinese language instructors of the University have organized a series of "Fun-Language Salon" activities between April and May of 2020, with the purpose of helping students to stay connected when everyone is physically separated from each other. Each Friday, international students participated as live streamers in online classrooms, where they become active rather than passive learners. In these settings, they shared their feelings through empathic reading

Table 11.2 Summary of the "Fun-Language Salon" activities

Time	Subject	Sharing method	Culture
First Session April 24, 2020	Chinese and Western dragons	"Online Chats"	Appreciation of Chinese and Western culture
Second Session May 1, 2020	Distant lands, my home	"Online Reading"	Sharing the beauty of Chinese
Third Session May 8, 2020	Understanding China through film	"Online Viewing"	Approaching Chinese cinema
Fourth Session May 15, 2020	Secrets of brands	"Online Translation"	Interpreting wisdom found in the Chinese language
Fifth Session May 22, 2020	The "Four Seas"—A panorama of world cultures	"Online Tours"	An overview of world cultures

experiences for achieving mutual understanding and joint learning. Total five activities were organized, which are summarized below (Table 11.2).

For example, through the topic of "longing for home", to define "my home" and "foreign lands", and similarities within differences in cross-cultural communication were highlighted: homesick is something experienced by all people regardless of their nationalities. This comprised a focal point of shared emotions that gave foreign students with free space for deeper sharing and room for abstract thinking. This facilitates students to analyze and link emotional themes in Chinese to similar timeless texts and achieve an empathic experience. To create an environment for sharing and highlight "significant form", individualized posters were created by every student participating in the reading exercise to build an individual and common sense of presence. Additionally, integration of graphics and texts was achieved through structural, phonetic, and lexical characteristics of Chinese characters. Students were introduced to the character 乡 (*Xiang*, village; hometown) after 家 (*Jia*), and then guided in comparing the similarities and differences between the words 家乡 (*Jiaxiang*) and 故乡 (*Guxiang*) to emphasize the delicate connotations behind the word 家乡 (Jiaxiang) in Chinese and establish a deep emotional resonance—to love your family and hometown.

In international Chinese language education, there is a need to develop a community of learners among students studying Chinese as a second language through an educational model entirely different from in-person instruction under the guidance of teachers. For learners, learning involves a transfer from previous experiences (Bransford, 2013, p. 60). Online Chinese lessons are significantly different from classroom instruction. In the online learning environment, which is very different from that previously experienced, a learner's inherent tendency is to compare, to reflect, and emotional transfer will reinforce the inconveniences of online lessons. For example, learners prefer face-to-face classroom teaching, which exposes certain disadvantages of online learning, thereby influences the conduct of online lessons. To address the disadvantages of online lessons, the Chinese reading and writing course conducted sharing and discussion activities themed "home-based learning". The empathy theory advocates interaction and dialogue with each other and the ability to gain understanding and consensus from mutual experiences. This is particularly important when teaching is undertaking remotely via digital platforms while students learn at home. Obsessed by the similar psychological anxiety, a communication platform is necessary to establish to understand each other's learning and psychological feelings about common topics, to bring in efficiency and effectiveness of online teaching and enhance teaching efficacy and learning quality.

3 The Role of Teachers and an Empathetic Model in Online Chinese Language Education

3.1 Role of Teachers in Teaching Online with Empathy

In online teaching environment, the form of teaching has changed. After professional training, Chinese teachers need to understand their new roles and personally practice online teaching.

Team Leaders (one-to-many): The role of online Chinese language instructors is analogous to the "T-Group" in psychotherapy, and what we commonly term as online group lessons. In this model, teachers act as the guides to many different Chinese language learners, where they focus more on acting as directors and organizers. As they put themselves in students' shoes, teachers should provide positive feedback on their progress in reading and writing during active reading and listening. They should use positive language to provide learners with adequate affirmation and encouragement to promote motivation and encourage them to complete online discussion and sharing activities.

Counselor (one-to-one): The role of these teachers is more inclined toward addressing students' questions on the course material, analogous to the "one-on-one therapeutic relationship" in psychological diagnosis and treatment interviews. Targeted individual attention allows interaction and dialogue between teachers and students to be more honest, private, and harmonized. The main purpose is to adapt to the tendency of each Chinese language learner to actualize his or her potential, provide an environment to facilitate their personal development, and thereby achieve constructive outcomes (Rogers, 1980, p. 104).

Interlocutors ("One-to-one" hotline operators): A dedicated group of Chinese language teachers are always available to discuss various questions with students, including knowledge-type queries and non-knowledge-type queries, especially technical inquiries and personal problems. Undoubtedly, this tests the ability of Chinese language teachers to play multiple roles. The teacher should have the ability to teach with empathy. Relevant questions can only be adequately answered and a solution might be reached when a teacher knows how to put him/herself in the student's shoes. Comments and feedback should emphasize interaction and empathy on the part of the teacher—both the teacher and the student should be "present". Use the "empathic design" of essay comments as an example: On the topic of the coronavirus—"I am just as anxious as you are right now"; on the topic of "Chinese is hard to learn online"—"trust your teacher, believe in yourself, and let's work hard together!"; on the topic of childhood—"I had the same childhood experiences like you had"; on the topic of food—"you are a gourmet of Chinese cuisine"; on the topic of "hometown"—"our hometowns will always be in our hearts", and so on. Comments should be carefully designed and sincerely conveyed by Chinese language teachers so that no learner should be ignored or neglected. This serves to constantly encourage students, meet their individual learning needs, and promote their motivation and enthusiasm for deeper learning.

During online lessons, Chinese language teachers should put themselves in students' shoes and try to understand their difficulties and feelings. Teachers should have the ability to empathize with his/her students and help students in their own learning journeys. In the online world where opportunities for empathy are boundless, both teachers and students will find that this world is more humanistic and more humane (Rogers, Carl Rogers on Encounter Groups, Rogers, 2006).

3.2 A Suggested Empathic Model of Online Chinese Language Education

In comparison with teaching face-to-face, teaching Chinese language online needs to have a much more substantial understanding of the psychological qualities and learning needs of Chinese language learners. Mutual understanding becomes even more important, especially when facing unpredictable challenges and difficulties such as technological issues, time differences, computer literacy, and self-motivation. Knowledge of the Chinese language is not sufficient for teaching online lessons. Instructors need to have a good understanding of psychology, knowledge of positive communication techniques, consciously practicing empathy, and involving in student's emotional development. These qualities could potentially break through the negative mindset that "it is difficult to teach Chinese online".

Figure 11.2 is a visualized model of empathy in online Chinese language education. As it shows that teaching Chinese language online requires both expertise in their professional field as well as extensive knowledge of multidisciplinary teaching methods. Chinese language instructors need to internalize the psychological theory of empathy as a pedagogical principle.

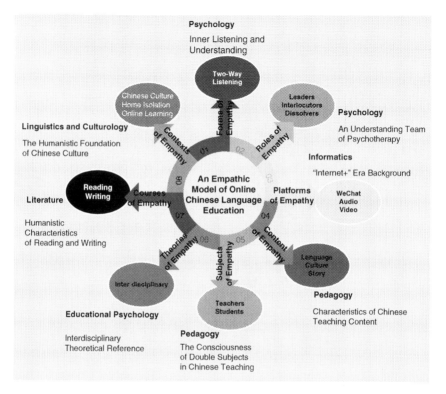

Fig. 11.2 An empathic model of online Chinese language education

4 Conclusion

In short, empathy theory helps to solve the issue of teacher-student interaction in an online Chinese teaching environment, achieve effective emotional communication between teachers and students, and gain a better understanding of the rich Chinese culture. The concept of empathy plays a positive role in the existing empathy teaching both inside and outside the classroom. In the post-pandemic era, international Chinese education especially needs cross-cultural engagement and communication. Online teaching with empathy and cultural exchange activities will continue. For the frontline teaching work, the perceived need to accelerate innovation in online learning is required, the professional development and continuous improvement of Chinese teaching quality should be further analyzed and researched, so that the interdisciplinary theoretical knowledge of pedagogy and psychology can be utilized to evaluate the learning behavior of Chinese language learners, clarify the role of teachers, and keep on improving the design of the optimal teaching form, to better serve the international Chinese education.

References

Bransford, J. B. (2013). *How people learn: Brain, mind, experience, and School* (Exp. ed., Vol. 1). (K. Cheng, Y. Sun, & X. Wang, Trans.). East China Normal University Press Ltd.

Chen, H. (2020). The influence of social emotion on teaching Chinese as a foreign language. *International Public Relations, 11*, 97–98.

Ciaramicoli, A. (2017). *The Stress Solution* (Vol. 3). (G. Mo, Trans.) Beijing United Publishing Co. Ltd.

Holmberg, B. (2003). Distance education based on empathy theory. In M. Moore & W. Anderson (Eds.), *Handbook of distance education* (pp. 79–86). Lawrence Erlbaum Associates.

Li, S. J. (2020). A Study on the relationship between learners' emotion and learning autonomy. *Journal of International Chinese Teaching, 3*, 56–64.

Lu, X. (2019). On children's empathy education. *Contemporary Family Education, 33*, 181–182.

Rogers, C. R. (1980). *A Way of being* (M. Shi, D. Zou, & Y. Zhang, Trans.). Houghton Mifflin.

Rogers, C. R. (2006). *Carl Rogers on encounter groups* (4th ed.). (B. Zhang, Trans.). China Renmin University Press.

Xue, Q. (2020). Construction and practice of empathy classroom in online teaching. *Computer Education, 10*, 28–31.

Zhao, X. (2020). The realization of empathy teaching in Chinese teaching. *Chinese Teaching and Research, 18*, 107–108.

Zimring, F. (1994). Carl Rogers (1902–1987). *The quarterly review of comparative education* (Paris, UNESCO: International Bureau of Education), vol. XXIV, no. 3/4, 1994, 411–422.

12

From Flipped/Blended to Fully Online: Lessons Learned and Strategies for the Future

Shenglan Zhang

1 Introduction

After spring break in March 2020, COVID-19 precautions meant that all courses at Iowa State University were moved fully online. This chapter reflects on the way two courses (a beginning-level course and an intermediate-level course) were successfully transformed from flipped/blended format to fully online format and suggests effective methods for future online language courses. Course components that were effective and those that presented challenges for students are identified. In addition, several methods are presented for designing foreign language courses online using a flipped format that would allow instructors to respond flexibly to similar challenges in the future.

This chapter is divided into four sections. The first section gives a description of the original flipped/blended courses. This overview

---

S. Zhang (✉)
Iowa State University, Ames, IA, USA
e-mail: shenglan@iastate.edu

provides a background for the transition process and the proposed redesign. Section two records the transition and integration process. The description of this process illustrates the approaches, activities, and technologies that were effective, less effective, and/or problematic and discusses how the issues were addressed. Section three reports student feedback. At the end of the semester, the instructor conducted a Zoom interview with each student to gather their overall impressions on which course components were effective and which less effective. In section four, the suggested methods for future fully online courses are proposed. A design for a future fully online course is presented, based on the researcher's experience and students' feedback, including a set of suggested practices for online course design.

2 A Description of the Original Flipped/Blended Courses

In the program, the lower-division courses have multiple class sections. Different instructors teach different sections at the same pace but not necessarily using the same teaching strategies or the same course format. Some sections of the beginning-level and the intermediate-level courses have been taught in a flipped/blended mode for three years. Flipped learning (Bergmann & Sams, 2012; Flipped Learning Network, 2014) has been shown to be successful in terms of giving students flexibility and efficiency in learning (Keengwe et al., 2014; Stone, 2012; Talbert, 2017; Zhang et al., 2017; Zhang & Jaramillo, 2021). All these courses are four credit hours, and the enrollment in each section is between 12 and 25 students. The textbook *Integrated Chinese* (the third edition) (IC) by Liu et al. (2009) is used in these courses.

The flipped/blended format is 3+1, that is, three face-to-face (FTF) meetings during the week and one asynchronous online component. This design was based on (1) Bloom's taxonomy of learning objectives and (2) the notion of receptive skills and productive skills in language learning. Bloom (1956) classifies the cognitive process of learning into six major categories starting from the simplest to the most complex. The six categories are knowledge, comprehension, application, analysis, synthesis, and evaluation. Bloom's guidelines were applied to determine what activities and assignments to put online. Online activities were designed to help learners enhance their knowledge, comprehension, and analysis of the content learned during FTF classroom time and to observe how their peers apply and synthesize what they have learned. Therefore, the activities that required simple learning processes are online, while content that focused on the more complex learning processes are taught in the FTF class meetings.

The notion of receptive and productive skills defines the different skill sets that are needed in language learning. The online components focused on improving the learners' receptive skills. The FTF instruction focused on the productive skills, which are more challenging to develop. Therefore, the FTF class meetings focused on speaking and writing, the two productive skill sets, the application and synthesis steps in Bloom's taxonomy. Speaking involves interaction among the learners and between the teacher and the learners. FTF is the most appropriate context for improving speaking skills. Due to the logographic feature of Chinese characters, Chinese writing, which presents a significant challenge to American students, also needs significant attention, especially at the beginning stages of Chinese learning. Drawing upon these two notions/theories, the class content was distributed to the different modalities, online and FTF, as follows (Table 12.1):

Table 12.1 Distribution of work online and FTF

Online (Thursdays/Friday/Weekend asynchronous)	Face-to-face (M, T, W)
* Vocabulary and grammar learning * Culture learning * Reading and listening comprehension practice * Using Open Educational Resources for supplemental learning (for intermediate level only)	* Speaking: – Pronunciation, conversation, self-expression * Writing: – Character writing (for beginners only), note writing, essay writing

2.1 The Design of the Online Components

Three different sets of videos were created using Camtasia and PowerPoint for the online components of the flipped/blended class (Zhang, 2018). The first set was an explanation of vocabulary and grammar. The length of each video varied between 7 and 15 minutes. These videos were designed and created based on Mayer's (2005) Cognitive Theory of Multimedia Learning (CTML). For each grammar point and word, the video provided explanation along with character, pinyin, and meaning and provided different examples that were used in different contexts with various images and animations. When the video presented challenging grammar, English was used in the video explanation. For the videos in the intermediate-level course, over 85% of teacher talk in the video was in Chinese. Following each important grammar point or important vocabulary word, there were activities for the students to do, such as writing down the answer to a question related to their real life, writing down the translation of a sentence related to the grammar they were learning, summarizing a linguistic phenomenon, and so on. For each chapter, there were two videos, one for each dialogue. (See Fig. 12.1 for a sample screen capture of the video.)

The second set of videos were short (about 31s to 1m 49s long) movies clips in which native speakers and advanced Chinese-as-a-Foreign-Language (CFL) learners acted out a scenario. The skits were based on what the students learned from each chapter and included the most important and the most challenging grammar points and new words.

Fig. 12.1 A screen capture of a video for the beginning-level course (left) and one for the intermediate-level course (right)

Not only did the skits use vocabulary and grammar that students were learning, but the skits were also funny and engaging. After the skits were written, the "actors," "actresses," and the researcher/instructor met to read and talk about each skit in depth before actors and students performed the skits and created the short movies. Each chapter had one to four movies.

While watching the two sets of videos, students were required to complete different tasks. For the first set of videos, they were asked to watch and take detailed notes; that is, they had to write down all the words and grammar points explained in the video with at least one or two examples in Chinese. In addition, they had to write down the answers to the questions embedded in the videos and write down any questions they might have for the teachers at the beginning of the FTF meeting on Monday. Their notes were graded by the instructor while the students took a quiz on the video's content in Monday's FTF class. The quiz also provided a check to see if the students had spent time viewing the video and reading the textbook.

For the second set of videos, that is, the short movies, the students were required to watch each video in groups or in pairs, transcribe it, write down their general views about the video, and create comprehension questions about the videos as if they were a teacher creating questions for their students.

The third set of videos were culture videos created by the researcher/instructor for the beginning-level courses only. Different topics such as education, calligraphy, hobbies, privacy, numbers, greetings, holidays, colors, and so on were addressed in the videos, along with a brief explanation of each topic using English with images. The videos were about 2–3 minutes long. One or two quiz questions each week came from the videos. These videos along with other supplemental materials were on the Canvas course site.

In the intermediate-level course, students were required to complete a different task: search for online resources, text, or multimedia texts to learn about the Chinese language or Chinese culture. The purpose of this task was to enable them to find useful resources for their self-regulated learning. See Appendix 1 for the form that they were required to fill out for this task.

2.2 The FTF Meetings

FTF meetings consisted largely of practicing speaking and sometimes writing. The learning process for a new chapter started on Thursdays (or Fridays/weekends) when the students were required to watch the videos. During the first FTF meeting on Mondays, the students asked questions they had about the videos, took a quiz (while the researcher/instructor checked and graded their notes), and then practiced speaking in pairs and groups, focusing on the grammar points and challenging vocabulary words introduced in the videos. During the second FTF meeting on Tuesdays, students started to create short dialogues using the vocabulary and the grammar they had learned in their pairs and in groups. During the third FTF meeting on Wednesdays, students practiced more comprehensive scenarios and completed writing exercises, either on the whiteboard or on their notebook.

2.3 Assignments and Assessments

Students had homework assignments starting on Monday. They first completed the listening and reading assignments in the workbook and then worked on the dialogue they were learning by Tuesday, and the grammar and written homework for the same dialogue by Wednesday. For the beginning-level course, students had VoiceThread activities to practice their pronunciation, tone, and formation of sentences. For all beginning-level to intermediate-level courses in the program, there was an after-class, one-on-one speaking session with an Undergraduate Native Speaker Assistant (UNSA).

Throughout the semester, a culture project was assigned during the second semester of the beginning-level courses and the intermediate-level courses. The projects were designed based on students' prior knowledge, available resources, and the social context. These projects included the following: (1) explore and research culture in small groups; (2) watch instructor-edited authentic movie clips, answer questions, and discuss online in small groups; (3) interview native speakers from China; and (4) reach out to the community to explore the language, the culture, and the people. Through these projects, the students had the opportunities to explore culture on the internet, on campus, and in the larger community (Zhang, 2019a, forthcoming; 2021).

Assessments included not only the Monday quizzes on each dialogue's vocabulary and grammar (and one or two items about the culture videos in the beginning-level courses), but also three exams, each of which had an oral section and a written section. The oral section was a group/pair performance task; that is, students wrote a skit together on a topic, asked native speakers to proof-read it, practiced it, and performed in front of the class with props without reading the skit. The written part consisted of grammar, translation, and reading comprehension which required them to be able to write characters. In addition, for both classes, students were required to write an essay after completing both the oral examination and the written examination.

3 The Transition and Integration Process

Three days before the spring break, the university decided that all classes would be taught online after spring break. From her prior experience, the researcher/instructor knew that online communication could be highly challenging and time consuming. She started planning right after being informed of the decision so that she could talk with her students about the plan before they left campus. She wanted to take advantage of the two FTF meetings left before break to help clarify for her students what class would be like and what would be expected of them when they met fully online. In addition, she also specified the formats their homework submission would need to follow after considering which submission formats were both convenient for the students to submit and for the instructor to grade. At that time, both classes had completed nine weeks' learning.

3.1 The Original Plan

Because these were language classes, practicing the four language skills remained the most important part of teaching and learning. To improve speaking and listening skills, the key is for students to have interaction with their teacher and their peers, to stay motivated, and to be purposeful in their practice. Therefore, synchronous meetings were adopted to replace the three FTF meetings. Zoom was chosen as the video-conference tool because it has all the functions needed for a successful class meeting such as breakout rooms, sharing screens, and so on.

Considering the size of the classes (14 students in beginning-level class and 17 in the intermediate-level class), the instructor was concerned that it would not be effective for student learning if all the students were hosted in one synchronous meeting. Therefore, she planned meetings in small groups of four or five students, with each group meeting for 15 minutes. Before their meeting time, each student would receive detailed information about how they needed to prepare to maximize the use of their time with the teacher and their group members. With this plan, the students were asked to form groups of 4–5 and sign up for the meeting time.

3.2 Transition

The transition period was short. Each day changes were made based on the practices the day before. During the first synchronous meeting, out of the five students, some were fully prepared, but most were not. The meeting did not go as expected; toward the end of the 15 minutes, the tasks the instructor had planned were not completed. When the next group started to join their meeting, the previous group had to leave, or the new group would be confused because they did not understand what was being done. Finishing the synchronous meetings for all groups required about 10 extra minutes beyond the scheduled class time. This experience showed that the small group synchronous meeting within a short time was not an ideal model. Furthermore, students expressed their opinions:

they would like to see all their class members with whom they had become familiar during the previous nine weeks. Class had to change.

Considering the unsuccessful experience with the first synchronous meeting and the students' feedback, the instructor decided that subsequent class meetings should be changed to whole class meetings. During the second meeting, all the class members were together. During the whole class meeting, the researcher/instructor guided the students to review the two chapters and practice some difficult words and grammar. Most importantly, the researcher/instructor encouraged the students to talk about their situation and how they felt in order to be sure that their feedback was incorporated into the class format and the teaching as the researcher/instructor explored the functions of Zoom as related to class meetings.

3.3 The Final Format

After the transition period of about one and a half weeks, the class format was settled. Each class section met four times a week as a whole class, Monday through Thursday. They still completed the asynchronous online component before coming to Monday's meeting. Each online synchronous meeting lasted 40 minutes.

Synchronous Meetings

Before the class started, every student was required to submit the notes they took while watching a required video on their own. A few minutes at the beginning of each meeting were spent talking about students' daily lives in Chinese or in English (depending on the skill level of the students). This small talk primarily addressed personal feelings and daily activities during the unique time. These discussions gave students a chance to communicate with their peers about their life, rather than only talking about their studies. (For most of the students, the Chinese class was the only class that met synchronously, and they really appreciated the opportunity to meet with their peers online.) The researcher/instructor also encouraged students to talk about the challenges they had with their learning and how they overcame the challenges.

During the formal learning, the researcher/instructor used mostly Chinese during the intermediate-level class meetings and about 80% in Chinese during the beginning-level class meetings. To ensure that all students at the beginning level were able to follow along, the researcher/instructor provided the English translation for some sentences that might have been too complicated for the students to understand. A word document (as a substitute for whiteboard in a physical classroom) was shared in Zoom. On this document, the instructor typed what she said in Chinese and the activities that were in process, the page numbers to turn to, and so on, to help students follow along. The students were not required to join the class with their video camera on; however, some students voluntarily used video. Those who used video seemed to be able to focus very well on tasks.

During the synchronous meetings, breakout rooms for pair and group work were used frequently. Sometimes students were randomly assigned to a group. At other times students of similar ability were assigned to the same breakout room so that they could talk more. The researcher/instructor tried her best to go to each room and see if they were on task and if they had questions.

In addition to practicing speaking in class, students also practiced writing, especially the beginning learners. They were asked to hand-write a short note in their notebook, then share the note with the class during the synchronous meeting. The problem with this approach was that it was very challenging to give feedback.

If there were things that students had questions about during class or if the researcher/instructor suspected that some students might be unclear about a topic, after class she sent the whole class an email clarifying to concepts and listing the tasks they needed to do after class.

Homework

Homework submission and grading became a significant challenge during the six weeks of online teaching. Students were encouraged to submit their homework online using whatever format they felt convenient and would make grading easy. As a result, most students tried their best to use the format that made their teacher's grading easier. They were required to submit assignments every day from Monday through Wednesday. The instructor used different methods for giving feedback, depending on the format in which students submitted the assignments. Giving students feedback in an electronic format, especially when students submitted their work in jpg/png/pdf formats, was very challenging. For example, the time spent on grading one student's homework using annotations in preview or pdf on a computer with no touchscreen function took at least five times longer than grading one student's paper homework submission. These time constraints made it difficult for the teacher to give feedback as promptly as she hoped. The feeling of getting buried in grading was overwhelming, and the thought that the students would not get timely feedback pushed her to find better ways.

The purpose of doing homework is to practice what the learners just learned and review what they learned in previous sessions. Submitting homework also holds the learner accountable. Feedback makes the learners aware of what they know or what they are able to do and what they do not know or what they are not able to do. Therefore, any new ways of collecting and grading homework should serve the purpose of completing, submitting, and getting feedback about the completed homework. Therefore, students were required to follow a few steps to ensure their learning through completion of the homework:

1) Submit homework by the due date.
2) Receive answer key.
3) Compare the key with their completed homework.
4) Write down all the mistakes they made, why they made the mistakes, and any questions they had.
5) Submit the summary of the mistakes and the reasons for those mistakes by another due date. The summary should not be vague, such as "I made a mistake in listening comprehension. I need to practice my listening more." The summary should be: "I thought … was true which was actually false because I misunderstood the use of the 无

论 … 都 …, this sentence xxx means …, which I mistakenly thought it meant."

In addition to the self-grading and reflection done by students, the researcher/instructor sent each student feedback on the notes they took when watching the videos, provided the answer to the questions they wrote down, and corrected mistakes in any example sentences in their notes. She encouraged students to submit their translation assignments, complicated written homework, and essays in MS Word format so she could use track changes to give feedback.

Assessments

The quizzes and the written exams became online open-book and open-note, with more items on the test than was the case for FTF classes. Most students could complete the tests with 85% or above accuracy, but if they did not learn outside of the tests, they could not do as well within the limited amount of time allowed for the assessments.

The spoken examination, which was originally a group assignment, had to be changed to an individual oral presentation. Due to the changes in the presentation format, the researcher/instructor redesigned the assignment so that students spent their time focusing on one assignment rather than multiple smaller assignments with different topics. Therefore, the students worked on the same topic in both the essay writing and the oral presentation. Since both the writing and the speaking focused on one topic, she had high expectations that students would do well on both tasks.

Projects

The Online Resources project in the intermediate-level class was successful. Although there was not time for students to share what they found with the entire class, they had a chance to talk with the instructor individually about what they discovered regarding online resources and what they planned to do in the future to continue learning on their own, either because there were no Chinese classes in the summer or because they had finished their formal learning of Chinese at the university.

Assistance

UNSAs for the classes provided virtual office hours so that students could practice speaking with them, in addition to the weekly one-on-one sessions originally scheduled. The instructor had office hours by appointment, but students did not utilize them often. Table 12.2 summarizes the comparison between the course before and after transition.

4 Student Feedback

To prepare well for the possibility of more fully online teaching in the future, the researcher/instructor conducted a short, individual interview with the students in both classes toward the end of the semester to get their feedback on the course. The interviews included their thoughts about (1) the projects/assignments and the methods for their delivery, (2) quizzes and exams, (3) synchronous meetings, and (4) challenges that they successfully addressed.

Generally speaking, all students were appreciative of the uneventful transition from a flipped/blended format to a fully online format. Most students said that out of all the courses they were taking, this course was the one that they liked the best and the one that transitioned most smoothly to fully online. They liked the fact that both the instructor and their peers were patient enough to explore the best ways to keep learning happening during the few days of transition. One student said to me,

> I can't imagine being on your end trying to figure all of this out. I think you've done a really good job. I really appreciate the effort that you put in. I've definitely still learned a ton in the online sessions. I have appreciated how you have changed things up when maybe things haven't gone as well.

Another student said,

Table 12.2 Comparison in course format before and after transition

	Before	After
Asynchronous online components	Videos on grammarVideos on vocabularyVideos on cultureShort movies on the use of challenging grammar and vocabulary	Videos on grammarVideos on vocabularyVideos on cultureShort movies on the use of challenging grammar and vocabulary
Accountability measures for learning online components	Note-takingQuizzesParticipation in class meeting	Note-takingQuizzesParticipation in class meeting
FTF focused on speaking and writing	Three 50-minute meetings per week	
Asynchronous meeting focused on speaking and writing		Four 40-minute meetings per week
Assignments submission and grading	Workbook on paper, teacher grading using red pen	Online submission twice (original completed work and comparison notes with answer keys), teacher grading completion of the two submissions
Assessments	Written: 50 minutes FTF closed book and closed notesSpoken: Group/pair work	Written: 50 minutes online with limited time but more test items, open book open notesSpoken: Individual
Projects	Yes	Remained the same
Assistance from UNSAs and instruction	Instruction office hours and one-on-one sessions with UNSAs	Instruction virtual office hours and UNSA virtual one-on-one sessions and office hours

[…] definitely for this circumstance that we are in, I think you made the most of having class, learning, and being productive. I'd say, out of all my classes, this one was the best and the one that was the most normal and consistent with what it was like on campus vs. not. … I think in this class I definitely continued my learning, and it really hasn't been hindered by having it online.

4.1 Course Structure

The students agreed that due to the flipped/blended feature of this course, the online transition turned out to be very easy, and the change did not affect their learning very much. They still were on time submitting their video notes, and their notes were still of the same high quality as before going online. Regarding the course structure, here are their views.

First, they liked the synchronous meetings not just for the purpose of learning by interacting and practicing their language skills but also for "being able to 'see' and hear other people's questions, just actually be together." One intermediate-level student said, "I know we were not in the classroom or together, but most of these people I have known for almost two years now. So, it is hard to not see them every day while you are still studying this."

Second, they liked the four synchronous meetings during the week plus one video watching session on their own. Since they had focused on speaking during the FTF meetings before the transition to fully online and the synchronous online meetings had the same speaking focus, class meetings felt almost the same as before the switch. When asked whether they preferred meeting three times a week for 50 minutes each meeting or meeting for four times a week for 40 minutes each meeting, most students liked the four times for 40 minutes option. The meeting time was shorter but more frequent, which gave them exposure to the language more frequently. However, some students said that if it were FTF, three times meeting would be the best because conflicts with other classes could be avoided.

Third, they appreciated the quick responses that the instructor provided when they had questions after class. The quick responses helped students who were dealing with several online courses be less frustrated. In addition, students appreciated the recap emails, which generally included assignment deadlines and requirements. Still, some beginning-level students mentioned that they did not find a comparable format to practice writing as they did in our FTF class when students were asked to write characters on the whiteboard.

4.2 Teaching Approach

All students appreciated the shared word document where the teacher wrote down notes and instructions during the synchronous meetings. These notes not only had the instructions for classroom activities but also most of the Chinese words, expressions, and sentences spoken by either the instructor or the students during the meetings. These notes gave them a very clear idea of what they were doing. They could see what the characters were and how they should express certain things in Chinese. These notes were an enormous help in their following along. Occasionally, due to tech problems, the students were unable to hear the instructor clearly, and sometimes the students got distracted by something else in their immediate environment. However, with the ongoing shared notes, students could get back on the right track very quickly. Additionally, students appreciated their instructor's repeating instructions when she thought that the students might have a hard time understanding them.

All students liked having breakout rooms. They enjoyed participating in speaking up in the whole class meetings, but breakout rooms gave them an opportunity to speak in Chinese in a more relaxing way. They "had less pressure to talk" with one or two peers rather than in front of the whole class. In addition, the breakout rooms to some degree made the online meeting more like having group discussion during the FTF meetings. One student put it this way:

> "[I]t (the breakout room) simulated being in the classroom, like, 'okay, grab a partner and talk about this' and again that makes it more normal and how we were always doing things."

Students liked how the time during the synchronous meetings was used. Students liked that they were called upon to answer questions and that sometimes the teacher waited for volunteers to answer questions. A few students expressed that it would be more efficient if the teacher called upon people to speak up all the time. One student said,

> [P]ersonally, I do not really want to speak up very much within Zoom calls but I'm more than happy to talk. So, I think, I'm trying, I mean, it's just

different than normal, I'm trying to be better at taking initiative and speaking up, but also, it's good when you call on people to. … When you call on me, I'm more than happy to read it or share my example, or whatever. It's just awkward, because I feel like, there is a pause, and everybody starts talking at once. You know, it's just weird being online. I think calling on people is fine too.

Another student commented,

[I]t's a little bit difficult—just not sure when I should jump in and speak or when other people are going to, but that's just the nature of doing synchronous meetings.

Most students appreciated that the instructor used as much Chinese as she perceived that the students would be able to understand if focused. Students said that most of their exposure to spoken Chinese happened during the synchronous meetings. They did not find much motivation to go to the UNSA sessions for extra practice, except for the required one-on-one sessions. So having the teacher talk in Chinese as much as possible greatly benefitted them in learning the language.

4.3 Assignments and Assessments

The students appreciated being given more time to complete the whole set of homework for a dialogue in the beginning-level class or one chapter for the intermediate-level class (for the week) rather than having different due dates for different parts of one set of homework for one chapter. They thought that "made it easier submission-wise by just doing it all in one," but "it definitely took more time management" on the students' end "of not just waiting till the last day." They perceived that the need for extra time management was a good way for them to grow. One student said, "[not just waiting till the last day to do the homework] was actually good because usually I do that, but I knew I couldn't with this one. It felt weird planning ahead, but I was able to effectively do that."

The students said that being given a finite amount of time to complete the quizzes and exams was beneficial for their learning because "if I had a large amount of time, I wouldn't study as much just because I would know that I could go back to look at my notes or watch the video or look at the book whatever. I can still do that with a finite amount of time but not for every question because I would run out of time." It "simulates most similarly to a normal classroom with having a finite amount of time, still needing to study, still needing to actually put effort prior to having the exam." One student said that she was anxious the first time taking the quiz within a finite amount of time because she was not good at typing Chinese, but "it worked out fine."

Two beginning-level students were not sure if the quizzes were useful because they could find all the answers in their notes or in the textbook. One student suggested replacing the quiz with a few questions at the end of each instructional video that they needed to answer by writing the responses down. The student suggested that the questions should be targeted at the most challenging elements in the video.

4.4 Students' Own Challenges

After the courses were put online, most students said that they had two challenges. One challenge was the lack of motivation to learn and the other was the lack of supportive environment. During the quarantine period, some students lacked structure in their days, and every day looked the same; therefore, the students had a hard time motivating themselves to excel at what they did.

Family members were supportive, but they sometimes did not understand what the student needed when they took an online course. For example, one student said that his parents and siblings would come over and ask him what he was doing and how he was taking an online course while he was synchronously having class. Sometimes students did not have a quiet place to take the class.

Other challenges included various tech problems. For example, one student did not have a stable internet connection at home. She had to go to relatives' and friends' homes to have the synchronous meetings. In this case, she was able to utilize some resources that the university was able to offer to her. She completed the course with a less-than-ideal grade, and she and the instructor felt she could have done better if she had a more supportive learning environment.

5 Future Plans for Flipped Online Courses

Flipped/blended learning during regular school semesters provides learners with flexibility in learning and allows the instructors to use the time during the FTF meetings to focus on speaking and writing (Zhang & Jaramillo, 2021; Zhang et al., 2017; Zhang, 2019b). When it was time to transition from flipped/blended to fully online, the transition proved to be less complicated and more natural than was true for those courses that were originally delivered fully FTF.

The flipped model of online courses in the last six weeks of the semester as described in this chapter seemed to provide students with both the opportunity for flexible learning—that is, learning on their own—and the opportunity to practice speaking skills and interact with a learning community. With enough preparation time, foreign language teachers can design, develop, and teach the fully online version of flipped/blended format courses well, with attention to the following seven critical points.

First, the 4s+1 course format is a good approach. Meeting more frequently for a shorter period of time could make learning more effective. The four-credit course could have four short synchronous meetings plus one asynchronous component. Meeting four times a week for 40 minutes at a time rather than meeting for three times a week for 50 minutes serves two purposes. (1) Being totally online and restrained at one's home creates the need for people to interact with others on a daily basis. In this situation, four meetings are better than three. (2) From the perspective of learning, more frequent synchronous meetings would give learners more chances to be exposed to the language and to practice speaking with others. Long online meetings can sometimes lead to disengaged learners.

Second, grammar, vocabulary, and culture explanations could be made into videos, and students could be required to watch them with measures put in place to ensure that they watch the videos closely. Creating these videos is a time-consuming process. It requires careful design, bearing in mind the CTML (Mayer, 2009, 2014) (for course/activity design examples, see Lan et al., 2015; Li, 2014; Wang & Crooks, 2015; Zhang, 2017, 2019a, 2019b). These videos should be short, concise, accurate, and engaging. Students tend to focus their attention for a limited amount of time when watching a video; therefore, the maximum length of any video should not exceed 15 minutes. It would be the best for any longer videos to be made into two or three 5- to 6-minute videos.

Because having a good understanding of the videos' content is critical for the practice sessions that take place during the four synchronous meetings, it is very important that the students watch the videos before the first meeting. There are at least three possible ways to hold the learners accountable for watching those videos. First, after explaining the use of challenging words or grammar points, instructors could insert questions in the video and require students to answer those questions in their notebook. Second, instructors could require students to take detailed notes while they watch the videos. Those notes, along with the answers to the inserted questions, should be submitted for grading before the first synchronous meeting. Third, instructors could have an accountability quiz at the beginning of the first synchronous meeting or ask accountability questions at the beginning of the first synchronous meeting. An alternative suggested by the students was adding more questions at the end of each video with the students required to answer those questions in their notebook.

Third, each of the four synchronous meetings should have different foci. For example, on Monday, you could focus on questions and answers, checking notes, warming up, and completing drills on challenging words and grammar. Tuesdays and Wednesdays could be spent on pair work and group work. Thursdays could be spent on review and writing. To make sure that synchronous meetings proceed well, it is necessary to make a few announcements at the beginning of the semester so that everyone knows that the learning community will work as a team. For example, instructors could encourage everyone to use video if they can so that they can see each other. Additionally, showing their faces could also help students be more focused. Additionally, instructors could encourage all students to find a quiet place for class time in order to minimize the interruption of class from any possible noise in their immediate environment. However, it is also necessary to make everyone aware that not everyone can find a quiet place for class. If there is any background noise from any student, students should understand that everyone is doing their best.

Fourth, instructors can improve synchronous meetings by following four rules. (1) Share a word document where the instructor can write down instructions for activities, page numbers the instructors would like the students to read or check, the correct phrases or sentences after the students give examples or practice saying anything, and Chinese sentences the instructor says that are complicated and may not be understood by all the students. With this shared document, students can better understand what is happening in class and be exposed to the written format of the target language more often. (2) Call upon students to answer questions when they are giving students the chance to practice speaking. Waiting for volunteers also works, but it is best for the instructor to indicate whether he/she will ask for volunteers or will call upon students for certain questions. Doing this will save time and help the class run more smoothly. (3) Use breakout rooms regularly so that the students can practice in small groups or in pairs. For everyone to benefit more, it is better to assign learners of similar language levels to the same group. It helps the students more if the instructor can step into the breakout room and stay for a minute or two to answer possible questions or to help those who need help. (4) Use as much of the target language as possible in synchronous meetings to give the students maximum exposure to the language. Unlike FTF meetings where body language plays an important role in helping the students understand the teacher even when they do not fully understand the teacher's Chinese, online meetings seem to be more challenging if the instructor uses the target language. However, because the instructor can write/type down what he/she says in the shared document, students can easily follow.

Fifth, as in FTF teaching or flipped/blended formats of teaching, assignments should require practice of listening and speaking as well as reading and writing. For speaking practice, one-on-one sessions with UNSAs work well. VoiceThread can also be used for the students to practice their speaking, with the added benefit that they can share what they produce with their peers. For listening, reading, writing, and grammar practice, the IC workbook is sufficient for daily practice. In addition, other writing assignments can be given, such as note writing or short essay assignments related to students' lives and what they are learning.

Assignments can be categorized into two groups when they are graded. One group could consist of assignments such as listening comprehension, reading comprehension, and simple grammar exercises. The other group could consist of any kind of complicated writing exercise, such as English-Chinese translation or short essay writing. The former group of assignments could use an alternative grading method (as described in section 3.3), that is, giving students the answer key for the questions and the transcripts of the dialogues for the listening practice and require them to submit a detailed evaluation indicating what mistakes they made, why they made such mistakes, and what they will do to fix those errors. This requires giving the students a firm deadline for completing the assignments before the answer key is sent to them. By doing this, students will be more engaged and more responsible for their own learning than they would be if they were simply given a grade. The second group of assignments, however, needs the instructor's detailed feedback. There are many ways for students to express the same idea when completing this type of assignment, so it is important to give feedback on how used the language in their writing and focus feedback on how to improve based on what language the students used.

Sixth, assessments need to assess the four skills, knowledge about grammar, and culture. For speaking tests, group performances are challenging online. Therefore, it is a good idea to combine the written assignment with the speaking assessment at the beginning and the intermediate level, because there is still not much distinction between the use of language in formal writing and in speaking at the early skill levels. Combining tasks allows the students to focus on one topic and accomplish both the speaking and the writing well. Rubrics should be given to students in advance when the instruction for the assignment/assessment is given.

For written tests, giving a finite amount of time for completion is crucial to motivate students to prepare and to learn well before the assessment starts. The quizzes over video content could be given in the format of a quiz with a finite amount of time or in the format of a few questions at the end of the video to test the students' knowledge about the grammar and the vocabulary covered in the video.

Seventh, instructors can send a recap email after each synchronous meeting to summarize the important and challenging points learned that day and to remind students of the important deadlines and requirements related to upcoming assignments and assessments. This email will ensure that the students do not miss anything and help students feel confident that they are on the right track.

These are preliminary suggestions. Each instructor should take into consideration their own available resources and immediate environment in designing synchronous, flipped online courses. The completion of the design and development of the courses does not symbolize an end but rather a beginning of an adapting and adjusting process based on continuous student feedback and teacher self-reflection. To help this process to run smoothly, three things are necessary. One is to be open to students' feedback on any aspect of course design and teaching. Second is to keep the course format, teaching routine, and assignment due dates consistent and to send emails or announcements to clarify tasks or to remind students of the task lists. The last but not the least is to stay connected with each of the individual students. Building rapport is critical in motivating the students to learn (Jiang & Ramsay, 2005). Spending a few minutes each day at the beginning of the class to encourage students to talk about their lives—either in English or in the target language—and replying to student emails with sincerity and promptness will greatly help students know that instructor not only cares about their learning but also cares about them as people.

6 Conclusion

This chapter gives a detailed description of how two flipped/blended courses were designed and successfully transitioned to fully online courses during an emergency situation, students' feedback on that transition, and ideas for creating a fully online course based on the flipped/blended model. This chapter is largely based on personal experiences and does not necessarily apply to every environment and every situation in which flipped/blended learning was adopted for a fully online context.

That being said, this chapter contributes to the knowledge base that instructors can access when they intentionally design an online language course. However, to make online language learning a total success, many questions still need to be answered, such as these: What tasks should teachers design to help beginning-level learners with writing without any FTF meetings? How do instructors teach true beginners successfully without any FTF meetings, considering the challenges that the tones and the character writing impose on the teaching of Chinese?

Appendix 1: Finding Online Resources and Learn Project: #_out of six

The Resource link (This link should directly go to the resource you used for learning.)
The resource title
The creator/author and their credentials
What you learned? Reviewed?
You can list the sentences you learned, the structures you learned/reviewed or got clarified, new vocabulary, new ways of saying things you know, mistakes you need to avoid, etc.
Your comments on this resource, such as whether it fits your Chinese level, whether their presentation is clear, interesting, what you would suggest they do, etc.
What specific aspect(s) of the Chinese language learning did you want to improve before you find this resource? Briefly explain the process of locating this resource.
What is your plan for the future regarding utilizing these resources you have found?

Complete 6 of these forms throughout the semester. It is due on Fridays in week 2, week 4, week 7, week 9, week 12, and week 14. You have reminders in the weekly plan. Send Zhang Laoshi your word document titled: [yourname_FORL_#outof6].doc

References

Bergmann, J., & Sams, A. (2012). *Flip your classroom: Reach every student in every class every day.* International Society for Technology in Education.

Bloom, B. S. (1956). *Taxonomy of educational objectives. Handbook I: The Cognitive Domain.* David McKay Co. Inc..

Jiang, W., & Ramsay, G. (2005). Rapport-building through CALL in teaching Chinese as a foreign language: An exploratory study. *Language Learning & Technology, 9*(2), 47–63.

Keengwe, J., Onchwari, G., & Oigara, J. (Eds.). (2014). *Promoting active learning through the flipped classroom model. A volume in the Advances in Educational Technologies and Instructional Design (AETID) Book Series. Information Science Reference, An Imprint of IGI Global.* Hershey.

Lan, Y. J., Fang, S. Y., Legault, J., & Li, P. (2015). Second Language Acquisition of Mandarin Chinese Vocabulary: Context of Learning Effects. *Educational Technology Research and Development, 63*(5), 671–690. Retrieved July 26, 2020 from https://www.learntechlib.org/p/175358/

Li, S. (2014). Literature circles with multimedia support in CFL teaching. *Journal of the Chinese Language Teachers Association, 49*(2), 27–44.

Liu, Y., Yao, T.-C., Bi, N.-P., Ge, L., & Shi, Y. (2009). *Integrated Chinese, Level 1 Part 1 & Level 2 Part 1.* Cheng & Tsui Company.

Mayer, R. E. (2009). *Multimedia Learning* (2nd ed.). Cambridge University Press. https://doi.org/10.1017/CBO9780511811678

Mayer, R. E. (2014). Research-based principles for designing multimedia instruction. In V. A. Benassi, C. E. Overson, & C. M. Hakala (Eds.), *Applying Science of Learning in Education: Infusing Psychological Science into the Curriculum* (pp. 59–70). Society for the Teaching of Psychology.

Stone, B. B. (2012). *Flip your classroom to increase active learning and student engagement.* Paper presented at the 28th Annual Conference on Distance Teaching & Learning. Madison, Wisconsin.

Talbert, R. (2017). *Flipped learning: A guide for higher education faculty.* Stylus Publishing, LLC..

Wang, Y., & Crooks, S. M. (2015). Does the personalization of multimedia instruction influence the effectiveness of decorative graphics during foreign language instruction? *Journal of Technology and Chinese Language Teaching, 6*(2), 29–38.

Zhang, S. (2017). Applying research-based multimedia design principles in designing and teaching beginning CFL learners Ba-construction online: A pilot study. *Chinese as a Second Language, 52*(3), 255–291.

Zhang, S. (2018, June). *Web-based video tutorial for grammar and vocabulary learning in beginning and low-intermediate level CFL courses: Learners' perspec-*

tives and preferences. Paper presented at the 10th International Conference on Technology and Chinese Language Teaching (TCLT10), Taipei, Taiwan.

Zhang, S. (2019a). Culture learning through multimedia authentic materials and ethnographic interview in a blended learning environment. *Journal of Technology and Chinese Language Teaching, 10*(2), 125–149.

Zhang, S. (2019b, July). *Learning from multimedia presentations in a flipped classroom—A Verbal Protocol Study.* Paper presented at the XXth International CALL Research Conference, Hong Kong, China.

Zhang, S. (forthcoming). Integrating Culture in Language Curriculum from Beginning- to Intermediate-Level in a Blended Learning Environment: A Design-Based Empirical Study. To appear in K. Nemtchinova (ed.). *Enhancing Beginner-Level Foreign Language Education for Adult Learners.* Routledge.

Zhang, S., & Jaramillo, N. (2021). Seamless Integration between Online and Face-to-Face: The Design and Perception of a Flipped-Blended Language Course. *International Journal of Computer Assisted Language Learning and Teaching, 11*(4), 1.

Zhang, S., Juvale, D., & Jaramillo, N. C. (2017). *A blended/flipped Chinese-as-a-foreign-language course: Design and perceptions.* The 33rd Distance Teaching & Learning Conference Proceedings (pp. 78-82). University of Wisconsin, Madison.

13

Instructors' Social, Cognitive, and Teaching Presences in Emergency Remote Teaching of Chinese Language in the United States: A Qualitative Study

Ching-Hsuan Wu and Lizeng Huang

1 Introduction

The COVID-19 pandemic suddenly moved most faculty and students in American institutions of higher learning from traditional classrooms to an emergency remote teaching (ERT) environment as a safety measure during the spring 2020 semester (Hodges et al., 2020). ERT in the present study refers to a temporary, hurried shift of instructional delivery to a fully remote virtual mode by removing all face-to-face teaching components and quickly setting up transitory educational access to instructional continuity as a result of a global pandemic disaster. This sudden online

C.-H. Wu (✉)
West Virginia University, Morgantown, WV, USA
e-mail: Chinghsuan.wu@mail.wvu.edu

L. Huang
The Ohio State University, Columbus, OH, USA
e-mail: huang.4295@osu.edu

© The Author(s), under exclusive license to Springer Nature Switzerland AG 2022
S. Liu (ed.), *Teaching the Chinese Language Remotely*,
https://doi.org/10.1007/978-3-030-87055-3_13

migration created a widespread paradigm shift in how instructors engaged their students cognitively and socially when they were urgently separated by time and space with scant resources, and many of these quick solutions to ERT were improvisational and emergent. This abrupt transition and weeks of not-fully-featured instruction together have made ERT meaningfully different from a well-planned online learning experience, and this less-than-ideal circumstance has also influenced how faculty members view the future of instruction and their needs for technological pedagogical support.

During ERT, faculty and students transitioned from a physical space that allowed face-to-face spontaneity to a virtual setting that operated in a reflective, text-based medium in a narrow preparation window. While the changes and quick adoption of virtual alternatives in response to the pandemic were tumultuous and disruptive, the rapid transition to remote classes also presented opportunities for faculty and students to experience what an online environment had to offer. They had the chance to reflect on how integration of technology made their ERT possible, what kind of technological, pedagogical structures helped them engage their students in social, cognitive, and teaching presences, and how this ERT experience impacted their future teaching. This unprecedented situation motivated the researchers to investigate faculty's emergency online instructional engagement strategies through the theoretical framework of Community of Inquiry (CoI) (Garrison & Vaughan, 2008) that would otherwise have been unavailable.

The construct of engagement in this study is defined as faculty's use of an online platform to organize their teaching presence, involve students in cognitive learning activities, and maintain social interaction in a virtual learning setting. Bolliger and Wasilik (2009) suggested that faculty's online teaching experience is complex and difficult to predict, and it can be even more challenging in the face of COVID-19. In addition, while the foremost purpose of an educational experience is to attain the teaching goals and achieve cognitive learning outcomes (Bair & Bair, 2011), are the primary instructional objectives different during ERT? As such, the purpose of this qualitative study was to develop an understanding and assess the process of how college faculty structured their teaching presence and enacted cognitive and social engagement with their students for instructional continuity of Chinese language instruction, a discipline that heavily depends on interaction to achieve learning outcomes. This study seeks to answer the following research question: What were faculty's ERT experiences in organizing social, cognitive, and teaching presences in an online environment to implement their Chinese language instruction?

2 Literature Review

Garrison and Vaughan (2008) stated that the foreground of an education is learner engagement; however, "interaction in and of itself is insufficient" (p. 31) for educational inquiry to occur. Inquiry is a process where learners "progress systematically from identifying a problem to resolving it" (p. 17), and as such, interaction in a learning community is purposeful, collaborative, and reflective. The conceptual framework of Community of Inquiry proposed by Garrison and Vaughan provided order and guidance to examine online educational processes and outcomes. Teaching, cognitive, and social presences are the three core, recursive elements in the framework, and the overlapped area of the three elements is the locus of a quality educational experience. An online learning community that embraces teaching, cognitive, and social presences features shared academic goals and mutual support, and through the instructor's effective design of learning opportunities, students can participate in the pedagogical process that supports knowledge construction (Shea et al., 2006).

The framework places its primary focus on academic purpose in a learning community and recognizes the importance of social dynamics in creating a supportive climate for student success. Social presence fosters interpersonal but purposeful student relationships in the learning community that promote student participation, build social cohesiveness for collaboration opportunities, and encourage a sense of responsibility and commitment to the academic interests that the community shares. Establishing social presence is essential at the outset of developing an educational community that supports emotional bonding and camaraderie. However, social presence does not structure the academic aspect of the learning community, and thus social engagement is insufficient to sustain the inquiry process or achieve the intended learning outcomes.

Cognitive presence is defined as "the extent to which learners are able to construct and confirm meaning through sustained reflection and discourse in a critical community of inquiry" (Garrison et al., 2001, p. 11). Cognitive presence is a systematic progression of critical thinking and includes four stages: identify questions, explore problems and gather relevant information, connect and integrate ideas, and test and apply solutions. Cognitive presence exists in both synchronous and asynchronous online tasks. Text-based communication in an asynchronous setting affords learners with time lag to reflect on the issues, intellectually engage with the content at a pace of their choosing, and produce permanent, precise written communication. A synchronous setting, on the other hand, invites spontaneity in student responses, and when in provocative discussions, students learn to exercise their critical thinking skills on the spot and "navigate emotionally-charged intellectual discussions" (Bair & Bair, 2011, p. 8) with careful instruction by an experienced teacher. The two cognitive engagement experiences are not interchangeable but are both valuable. Cognitive presence alone, however, is not adequate to sustain a critical learning community. Garrison et al. (2000) explained "high levels of social presence with accompanying high degrees of commitment and participation are necessary for the development of higher-order thinking skills and collaborative work" (p. 94) at the heart of cognitive presence.

Online teaching presence is orchestrated by three elements: effective design of learning opportunities, facilitation of productive discourse to maintain focused learner engagement, and structure the direction of cohesive, progressive cognitive and social processes (Garrison & Arbaugh, 2007; Shea et al., 2006). That is, teaching presence structures the process and opportunities for cognitive and social presences to grow and advance. The results in Bair and Bair (2011) showed that online teaching can help students stay more focused when it is as flexible as it is structured. While online learners enjoy freedom to work at their own pace, they do not necessarily have the self-discipline to thrive in the online flexibility. Hence, learners often request, for example, reminders of deadlines or pre-assigned partners for collaboration (e.g., Bair & Bair, 2011; Martin &

Bolliger, 2018). For these students, teaching presence in offering a high degree of course structure and inflexible requirements become even more critical for student success. Ironically, as Bair and Bair shared, "what allowed these students to complete the online course successfully was re-creating qualities of a face-to-face class and eliminating the more central elements of an online course" (para. 38). This observation also reinforces the binding nature of teaching presence in a virtual Community of Inquiry, as seen in the study of Chen et al. (2017). In their study, the productivity in online discussions was enhanced and positively influenced elements of CoI when the well-structured protocol-based discussion strategy with well-defined goals, rules, and deadlines was used. Patterns commonly observed in teaching presence include: engage in learners, keep learners focused, set a climate for learning, diagnose misperceptions, identify areas of agreement, seek to reach consensus, focus on discussion, assess understanding, reinforce student contributions, impart knowledge, present content and questions, netiquette (i.e., the acceptable way when communicating over the Internet), communicate expectations, and provide clear instruction (Shea et al., 2006).

While CoI has been applied to study both in-person and online teaching environments, the framework has not yet been widely researched in an ERT context. As such, the results of the present study aim to add to this dimension of the literature.

3 Methodology

3.1 Participants

With the approval of institutional review board (IRB) from the authors' universities and the participants' consent, five participants were purposefully sampled for diversity to produce the most representative sample (Teddlie & Tashakkori, 2008) within the limits. The researchers started with a list of twenty contacts of colleagues who were college instructors of Chinese language during the time of the study in the United States. Subsequently, the twenty contacts were cross-grouped based on their age, gender, position title, and institutional types. From those who agreed to participate in the study, one or two representatives from each group were selected to form the purposive sample. The participants were recruited from four different types of institutions of higher education in the United States: state research-focused, state teaching-oriented, private research-focused, and private liberal arts. The participants were all native speakers of Chinese from either China or Taiwan. The participants included male and female Chinese language instructors, who were between the ages of twenty-eight and sixty-five with different ranks from Instructor I to Full Professor at various stages of their careers in a Chinese language program at their institutions.

3.2 Interview Questionnaire Instrument

Based on the conceptual frameworks of CoI (Garrison & Vaughan, 2008), an open-ended, detailed, semi-structured interview instrument was constructed and employed to guide the video conference interviews for data collection. The interviews were conducted by the first author. The core questions were as follows:

- Can you share your overall ERT experiences?
- How did you organize your ERT teaching to engage your students socially and cognitively?
- What were strategies that you used to deliver your teaching to achieve both social and cognitive purposes?
- What were the challenges, if any, in the areas of course presentation, content delivery, student-teacher rapport development, and technology use that you experienced during ERT?

Depending on the narratives of the participants, follow-up questions were raised. The instrument was field tested for content validity of the questions and questioning strategies with three college professors, who had expert knowledge about the population and research topic. Based on the three sets of the feedback at three points in time, the instrument was refined to avoid ambiguity and reduce repetition of the questions.

3.3 Data Analysis

The interview content was member checked; documented through field notes, video recordings, and analytic memos; and coded using the first and second coding cycles (Saldana, 2009) for emergent, repeated themes and explanations. The structural coding was applied during the initial round of coding to label and gather lists of major topics relevant to the theoretical propositions within individual participants and interviews. The second round cross-examined the five interviews to look for repeated, focused topics, and the third and final round analyzed interactions among thematic sub-datasets and synthesized them. The final codebook was checked for consistency and repeatability to increase reliability across the coders (Trochim, 2006) by additional two colleagues who hold university-level foreign language teaching positions. In addition to reliability, the aforementioned two colleagues examined the validity of the findings by verifying how the findings were supported by the evidence in the data set (Guion, 2002).

4 Findings

The findings show that the participants all believed they possessed necessary, sufficient technological skills to urgently transition into ERT as college Chinese language instructors. Although the participants all had varying degrees of experience integrating technology in their teaching in traditional classrooms, ERT was the first time for all five participants to teach in a non-face-to-face environment. Their commonly used pedagogical technologies prior to ERT included emails, presentational slides (e.g., Keynote and PowerPoint), websites (e.g., YouTube and Google Images), and document processing applications (e.g., Word, PDF, and Office Lens). The five participants were all involved in ERT during the spring 2020 semester, and all expressed that they kept the same academic standards and requirements during ERT and maintained academic progress as their primary teaching objective. Their ERT class sizes ranged from eight to thirteen students, and the classes were across all Chinese proficiency levels from elementary to advanced, including both second language and heritage learners. In terms of teaching methods, all five participants described themselves as users of communicative teaching approaches and emphasized the importance of interaction in their class activities.

4.1 Social Presence

In this study, social presence refers to the sense of social and emotional togetherness shared between faculty and students in an ERT community. The findings are thematically grouped below.

Collaboration: The five participants all emphasized the importance to maintain faculty-student rapport during ERT. As such, the participants were asked why the social presence was critical in their ERT teaching and how they engaged their students socially. One reason shared by all the participants was to obtain students' support for faculty's teaching practice, and all the participants enacted their social presence by inviting students to collaborate on structuring their ERT experience during the course suspension periods before ERT began. In reflecting on how collaboration affected the enactment of social presence, Participant One shared, "The communication and invitation for students to collaboratively structure the ERT experience extended the emotional connections between my students and me during the suspension days." Participant Two's comment on students' involvement in planning ERT is as follows:

> The collaborative conversations and exchanges of ideas helped me gain student support for the changes necessitated by ERT. The process also helped me evaluate the level of practical resources that my students had for their Chinese studies, such as how their home situations afforded learning opportunities for them in terms of time, space, and equipment.

Tailored assistance: When being asked how their social presence benefited their teaching in addition to gaining students' support, three participants expressed that a strong sense of "togetherness" enabled them to find out students' needs and offer immediate assistance. Three participants reported that a few of their students needed to take on additional responsibilities for house chores or caring for their younger siblings, who were also home due to school closures caused by COVID-19, and these duties may have interfered with their learning in different ways. The participants explained that tailoring accommodations for students was a strategy not only for a practical academic gain but also for a social interconnectedness with their students. To find out if the students struggled in any way at home during ERT, for instance, Participant Four sent out weekly greeting emails with encouraging words and offered additional assistance. Participant Four explained, "I believe my efforts to increase my availability were meaningful for my students more in an emotional sense than they were academic because what seemed to matter more during the pandemic was my students knew I cared."

Rapport: The participants were asked to comment on how ERT reduced their social presence in any way. The five faculty participants unanimously expressed their confidence in having sustained student academic commitment and positivity in the faculty-student interpersonal relationships during ERT. As Participant Five put it, "Absolutely! Our strong bond never went away." The faculty participants used different strategies, such as warm-up greetings, humor, discussions on topics of mutual interest, and constant presence, to socially engage their students and attributed the positive results primarily to the strong social dynamics in their learning community that had been cultivated steadily prior to the COVID-19 pandemic. Participant One had shared the following reflection, in which reassurance and care were strategically demonstrated through verbal communication and actions.

> The students rested assured that I was as available as before the pandemic if not more. I tried to be even more responsive to their emails and social media messages. The students understood I cared about them, and they were supportive of and cooperative with me during ERT. We had a strong rapport that had been cultivated over years, and we simply continued to build on it throughout ERT. However, I do feel worried about what would happen if the pandemic continues into the Fall semester. I will have new students, with whom I won't have any pre-existing relationship to build on.

In that case, I wonder if we can still feel as connected if we have never met in person.

Technologies: The faculty participants reported that the elimination of face-to-face interaction did not reduce their social presence. Consequently, the participants were asked how they kept up with their social presence when in-person contact was unavailable. The participants stated that technology-mediated communication during ERT afforded easy access to social engagement activities to continuously develop faculty-student rapport that had already been previously established. Specifically, as Participant Two narrated, "More frequent group and individual email exchanges with an occasional use of emoji, memes, and Graphics Interchange Formats (GIFs) actually made our communication more fun and intimate with the younger generation." The participants all agreed that emails were the primary text-based technology to keep communication formal, instant, clear, efficient, and affective during ERT. On the other hand, in commenting on the use of videoconferencing, Participant Three shared that "Videoconferencing technology made ERT teaching safe, easy, and convenient. We still could laugh together, and we often took group pictures on the screen. We could also compliment on each other's outfits and hair. As such, I don't think ERT placed an emotional distance among my students and me."

Cultural sensitivity: In commenting on the ways that social presence could be integrated into class activities, Participant Two shared how the topic of mask-wearing, a potentially provocative issue, was strategically approached during the class discussions by guiding the students to reflect on the topic in an effort to foster cultural sensitivity in students and to further connect their community of learning.

> Once we learned that our Chinese class needed to become virtual, the students and I talked about the importance of our healthcare and contemplated on how and why wearing a mask in public could possibly raise questions in our small town and across the country in general. Many of my students just returned from their study-abroad programs in China and thus understood why people wore a mask as a preventative measure and respectful gesture. They shared my value and encouraged me to feel at ease

about wearing a mask in the US. The relevant topics continued throughout ERT and also inspired us to revisit the meaning of democracy. The support from my students was reciprocated and appreciated. I feel our mutual understanding was further fostered, and my students and I became even more connected as a result of ups and downs that we shared together during ERT.

Moreover, Participant Five reported that some of the international students traveled back to their home countries during the transition and thus had access to images, videos, and personal experiences of their local COVID-19 situations. In an effort to engage the class in intellectual discussions, social connections, and interpersonal support, the faculty participant tactfully integrated news into the teaching by having the students present how the pandemic was situated in different regions as a course project. According to the participant, this activity served as a window for the students to virtually witness how the pandemic affected people locally and globally and connected their personal worlds (e.g., how the pandemic affected individuals at a personal level and how individuals reflected on it) with the shared world (e.g., the class collaborated to construct knowledge-based facts about the pandemic at a community level). According to Participant Five, this strategy fostered social engagement among faculty participants and the students through class cognitive interactivities.

4.2 Cognitive Presence

The operational definition of cognitive presence in this study, modified from the work of Garrison et al. (2001), is the extent to which faculty participants helped their students identify inquiries related to Chinese learning, explore the issues individually or collaboratively with sustained critical reflection, integrate discoveries with existing ideas to construct new meanings, and apply newly gained knowledge to their educational contexts. In enacting their cognitive presence to engage their students to practice oral skills in addition to other aspects of Chinese proficiency, all the participants chose synchronicity as their principle technological medium to implement their classroom activities in a real-time setting to support students' language development.

Spontaneous interaction: All the participants emphasized the vital role of spontaneous interaction with visual-audio aids in their use of communicative language teaching approaches and thus considered synchronous teaching fundamental for their enactment of cognitive presence during ERT. When asked to discuss engagement strategies in terms that improve students' language skills during ERT, Participant Three noted the following:

> Development in students' oral proficiency was our primary learning objective. The videoconferencing tools enabled me to continuously engage my students in interactive, fast-paced language practice. In class, I contextualized our language application activities and elicited improvisational responses from my students. Without synchronicity, I wouldn't have been able to offer clear instruction, timely drills, foster automaticity in their language output, or evaluate the spontaneity of interactive communication in students' language skills.

Corrective feedback: The participants were asked to describe their strategies in engaging their learners cognitively in their synchronous teaching. Four participants considered their timely provision of corrective feedback on varying aspects of students' language use as one important function of a language teacher. Corrective feedback is a form of negative feedback and is offered when a second language learner's use of the target language is not considered native-like. Corrective feedback can either implicitly or explicitly inform students about the comprehensibility in their output, and some corrective feedback includes acceptable examples of target language use (Wu, 2020). In addressing the necessity of instant pronunciation correction during the class, for example, Participant Two noted that "One's pronunciation leaves an audience a first and lasting impression, and instant feedback can help students improve tones and pronunciation. Hence, it was critical that our class continued synchronously throughout ERT so I could offer timely feedback."

Adaptive questioning: Four participants shared that with real-time interaction through videoconferencing, they were able to strategize adaptive questioning techniques to engage their learners and scaffold students' language skills and organization of ideas. The following description from Participant Five shows that the instructor's cognitive presence was a systematic progression that invited the students to exercise critical thinking from identifying questions to integrating viewpoints and then applying solutions during the process of scaffolding, as suggested by Garrison et al. (2001).

> When the class started, we would quickly skim through Chinese news on a website through the shared screen on Zoom. While they were at an advanced level in their Chinese proficiency, the students' proficiencies can be heterogeneous, and they didn't always catch all the details in a news story. After they had the chance to glance over the news article, I would ask them content questions, starting with general ones. Depending on the answers from the students, I would adapt my questions to clarify confusing points, guide them to uncover the messages between the lines, and help them structure their ideas to present their arguments. Instantaneous interaction on Zoom enabled us to negotiate meanings, and this process played a major part in growing students' reading and speaking skills.

Group work: Collaboration in small groups was reported to be difficult to replicate during ERT. The participants reported challenges in their implementation of group work using virtual breakout rooms to encourage discussions. They were unable to visit, support, or supervise student work of multiple groups simultaneously, and instead, they needed to exit one room in order to enter the next. When the faculty participants finally made it to the last few groups, the students usually would have already finished the work and stayed in the breakout rooms quietly on the screen. This situation was particularly a problem with lower-level Chinese classes, in which the students did not have the language skills necessary to sustain longer conversations until the instructor arrived. After a few attempts, all the participants needed to discontinue the group work in this format in their classes.

4.3 Teaching Presence

Teaching presence refers to teachers' creation of opportunities for cognitive and social presences to grow and advance. The participants were asked how they organized their overall teaching structure so their students could stay socially and cognitively engaged during ERT. Four of the five participants kept the class size and meeting date, time, and duration intact during ERT and taught the students on the videoconferencing platform. Participant Four split the classes into halves and taught these smaller groups synchronously with a similar number of contact hours with the help from a graduate teaching assistant. All the participants stated that overall the preparation for ERT was not a difficult task. Participants One, Two, and Five described their ERT experience in organizing their teaching presence as "easy and breezy." Subsequently, the participants were asked to elaborate on the strategies that made their organization of teaching presence "easy and breezy."

Comparability in course structures: All the five participants reported that students' learning outcomes remained important during ERT and that they had technological knowledge and skills necessary to strategically create a comparable course structure with what they had prior to the pandemic. Specifically, the participants expressed that they were able to apply their pre-existing digital literacy to easily perform the following tasks: organize the learning opportunities; facilitate cohesive cognitive and social engagement activities; motivate students to progress through academic tasks; keep students on track with the curricula; maintain the same expectations of learning outcomes; hold office hours virtually; and practice timely communication via emails, instant messages, and phone calls during ERT. Participant Three shared the following narrative in response to why it was important to keep the course structure comparable:

> During the course suspension period, my focus was on the overall structure of my ERT, not any particular technologies. I was confident that what I knew about technology was enough for my ERT pedagogical needs. Decades ago, there were not many technological tools available to help students learn Chinese, but students could still excel under their teachers' guidance. Hence, teaching designed by the instructor as a content and

pedagogy expert is more important than the instructional technologies when priorities need to be set in a hurry. I held myself accountable for offering my students a productive ERT learning experience so they could successfully advance to the next Chinese level. In order to keep a similar course structure in the best interest of my students, I chose to teach synchronously during ERT.

To elaborate on comparability, Participant Four added, "I felt stability was what was needed the most at the time, including teaching objectives and learning outcomes. In order to enhance comparability, I even wore the same clothes and hair style on the screen."

Technologically effective: The participants were asked to discuss their technological knowledge and skills in the context of teaching presence. In response, Participant Three made the following comment:

> I am aware of commonly used technological tools in teaching foreign languages and am able to proficiently use a few of them in my classroom. While I believe periodical professional development in this regard is important, I am also clear I am a user of these tools, not a researcher. That is, I use technologies that I feel comfortable with, and I don't think I need to be an expert on a wide range of technologies. This principle served me well throughout ERT. My primary focus was to ensure my students continued to advance in their Chinese skills during the pandemic. I used familiar technologies to design our virtual learning so the aspect of technology was considered facilitative, instead of onerous when the situation on its own was already disastrous.

This observation was echoed by the comment from Participant Five, "less is more." In this case, Participant Five had elected to develop technological proficiency over just one virtual bulletin board and continued to rely on it systematically and dominantly to structure the teaching presence in both synchronous and asynchronous settings during ERT. In addition, Participant One reported that the "traditional" technologies (e.g., PowerPoint slides and YouTube) in combination with Zoom worked well to maintain the class rhythm throughout ERT. The use of simple technologies did not further burden the students and faculty to develop technological proficiency over new online tools in such an emergency, as Participant One noted below:

> Overall, we didn't need any new technologies, except for Zoom, to complete our courses during ERT. While I am not particularly well-versed in pedagogical technology, the selected tools I felt comfortable to operate were sufficient to effectively deliver synchronous sessions, keep academic rigor, interact with students, and achieve most, if not all, of our instructional objectives without any issues.

The strategies used to structure the learning opportunities in the findings above concern the employment of a smaller number of technologies with a higher level of familiarity that the participants had with the tools. A skillful application of pedagogical technology required the faculty to practice tool functions frequently, as Participant Five stated, "As part of my own professional development, I research and practice using pedagogical technological tools in my own time just to stay tuned even when I don't teach online."

Active teaching role with more preparation: The participants were asked to reflect on differences in their teaching role between in-person and ERT teaching. The five participants reported that their faculty roles remained the same in terms that they continued to actively structure their teaching presence to facilitate students' cognitive and social activities. However, their overall workload increased during ERT, and three participants found themselves offering technical support to students as part of their "new" teaching responsibility. The expectation for teaching presence in the virtual learning environment was unfamiliar to the faculty participants especially because the abrupt transition left them insufficient reaction time. Therefore, to continue the instructional flow, they invested additional time to create a virtual learning environment that allowed most comparable communication opportunities and learning outcomes during ERT.

Participant Two shared that "The ERT environment challenged our creativity and adaptability to virtually organize our teaching presence in terms that designed, facilitated, and directed cognitive and social processes for our students." To rise to the occasion, all the participants agreed that increased preparedness and organization were a must for them to engage their students academically and socially in the absence of physical presence, social cues, and norms of the traditional classroom. The findings show that the areas where the workload surged were the following: a greater amount of time in digitally collecting and grading assignments; elevated availability to assist students during office hours, via written communication, and through phone calls; a deeper commitment in enhancing digital literacy; and further proficient technological pedagogical skills in seeking, converting, and organizing teaching materials in a manner conducive to synchronous learning. Pertaining to the higher level of preparedness, Participant One shared the following narratives:

> As soon as I knew ERT was put in place, I went online to learn about different functions of Zoom. I couldn't enter ERT as if I were walking into a regular classroom. The knowledge and instruction that I used to be able to keep only in my head and then just verbally convey them in front of my class now needed to "be visually on display." I reviewed the teaching materials, made plans about how my teaching could be best transformed and represented online, and reorganized the materials. I felt I wouldn't have been able to engage my students as successfully had I not had this additional preparation.

Moreover, Participant Four recorded a series of mini lectures on grammar and vocabulary to supplement the regular synchronous sessions in case the instructional clarity was compromised in a virtual setting. Furthermore, all the participants responded to students in the forms of emails, voice comments, messages, and written feedback more promptly, frequently, and thoroughly during ERT in an attempt to offer immediate accommodation, engage students in the ERT environment, and enhance teaching presence. Participant Two stated that "I believe frequent communication, reciprocity, and cooperation between my students and me was a successful strategy that I used to hold everyone together and keep us on task throughout ERT."

Impact on future teaching: The participants were asked to discuss how ERT experience has changed their ideas of teaching presence. In response, Participant Four reported that "I still think face-to-face teaching and a strong presence of teachers are the way that foreign languages should be taught. However, my ERT experience was better than I had imagined so I would be willing to consider offering courses virtually in the future." Participant Five shared a similar view:

> My students and I discussed our ERT experience at the end of the semester, and we both agreed it was enjoyable and convenient. I never thought I would say this but now I am exploring the option of offering my Chinese classes in a hybrid mode, in which students and I can meet in person once a week and then arrange the rest of the weekly meetings synchronously.

5 Discussions

The following discussions are organized and analyzed by the three core, recursive elements in the CoI framework (Garrison & Vaughan, 2008).

5.1 Social Presence

The importance of social presence was a recursive theme during the interviews, and this observation is in an agreement with Garrison and Vaughan's (2008) recognition of the essential role of social dynamics in creating a supportive climate for student success in a Community of Inquiry. The findings suggest two driving forces for instructors to strategize their social presence during ERT: pedagogical reasons and emotional connections. The faculty participants' social presence operated as a means to seek pedagogical information to revise their teaching plans during ERT and build an emotional network that connected individuals and supported student learning. Pedagogically, it was essential for student success that instructors considered contextual cues and then adapted their teaching to these emergent student characteristics related to ERT (i.e., students could be in different time zones or camera shy). Emotionally, the participants' incorporation of student feedback in structuring their online learning seemed to further connect the faculty participants and their students in the sense that they were all in the undesirable situation together. This emotional connection may have contributed to the participants' "easy and breezy" ERT experience. This finding aligns with the result in Liu's (2020) study that instructors' incorporation of student feedback in structuring a Chinese learning experience can be a motivational teaching strategy in keeping students emotionally engaged with the program and creating a successful learning experience for students. This perspective is also supported by the observation of Handelsman et al. (2005) that the level of student engagement with their instructor, peers, and content can be a significant predictor for their academic achievement.

Independent from instructors' motivation for social presence, the discoveries of this study suggest that instructors should consider employing the following three formats to maximize their social engagement opportunities: consistent interaction (e.g., greetings when an instructional session begins to find out how school is going), organized engagement (e.g., a forum for students to share their personal experience about COVID-19 across nations and cultures and engage in critical discussions), and as-needed interactivity (e.g., additional dialogues with students during office hours, after class, or via emails to find out how additional tailored academic and personal accommodations can be rendered).

Some characteristics of Chinese language classes can explain why the five participants were at ease about faculty-student interconnectedness in the absence of face-to-face communication during ERT. First, Chinese language courses typically have smaller class sizes to allow for individual attention, and activities often engage the instructor and students in constant interaction with one another to practice students' oral communicative language skills. Second, when cultures in Chinese-speaking areas are introduced and compared with students' own cultures, students become aware of other perspectives and learn to understand others in their learning community. Such a mutual understanding and cultural sensitivity can develop empathy among individuals. Third, the sequential nature of Chinese language courses and study-abroad programs offer opportunities for students and faculty in the program to create long-term social and academic experiences on a continuum and develop a strong rapport over years. This discipline-specific instructional context has built a platform for the faculty and students to consistently develop bonding, share academic interests, and sustain social connections despite the interruption caused by COVID-19. Moreover, Moore (1993) indicates that, among other factors, the extent and nature of learner-instructor interaction vary depending on instructor's personality, teaching rationale, and student needs. Hence, the positive social presence reported in this study can also be attributed to personal characteristics of the participants and their students in addition to the strategies applied and the pre-existing strong social dynamics.

5.2 Cognitive Presence

The engagement strategies in the participants' enactment of cognitive presence all involved intense verbal interactivity between instructor and students. The interactivity in speaking practice (e.g., adaptive questioning and oral proficiency enhancement), corrective feedback, and critical reflection (e.g., discussions on news) was observed to be an effective strategy to keep students engaged with and focused on the learning objectives. The findings regarding the faculty's use of corrective feedback in relation to student engagement align with the result in the study of Martin and Bolliger (2018) that students found prompt faculty feedback to be the most effective strategy in engaging them in learning. Chickering and Gamson's (1987) also included faculty's prompt assessment and feedback on student knowledge and competence in the seven important principles of good educational practice. In addition, the impact of the participants' use of the spontaneous verbal-exchange engagement strategies, as seen in adaptive questioning and reflections on the COVID-19 and democracy, corresponds to the finding in Martin and Bolliger's study (2018) that engaging students in discussions that involve students exercising deep reflection on the topic is the most valuable strategy in enhancing online student-content and student-student interaction. The implication of this observation is for instructors to consider the application of interactivity to other aspects in their teaching. For example, enhanced interactivity among students themselves in and outside instructional hours can further engage students in both social and cognitive contexts in their learning community. Interactivity between students and teaching content can also encourage critical reflection and meaning construction.

Videoconferencing technologies in this study provided an online synchronous teaching environment. With their functions such as chat rooms, shared screens, whiteboards, polls, and other communication tools, videoconferencing resembles face-to-face classrooms in a number of ways (Lee, 2009), such as spontaneous interaction in language conversation practice. The engagement strategies that the faculty participants adopted to enact their cognitive presence during ERT were centered on real-time interactivity. According to the participants, the process of instant instructor-student interaction could cognitively engage their students when the students performed the following tasks: negotiate meaning, consider corrective feedback from their instructors, attempt to revise their own knowledge and applications of the language forms based on the corrective feedback, and improve spontaneity, comprehension, and organization in their Chinese language use. Such gradual development of individual students' personal understanding of the subject matter via planned and unplanned interactions with the faculty participants, peers, and content was one important undertaking of classroom instruction (Laurillard, 2000) and of the participants' pedagogical approaches. The faculty participants' decisions in choosing synchronicity and communication tools equipped in videoconferencing (e.g., to use the chat room function to visualize students' mistakes in oral output) to accomplish their teaching objectives reflected the participants' discipline-specific technological knowledge that integrated their knowledge in foreign language teaching methodology.

The participants reported that the technical situation of breakout rooms made peer collaboration less effective in a virtual classroom than it would have been in a traditional classroom, where the instructor could move among groups quickly and easily. The concept of collaborative learning stresses an added value in multifaceted insights that individuals can share with a group. When collaboration takes place, individual learners' contributions enable the group to arrive at new or changed perspectives that otherwise might not have been possible to achieve by the individuals on their own (Donato, 2004). Collaboration is a commonly used teaching strategy in language classrooms in the format of, for instance, discussions, debates, and group projects to help students develop interpersonal language skills, process diverse views, and shape ideas. During ERT, however, the implementation of simultaneous multiple small group collaborative activities was a challenge in this study. Nevertheless, this challenge presents pedagogical implications for instructors to reconceptualize on-the-screen student collaboration in groups. One of the primary functions of group work is for students to benefit from interaction, idea exchange, and critical thinking. With this end in mind, when simultaneous multiple small group work is limited in virtual classes, instructors should consider making the most of collaborative activities with the entire class present, such as debates, moderated class discussions, and a variety of small interactive tasks that require brief turnaround times. These collaborative activities with the whole class suggest that a variety of personalities and perspectives can be more effective in developing cognitive presence than in a group composed with less diverse insights (Garrison & Arbaugh, 2007). Additionally, as suggested by Chai et al. (2013), in promoting collaboration among students through technologies, Chinese language instructors should explore the usefulness of online discussion forums and mind-mapping tools (e.g., Mindmeister and Miro). According to Chai et al., these tools can concurrently unlock ideas of students, engage students in collaboration in a graphical way, and enhance the abilities of learners of Chinese to interact while they analyze, comprehend, synthesize, recall, and generate new thoughts.

5.3 Teaching Presence

Synchronicity as a teaching platform contributed to the sustainability and continuity of the participants' cognitive and social presences during ERT according to this study. However, teaching synchronously required a high level of technological pedagogical content knowledge of faculty participants. For instance, in a face-to-face environment, instructors can simultaneously write down planned or unplanned information on the blackboard as they teach and show visual aids without having to switch modes. On the other hand, in a virtual setting during ERT, the faculty participants often needed to multitask in switching settings quickly on the computer in order to navigate through functions such as writing with a marker on the screen, moving the mouse cursor, sharing the screen, taking a poll, and admitting students into the virtual classroom. To facilitate these tasks synchronously, prior to the class, the faculty participants needed to plan for digitalization and organization of the sequence of their teaching materials in terms that closely aligned with the teaching agendas to avoid sporadic idle time due to technological transitions. This observation illustrates the participants' teaching presence with regard to "the selection, organization, and primary presentation of course content as well as the design and development of learning activities" (Garrison et al., 2000, p. 90). It also demonstrates the faculty participants' technological content knowledge in applying technology to change the presentation of the subject matter in a pedagogically beneficial manner (Mishra & Koehler, 2006) so they could offer student learning opportunities during ERT comparable with those offered in their face-to-face teaching.

Bair and Bair (2011) suggested that educators often experience a role change from an instructor to a less visible facilitator when they transition to an online environment. However, the participants in the study reported that they remained active and visible and continued their instructor-student dynamics throughout ERT. This observation can be attributed to the fact that ERT was a continuation of the first half of the spring 2020 semester and was intended to finish the remaining coursework with as little interruption as possible. Hence, the faculty participants virtualized their teaching by shifting the meeting place online but keeping the other instructional elements minimally changed, including tangibles (e.g., due dates of the assignments and class meeting times) and intangibles (e.g., expectation of students' progress and active engagement in a Zoom classroom). Keeping the ERT learning experience comparable to what it was before the pandemic required the faculty participants to stay present, visible, and active in a similar fashion. This explains why a role change of the faculty was not evident in the present study.

The comparable course arrangement during ERT entailed well-detailed, per-session learning goals and schedules for required meetings. Hence, flexibility, one characteristic often observed in online courses that allows students to learn at their own pace (e.g., Tang & Chaw, 2016), is not as evident in the virtual learning in the present study. However, a more structured virtual learning experience during ERT likely worked to the students' advantage because it consisted of most face-to-face instructional mechanisms to support students and avoided more disruptive changes than what the students were already experiencing. This result can be supported by the findings from the studies of Bair and Bair (2011) and Martin and Bolliger (2018), in which the learners of online courses found a clear structure and inflexibility to be helpful in making them less vulnerable to distraction. These undertakings that were to create an ERT learning experience compatible with what the students had had prior the pandemic suggest that ERT was rather a different delivery mode to continue the course than an independent online course unit. The dissimilarities that ERT shares with regular online teaching (e.g., a more structured learning experience) and the positive ERT experiences (e.g., maintaining academic rigor) can help faculty members put virtual learning in perspective. Since "there is no single technological solution that applies for every teacher, every course, or every view of teaching" (Mishra & Koehler, 2006, p. 1029), instructors who are interested in online teaching should develop their own "nuanced understanding of the complex relationship between technology, content, and pedagogy" and use this understanding and these technologies in constructive ways to design "appropriate, content-specific strategies and representations" (p. 1029) in their course delivery.

For the faculty participants to carry on their active teaching role and keep the course structures comparable, the faculty participants needed to adapt the teaching materials quickly to accommodate to virtual learning by reformulating the subject content through the use of technology (e.g., recorded mini lectures and interactive annotations on Zoom). In this study, the five participants all possessed proficient technological pedagogical content knowledge to immediately coordinate their virtual teaching presence that focused on keeping their students on track and attaining learning outcomes. Such an instructional task wouldn't have been accomplished had the faculty participants lacked necessary technological literacy. This reflects a teaching dynamic that places the faculty participants' proficiency in technology use on the same level with pedagogy and content in their professional skills, a different hierarchy from a traditional classroom. Functioning within this new dynamic with added responsibilities in technology use, the participants in this study were found to continuously prioritize student success and instructional stability during ERT. Consequently, according to the participants, a greater investment of time and work from the faculty was required to achieve the teaching and curricular goal. This finding is congruent with the results in the study of Chai et al. (2013) that Chinese language instructors spent additional time preparing for their teaching and offering technical support to their students when using information and communication technology to organize their teaching. This result suggests a challenge for the future virtual teaching environment to consider: how should faculty's increased workload be addressed by their institutions?

6 Summary of Pedagogical Implications and Future Research

Regarding organizing social presence in a virtual teaching environment where visual cues are reduced, instructors should reframe the concept of social presence and develop compensating strategies and take advantage of, for example, the reflective and explicit nature of the text-based communication to engage their learners in activities of higher-order thinking. Moreover, instructors can structure their social presence with pedagogical purposes in mind, and their social engagement with students should also be inspired by genuine emotions of caring. The findings suggest that instructors maximize their social presence opportunities through consistent interaction, organized engagement, and as-needed interactivity.

Simultaneous multiple small group work was reported to be a challenge when the participants enacted their cognitive presence through collaboration using breakout rooms during videoconferencing. The study suggests that instructors reconceptualize the idea of on-the-screen collaboration and pedagogically tailor it to their specific context. Instructors can make the most of collaborative efforts with the whole class present. Such collaboration with more individuals engaged suggests that diverse personalities and perspectives can be more effective in developing cognitive presence than in a group composed with less varying insights

(Garrison & Arbaugh, 2007). Moreover, the engagement strategies associated with the participants' cognitive presence all involved a high degree of interactivity between instructor and students. This emphasizes the importance of interactivity in student engagement in foreign language classrooms. Hence, instructors should consider creating learning opportunities that afford the most interactivity among instructors, students, and subject content to further cognitive engagement in their classrooms.

The enactment of technology-mediated teaching presence was not a challenge for the participants in the study, and they attributed their successful ERT experiences to their pre-ERT discipline-specific technological skills that they had selectively and consistently cultivated over time. Their success, on the other hand, suggests that technology can be a site of struggle for instructors because their technological skills can decide the quality of teaching (Warschauer, 2000). The implication from this observation is that continuous growth in faculty's technological literacy through self-directed learning or institutional professional development is imperative and that the depth of instructors' knowledge on selected technologies has a greater utility than the breadth. Moreover, during ERT, the participants' proficiency in technology use functioned on the same level with their pedagogical skills and content knowledge, which shows a different hierarchy from a face-to-face classroom. The participants also reported that ERT required them to invest a greater amount of time and effort to achieve the same teaching objectives than a traditional classroom would have. While remote teaching was found to be more demanding in skills and effort, the faculty participants' positive ERT experiences encouraged them to explore options to offer their Chinese language classes online. These results implicate important questions for teacher education programs, university administrators, and program directors to address:

- How should teacher education programs prepare teacher candidates with integrated technological knowledge and skills for virtual teaching?
- How do university administrators regulate faculty's increased workload with regard to online teaching assignments?
- How do program directors redesign their curriculum to reflect both the advantages and disadvantages of virtual language instruction?

The faculty participants' ERT experiences synthesized in this project can serve as a suggestive indicator of what additional support is necessary for the development of foreign language instructors' knowledge and skills in pedagogical technologies. More research is necessary to identify structures of ongoing institutional professional development that not only imparts the technological skills but also creates a learning culture that encourages faculty to stay current with useful pedagogical technologies. In addition, studies are needed to investigate the paradigm shift in foreign language education that stem from post-ERT perspectives of language faculty and to propose directions in curriculum design, teacher preparation, and language pedagogy that best reflect this paradigm shift. Moreover, this study reported the faculty's overall engagement strategies during ERT, and additional research is necessary to uncover how other parameters in a teaching environment (e.g., proficiency levels, types of institutions, and instructors' personalities) would impact faculty's implementations of engagement strategies. Finally, teaching strategies are context-dependent and can reflect instructors' cultural traditions and other conditions in the classroom (Liao et al., 2017; Romig, 2009). This study offers information regarding how Chinese language instructors applied a number of engagement strategies to organize student learning at different American four-year universities. With these new insights pertaining to Chinese language teaching and learning in the U.S. college classrooms, comparative studies can be conducted to offer additional perspectives on how teaching approaches reflect instructors' cultural and educational backgrounds.

7 Conclusion

This qualitative study sought to answer the research question: What were faculty's ERT experiences in organizing social, cognitive, and teaching presences in an online environment to implement their Chinese language instruction? The findings and discussions were organized by and analyzed with the theoretical frameworks of CoI (Garrison & Vaughan, 2008). When interpreting the results, readers are advised to consider the limitations of the study. The most limiting aspect is the small, non-randomized sample, and as a result, the findings cannot be generalized. In addition, the single source of data (interviews) is a limit in this study. Moreover, while subjectivity is expected because the participants were asked to discuss their ERT experiences, it can present a limiting factor along with potential recall errors. Hence, the narratives in the data should not be regarded as objective accounts but rather the participants' subjective interpretations of the situation and their experiences. Nevertheless, the study results are important in the following theoretical and practical aspects. First, how the faculty participants organized their social, cognitive, and teaching presences in this study can add empirical insights to the literature germane to engagement strategies in videoconferencing-mediated foreign language classrooms in general and in synchronous Chinese language classrooms in particular. Second, the faculty participants' use of technologies to support their virtual social, cognitive, and teaching presences during ERT can contribute a new understanding of the theoretical frame of CoI, which was originally based on a non-virtual learning context. Third, the analyses of the participants' integrated knowledge of technology, content, and pedagogy provide a synthesized view of technology-mediated Chinese language teaching. The specific data samples suggest a means for language instructors to self-examine their rationales in technology use in conjunction with their pedagogical grounds and other aspects of their teaching practices. Fourth, the faculty participants were able to function in technology use on similar levels with their content knowledge and pedagogical skills to make ERT a positive teaching experience in this study. This observation reinforces the important curricular role that the technology component plays in teacher education and in-service professional development. Fifth, the faculty participants had positive ERT experiences and became interested in exploring online teaching options. This emerging direction of faculty's instructional interest may be the beginning of a paradigm shift in Chinese teaching and learning and warrants further studies in Chinese language curriculum design, teacher preparation, and pedagogy.

References

Bair, D., & Bair, M. (2011). Paradoxes of online teaching. *International Journal for the Scholarship of Teaching and Learning, 5*(2), 1–15.

Bolliger, D. U., & Wasilik, O. (2009). Factors influencing faculty satisfaction with online teaching and learning in higher education. *Distance Education, 30*(1), 103–116.

Chai, C. S., Chin, C. K., Koh, J. H. L., & Tan, C. L. (2013). Exploring Singaporean Chinese language teachers' technological pedagogical content knowledge and its relationship to the teachers' pedagogical beliefs. *Asia-pacific Education Researcher, 22*(4), 657–666.

Chen, B., deNoyelles, A., Patton, K., & Zydney, J. (2017). Creating a community of inquiry in large-enrollment online courses: An exploratory study on the effect of protocols within online discussions. *Online Learning, 21*(1), 165–188.

Chickering, A. W., & Gamson, Z. F. (1987). Seven principles for good practice in undergraduate education. *AAHE Bulletin, 39*(7), 3–7.

Donato, R. (2004). Aspects of collaboration in pedagogical discourse. *Annual Review of Applied Linguistics, 24*, 284–302.

Garrison, D. R., Anderson, T., & Archer, W. (2000). Critical inquiry in a text-based environment: Computer conferencing in higher education. *The Internet and Higher Education, 2*(2–3), 87–105.

Garrison, D. R., Anderson, T., & Archer, W. (2001). Critical thinking, cognitive presence, and computer conferencing in distance education. *American Journal of Distance Education, 15*(1), 7–23.

Garrison, D. R., & Arbaugh, J. B. (2007). Researching the community of inquiry framework: Review, issues, and future directions. *The Internet and Higher Education, 10*(3), 157–172.

Garrison, D. R., & Vaughan, N. D. (2008). *Blended learning in higher education: Framework, principles, and guidelines*. Jossey-Bass Publishers.

Guion, L. (2002). Triangulation: Establishing the validity of qualitative studies. *EDIS, 2002*(6), 3.

Handelsman, M. M., Briggs, W. L., Sullivan, N., & Towler, A. (2005). A measure of college student course engagement. *The Journal of Educational Research, 98*(3), 184–191.

Hodges, C., Moore, S., Lockee, B., Trust, T., & Bond, A. (2020, March 27). The difference between emergency remote teaching and online learning. *Educause Review*. https://er.educause.edu/articles/2020/3/the-difference-between-emergency-remote-teaching-and-online-learning

Laurillard, D. (2000). New technologies and the curriculum. In P. Scott (Ed.), *Higher education re-formed* (pp. 133–153). Falmer Press.

Lee, C.-Y. (2009). A case study of using synchronous computer-mediated communication system for spoken English teaching and learning based on sociocultural theory and communicative language teaching approach curriculum [Unpublished doctoral thesis], Ohio University, Ohio.

Liao, W., Yuan, R., & Zhang, H. (2017). Chinese language teachers' challenges in teaching in U.S. Public Schools: A dynamic portrayal. *Asia-Pacific Edu Research, 26*(6), 369–381.

Liu, S. J. (2020). Learning the Chinese language on a non-traditional path: A case study. *The Language Learning Journal.* https://doi.org/10.1080/09571736.2020.1811370

Martin, F., & Bolliger, D. U. (2018). Engagement matters: Student perceptions on the importance of engagement strategies in the online learning environment. *Online Learning, 22*(1), 205–222.

Mishra, P., & Koehler, M. (2006). Technological pedagogical content knowledge: A framework for teacher knowledge. *The Teachers College Record, 108*(6), 1017–1054.

Moore, M. J. (1993). Three types of interaction. In K. Harry, M. John, & D. Keegan (Eds.), *Distance education theory* (pp. 19–24). Routledge.

Romig, N. (2009). Acculturation of four Chinese teachers teaching in the United States: An ethnographic study. Doctoral dissertation, Michigan State University. www.lib.msu.edu

Saldana, J. (2009). *The coding manual for qualitative researchers.* Sage Publications Ltd.

Shea, P., Li, C. S., & Pickett, A. (2006). A study of teaching presence and student sense of learning community in fully online and web-enhanced college courses. *The Internet and Higher Education, 9*(3), 175–190.

Tang, C. M., & Chaw, L. Y. (2016). Digital literacy: A prerequisite for effective learning in a blended learning environment? *The Electronic Journal of e-Learning, 14*(1), 54–65.

Teddlie, C., & Tashakkori, A. (2008). *Foundations of mixed methods research: Integrating quantitative and qualitative approaches in the social and behavioral sciences.* Sage Publications, Inc.

Trochim, W. (2006). *Research methods knowledge base.* https://conjointly.com/kb/

Warschauer, M. (2000). The changing global economy and the future of English teaching. *TESOL Quarterly, 34*(3), 511–535. https://doi.org/10.2307/3587741

Wu, C. (2020). Analysis of learner uptake in response to corrective feedback in advanced foreign language classrooms. *Applied Linguistics Research Journal, 4*(4), 1–29.

14

Reconfiguration of L2 Chinese Learners' Ecologies of Resources During the COVID-19 Pandemic in China and the US

Bing Mu, Chunyan Ma, and Ye Tian

1 Introduction

COVID-19, whose outbreak was first reported in China by the end of 2019, rapidly spread to every corner of the world in the first half of 2020. Such a global pandemic abruptly altered the landscape of people's lives in almost every aspect imaginable. Students, instructors, and administration around the globe faced unprecedented challenges as traditional face-to-face instruction came to a sudden halt due to the potential threat it could

---

B. Mu (✉)
University of Rhode Island, Kingston, RI, USA
e-mail: mubing@uri.edu

C. Ma
Zhejiang Sci-Tech University, Hangzhou, China
e-mail: machunyan@zstu.edu.cn

Y. Tian
University of Pennsylvania, Philadelphia, PA, USA
e-mail: tianye1@sas.upenn.edu

© The Author(s), under exclusive license to Springer Nature Switzerland AG 2022
S. Liu (ed.), *Teaching the Chinese Language Remotely*,
https://doi.org/10.1007/978-3-030-87055-3_14

pose to all parties concerned. In the face of this challenge, schools around the world had no choice but to take emergency measures and switch to remote teaching. As a result, the resources with which students interacted as forms of learning assistance were inevitably restructured to better adapt to the new global environment.

This study aims to address the following research question: How were L2 Chinese learners' ecologies of resources reconfigured in the face of the global pandemic in China and the US? First, this study identifies what types of resources were available to the L2 Chinese learners in China and the US during this global crisis, and then investigates how these types of resources interacted with the L2 Chinese learners to support their learning. The answers to this question can provide language pedagogues with not only a broad picture of the resources available to learners as learning assistance amidst the global crisis, but also food for thought on how to restructure learners' learning environments in the post-pandemic era to achieve better learning results.

2 Theoretical Framework

Advances in technology in the past several decades have not only rendered the learning contexts more technology rich, but also increasingly learner centered (Sun, 2018). To address the complex learning system afforded by the technology-rich environments, Luckin (2010) proposed an ecology of resources model, where learners as the active participants in the learning process are surrounded by a variety of resources with which the learners can interact. Grounded in Vygotsky's (1978) Zone of Proximal Development, the ecology of resources model conceptualizes the resources with which learners interact as potential forms of learning assistance.

In the ecology of resources model, the learner is at the center and surrounded by the resources that are variously located and yet interrelated. The resources that a learner can interact with as learning assistance encompass a rich mix of elements, and these elements can be roughly grouped into four categories: knowledge and skills, people, tools, and environment. Specifically, knowledge and skills refer to the learner's subject of learning, for example, mathematics, chemistry, psychology; tools incorporate books, pens and paper, and technology; people refers to instructors and other students who know more about the knowledge or skills than the learner; and environment includes location and surrounding environment with which the learner interacts, for example, a school classroom, a place of work, and so on. According to Luckin et al. (2013), "to support learning, it is necessary to identify and understand the relationships between the different types of resource with which the learner interacts. In addition, it is necessary to explore the way a learner's interactions with these resources is, or might be, constrained" (p. 36).

Learners' interactions with the available resources are not experienced directly by the learners, but oftentimes mediated or filtered by the action of others. For example, learners' interactions with certain knowledge and skills are usually filtered through some kind of organization, such as a particular curriculum and pedagogy. The tools available to the learner are usually filtered or mediated through school rules and protocols; for example, some classrooms prohibit the use of cell phones or laptops, while such use may be encouraged in other classrooms. People that the learner interacts with for learning assistance are filtered through space and time, in the sense that a teacher may only be available during a class or office hours and can be reached via email. Environment, on the other hand, is mediated by the environment's organization; for example, certain schools may have certain timetables and regulations, which could impact the ways in which learners interact with their environment. This said, it is necessary to take into account the filter elements when examining learners' interactions with the available resources to support their learning. Figure 14.1 demonstrates the different elements in ecology of resources model and how the different elements interact with the learner and among themselves.

To adopt ecology of resources as a theoretical and analytic construct, it is first necessary to identify the different types or categories of resources available to learners. Second, the significant role of interaction between learners and the resources needs to be recognized, which includes not only the more knowledgeable and able members of a society, such as instructors, other students, and parents, but also a variety of tools and technologies that could assist the learner at a particular point in time.

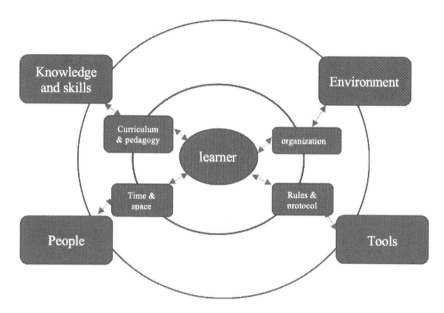

Fig. 14.1 Learners' ecology of resources

Meanwhile, it is key to recognize that these resources do not exist independently of one another. Rather, it is their interactions with the learners and with each other that effectively support the learning process, and such interactions are mediated by various filter elements.

3 Methodology

A case study was applied to give a closer examination of the research question. In the context of educational research, this approach allows for a deeper understanding of the interactions among educational organizations, learning environments, and participants within the organization and the environment (Erickson, 1986). Guided by the principle of information-oriented selection (Flyvbjerg, 2006) and convenient sampling (Henry, 1990), three L2 Chinese language classes were carefully chosen to maximize the utility of information from relatively small samples when time is of the essence:

- An intermediate-level comprehensive Chinese language class at an Ivy League University in the US (pseudonym "U1");
- A beginning-level comprehensive Chinese language class at a public research university in New England, US (pseudonym "U2"); and
- A beginning-level Chinese speaking and listening class at a provincial university in Hangzhou, China (pseudonym "U3").

There were 13 students in the Chinese language class at U1, 10 students at U2, and 19 students at U3. The majority of the L2 Chinese learners at U1 and U2 were American students, with three international students at U1 from Japan, Korea, and Ecuador. The L2 Chinese Learners at U3 were all international students from nine different countries, including Turkmenistan, Tajikistan, Kazakhstan, Ghana, Democratic Republic of Congo, Libya, Gabon, Ecuador, and Switzerland. The Chinese language class at U1 met four times a week from Monday to Thursday, 50 minutes a session. Class at U2 met three times a week on Monday, Wednesday and Friday, 50 minutes a session. The Chinese speaking and listening class at U3 met three times a week on Monday, Wednesday, and Friday, 90 minutes a session.

This study adopted the complete participant observation (Burgess, 1984; Erickson, 1986) as the main research method, as all three authors were already members of these particular research sites. The research data were collected from February to July 2020 by the authors who worked as the Chinese instructors of these three classes. This position allowed for relevant data, for example, school emails, teaching guidance, course arrangements, and instructors' reflections to be collected, coded, condensed, and analyzed based on the qualitative methodological approach as recommended by Miles et al. (2014). Finally, recurring and explanatory themes were selected to report findings, focusing on the L2 Chinese learners' ecologies of resources and how they were reconfigured in the face of the global pandemic that abruptly transformed people's lives worldwide.

4 Findings

The ecology of resources model encompasses four main categories, namely, environment, tools, people, and knowledge and skills. This section reports answers to the question of how L2 Chinese learners' ecologies of resources were reconfigured in the global pandemic through a systematic examination of these four categories.

4.1 Environment

The COVID-19 pandemic changed the living and learning environment of millions over a very short period of time. Luckin et al. (2013) argue that "a learner's access to their environment is mediated by that environment's organization and any rules and conventions that apply to it" (p. 36). Thus, to understand the new learning environment, it is crucial to examine the policies issued by the universities to cope with the ongoing global crisis.

Environment in the US Universities

Policies issued by universities in the US aimed to "create and maintain an environment conducive to personal health and wellness while ensuring the continuity of education and research" (U2's President's Office, March 11, 2020). In response to this policy, both universities canceled face-to-face instruction and mandated that all classes be delivered remotely. The decision for this transition was made during the Spring Break in both US universities in March 2020, when the majority of the students were either visiting their hometowns or traveling. As a result, both schools encouraged their students to remain at home for the remainder of the semester. For this reason, students' living environment moved from campus to their individual home and the location of teaching and learning from school classrooms to the virtual world.

Three themes emerged from a close examination of the two universities' school emails and the correspondence between instructors and students. First and foremost, *safety*. Building a safe environment for students in and outside of the classroom was the most important task undertaken by both universities. To ensure students' safety, all in-person events that involved large gatherings of participants were cancelled, including face-to-face instruction, sporting and athletic events, commencements, and so on. After learning that some students' family members or the students themselves were infected with the virus, instructors reassured them not to worry about their grades or assignments but prioritize their safety and health.

Second, *support*. Learning does not simply take the form of lectures, but also is supported by the infrastructure to support student success, such as library resources, co-curricular activities, and other social supports (Hodges et al., 2020). In the face of the disruption to both face-to-face education and the infrastructure that exists around it, both US universities provided various supports to ensure safety of the students and the continuity of instruction, including cancelling an extra week of classes before the transition to allow more time for preparation; providing on-campus housing for those when staying at home was not possible or prudent; providing free tablets, laptops, and internet for students in need; setting up an information hotline for students on health services; giving various workshops and webinars for students to share experiences; and asking instructors to be more accommodating and simplify their teaching requirements and methods, and so on.

Third, *accessibility*. Compared with the traditional face-to-face instruction, remote instruction requires more resources, especially technological resources, to support the learning process. These technological resources include but are not limited to a stable internet, PC or laptop, printer, and a quiet place to take classes and study. Access to these resources was, to a large extent, confined by the vast difference of socioeconomic status among students. In addition, as students were scattered across the country or even in different countries when the pandemic hit the US, the geographical and temporal constraints for taking online classes became an issue that needed to be addressed.

As a result, both US universities highlighted *accessibility* and encouraged the instructors to provide instruction readily and reliably to all students. For instance, U1 reminded the instructors that "your students might be in diverse time zones or have only intermittent access to reliable internet service, both of which would make it difficult for them to participate synchronously"; therefore, it was recommended that instructors keep their newly created online courses "simple and readily supportable by SAS computing" (U1's SAS Dean's Office, March 13, 2020). The school-wide announcements and workshops following the school email shortly thereafter also reiterated the same principle. In one announcement, this principle was emphasized with all capitalized and bold letters: "**A STRONG REMINDER ABOUT TECHNICAL ASPECTS: KEEP IT AS SIMPLE AS POSSIBLE**" (U1's SAS Dean's Office, March 19, 2020). This principle of "simplicity," to a large degree, limited the available choices at U1 and constrained the Chinese language instructors' use of certain technological tools, which inevitably shaped how remote teaching was conducted in that institution.

The three principles of safety, support, and accessibility promoted in the US universities aimed to create a learning environment that was supportive, inclusive, and equitable in the midst of a global crisis. While students were provided with a full range of support and learning assistance encompassing physical, mental, material, and intellectual considerations, students' learning was mediated by the university policies highlighting accessibility, which laid emphasis on the simple and reliable access on the one hand and constrained and limited the available options that instructors could choose from on the other.

Environment in the Chinese University

When the pandemic broke out in China in late January 2020, most Chinese universities were on winter break, and the majority of their international students had returned to their home countries. By that time, COVID-19 had not yet spread to the rest of the world. As a result, some students chose to cancel or postpone their trip back to school for safety. The spread of the virus in China caused U3's lockdown, and the start of the spring semester originally scheduled on February 9th was postponed. During the lockdown, instructors started to prepare for the transition to online teaching. Although the online courses for Chinese domestic students began as early as February 24th, the Chinese language courses for international students were further postponed because most of the students had not returned to campus and the administration had little knowledge of those students' learning environments. The online Chinese language courses for international students started on April 13th after students' petitions at the beginning of April. In May, when the virus was largely under control with no new cases for three consecutive months in Hangzhou, U3 decided to let students voluntarily return to school for normal face-to-face classroom teaching. Students not willing to go back to the classroom could continue to attend online classes. After their return, students were still required to stay on campus, and couldn't leave campus without the school's permission. Under such circumstances, as of May 18, Chinese language classes for international students resumed face-to-face instruction, with 15 students in the classroom and 3 students attending the same class remotely.

Similar to US universities, safety and support were strongly advocated in the Chinese university. To ensure safety, the international students who chose to stay in China were not allowed to leave campus other than for some exceptional reasons, such as seeing the doctor, going to the bank, repairing their computers or cellphones, and so on. The campus lockdown had successfully protected the safety of the international students by keeping the virus out. While students were kept safe on campus, the university admin took a series of measures to support their living and learning environment. To help maintain their normal lives, the school's cafeterias, libraries, and hospital remained open during the school lockdown. The international students' office remained open to deal with any unexpected situations. Students' dorms were sterilized with disinfectants regularly, and students were provided with free masks, disinfectant, and hand sanitizers. In addition, each student was given a thermometer to closely monitor any fever. Training was also offered to students on pandemic prevention.

To assist instructors with smooth transition to remote instruction, the academic affairs office at U3 provided instructors with online training and Q&A sessions on various teaching software and classroom operating systems since February 9, the date that the university was scheduled to start its spring semester. While both US universities emphasized accessibility, the Chinese university granted instructors more freedom in choosing technological tools and the mode to deliver their classes. For example, while the university provided various resources for the instructors, it was entirely up to the individual instructor to choose which platform or software to use for teaching. In addition, the school also encouraged the instructors to be more innovative with their use of technology and experiment with new technologies that they hadn't used before. Furthermore, since the school admin believed that the pandemic would soon abate at that time, they even allowed instructors to postpone teaching to a point when it was safe for students to return to school to resume face-to-face instruction.

The contrastive policies between the two US universities and the Chinese university in Hangzhou mediated learners' interaction with the different learning environments in the US and China. Compared with the diverse socioeconomic status and the scattered presence of students around the world at the US universities, the international students' learning environment in China was comparatively unified and readily manageable. When online Chinese language courses for international students started, the campus lockdown mandate was still in effect. Students in this particular class were all physically on campus with easy access to the internet provided by the school. Such an environment supported the instructors' innovative use of technological tools in their virtual classroom. Therefore, the U3 university admin in China encouraged the instructors to take the opportunity to explore the affordances and possibilities of the remote instruction.

4.2 Technological Tools

Entering the twenty-first century, technology has been playing an increasingly significant role among foreign language learners in and outside of the classroom. Technological tools, as teaching aids, have already been widely applied to assist teaching, either in face-to-face, or blended or hybrid, or a fully online context (Chun, 2016). The benefits of using technologies include enhanced input and comprehension, output and interaction, feedback, affect and motivation, metacognition, and metalinguistic knowledge (Golonka et al., 2014).

Different from "online teaching" featured with careful instructional design and innovative use of technological tools (Hodges et al. 2020; Nilson & Goodson, 2017), the emergent shift to remote delivery focused on providing simple and reliable access to instruction during a global crisis. The following subsection presents the different technological tools utilized in the virtual classrooms in the new learning environment and the way students interacted with them to assist their learning.

Technological Tools Utilized in the US Universities

Three technological tools were selected for a close examination of their functions and the students' interactions therewith. These three were the only ones employed at U1 for the consideration of reliable accessibility. For U2, these three were used most frequently, although a few others were also in use due to the tradition of incorporating technological tools in the classroom in its Chinese language program.

Course Management System. During the transition from face-to-face instruction to remote, course management systems played a key role. In asynchronous teaching, course management systems became the most important tool to connect instructors and students. The course management systems utilized at U1 and U2 were Canvas and Sakai respectively, and these two systems share some similar features. On the course websites, instructors can post course-related materials, such as announcements, syllabi, schedules, scanned pages of textbooks, webpage links, course recordings, and audio and video files. Discussion board is available to facilitate communications between students and instructors and among students themselves. Moreover, course management systems can also be used to design online assignments, administer quizzes remotely, and automatically analyze and record students' grades. The course management systems function as information hubs for students, and almost everything students need to succeed in the class can be found here. Although course management systems played a big role in students' learning before the transition to remote mode, the frequency and extent of the interactions between students and the course management systems during the pandemic increased substantially, and the course management systems replaced part of the functions of other tools, such as books, pens and paper. In addition, both U1 and U2 used the course management systems for exams when the pandemic rendered in-person contact unsafe.

Zoom. As a cloud-based peer-to-peer software platform, Zoom is used for teleconferencing and telecommuting, where learners can have real-time instruction, practices, feedback, and discussion. It provides video/audio communication for synchronous teaching, breakout rooms for small group discussions, whiteboard for handwriting, chat for typing, and screensharing for instructors and students to share anything on their computers, such as course management system websites, PowerPoint slides, and YouTube videos. Instructors can also record their synchronous sessions via Zoom for those who cannot make it to the virtual classroom during their regular meeting time. The advantage of using Zoom for synchronous online sessions is that it successfully simulates the face-to-face interaction by not only allowing multiple people to talk simultaneously but also enabling pair work among students via its breakout room function. In addition, it also supports functions not readily accessible in the face-to-face context, such as "annotate" to encourage instructors and students to interact through drawing or typing and "chat" to answer questions in a written format, thus a good exercise for typing characters. During the pandemic when remote delivery was conducted, Zoom was utilized on a daily basis for synchronous teaching at both U1 and U2.

Quizlet. Quizlet is a popular online study application for vocabulary, which incorporates various functions of flashcards, games, and tests. After the new vocabulary of each lesson is created, Quizlet can provide learners with various options to study through flashcards, multiple choices, fill-in-the-blank, matching the Chinese-English equivalents, tests, and so on. After the transition to remote instruction, both universities used Quizlet to replace the original vocab quizzes in the classroom, where students were required to take the test in Quizlet, and their test scores were recorded as part of their final grades. In this case, students' interaction with Quizlet was not limited to using it as a self-study tool, but also as an assessment tool that bears stakes in the learning process. In addition, at U2, Quizlet live was frequently used in their virtual classroom where students were grouped by Quizlet randomly and competed with other groups. While Quizlet live was also frequently employed in face-to-face instruction before the crisis at U2, the function shifted from entertaining and educational to community building. The instructor specifically chose to do Quizlet live in the classroom because being grouped together and accomplishing a task as a group against others can help build a sense of belonging and membership, when this sense of connection and support is highly valuable during a crisis.

Technological Tools Utilized in the Chinese University

After the temporary transition to remote instruction in China, quite a few classroom management systems emerged as candidates, including Tencent conference system (腾讯会议系统), Zoom, Rain Class (雨课堂), Tencent Class (腾讯课堂), DingTalk (钉钉), and so on. After careful consideration, DingTalk was chosen as the teaching platform for the Chinese language class at U3. There were two main reasons to choose DingTalk over other classroom management systems. First, as one of the most widely used collaboration platforms in China, DingTalk has been constantly evolving to better serve the needs of different students and instructors; second, DingTalk is a free one-stop platform integrating various functions, including sign-in, assignment, notification, lecture, meeting, playback, file storage, and so on. Besides these basic functions, DingTalk also supports functions unavailable on other platforms, such as storing and sharing large files, one-click reminder for unfinished assignments, and daily challenges. Here are the most frequently used functions of DingTalk in the listening and speaking class at U3.

Class Live Broadcast (课堂直播). After the instructor initiates the live broadcast, students can interact with the instructor via typing, sending voice messages, or "connecting through camera" (连麦). Live broadcast also supports playback, which means that if a learner misses something, s/he can make up his/her work by watching the videos. This function is particularly useful for an instructor's explanation of language points and the listening part in a listening and speaking class. In the listening and speaking class, when the instructor plays the recording, students can reply with the selected answers in real time. One drawback of this function is that the instructor cannot see the students; therefore, the instructor is unable to know if a student fully understands something soon enough and will have to wait until the drilling section to have a better understanding.

Online Classroom (在线课堂). Online classroom supports real-time interaction between the instructor and the students and among the students themselves. The instructor can choose to deliver the class either through audio or video. The computer can also import class handouts to facilitate students' viewing. This function is particularly suitable for drill practice. For example, in listening and speaking class, the instructor can use this function to have students take turns to read new words, provide corrective feedback, or have students act out the text in roles. There are also functions in online classroom that cannot be realized otherwise, for example, the online live broadcast of making rice dumplings during the Dragon Boat Festival, or a live broadcast of cooking beef fried rice and Chinese scallion pancakes when food is mentioned in the text.

Assignment (家校本). Assignment is a platform for homework assignment, completion, and feedback. Its advantages are as follows:(1) instructors can monitor whether students have carefully previewed the lesson and completed the assignment; (2) as soon as the students submit their assignment, the instructor can provide timely feedback; (3) high-quality assignments can be shown to the entire class to motivate students and provide an opportunity for peer learning; (4) for students who have not handed in their assignment, the instructor can send out a one-click reminder. Timely practice and feedback can deepen the internalization of students' knowledge and skills. Meanwhile, this function can also keep track of students' submission of assignments throughout the entire semester. This not only facilitates the teaching management but also provides a proof for students' daily grades.

Daily Challenge (打卡). The instructor can specify the content for students' daily challenge, for example, reading aloud. Instructors can also set a cycle, for example, one month, and DingTalk will automatically record students' daily challenge and rank them every day. Instructors and students can give thumbs up, and instructors can also provide comments. By the end of the cycle, the system will issue gold, silver, and bronze medals to the top three students. Instructors can use the daily challenge as students' homework and export the results at any time. The results can be sent to DingTalk group for reminder and supervision. This function plays a positive role in students' after-school practice of language points and deepens the internalization of their knowledge and skills.

Sign-in (签到) and **Notification** (通知). These two functions are mainly used for student management in and outside of the classroom. Teachers can click the "sign-in" button at any time during the class, and students are supposed to respond within 30 seconds. This is to check whether students are listening attentively. If a student fails to sign in on time, it is very likely that the student is doing other things with their cellphone on. The "notification" function is used to publish notices after class. Instructors can check whether students have viewed the notice. Students can click "Confirm" after viewing them, indicating that they have no question with the contents of the notices. For important ones, the system can be set for signature confirmation. All the statistical functions in the system free the instructors from the tedious and repeated scoring calculation and statistics.

4.3 People

In the ecology of resources model, people refer to the more knowledgeable and able members of a society, such as instructors, other students, and parents, with whom learners interact as learning assistance. This subsection examines learners' interactions with their instructors, fellow classmates, and other people in their immediate social circle, specifically how their interaction changed in the remote context and how such changes enhanced and/or constrained learners' learning.

First, after the abrupt migration to remote delivery, learners' interactions with their instructors and fellow classmates changed from face-to-face interactive mode to remote format mediated by space, time, and various tools of the internet, laptops, cameras, and so on. The change of location from the traditional classroom to virtual environment has deprived the interactions between the instructors and the students of physical vicinity. While the various technological tools, such as Zoom, have made the virtual interaction as similar as possible to the face-to-face format, the lack of physical vicinity has made the transition challenging. For example, some activities afforded by physical vicinity in the traditional classroom, for example, asking a student who sits next to you for a quick answer to a question in a low voice, was not readily achievable in an online format, because doing so would inevitably disrupt the classroom order and process. One student from U1 complained about that in a program-wide survey: "the virtual learning has been very difficult for me. I feel like I am losing a lot of comprehension and time to practice speaking with peers. It sometimes is hard to hear clearly, and I can no longer rely on more peers to ask a quick clarification about a term or topic. I feel bad interrupting class to ask for clarification when it seems like everyone understands."

Second, the mediation of technology can sometimes play the part of a double-edged sword. In the synchronous sessions, the instructors usually asked the students to turn on their cameras so that they could see the instructor and each other. By doing so, the communication process can be supported by the various para-linguistic cues that students could hear and the extra-linguistic signs that they could see. All of these elements intertwine together to create context to facilitate the interpretation of the language in use. Two students at U1 and U2, however, did not have cameras on their laptops, thus failing to make full use of the rich resources that an online environment could afford. Consequently, the interactions between these students and the instructor and their interactions with the rest of the class were also impaired. On the other hand, the use of certain platforms deepened the connection between students and the instructors, resulting in a greater authenticity of written and spoken communication. One example is the use of the "chat" function for typing Chinese characters when using Zoom to deliver synchronous teaching. In a traditional classroom, students' and instructors' interactions normally take the form of oral, that is, instructors ask questions and students answer. In the online format, the instructor can ask the students to answer it either orally or in written form by typing the answer in the chat box. This particular function made written communication more convenient and meaningful.

Besides instructors and classmates, another group of people providing valuable learning assistance to L2 Chinese learners lies in their social circle. At US universities the L2 Chinese learners can interact with tutors and heritage speakers with whom they have a personal relationship; at the Chinese university learners can interact with their local friends and native speakers on a regular basis. The migration to online learning caused by the pandemic, however, limited learners' access to this group of people as their learning resources. Before the pandemic outbreak, students at U1 and U2 were provided with opportunities to interact with language tutors to practice speaking Chinese for a certain amount of time on a weekly basis. By doing so, students had a chance to hang out with someone of similar age and with common interests, which often resulted in the improvement of their linguistic proficiency and the development of personal bonds and friendship. In a similar vein, the Chinese language learners at U3 could hang out with their local friends and interact with native speakers to make full use of the rich local resources while in China. Furthermore, by personally participating in the target culture and being immersed in environment rich in naturally occurring interactions, learners could not only maximize their proficiency gains but also develop their intercultural communicative competence (Chai, Cornelius, & Mu, 2018). The on-going pandemic, however, significantly limited people's social interactions, which consequently constrained L2 Chinese learners' interactions with this group of people as learning assistance in both the US and Chinese universities.

4.4 Knowledge and Skills

Although the subject of learning for L2 Chinese learners, that is, Chinese language, remained the same at these three universities during the global pandemic, the content of what should be covered and how to cover it in the midst of a global crisis differed greatly from the normal days.

For instance, in response to the abrupt migration to the online learning environment that significantly restructured the interactions between students and instructors and the way classes could be delivered, the administrators of U2 urged vigorously and resolutely that the goal of emergency remote teaching was not innovative online course design, but bare bone remote delivery to salvage bare minimum learning opportunities due to a pandemic. Therefore, instructors should "**Identify priorities, set realistic goals, determine tools**" **(bolded by the authors)** (U2's A & S Dean's office, March 11, 2020). Guided by this principle, instructors were urged to deliver only the absolutely essential and necessary knowledge and skills that students should acquire in a specific class and figure out how to deliver them effectively in a remote format.

Similar phenomenon can also be found in U1 and U3 where Chinese learners' access to knowledge and skills were consequently confined to the absolutely essential and necessary. For example, students' homework load was reduced, the submission and deadlines of various assignments and homework became more flexible, the examinations were further simplified both in format and content, the requirement of handwriting characters was slackened, and students were encouraged to take the opportunity to practice character typing as an alternate skill. In addition, students were encouraged to explore some functions that could promote their self-study abilities, for example, the use of machine translation and speech recognition "to enhance learners' awareness of self-correction on grammar, pronunciation, and word choice errors" (Tian, 2020, p. 20).

In the meantime, COVID-19 related knowledge was incorporated into the Chinese instructions at all three institutions, where students were instructed not only with the key vocabulary related to COVID-19, but also how to use these words or terms to discuss their lives during the pandemic. For instance, instead of the normal movie appreciation and presentation activities, students at U1 were required to watch the documentary films that discussed how China controlled the COVID-19 pandemic.

5   Discussion

The research question addressed how the L2 Chinese learners' ecologies of recourses were reconfigured amidst the global pandemic. Four categories of resources available to learners were examined, that is, environment, technological tools, people, and knowledge and skills. The findings show that the available resources with which learners interacted to support their learning were significantly restructured due to the public health crisis. Universities in both countries cancelled face-to-face instruction and switched to temporary remote delivery to protect students' health and wellness. To support the emergency remote instruction, various technological tools were employed to support learners' acquisition of absolutely essential and necessary knowledge and skills. During this process, the interactions between students and the people who could assist their learning were significantly reshaped. From this perspective, it is evident that these four categories of resources do not exist independently of one another. Instead, they interact with each other to form an ecology that provides meaningful learning assistance to the L2 Chinese learners.

This study first examined the L2 Chinese learners' learning environment in the two American universities and one Chinese university. A close look at the policies revealed common themes of safety and support to ensure continuity of instruction while protecting students' health. In terms of how to deliver remote instructions, these two countries underlined different principles. The US universities highlighted accessibility to ensure easy and reliable access to remote instruction by all students, by taking into consideration their socioeconomic disparity and geographical and temporal constraints. The Chinese university, on the other hand, granted instructors more freedom in how to deliver their classes and encouraged their instructors to take the opportunity to explore the affordances and possibilities of the remote instruction. The difference in the principles of how to approach remote instruction was rooted in the different learning environment in these two countries: while the majority of the American students stayed at their individual home to take online classes, the international students in China all stayed at their dorms, which made their learning environment comparatively unified and readily manageable. Such an environment supported the instructors' innovative use of technological tools in their virtual classrooms.

In examining the technological tools adopted in the emergency remote instruction in these three universities, findings show that before the global pandemic, technological tools were widely applied to the foreign language teaching and learning but mainly as teaching aids. The disruption to face-to-face instruction by the global pandemic has made the use of technology essential in the remote context, whether it be synchronous or asynchronous. What's more, the global pandemic restructured the types of technological resources that learners used to support their language learning. Before this global pandemic, Lai et al. (2018) documented that the technological resources that language learners utilized the most were receptive ones, such as movies, music, and news; on the other hand, those that engaged learners in language communication such as online chatting and conferencing tools were least frequently employed. This study revealed that the pandemic significantly reconfigured the ecology of resources in L2 Chinese classrooms in that the technological resources that Chinese language instructors and students employed the most were the ones that can engage learners in language communication in a real-time fashion, for example, Zoom, WebEx, DingTalk, and other conferencing tools of similar nature, and these technological resources were utilized on a daily basis for most L2 Chinese classrooms conducted synchronously. A close examination of the technological tools adopted in China and the US also revealed that the US and Chinese universities tend to employ different media in achieving their respective teaching goals. The tools that the US universities use tend to target one function, for example, Quizlet at vocab acquisition and Zoom at online classroom, while the technological tools developed in China tend to incorporate various functions in one application, for example, DingTalk can achieve the different functions of live broadcast, online classroom, sign-in, daily challenge, assignment, and so on.

People is the third category of ecology of resources examined. This study not only delved into how the L2 Chinese learners interacted with their instructors and fellow classmates in the online format, but also examined how the interactions between the L2 Chinese learners and those in their immediate social circle were hindered by the on-going pandemic. The result showed that the interactions between students and those who could provide them with learning assistance were mediated by time, space, and technology, which both constrained and enhanced students' learning. On the plus side, the use of certain platforms created more opportunities for students to practice certain uses of language. On the other hand, the reliance on technology for communication deprived learners' interactions with instructors and classmates of physical vicinity, and also limited learners' social interaction with those in their social circle. In addition, the use of technologies also created challenges for students when their technological tools on hand did not support certain features adopted in the classroom.

In terms of knowledge and skills that supported learners' learning during a pandemic, remote delivery was considered as a means to salvage the minimum learning opportunities in a global crisis. As a result, the L2 Chinese learners' knowledge and skills acquired were confined to the absolutely essential and necessary ones due to the threat and challenges that the pandemic has posed to both the instructors and learners. Students were given not only more flexibility in the process of learning but also more opportunities to explore the tools that could assist their self-study.

6 Limitations and Future Research

This study examined how L2 Chinese learners' ecologies of resources were reconfigured during the global pandemic in China and the US. Three classes from two US universities and one Chinese university were selected and examined as a case study. Consequently, this research only aimed to provide a contextualized understanding, and generalization within this study merits careful attention. Another drawback is that complete participant observation was adopted as the main research methodology, and the research is largely based on the instructors' observation and reflections. To include more stakeholders' voices, more effective and panoramic research methods are needed, such as interviews of the university admin, other instructors, and students. Another thing to note is that this research examined a dynamic process during the first half of 2020, which continues to evolve on a daily basis. As many universities were continuing the remote instruction in the second half of 2020, the research result may need updating.

As COVID-19 has still been a threat to many parts of the world, more robust research on teacher training, textbook development, and technology application that supports remote instruction is needed. In addition, the emergency remote instruction experience has demonstrated that online teaching is more than extending the classroom via technology to the virtual world or creating a digital environment via technical supporting systems. Therefore, more research is needed on the very nature of remote instruction, and the affordances and constraints thereof. Meanwhile, it is also worth studying how to transform the experiences and lessons learned from the emergency remote instruction into regular online teaching and face-to-face instruction in the post-pandemic era.

References

Burgess, R. G. (1984). *In the field: An introduction to field research*. Allen & Unwin.

Chai, D., Cornelius, C., & Mu, B. (2018). *Action! China: a field guide to using Chinese in the community*. Routledge.

Chun, D. M. (2016). The role of technology in SLA research. *Language Learning & Technology, 20*(2), 98–115.

Erickson, F. (1986). Qualitative methods in research on teaching. In M. C. Wittrock (Ed.), *Handbook of research on teaching* (3rd ed., pp. 119–161). Macmillan.

Flyvbjerg, B. (2006). Five misunderstandings about case-study research. *Qualitative Inquiry, 12*(2), 219–245.

Golonka, E. M., Bowles, A. R., Frank, V. M., Richardson, D. L., & Freynik, S. (2014). Technologies for foreign language learning: a review of technology types and their effectiveness. *Computer assisted language learning, 27*(1), 70–105.

Henry, T. (1990). *Practical sampling*. Sage Publications.

Hodges, C., Moore, S., Lockee, B., Trust, T., & Bond, A. (2020). The difference between emergency remote teaching and online learning. *Educause Review, 27*, 1.

Lai, C., Hu, X., & Lyu, B. (2018). Understanding the nature of learners' out-of-class language learning experience with technology. *Computer Assisted Language Learning, 31*(1–2), 114–143.

Luckin, R. (2010). *Re-designing learning contexts: Technology-rich, learner-centered ecologies*. Routledge.

Luckin, R., Clark, W., & Underwood, J. (2013). The ecology of resources: A theoretically grounded framework for designing next generation technology-rich learning. In R. Luckin, P. Goodyear, B. Grabowski, S. Puntambekar, N. Winters, & J. Underwood (Eds.), *Handbook of design in educational technology* (pp. 33–43). Routledge.

Miles, M. B., Huberman, A. M., & Saldaña, J. (2014). *Qualitative data analysis: A methods sourcebook*. SAGE Publications.

Nilson, L. B., & Goodson, L. A. (2017). *Online teaching at its best: Merging instructional design with teaching and learning research*. John Wiley & Sons.

Sun, S. Y. (2018). Student configuration and place-making in fully online language learning. *Computer Assisted Language Learning, 31*(8), 932–959.

Tian, Y. (2020). The Error Tolerance of Machine Translation: Findings from a Failed Teaching Design. *Journal of Technology and Chinese Language Teaching, 11*(1), 19–35.

Vygotsky, L. S. (1978). *Mind in society: The development of higher psychological processes*. Harvard University Press.

15

Perspectives of Instructors and Students on Online Chinese Teaching and Learning in 2020: Preliminary Findings

Shijuan Liu, Yanlin Wang, and Hong Zhan

1 Introduction

According to Allen and Seaman (2017), there were over six million students, more than one in four students, enrolled in at least one distance course in American higher education in Fall 2015. Inside Higher Ed's 2019 *Survey of Faculty Attitudes on Technology* showed that 46% of surveyed faculty members taught online courses versus 30% in 2013, which demonstrates a slow but steady increase in positive attitudes toward

---

S. Liu (✉)
Indiana University of Pennsylvania, Indiana, PA, USA
e-mail: sliu@iup.edu

Y. Wang
Texas Tech University, Lubbock, TX, USA
e-mail: yanlin.wang@ttu.edu

H. Zhan
Embry-Riddle Aeronautical University, Prescott, AZ, USA
e-mail: zhan121@erau.edu

© The Author(s), under exclusive license to Springer Nature Switzerland AG 2022
S. Liu (ed.), *Teaching the Chinese Language Remotely*,
https://doi.org/10.1007/978-3-030-87055-3_15

online learning among professors (Lederman, 2019). Accordingly, there has been increasing interest in online education since the late 1990s in accordance with the internet's rapid development (e.g., Moore & Anderson, 2003; Rudestam & Schoenholtz-Read, 2009). Online teaching and learning have been studied from various aspects such as design and teaching guidelines (Thormann & Zimmerman, 2012; Vai & Sosulsk, 2016), activities (Bonk & Zhang, 2008), assessment (Koç et al., 2015; Liu, 2009; Palloff & Pratt, 2008), asynchronous discussions (Hiltz & Goldman, 2004), synchronous teaching and learning (Finkelstein, 2008), and Massive Open Online Courses (MOOCs) (Bonk et al., 2015).

Before the COVID-19 pandemic, there are some institutions and programs offering Chinese courses fully online. For example, Beijing Language and Culture University offers a series of Chinese courses through eBLCU (网上北语) (http://chinese.eblcu.com/); the Open University of China offers MyEChinese (https://s.myechinese.com/app/public/products); Florida Virtual School (https://www.flvs.net/) and Michigan Virtual (https://michiganvirtual.org/) offer fully online Chinese courses to high school students. There are also several Chinese MOOCs offered through XuetangX (学堂在线) (http://www.xuetangx.com/global), Coursera (https://www.coursera.org/), or edX (https://www.edx.org/). Additional training programs for online Chinese teaching and learning include the U.S. federally funded STARTALK programs (Liu, 2018). However, before 2020 face-to-face instruction remained the primary and preferred method for language education across all levels from preschool to graduate school. As Li (2019) pointed out, despite the increasing number of student enrollments in online courses and abundant research in online education, many stakeholders in language education including some instructors and students remained skeptical of the quality and effectiveness of teaching and learning language online.

Consequently, although many empirical studies (e.g., Kim et al., 2005; Liu et al., 2007; Liu et al., 2010; Martinez et al., 2006) have investigated teaching and learning other subjects online, there was little research on fully online language teaching and learning (Lai et al., 2008; Vorobel & Kim, 2012). While some literature could be found on online Chinese teaching and learning before the pandemic, such as Bai et al. (2019), Li (2007), Li and Jiang (2017), Tseng et al. (2019), and Zheng (2001), the amount is still very limited. Additionally, most of the existing empirical studies on online Chinese language teaching and learning are case studies investigating issues related to specific courses (e.g., Stickler & Shi, 2013; Sun et al., 2013; Wang, 2012). As Liu (2020a) pointed out, the relative paucity of empirical research on online Chinese language teaching and learning was likely associated with the shortage of experienced instructors and students familiar with the online Chinese language teaching and learning.

The online teaching and learning experience has become pervasive since the COVID-19 pandemic first hit Mainland China and then quickly spread to other countries. The World Health Organization (WHO) officially declared the COVID-19 pandemic on March 11, 2020 (WHO, 2020). Consequently, starting with China in January 2020, programs from kindergarten to doctoral levels in various countries were forced to transition to fully online instructional activities to better adhere to social distancing guidelines and mitigate the spread of the virus. Giannini et al. (2020) stated that schools in over 190 countries had closed by May 13, 2020, affecting 90% of the world's student population.[1] Zimmerman (2020) has suggested reflecting on these worldwide challenges from coronavirus as opportunities for conducting global online learning experiments.

Amid the pandemic, how did Chinese language instructors and students in different countries perceive their online teaching and learning experiences? What were their perceptions, perspectives, and practices? This chapter reports partial findings of the survey study that we conducted in 2020 on these overarching questions.

---

[1] The global monitoring of school closures caused by COVID-19 including the visualized evolution over time is available at https://en.unesco.org/COVID19/educationresponse.

2 Methodology

2.1 Instruments

The two surveys used for data collection were developed by the three authors together. One survey was for Chinese language instructors, and the other was for Chinese language students. The following section describes these two surveys.

Instructor Survey

The instructor survey included 4 sections and 28 questions.

- **Section 1: General Questions.** Included seven questions: country/region and type(s) of institutions where the instructors taught in Spring 2020; number of weekly contact hours before and after the pandemic transition; the Learning Management Systems (LMS) used to manage their courses; frequently used tools for real-time/synchronous communication; and other technical tools often used to teach Chinese online.
- **Section 2: Perspectives.** Included eight questions: how instructors perceived student learning outcomes and their own teaching effectiveness in online courses versus onsite; instructors' willingness and confidence to teach fully online courses in the future; their preferred instructional modes; and perceived impacts of their online teaching experiences on their future teaching, as well as their likes and dislikes regarding online teaching.
- **Section 3: Practice.** Included seven questions: activities that instructors found most effective at improving students' language skills; effective strategies for increasing student-to-student interactions; strategies for managing online courses and designing online oral and written assessments; instructors' concerns regarding student dishonesty and plagiarism online, as well as relative mitigation strategies; and other problems encountered teaching online.

- **Section 4: Demographic information.** Included six questions: gender identity; age; highest academic degree received; previous teaching experience; familiarity with online teaching; and venue(s) from which they received training in online teaching.

Student Survey

The structure of the student survey mirrored the instructor survey and included 4 sections and 21 questions.

- **Section 1: General Questions.** Included five questions: country/region and the type(s) of institutions where they studied Chinese in Spring 2020; the level(s) of the Chinese language classes taken; technology tools they favored for real-time/synchronous communication; and other tools they liked to use in learning Chinese online.
- **Section 2: Perspectives.** Included seven questions: students' perception of their learning outcomes online compared to onsite; students' satisfaction with their online learning experience; their willingness to take fully online courses in the future; their preferred types of online courses; and what they liked and disliked most about online learning.
- **Section 3: Practice.** Included five questions: effective activities for improving students' language skills; helpful strategies for increasing their interaction with their classmates in Chinese; other useful learning strategies for online learning; and challenges encountered.
- **Section 4: Demographic information.** Included four questions: gender identity; age; types of Chinese classes previously taken; and whether they had taken any fully online courses prior to 2020.

Both surveys were developed in Qualtrics and administered electronically. The instructor survey was for Chinese language instructors teaching at any level. The student survey was targeted toward college students, but interested high school students were also allowed to participate. To encourage and maximize participation, subjects were not forced to answer every question and could choose to skip any question.

2.2 Data Collection and Analysis

After receiving official IRB approval in late April 2020, the researchers sent out the survey link via the listserv of the Technology and Chinese Language Teaching (TCLT), social network platforms like WeChat groups for Chinese language teachers from different countries, and through personal and/or professional contacts. Interested Chinese instructors were asked to fill out the instructor survey and forward the student survey to their students.

In this chapter, we only analyzed data collected before June 1, 2020, with a focus on the quantitative data. The data were mainly analyzed with Qualtrics built-in tools, Excel, and SPSS. Relative findings and data collected after June 1, 2020, will be reported in future articles.

3 Findings

3.1 Findings from the Instructor Survey

This section reports our findings from the instructors' responses to the following selected survey questions: (1) demographic information; (2) background information related to online teaching; (3) instructors' perceived teaching effectiveness and student learning outcomes in online courses compared to onsite, and instructors' future preference regarding the type(s) of courses to teach; (4) their willingness and confidence to teach fully online courses in the future; (5) the impact of their online teaching experiences on their future teaching; (6) which Learning Management Systems (LMS) they used, tools used for synchronous/real-time communication, and other tools used for online teaching; (7) how much instructors were concerned about plagiarism and dishonesty; and (8) the number of contact hours they had with students before and after the pandemic transition.

(1) Demographic Information

15 Perspectives of Instructors and Students on Online Chinese... 355

Among the 78 instructors who shared information on where they worked in Spring 2020, 65 (83.33%) of them were from the United States, 6 (7.69%) from China, and the rest were from Australia, Argentina, Canada, Ecuador, Singapore, and the U.K. Among the 68 respondents who provided gender identity information, 56 (82.35%) were female. Among the 70 instructors who revealed their age, nearly one-third of them were between 41 and 50 years old. Nearly one-quarter (24.29%) were 31–40 years old and 22.86% were 51–60 years old. Nearly all (66 out of 68) respondents reportedly held master's degrees (55.88%) or doctorate degrees (41.18%).

Regarding the types of institutions where the surveyed instructors taught in Spring 2020, among 88 responses, nearly 60% taught at four-year institutions and 19.32% taught at high schools. The other respondents taught at two- and three-year colleges, middle schools, or elementary schools. In total, 125 responses were recorded for the proficiency-level courses they taught. Nearly 40% of them reportedly taught beginning-level courses, 33.6% taught intermediate-level courses, and 24.8% taught advanced-level courses.

(2) Background Related to Online Teaching (Experiences, Familiarity, and Training)

Out of 84 instructor responses on teaching experience, only four of them had fully online teaching experiences before the pandemic transition; the majority had face-to-face class teaching experience (67.82%) or hybrid/blended teaching experience (27.59%).

Nonetheless, most reported to be somewhat familiar (27.94%), familiar (22.06%), or mostly familiar (11.76%) with online teaching before the pandemic transition, and the others reported to be less familiar (27.94%) or least familiar (10.29%).

Among the 123 responses regarding venues for online teaching related training, about one-third of the instructors had received internal training from their working institution, and more than 40% had received training from external workshops, symposiums, and/or conferences. Nearly one-fourth had received training from their formal education Master's program (9.76%), doctoral program (8.94%), or undergraduate program (5.69%).

(3) Perceived Student Learning Outcome, Teaching Effectiveness, and Future Preferences

The majority of the instructors also perceived student learning outcomes of online courses to be slightly lower (54%) or much lower (31%) compared to onsite (see Table 15.1 for details). Interestingly, while more than 20% of the students believed online learning outcomes were about the same as onsite, only about 9% of the instructor participants agreed.

Similarly, a majority of the 78 instructors perceived their online teaching as slightly less effective (52.56%) or much less effective (26.92%) compared to teaching onsite. Fewer than 10% of the instructors perceived online teaching as more effective (6.41%) or much more effective (2.56%) than teaching onsite. About 12% of the instructors perceived the same effectiveness between online and onsite. If given a choice, less than 20% of instructors would choose to teach fully online and about 40% would choose face-to-face or hybrid (also 40%). Details are shown in Table 15.2.

(4) Willingness and Confidence of Teaching Future Online Courses

A majority of the 78 instructor participants indicated that they were somewhat willing (28.21%), moderately willing (26.92%), or very willing (19.23%) to teach fully online courses. About 24% of the instructors reported that they were not very willing to teach online and only one

Table 15.1 Student learning outcomes online versus onsite

What do you think of students' learning outcomes in the online teaching mode compared to the onsite teaching mode?	Count	Percentage
Online is much lower than onsite	24	30.77
Online is slightly lower than onsite	42	53.85
Online is about the same as onsite	7	8.97
Online is higher than onsite	4	5.13
Online is much higher than onsite	1	1.28
Total	78	100

Table 15.2 Faculty preference(s) for instructional modes

If you have a choice, what type of course(s) are you willing to teach in the future? Please choose all that apply.	Count	Percentage
Face-to-face classroom teaching	51	38.93
Hybrid course (some hours onsite and some hours online)	50	38.17
Fully online course with real-time meetings	21	16.03
Fully online course without real-time meetings	7	5.34
No preference	2	1.53
Total	131	100

instructor reported to be not at all willing. Similarly, a majority of the 78 instructors indicated that they were moderately confident (41.03%), somewhat confident (30.77%), or very confident (19.23%) in teaching fully online courses in the future. Only about 10% reported to be not very confident (six instructors) or not at all confident (one instructor).

(5) Impact on Future Teaching

Regarding the impact of this online teaching experience on their future teaching, "use more technology" was ranked the highest benefit (47.20%), followed by "more organized" (25.60%) and "better time management" (22.40%). Six instructors also shared other impacts, such as "appreciate the face-to-face teaching time more", "prioritize essential skills such as building more consistent routines, training pronunciation", "more flexibility", "teach in the classroom and have some students online if needed", and "well-thought and carefully designed asynchronous learning particularly flipped learning".

(6) LMS, Synchronous Tools, and Other Technical Tools Used

Among the 79 instructors who shared information on the LMS they used for teaching, 22 of them (28%) used Canvas, 18 (23%) used Blackboard, and 9 (11%) used Google Classroom. The listed other LMS platforms included Sakai, D2L (Desire2Learn), Moodle, Schoology, systems developed by individual institutions such as LuAmiNus and LATTE, and tools developed in China like Chaoxing (泛雅超星学习通).

Regarding synchronous/real-time communication tools, many instructors chose more than one tool and a total 107 responses were recorded. Zoom was used most frequently (46.73%), followed by WeChat (14.95%), Blackboard Collaborate Ultra (11.21%), Google Hangouts (10.28%), and Microsoft Teams (6.54%). Other tools included Skype, Google Meet, Facetime, WebEx, QQ, and Tencent Meeting (腾讯会议).

Analysis of the 130 instructor responses showed that Quizlet was most frequently used (22%), followed by Kahoot (18%), and Flipgrid (8%). Other listed tools included Padlet, Gimkit, Edpuzzle, Youtube, Nearpod, Google Forms, Quia, Playposit, Loom, Voicethread, Can-8 Dingding, Scribble.io, Instagram, CoSpaces, Goformative, Bookcreator, Notability, Onenote, Class Notebook, SharePoint, Screencastify, Camtasia, Slack, Lino, Studystack, Powtoon, Bingo maker, and Classroom Screen.

(7) Concerns Regarding Plagiarism and Dishonesty

Among the 67 instructors who responded to how concerned they were about plagiarism and dishonesty, more than 60% of them indicated they were somewhat concerned (29.85%), moderately concerned (16.42%), or very concerned (16.42%), while the other nearly 36% reported to not be very concerned. Only one instructor reported to not be concerned at all.

(8) Comparison of the Number of Contact Hours Before and After the Pandemic Transition

Seventy-nine instructors reported their number of weekly contact hours before and after the transition. The average was 11.39 hours (SD = 10.82) before the pandemic transition versus 7.64 hours (SD = 6.34) after the pandemic transition. The reduced average number of hours was statistically significant based on the paired sample t-test, $t(78) = 3.46, p < .001$.

3.2 Findings from the Student Survey

This section reports our findings from the student responses to the following selected questions: (1) demographic information; (2) background information related to online learning; (3) students' perceived learning outcomes in online courses versus onsite, and their preference for the type(s) of courses to take in the future; (4) students' overall satisfaction with online courses and their willingness to take fully online courses in the future; (5) their perceived impact of online learning experiences on their future Chinese learning; and (6) technological tools they liked most for real-time/synchronous communication, and other tools they liked for learning Chinese online.

(1) Student Demographic Information

Among the 133 students who provided information on where they studied Chinese in Spring 2020, 87 (65.4%) were in the United States, 26 were from Singapore (19.5%), and 10 were from China (7.5%). There were also participants who reportedly studied in Australia, South Korea, South Africa, Vietnam, Russia, and Yemen. More than two-thirds (66.67%) of the student respondents were female. The average age of the 98 students who revealed their age was 21 years old. The oldest age was 36 and the youngest was 16.

The majority (86.39%) of the respondents studied at a four-year university/college, and the rest studied at a two-/three-year university/college (8.16%) or other types of institutions (5.44%) such as high school. Most of them took beginning-level courses (41.38%) or intermediate-level courses (37.24%). Fewer students took advanced courses (17.93%) or other courses (3.45%) in Spring 2020.

(2) Background Information Related to Online Learning

In answering the question *Did you take any fully online courses (not necessarily Chinese) before the transition to the online delivery mode in the Spring 2020 semester/quarter*, among the 99 responses, 68 (68.6%) chose "No". Among the 118 responses for what type(s) of Chinese language

Table 15.3 Types of classes taken before the transition

What type(s) of Chinese language teaching modes did you experience before the transition to the online mode in the Spring 2020 semester/quarter? (Please choose all that apply)	Count	Percentage
Face-to-face classroom teaching	90	76.27
Hybrid course (some hours onsite and some hours online)	20	16.95
Fully online course with real-time meetings	5	4.24
Fully online course without real-time meetings	3	2.54
Total	118	100

Table 15.4 Student's perceptions on comparison of learning online versus onsite

Do you think you learn more or less Chinese in an online course compared to an onsite course?	Count	Percentage
Learning much less online than onsite	33	27.73
Learning slightly less online than onsite	57	47.90
Learning about the same online as onsite	25	21.01
Learning more online than onsite	4	3.36
Learning much more online than onsite	0	0.00
Total	119	100%

courses they had experienced before the pandemic transition, less than 7% reported to have studied fully online (see Table 15.3 for details).

(3) Perceived Learning Outcomes and Preference for Future Type(s) of Course

Among the 119 students who responded to this question, more than two-thirds perceived learning slightly less (47.9%) or much less online (27.7%) when compared to learning onsite. About one-fifth reportedly perceived learning about the same online compared to onsite. (See Table 15.4 for details.)

If given a choice, nearly 60% of the students indicated that they would choose face-to-face classes. Less than 10% would choose to learn entirely online. (See Table 15.5 for details.)

Table 15.5 Student's preference(s) for instructional modes

If you have a choice, what type(s) of Chinese language courses would you prefer to take in the future? (Please choose all that apply)	Count	Percentage
Face-to-face classroom teaching	93	59.24
Hybrid course (some hours onsite and some hours online)	46	29.30
Fully online course with real-time meetings	12	7.64
Fully online course without real-time meetings	3	1.91
No preference	3	1.91
Total	157	100

(4) Overall Satisfaction and Willingness to Take Future Online Courses

Among the 118 students who shared their responses, more than 60% reported that they were either somewhat satisfied (40.68%) or extremely satisfied (19.49%) with their online Chinese learning experience. About 19% were somewhat dissatisfied (16.95%) or extremely dissatisfied (1.69%), whereas 21.19% remain in the middle (neither satisfied nor dissatisfied).

When asked whether they were willing to take fully online courses in the future, nearly 70% of them indicated that they were moderately willing (27.12%), somewhat willing (25.42%), or very willing (16.10%). Very few (6.78%) indicated that they were not all willing.

(5) Impact on Future Learning

Regarding the impacts of their online experiences on future Chinese learning, more than 40% of the 165 recorded responses chose "use more technology" (41.21%), followed by "better time management" (30.91%), and "more organized" (20.61%) as a benefit.

Among the 12 students who chose the "other" option and provided an explanation, 3 shared a perceived negative impact of online learning, including reasons such as "less progress", "this class illustrates the need for less technology in Chinese classes and places a stronger emphasis on face to face classroom learning," and "I feel as though I have lost some of my ability to speak because there was no in-class setting to practice." Two other students seemed to indicate neutral responses—"I am not sure it will yet" and "it won't impact me that much."

The other seven students listed positive impacts, including "increased practice at home", "able to find more resources online for language learning", "maybe accelerate my learning process", and "appreciate speaking with my Chinese friends more often". One student further elaborated "I really liked how online courses felt more one-on-one than an in-person class. Plus, I valued learning in my personal environment where I felt most comfortable. This made me go out of my way to learn the language because I wasn't 'forced' to physically go to class to check an attendance box."

(6) Tools Used for Synchronous Communication and Online Learning

Consistent with the findings from the instructor responses on tools used in online teaching, among the 243 total responses to the question regarding real-time/synchronous communication tools, nearly half (46.91%) of the responses chose Zoom, followed by WeChat (18.52%). Some students also listed the conferencing tools provided by Learning Management Tools, such as Blackboard Collaborate Ultra (7.00%) and Canvas Conference (4.93%). In addition, the other listed popular tools included Skype (6.17%), Google Hangout (4.12%), Microsoft Teams (3.70%), and FaceTime (2.47%). There were also other tools listed such as Google Meet, Snapchat, WhatsApp, QQ, Tencent Meeting (腾讯会议), Chaoxing (超星学习通), and Classin.

Among the 192 total responses to the question on other tools they liked to use in their online learning, 82 students (42.71%) chose Quizlet, followed by Kahoot (36.98%), Voicethread (4.69%), and Flipgrid (4.17%). Other respondents listed tools like Edpuzzle, Gimkit, Quia, Youtube, Google Dictionaries, WeChat, QQ, Skribbl.io, and Textivate.

4 Discussions and Implications

Findings from this study revealed that only very small percentages of the instructor participants (5%) and student participants (7%) had prior experience teaching and learning Chinese language online before 2020, which is consistent with the researchers' assumption before conducting the survey and the literature (e.g., Liu, 2020a).

On the other hand, more than 60% of the instructors reported to be familiar with online teaching (from somewhat familiar to most familiar). One possibility to explain their familiarity with online teaching is the training they had received through a variety of venues. Another might be that their teaching experience in other delivery modes helped familiarize them with the online mode. Even though some instructors reported to have only had face-to-face teaching experience, it is possible that they have integrated abundant technologies and included many online elements (such as LMS and WeChat) in their teaching before the pandemic. Their familiarity with various technological tools likely assisted them with the urgent switch to fully online teaching. Similar observations were discussed in some chapters of this book, such as Chap. 7 (by Jiang) and Chap. 12 (by Zhang). According to Wu and Huang (in Chap. 13 of this book), while it was the first time for each of the five instructor interviewees teaching fully online during the pandemic, they all believed that they possessed necessary and sufficient technology skills because they had experience integrating technology in their teaching in other modes.

Overall, the majority of the student participants were satisfied with their online learning experiences, though their satisfaction degree varied (from somewhat satisfied to extremely satisfied). This finding is consistent with what was found in several chapters of this book, such as Chap. 5 by Ma, and Chap. 4 by Romagnoli and Ornaghi. Additionally, surveys conducted by Su (2020) and Zhu (2020) also reported student overall positive ratings of their online learning experiences in Spring 2020. Xu et al. (2021) further found that the degree of satisfaction of learning Chinese online differed among degree-seeking and non-degree-seeking students; specifically, degree-seeking students were found to be more satisfied. Their analysis showed that student satisfaction was affected by several factors, such as instructional materials, student-faculty interaction, and emotional support. One interesting quote from their study reads, "although online was not the best option, instructors did very well. They have done all that they could do, so I do not have any complaints" (p. 42. *translated from Chinese*). In other words, students' overall satisfaction should be interpreted with context and caution.

Regarding perceived student learning outcomes, the majority of both instructors (84.62%) and students (75.63%) perceived student learning outcomes in online environments to be lower (slightly or much) than onsite. This finding is different than what several other studies have found, though those studies were not specifically on teaching and learning of the Chinese language online. For example, Best Colleges (2019) claimed that more than two-thirds of the online students who identified employment as their primary goal considered distance education to be better than or equal to on-campus options. Means et al. (2010) found that on average students in online learning conditions performed modestly better than those receiving face-to-face instruction, based on their review of more than one thousand empirical studies (most at the postsecondary level) on online learning from 1996 to 2008. There were fewer studies in the literature (e.g., Coates et al., 2004) reporting online student learning outcomes as inferior to onsite, but often with stated caveats.

On the other hand, numerous studies found that there was no significant difference in student outcomes between online and onsite, such as those listed in *The No Significant Difference* database of the DETA Research website (https://detaresearch.org/research-support/no-significant-difference/). The database was first established in 2004 as a companion piece to the book *The No Significant Difference Phenomenon* by Thomas L. Russell (2001). Moore and Thompson (1990) claimed that distance education was effective in terms of achievement of learning and attitudes expressed by students and teachers, which has since resonated across other studies (e.g., Bernard et al., 2004). Many scholars (e.g., Arias et al., 2018; Kryczka, 2014; Ni, 2013) further suggested taking into consideration a variety of factors/variables (e.g., course design, student commitment, and learning styles) when comparing online and onsite teaching and learning.

15 Perspectives of Instructors and Students on Online Chinese…

In this study, the perceived lower learning outcomes in online modes can be viewed together with the reduced number of contact hours after switching from onsite to online formats due to the pandemic. It seems logical to argue that the lower learning outcomes resulted from the fewer contact hours that the students had with their instructors after the pandemic transition. One related finding from Wu and Huang's study (Chap. 13 in this book) is the importance of synchronous interactions in language classes. Instructors are advised to include some synchronous interaction sessions with students regardless of the delivery mode from both the social and cognitive perspectives.

It is also worth pointing out that the findings of this study on the perceived online learning outcomes need to be interpreted with caution when linking to relevant literature on online education. First, students and instructors in this study did not self-select the online mode but were forced to embrace it due to the pandemic. In many institutions across countries, instructors were only given one week or even one weekend to urgently switch to online teaching in the middle of the semester/quarter (see descriptions in Chap. 7 by Jiang from Australia and Chap. 2 by Zahradnikova from Czech Republic). This is also why Hodge and coauthors (Hodges et al., 2020) advocated using the term "emergency remote teaching" (ERT) to specify the urgent situation and differentiate it from regular online courses which are usually more prepared and better planned. Second, one must consider the mental challenges caused by the pandemic, such as depression, anxiety, fear, as well as financial pressure and family-related concerns. These unexpected difficulties could have negatively affected student and instructor performances and their perceptions of their experiences.

Another notable finding is that while more than 20% of the students believed they received about the same quality of education through online classes versus onsite, only fewer than 9% of the instructors agreed. This disparity might be explained by instructors having higher expectations for learning outcomes than students. Instructors' high expectations were also reflected in their self-evaluations of their own teaching effectiveness. About 80% of them self-reported that their teaching became less effective after the pandemic transition to online formats.

Regarding future instructional modes, a majority of both instructors and students chose face-to-face and hybrid/blended as their first and second choices respectively. However, differences exist between these two groups. In contrast with about 60% of the student responses opting for the face-to-face mode, only fewer than 40% of instructors chose it. The number of instructors who voted for face-to-face was equal to those who voted for hybrid. Similarly, fewer than 10% of the student responses chose the fully online mode, whereas more than 20% of the instructors chose the same mode. A similar pattern is also seen in the willingness to teach/take fully online courses in the future, indicated by 74% of the instructors and 69% of the students. The slightly higher percentage of instructor willingness seems consistent with the confidence levels reported by over 90% of the instructors regarding future online teaching.

Many students and instructors preferred the hybrid mode, and many instructors felt confident and willing to teach online. Thus, institutions were advised to provide multiple delivery modes for students to choose from and allow instructors to have flexibility in course design and instruction delivery. At institutions where there was a limited number of instructors and enrolled students, to maximize resources and meet diverse student needs, hybrid flexible modes can be considered in addition to regular instructional modes, as suggested by Liu (2020b). This provides students with more flexibility in choosing how to learn (e.g., onsite and/or online, synchronously and/or asynchronously) on a weekly or even daily basis.

Additionally, regarding the impact of online experience on future teaching/learning, "use more technology" received the most votes from both instructors and students. Although the COVID-19 pandemic undoubtedly caused huge disruptions to many aspects of human society, including education globally, the experiences and lessons that instructors and students learned from coping with the ERT and their perceived impacts on future teaching and learning can be considered the silver lining of the pandemic.

Regarding plagiarism and cheating, while more than half of the instructors showed differing degrees of concern, more than 37% of them did not. Liu (2020a) suggested instructors focus their time and energy on developing more individualized assignments and making assessment more useful for student learning. Liang (2021) further shared strategies and examples of how she allowed students in her upper-level Chinese courses to complete assignments and exams with access to many materials. She invited students to play more active roles in their assessments (e.g., co-writing test items). She found that her students had high satisfaction and they were able to develop and demonstrate higher-level proficiency.

Finally, it is worth mentioning that although the instructors and students were not from the same institutions, they shared similar views (e.g., both groups perceived lower student learning outcomes after the switch from onsite to online) and reported many similar situations. For instance, Zoom was most frequently used for real-time communications followed by WeChat, as reported by both instructors and students. The similarities, including tool usage, might be due to the homogeneity of respondents. Most of the instructor (83.33%) and student (65.41%) participants were from the same country, predominantly the United States.

5 Limitation, Future Research, and Conclusion

This chapter reports the preliminary findings of two surveys conducted in May 2020. Different from other surveys conducted at one institution or in one region/country, this study spanned students and instructors around the world. Although the data we collected before June 1 were still mainly from the United States, there were about 16% of instructors and 35% of students from other countries. Exploring the perspectives of instructors and students from different institutions and different regions/countries helps to provide a larger picture and more comprehensive view of the issues investigated.

Due to space limitations and other constraints, this chapter only reported findings from the analysis of partial questions from the two surveys. The sample size reported in this chapter is yet not large enough to represent the global population of Chinese language instructors and students. Moreover, even though the titles of both surveys and of this chapter use the word "online", readers are cautioned against equating the Spring 2020 ERT to normal online teaching and learning, as distinguished in Hodges et al. (2020). Readers should also be aware that student perceptions and experiences of online learning could be affected by how the individual course was taught and their personal situations (such as home internet accessibility); similarly, instructors' perceptions and experiences from online teaching were likely intertwined with their specific situations, such as the policy of their institutions, available technology, and pedagogical resources.

In addition to completion of further analysis of the data collected through the two surveys, the researchers plan to interview some purposively sampled instructors and students on their in-depth perspectives on selected issues (e.g., interactions and assessments), especially after they have experienced online teaching and learning for over a year. Given that most available studies have been on ERT teaching and learning at the college level, such as Jin et al. (2021) and most chapters in this book, it would be valuable to compare the perspectives and experiences of college students and instructors to those of K-12 settings. It will also be necessary and beneficial for the field to conduct meta-analysis research to examine findings across multiple studies associated with remote Chinese teaching and learning.

To conclude, this chapter enriches the research on online education and particularly expands literature concerning teaching and learning Chinese language online. Findings of this study also help practitioners in planning and designing future curriculum and programs. More research is expected to advance the practice further and expand research in the field of online Chinese language education.

References

Allen, I. E., & Seaman, J. (2017). Digital learning compass: Distance education enrollment report. https://onlinelearningconsortium.org/read/digital-learning-compass-distance-education-enrollment-report-2017

Arias, J., Swinton, J., & Anderson, K. (2018). Online Vs. Face-to-Face: A comparison of student outcomes with random assignment. *e-Journal of Business Education & Scholarship of Teaching, 12*(2), 1–23.

Bai, J., Li, C., & Yeh, W. C. (2019). Integrating technology in the teaching of advanced Chinese. *Journal of Technology and Chinese Language Teaching, 10*(1), 73–90.

Bernard, R., Abrami, P., Lou, Y., Borokhovski, E., Wade, A., Wozney, L., Wallet, P., Fiset, M., & Huang, B. (2004). How does distance education compare with classroom instruction? A meta-analysis of the empirical literature. *Review of Educational Research, 74*(3), 379–439.

Best Colleges. (2019). *2019 Online education trends report.* https://res.cloudinary.com/highereducation/image/upload/v1556050834/BestColleges.com/edutrends/2019-Online-Trends-in-Education-Report-BestColleges.pdf

Bonk, C., Lee, M., Reeves, T., & Reynolds, T. (Eds.). (2015). *MOOCs and open education the world.* Routledge.

Bonk, C. J., & Zhang, K. (2008). *Empowering online learning: 100+ activities for reading, reflecting, displaying, and doing.* John Wiley Sons.

Coates, D., Humphreys, B. R., Kane, J., & Vachris, M. (2004). "No significant distance" between face to face and online instruction: Evidence from principles of economics. *Economics of Education Review, 23*(5), 533–546.

Finkelstein, J. (2008). *Learning in real time: Synchronous teaching and learning online (Jossey-Bass Guides to Online Teaching and Learning Book 5).* Jossey-Bass.

Giannini, S., Jenkins, R., & Saavedra, J. (2020, May 13). *Reopening schools: When, where and how?* https://en.unesco.org/news/reopening-schools-when-where-and-how

Hiltz, S., & Goldman, R. (2004). *Learning together online: Research on asynchronous learning networks.* Lawrence Erlbaum Associates.

Hodges, C., Moore, S., Lockee, B., Trust, T., & Bond, A. (2020, March 27). The difference between emergency remote teaching and online learning. *Educause Review.* https://er.educause.edu/articles/2020/3/the-difference-between-emergency-remote-teaching-and-online-learning

Jin, L., Xu, Y., Deifell, E., & Angus, K. (2021). Emergency remote language teaching and U.S.-based college-level world language educators' intention to adopt online teaching in postpandemic times. *The Modern Language Journal, 105*(2) https://doi.org/10.1111/modl.12712

Kim, K. J., Liu, S., & Bonk, C. J. (2005). Online MBA students' perceptions of online learning: Benefits, challenges, and suggestions. *Internet and Higher Education, 8*(4), 335–344. Lai, C., Zhao, Y., Li, M. (2008). Designing a distance foreign language learning environment. In S. Goertler & P. Winke (Eds.), *Opening doors through distance language education: Principles, perspectives, and practice* (pp. 85–108). CALICO Monograph Series.

Koç, S., Liu, X., & Wachira, P. (Eds.). (2015). *Assessment in online and blended learning environments* (pp. 77–101). Information Age Publishing.

Kryczka, S. (2014). *The graduate student learning experience in online, hybrid, and onsite courses*. Unpublished doctoral dissertation, Northeastern University. https://repository.library.northeastern.edu/files/neu:336592/fulltext.pdf

Lai, C., Zhao, Y., & Li, M. (2008). Designing a distance foreign language learning environment. In S. Goertler & P. Winke (Eds.), *Opening doors through distance language education: Principles, perspectives, and practice* (pp. 85–108). CALICO Monograph Series.

Lederman, D. (2019). *Professors' slow, steady acceptance of online learning: A survey.* https://www.insidehighered.com/news/survey/professors-slow-steady-acceptance-online-learning-survey

Li, J. (2019). Online Chinese program evaluation and quality control. *International Chinese Language Education, 4*(3), 62–70.

Li, J., & Jiang, Z. (2017). Students' perceptions about a flipped online Chinese language course. *Journal of Technology and Chinese Language Teaching, 8*(2), 25–38.

Li, S. (2007). *The characteristics of online Chinese language teaching and learning in higher education: Perceptions of teachers and students*. Unpublished doctoral dissertation of Alliant International University.

Liang, H. (2021, April 17). Remote language teaching and learning: Opportunities and challenges for testing. Presentation given at the 2021 Annual Conference of Chinese Language Teachers Association, held virtually online via Zoom, April 8–18. https://clta-us.org/clta-annual-conference/

Liu, S. (2009). Assessment in online courses. In P. Rogers, G. Berge, J. Boettcher, C. Howard, L. Justice, & K. Shenk (Eds.), *Encyclopedia of distance learning* (2nd ed., pp. 103–107). Idea Group, Inc..

Liu, S. (2018). Teaching and learning Chinese language online: What and why? *International Chinese Language Education, 3*(2), 11–26.

Liu, S. (2020a). *Similarities and differences between teaching and learning of the Chinese language online and onsite: Opportunities and challenges*. Invited presentation given at the "A Series of Zoom Presentations on Remote Chinese Teaching", organized by DoIE Chinese Language & Exchange Programs, San Francisco State University, May 29, 2020.

Liu, S. (2020b). *Online, remote, hybrid/blended, hyflex: A brief discussion on teaching in different delivery modes*. Invited talk given for the 6th Online Chinese Teaching Forum and Workshop (OCTFW) and Chinese Teachers Association of Michigan Conference. Organized by the Confucius Institute of Michigan State University, via Zoom, November 14, 2020.

Liu, S., Kim, K. J., Bonk, C. J., & Magjuka, R. (2007). Benefits, challenges, and suggestions: What do online MBA professors have to say about online teaching? *The Online Journal of Distance Learning Administration, 10*(2). http://www.westga.edu/~distance/ojdla/summer102/liu102.htm

Liu, X., Liu, S., Lee, S., & Magjuka, J. (2010). Cultural differences in online learning: International student perceptions. *Educational Technology & Society, 13*(3), 177–188.

Martinez, R., Liu, S., Watson, W., & Bichelmeyer, B. (2006). Evaluation of a web-based Master's degree program in a Midwestern research university. *Quarterly Review of Distance Education, 7*(3), 267–283.

Means, B., Toyama, Y., Murphy, R., Bakia, M., & Jones, K. (2010). *Evaluation of evidence-based practices in online learning: A meta-analysis and review of online learning studies.* Available from the U.S. Department of Education at http://www.ed.gov/rschstat/eval/tech/evidence-based-practices/finalreport.pdf

Moore, M., & Anderson, W. (Eds.). (2003). *Handbook of distance education.* Lawrence Erlbaum Associates.

Moore, M. G., & Thompson, M. M. (1990). *The effects of distance learning: A summary of literature.* ERIC Document Reproduction Service No. ED 330 321.

Ni, A. (2013). Comparing the effectiveness of classroom and online learning: Teaching research methods. *Journal of Public Affairs Education, 19*(2), 199–215.

Palloff, R., & Pratt, K. (2008). *Assessing the online learner: Resources and strategies for faculty (Jossey-Bass Guides to Online Teaching and Learning Book 13).* Jossey-Bass.

Rudestam, K. E., & Schoenholtz-Read, J. (Eds.). (2009). *Handbook of online learning* (2nd ed.). Sage Publishing.

Russell, T. L. (2001). *The no significant difference phenomenon: A comparative research annotated bibliography on technology for distance education* (5th ed.). ARELLO Education and Technology Division.

Stickler, U., & Shi, L. (2013). Supporting Chinese speaking skills online. *System, 41*(1), 50–69. http://eprints.lse.ac.uk/49513/

Su, Y. (2020). *Teaching Chinese online to non-degree seeking students.* Presentation given via Zoom on July 18, 2020, organized by Beijing Language and Culture University Publishing House.

Sun, M., Chen, Y., & Olson, A. (2013). Developing and implementing an online Chinese program: A Case Study. In B. Zou, M. Xing, Y. Wang,

M. Sun, & C. Xiang (Eds.), *Computer-assisted foreign language teaching and learning: Technological advances* (pp. 160–187). IGI Global. https://doi.org/10.4018/978-1-4666-2821-2.ch010

Thormann, J., & Zimmerman, I. (2012). *The complete step-by-step guide to designing and teaching online courses.* Teachers College Press.

Tseng, M., Gao, Y., & Cai, L. (2019). Enhancing interaction through the effective incorporation of technology tools for a virtual Chinese language classroom. *Journal of Technology and Chinese Language Teaching, 10*(1), 91–113.

Vai, M., & Sosulsk, K. (2016). *Essentials of online course design: A standards-based guide.* Routledge.

Vorobel, O., & Kim, D. (2012). Language teaching at a distance: An overview of research. *CALICO, 29*(3), 548–562.

Wang, Y. (2012). E-language teaching and learning in Australia: A case study. http://www98.griffith.edu.au/dspace/bitstream/handle/10072/48843/80825_1.pdf;jsessionid=3C9D4A47655AD2A416FBD375283C6ECB?sequence=1

World Health Organization. (2020). *Archived: WHO timeline – COVID-19.* https://www.who.int/news/item/27-04-2020-who-timeline%2D%2D-COVID-19

Xu, L., Chen, Y., & Shi, S. (2021). An analysis of international students' experiences of online courses: Based on a survey of international students at a Chinese university. *Journal of International Chinese Teaching, 1,* 39–49. [徐来, 陈钰, 施妤婕 (2021),国际学生汉语课程线上学习体验调查分析——以国内某高校国际学生为例,《国际汉语教学研究》, 2021年第1期, 39–49页].

Zheng, Y. (2001). Network in the classroom and classroom on the network. *Chinese Teaching in the World, 4,* 98–104. [郑艳群(2001).课堂上的网络和网络上的课堂 – 从现代教育技术看对外汉语教学的发展 《世界汉语教学》, 第4期, 98–104页].

Zhu, R. (2020). *Chinese language teaching in Beijing Normal University under Pandemic.* Presentation given via Zoom on July 18, 2020, organized by Beijing Language and Culture University Publishing House.

Zimmerman, J. (2020, March 10). Coronavirus and the Great Online-Learning Experiment. *Chronicle of Higher Education.* https://www.chronicle.com/article/coronavirus-and-the-great-online-learning-experiment/

Index[1]

A

Academic syllabus, 93
Accessibility, 15, 45, 116, 331, 332, 334, 335, 343, 368
Accountability, 288
Activities, viii, 3, 4, 9, 11, 13, 17, 18, 25, 27, 28, 31–33, 36–38, 42, 43, 47, 49, 61, 70, 86–89, 91–93, 96, 101, 107, 111, 112, 116, 127, 128, 138, 147–148, 151–154, 156–157, 170, 173, 177, 184, 188, 189, 191, 192, 194, 196–198, 206, 219, 236, 239–248, 255–264, 266, 270–272, 274, 277, 278, 287, 289, 296, 302, 304–306, 308, 310, 313, 316, 317, 319, 331, 340, 342, 350–353
Africa, 6, 7, 60, 135–159, 256
Age, 85–107, 154, 184, 299, 300, 341, 353, 355, 359
Annotation, 60, 135–139, 147, 157, 162, 279, 318
Anxiety, 24, 31, 32, 35–38, 42, 45, 47, 66, 74, 75, 117–119, 134, 179, 199, 200, 255, 261, 263, 365
Applications, 9, 28, 46, 59, 77, 146, 210, 219, 253–256, 271, 301, 306, 310, 314, 315, 336, 344, 345
Asia, 7, 8, 60, 111, 256

---

[1] Note: Page numbers followed by 'n' refer to notes.

Assessment, 18, 20, 27, 31–33, 37, 43, 44, 49–50, 91, 105, 114, 125, 135–140, 148–149, 155, 157, 159, 172, 174–179, 183, 184, 187, 188, 190–192, 194, 195, 197–200, 238, 239, 242, 248, 274–275, 280, 282, 285–286, 290, 291, 314, 336, 350, 352, 366–368

Assignments, 15, 16, 18, 25, 30–35, 42–47, 49, 57, 60, 61, 70, 71, 76, 97, 106, 116, 125, 126, 128, 132, 151, 177, 179, 187, 188, 190, 194, 197, 207, 209, 215, 217, 271, 274–275, 279–283, 285–286, 289–291, 311, 317, 320, 331, 335, 337, 338, 342, 344, 366, 367

Asynchronous, 12, 17, 23, 24, 30, 42, 88, 90, 94, 97, 103, 106, 140, 181, 186, 187, 193, 198, 207, 209, 214–216, 218, 235–239, 241, 242, 270, 271, 277, 282, 287, 298, 309, 335, 344, 350, 357

Attendance, 19, 35, 65, 68, 135–144, 160, 200, 217, 242, 362

Attention, vii, 13, 16, 18, 24, 31, 33–40, 42–49, 67, 85, 86, 153, 156, 206, 254, 255, 264, 271, 287, 288, 313, 345

Audio conferencing, 30, 35, 43

Australia, 6, 8, 10, 167–179, 184, 185, 355, 359, 365

Authentic material, 95, 104

Automatic feedback, 220

B

Background, viii, 19, 60, 150–151, 184, 237, 270, 289, 321

Background information, 126, 136–139, 168–172, 237–238, 354, 359–360

Before the pandemic, 206–207, 222

Benefits, 12, 13, 26, 44, 46, 47, 74, 75, 97, 126, 194, 248, 289, 316, 334, 357, 361

Blackboard Collaborate, 238

Blackboard Learn, 238

Blended, viii, 4, 5, 11, 12, 14, 17, 24, 73–75, 113, 201, 214, 224, 226, 236, 239, 269–292, 334, 366

Blended class, 207, 208, 272

Blended learning, 8, 24, 26, 42, 46, 88, 89, 170, 185, 200, 287, 291

Blended teaching, 3, 46, 248, 355

Blended teaching and learning, 112, 248

Blended teaching mode, 73–76, 149

Breakout room, 60, 105, 135–139, 146, 147, 154, 156, 162, 163, 177, 178, 244, 276, 278, 284, 289, 307, 315, 319, 336

Broadcast, 4, 337, 338, 344

C

Camera, 40, 60, 69, 104, 119, 152, 153, 155, 162, 278, 312, 337, 339, 340

Camp/camps, 19, 138

Campus, 18–20, 26, 111–114, 122–124, 127, 128, 130, 132,

137, 138, 170, 184, 199, 275, 282, 330, 333, 334
Cantonese, 237, 242, 246
Cantonese as a second language, 242, 246
CEFR, 205
CGIL, 92, 92n3, 93
Challenges
　of distance learning, 40, 41, 43, 46
　of learning Chinese, 26
Chaoxing, 256, 357, 362
Character, v, vi, 7, 12, 13, 26, 32–34, 38, 40, 42, 44, 45, 47, 48, 58, 71, 72, 76, 90, 91, 97, 103, 105, 125–129, 132, 135–139, 146, 152, 153, 155, 157, 171, 174, 179, 187, 191, 257, 262, 272, 275, 283, 284, 336, 340, 342
Character writing, 61, 70, 72, 76, 125, 148, 155, 292
Chat, 25, 26, 33, 35, 38, 39, 43, 60, 68, 87, 88, 96, 97, 102, 103, 105, 106, 152, 179, 246, 336, 340
Chat Room, 87, 135–139, 146, 152, 155, 156, 162, 246, 315
China, v, vii, x, 7, 9, 89, 135–138, 171, 182, 255, 257, 258, 274, 300, 304, 325–346, 351, 355, 357, 359
Chinese as a foreign language, 171, 172
Chinese as a Second Language (CSL), 205, 206, 236, 238–240, 242–248, 259, 263
Chinese characters, 7, 12, 13, 25, 26, 29–31, 33, 38, 41–43, 47, 48, 58, 70–72, 90, 91, 125–129, 132, 146, 153, 157, 171, 174, 179, 187, 257, 262, 271, 340
　instruction, 33, 38
Chinese culture, 135–139, 154, 183, 266, 273
Chinese discipline, 178
Chinese language, v, vii, viii, 4, 6–11, 13–20, 23, 25, 28, 29, 45, 57–77, 86, 89–91, 94–98, 167–179, 182, 183, 186, 188, 206–207, 210, 211, 213, 219, 237, 255, 256, 259–261, 264, 265, 267, 273, 295–322, 328, 329, 332–335, 337, 341, 344, 351–353, 359, 363, 364, 367, 368
Chinese language education, vii, viii, 7–9, 20, 59, 204–207, 253–267, 368
Chinese language teacher, 29, 59, 67, 77, 205, 206, 220, 264, 265, 354
Chinese Linguistic Society, 205
Chinese program, 8, 94, 168–169, 173, 182, 185
Classin, 238, 362
Classroom, 5, 11, 13, 14, 18, 20, 33–36, 40, 42, 46, 57–60, 65–69, 71, 73, 74, 76–79, 89–94, 102, 106, 115, 121–123, 170, 177, 186, 200, 201, 205–207, 218, 236, 238, 239, 242, 244, 247, 254, 261, 263, 266, 271, 278, 283, 284, 286, 295, 301, 309, 311, 315, 317, 318, 320–322, 327, 330, 331, 333–340, 343–345, 357, 361

Classroom activities, 147, 206, 240, 242–245, 284, 306
Classroom games, 135–139, 154, 157
Classroom management, 140, 177, 337
Class size, 87, 104, 107, 205, 301, 308, 313
Cognitive presence, 9, 196, 197, 298, 305–307, 314–316, 319, 320
Collaboration, x, 25, 114, 137, 147, 197, 297, 298, 302, 307, 315, 316, 319, 337
Collaborative language activities, 244
Communication, 2–4, 18, 19n3, 24, 27, 31–35, 38–40, 45, 49, 76, 87, 88, 97, 107, 114, 116–117, 128, 133, 147, 151, 155, 156, 171, 181, 187, 190, 198, 206, 219, 221, 246–248, 254, 259, 261–263, 265, 266, 275, 298, 302–304, 306, 308, 310, 311, 313, 315, 319, 335, 336, 340, 344, 352–354, 358, 359, 362, 367
Community of Inquiry (CoI), 9, 296–300, 312, 321, 322
Comparable, viii, 12, 58, 87, 113, 132, 159, 283, 308, 310, 317, 318
Competitive learning, 156
Complex sentence structures, 245
Computer assisted language learning (CALL), 172, 235
Concerns, 12, 71, 87, 105, 112, 116, 118, 151, 215, 217, 241, 310, 352, 358, 365, 366

Conference/conferences, 12, 18–20, 19n4, 146, 156, 198, 206, 211, 300, 337, 355
Confidence/confident, 14, 36, 74, 96, 115, 132, 154, 158, 179, 215, 291, 303, 308, 352, 354, 356–357, 366
Confucius Institute at University of Mauritius (CI-UoM), 7, 8, 135–140, 144, 150, 151, 157–159
Connection, 2, 5, 12, 28, 30, 35, 40, 42, 43, 58, 68, 76, 97, 101, 103, 105, 106, 118, 135–139, 144, 145, 151, 152, 156, 196, 198, 207, 209, 217, 241, 286, 302, 305, 312–314, 337, 340
Contact hours, 59, 59n2, 237, 308, 352, 354, 358, 365
Contact teaching, 118, 121, 124–126
Context, vi, 16, 29–30, 58–61, 64, 66–69, 123, 167, 185, 211, 220, 258, 271, 272, 274, 291, 299, 305, 309, 313, 314, 319, 322, 326, 328, 334, 336, 339, 340, 344, 364
Contingency strategies, 248
Continuum, viii, 4, 11, 313
Copyright law, 210
Coronavirus, vii, xi, 167, 236, 264, 351
Coronavirus disease 2019 (COVID-19), vii, 3, 16, 42, 47, 61, 85–107, 111, 139, 167, 172, 173, 191, 195, 199–200, 203, 206–210, 216, 221, 236, 245, 255, 269, 296,

303, 305, 313, 314, 325, 332, 342, 345, 351n1
Corrective feedback, 34, 39, 47, 306, 314, 315, 338
Counselor, 264
Course, 67
Course management system (CMS), 11, 25, 30, 32, 335, 336
Coursework, 97, 135–139, 146, 148–150, 155, 317
COVID-19 pandemic, vi, vii, 3, 6, 8–10, 23, 24, 27, 30, 45, 46, 57, 77, 91–97, 135–159, 167–179, 199–200, 203–223, 239–241, 247, 257, 261, 295, 303, 325–346, 350, 351, 366
Credit-hour, 205, 270
Crisis/crises, v, vi, xi, 3, 18, 20, 25, 57, 91, 113, 134, 220, 247, 248, 326, 330, 332, 335, 337, 341, 343, 345
Critical, 18, 64, 86, 88, 91, 93, 95, 96, 100, 101, 104, 105, 157, 172, 195, 247, 287, 288, 291, 298, 299, 302, 305–307, 313–316
CRUI, 92
Cultural sensitivity, 304, 313
Culture, vi, 26, 95, 96, 151, 154, 182, 183, 237, 257, 258, 266, 273–275, 282, 287, 290, 313, 321, 341
Curriculum, 27, 29, 32, 46, 58, 77, 122, 125, 137, 145, 153, 157, 171, 182, 221, 237, 247, 320, 327, 368
Curriculum design, 46, 220, 221, 238, 248, 321, 322
Curriculum planners, 235, 238

Czech Republic, 6, 7, 10, 23–47, 365

D

Debates, 244, 316
Degree of acceptance, 213
Degree of expectation, 216
Degree of satisfaction, 104, 204, 214–216, 363
Demographic information, 140–142, 353–355, 359
Dependent clause, 245
Design/designed, 3, 9, 16, 17, 25, 30, 44, 46, 47, 62–63, 77, 86, 95, 137, 140, 155–159, 169, 174, 174n4, 182, 188, 189, 192–195, 199, 207, 213, 220–222, 238, 248, 254, 257, 261, 264, 265, 267, 269–274, 287, 291, 292, 297, 298, 308–310, 317, 318, 321, 322, 335, 342, 350, 357, 364, 366
Dialogue in the virtual space, 218
Dictation, 32, 37, 38, 41, 43, 44, 48, 70, 72, 128, 129, 132, 170, 174n4
Different countries, vii, 10, 329, 331, 351, 354
Differentiated learning, 135–139, 152
Digital, 13, 25, 32, 35, 43, 44, 58, 67n4, 74, 85, 144–146, 151, 207, 210, 219, 263, 346
Digital divide, 220
Digital literacy, 308, 311
Digital technology/digital technologies, 17

Digital tool, 11, 15, 18, 26, 43, 57–61, 70, 75–77
DingTalk, 139, 337–339, 344
Disaster, vin2, 13, 14, 74, 104, 132, 247, 295
Discussions, 2, 5, 13, 16, 25, 26, 41–46, 60, 61, 64–77, 87–89, 104–106, 112, 130–132, 135, 147, 156–158, 190, 193, 241, 242, 246, 247, 254, 259, 263, 264, 277, 284, 298, 299, 303–305, 307, 312–319, 321, 335, 336, 342–345, 350, 363–367
Dishonesty, 61, 352, 354, 358
Distance education, 2, 8, 24, 25, 40, 64, 113, 186, 207, 216, 221, 247, 248, 254, 364
Distance language learning (DLL), 24–25, 27–28
Distance teaching, 29, 30, 57, 91–93, 104, 107, 207, 210, 214, 216
Distraction, 13, 68, 76, 141, 154, 255, 318
DLL, *see* Distance language learning

E

Ecology of resources, 9, 326–328, 330, 339, 344
Educational environment, 204, 221, 222
Educational resource gap, 220
Educational technology, 181, 235, 237
Education reform, 237
Effective language activities, 247, 248

Effectiveness, 16, 157, 217, 240, 263, 350, 352, 356–357, 365
Efficacy of online training, 105
E-learning, 91, 107, 181, 206, 207, 216, 237–240, 248
E-learning habit, 245
Electronic devices, 13, 65, 69, 76, 145
Emergency, vii, 3, 11, 14, 25, 57–77, 87, 99, 107, 113, 122, 133–139, 151, 156–159, 167, 173, 176, 203, 291, 296, 310, 326, 343, 345, 346
Emergency online teaching, 57, 62, 173
Emergency remote teaching (ERT), vii, 3, 7–9, 11–13, 15, 16, 18, 23, 24, 27–32, 34–36, 41–43, 45–47, 57, 60, 98, 99, 111–135, 157, 159, 172–173, 203–205, 208–222, 247, 248, 295–322, 342, 365, 366, 368
Chinese, 23–47, 111–134, 139, 220
Emoji, 304
Empathetic language, 258–260
Empathic listening, 259–261
Empathy, 9, 17, 34, 45, 47, 253–267, 313
Empirical studies, viii, 16, 350, 351, 364
Engagement, 9, 157, 188, 194, 198, 261, 266, 296–298, 304–306, 308, 313–315, 317, 319–322
Engagement strategies, 9, 296, 306, 314, 315, 320–322
Engaging, 12, 42, 152, 157, 174, 177, 179, 185, 189, 196, 197, 273, 288, 314

Index

Entirely online, 6, 113, 172–174, 178, 179, 360
Environment, 8, 12, 17, 26, 38, 43, 44, 46, 94, 113–121, 125, 141, 145, 151, 153, 154, 156, 157, 159, 167, 170n3, 172, 185–200, 204, 209, 215, 217, 221, 222, 241, 244, 254, 262–264, 266, 284, 286–288, 291, 295–297, 299, 301, 310, 311, 315–317, 319, 321, 326–328, 330–335, 339–343, 346, 362, 364
ERT, *see* Emergency remote teaching
Europe, x, 6, 111, 205, 256
Evaluation, 8, 25, 28, 86, 93, 116, 135–140, 155, 173–174, 194, 195, 203, 215, 259, 261, 271, 290
Examination, 29, 91, 115, 116, 126, 128, 130, 132, 133, 136–139, 149, 169, 199, 208, 220, 222, 275, 280, 328, 330, 335, 336, 342, 344
Exchange students, 237

FaceTime, 358, 362
Face-to-face class, 25, 33, 35, 39, 46, 68, 88, 141, 149, 150, 152–154, 159, 200, 204, 208, 215–218, 273, 299, 355, 360
Face-to-face classroom teaching, 236, 242, 263, 333
Face-to-face (F2F), 4, 13, 14, 17, 18, 24, 25, 27–29, 35, 38, 42, 45–47, 57–59, 61, 62, 64, 68, 71, 73, 76, 85–88, 94, 96, 99, 122, 128, 135–140, 149, 150, 153, 154, 156, 159, 168, 172–177, 179, 182–184, 186, 191, 195, 196, 198, 200, 216–218, 235, 237–239, 242, 244, 247, 265, 270, 295, 304, 311, 313, 315–318, 320, 331, 334, 336, 339, 340, 356, 357, 361, 363, 366
Face-to-face instruction, 14, 41, 219, 325, 330, 331, 333–335, 337, 343, 346, 350, 364
Faculty, viii, 25, 138, 140, 153, 168, 203, 206, 211–214, 217, 241, 295–297, 302–305, 307, 309, 310, 312–322, 349, 357
Faculty development (FD), 206, 210
Fatigue, 13, 38, 45, 118, 133, 217
Feedback, 4, 9, 15, 24, 25, 30, 32, 34, 35, 45, 61–63, 69, 71, 76, 87, 88, 90, 96, 97, 99–101, 103, 106, 119, 126, 128, 152, 154, 156, 171, 173–178, 186, 188, 190, 193–200, 220, 239, 242, 244, 248, 261, 264, 270, 277–287, 290, 291, 300, 306, 311–315, 335, 336, 338
#FeesMustFall, 112
Figure, 36, 86, 93, 104, 120, 121, 168, 216, 253, 281, 342
Finding/findings, 7–15, 17, 28, 37, 40, 45, 46, 59, 64–75, 97, 99, 126, 133, 141–155, 159, 176, 204, 211–218, 301–314, 318, 319, 321, 322, 329–343, 349–368
First Generation Students (FGS), 205, 215

Flexibility/flexible, 5, 14, 15, 17, 24, 45, 65–66, 75, 77, 141, 270, 287, 298, 317, 342, 345, 366
Flipped/blended, 9, 18, 269–292, 357
Flipped classroom, 89, 207
Focus, x, 2, 12, 14, 40, 44, 64, 69, 90, 123, 132, 143, 153, 168, 170n2, 182, 188, 219, 239, 245, 246, 248, 256, 264, 278, 283, 287, 288, 290, 297, 299, 308, 309, 354, 366
Focus group discussion, 246, 247
Fortune, vi, vin2, vii
Framework, viii, 9, 188, 296, 297, 299, 300, 312, 321, 326–328
Freshmen, 205, 215–217, 220
Full-time academic staff, 206
Fully online, vii–ix, 4–6, 9, 11, 14, 16–19, 19n4, 58, 60, 73, 74, 176, 179, 217, 269–292, 334, 350–357, 359–361, 363, 366
Future preferences, 354, 356–357
Future teaching, 18, 62, 296, 311, 352, 354, 357, 366

G
Gamified learning, 135–139, 147, 154, 156
Germany, 6, 7, 10, 11, 15, 58, 59, 67, 67n4, 68, 72, 75, 77
Global, vii, 20, 28, 57, 91, 248, 295, 325, 326, 329, 330, 332, 335, 341–345, 351, 351n1, 367
Google Classroom, 50, 61, 135–139, 146, 155, 161, 238, 357
Google Meet, 92, 238, 358, 362

Grammar, 26, 29, 30, 33, 42, 60, 68, 73, 75, 76, 79, 96, 97, 126, 135–139, 147, 153, 188, 191, 194, 206, 271–275, 277, 282, 287–290, 311, 342
Graphics Interchange Formats (GIFs), 153, 304

H
Handwriting, 12, 13, 26, 27, 32, 33, 35–38, 40, 41, 43–45, 47, 50, 70–73, 76, 78, 79, 91, 126–128, 132, 174, 179, 336, 342
Handwritten, 30, 32, 33, 35, 43, 44, 47, 60, 61, 70, 125–128, 132, 155
Hierarchy, 318, 320
History, 8, 16, 94, 152, 182, 183
Homework, 18, 30, 33, 34, 40, 45, 60, 61, 71, 75, 76, 78, 79, 135–140, 146, 148–150, 155, 163, 164, 185, 259, 260, 274, 275, 278–280, 285, 338, 339, 342
Hong Kong, 3, 7, 8, 235–248
HSK, 97, 135–139, 141, 142, 160, 169
Human beings, vi
Human society, 4, 20, 366
Hybrid, viii, 4, 5, 14, 15, 17, 24, 27, 113, 216, 312, 334, 355, 356, 366
Hybrid-blended, 214
Hybrid class, 207, 217
Hybrid flexible (HyFlex), 5, 214, 366

Index

ICT utilization, 203, 204, 210
Impact, 15, 18, 32, 43, 44, 57, 69, 151, 191, 195, 200, 208, 311, 314, 321, 327, 352, 354, 357, 359, 361–362, 366
Implications, 41–46, 107, 133, 156–158, 204, 314, 316, 319–321, 363–367
Independent clause, 245
Individual needs, 178
Inflexibility, 318
Information and communication technologies (ICT),), 203, 204, 206, 207, 210, 216, 217, 219, 220, 239, 240, 246, 319
Informatization, 219
Innovation, 20, 187, 256, 266
Institutional Research (IR), 210
Institutional supports, 43
Instruction, 2, 3, 6, 10–12, 14, 16–18, 19n2, 24–26, 29–34, 36, 38, 39, 41–46, 85, 95, 97, 113, 128, 195, 206, 215, 217, 219, 237, 244, 245, 254, 263, 271, 284, 289, 290, 296–299, 306, 311, 315, 320, 321, 325, 330, 331, 333–337, 342, 343, 345, 346, 350, 364, 366
Instructional design, 182, 207, 223, 335
Instructional modes, 4, 10, 14, 16, 17, 214, 352, 357, 361, 366
Instructors, vii, 2, 4, 6–18, 20, 24, 27–36, 38–40, 43–46, 48, 58, 85, 87, 92, 93, 95, 96, 105, 107, 113, 117, 119–121, 125, 127, 133, 138–140, 146, 150–155, 168, 171, 178, 218, 219, 239–241, 245–248, 261, 264, 265, 269, 270, 273–281, 283–285, 287–292, 295–322, 325, 327, 329–345, 349–368
Integration, viii, 186, 221, 262, 270, 275–281, 296
Integration process, 270, 275–282
Interaction, 2, 12, 18, 24, 25, 30, 39, 42, 43, 45, 57, 58, 61, 66–71, 75, 78, 87–90, 93, 95, 97, 99, 103–107, 113, 114, 117, 118, 121, 122, 125, 128, 133, 135–139, 141, 147, 151, 154, 157, 161, 184–187, 190, 193, 194, 196–198, 204, 205, 217–219, 244, 255, 259–261, 263, 264, 266, 271, 276, 296, 297, 301, 302, 304, 306, 307, 313–316, 319, 327, 328, 334–336, 338–341, 343–345, 352, 353, 364, 365, 368
Interactive, 12, 17, 25, 32, 70, 106, 112, 123, 156, 174, 179, 190, 198, 217, 240, 244, 254, 256, 306, 316, 318, 339
Interactivity, 105, 187, 305, 313–315, 319, 320
Interlocutors, 264
International Chinese education program, 236
Internationalization, 204, 237
International undergraduates, 237
Internet, vii, viii, 2–5, 12, 16, 28, 30, 35, 42, 58, 60, 67, 67n4, 68, 73, 76, 78, 97, 101, 105, 116, 118, 119, 135–139, 141, 144, 145, 151, 152, 155, 158, 159, 171, 177, 181, 209, 217, 241, 275, 286, 299, 331, 332, 334, 339, 350, 368

Internet access, 117, 158
Interview, 7, 8, 17, 28, 30–37, 41, 174–178, 264, 270, 274, 281, 300, 301, 312, 322, 345, 368
Italian academics, 93
Italian universities courses, 86
Italy, 6, 7, 85, 86, 91, 92, 94

J

Japan, 4, 7, 8, 13, 17, 184, 203–222, 246, 329
Japanese universities, 203–223

K

Knowledge and skills, 9, 20, 210, 308, 309, 320, 321, 326, 327, 330, 338, 339, 341–342, 345

L

Language courses, vii, 7–9, 11, 13–17, 19, 29, 30, 44, 59–61, 64, 76, 87, 89–91, 94–96, 123, 138, 168, 169, 173, 182, 186–188, 207, 222, 237, 238, 241, 269, 292, 313, 332–334, 360
Language education, 20, 25, 187, 211, 248, 321, 350
Language games, 244–246
Language teaching theory, 235
Learner autonomy, 24, 217, 219, 220
Learning, vii, 2, 23, 57–77, 85–107, 111, 135–159, 168, 181–201, 203–223, 237, 254, 270, 295, 326, 349–368

Learning Management System (LMS), 11, 57, 138, 146, 170n3, 181, 183, 207, 209, 210, 219, 220, 260, 352, 354, 357–358, 363
Learning outcomes, 7, 27, 87, 171, 183, 191, 197, 255, 296–298, 308–310, 318, 352–354, 356, 359, 364, 365, 367
Lectures, 4, 16, 19, 24, 44, 75, 85, 112, 115, 117, 123, 126, 127, 139, 141, 145, 146, 150, 151, 153, 173, 183, 184, 196, 200, 201, 208, 217, 242, 311, 318, 331, 337
Limitations, 27, 30, 36, 41–46, 68, 76, 123, 133–134, 145, 158, 221–223, 241, 321, 345–346, 367–368
Listening, 34, 40, 43, 62, 67, 73, 79, 97, 102, 138, 178, 185, 191, 193, 239, 259–261, 264, 274, 279, 289, 290, 329, 337–339
Listening comprehension, 170, 238, 239, 246, 279, 290
Listening skills, 184, 199, 240, 276
Lockdown, 68, 99, 112, 121, 125, 129, 132, 133, 135–141, 146, 148, 150, 158, 160, 161, 167, 191, 199, 200, 332–334
Low-tech, 116
L2 Chinese learners, 325–346
Luckin, R., 326, 327, 330

M

Mandarin as a second language, 242
Massey University, 8, 181–201

Massive Open Online Courses (MOOCs), 64, 89, 90, 113, 122, 183, 350
Materials for asynchronous self-study, 103, 106
Mauritius, 6, 7, 135–159
Memes, 304
Mental health challenge, 118, 119
Methodology, 62–63, 139–140, 159, 299–301, 315, 328–329, 345, 352–354
Microphone, 35, 119, 152, 154, 162
Microsoft Teams, 39, 92, 95–97, 117, 238, 358, 362
Milan, 98
Misfortune, vi, vin2, vii
Model, 186, 207, 216, 221, 239, 256, 259, 260, 263–266, 276, 287, 291, 326, 327, 330, 339
Monitor the level of learning, 103, 106
Moodle, 11, 25, 26, 30, 32–34, 61, 70, 71, 181, 183, 238, 357
Motivation, 40, 44, 47, 68–71, 76, 107, 124, 133, 150, 157, 172, 184, 194, 248, 261, 264, 265, 285, 286, 313, 335
Movement, 8, 13, 33, 91, 154, 238
Multiple choice questions, 63, 98, 101, 238
Mute, 135–139, 151, 155

N

Network-Based Language Teaching (NLBT), 214
Network infrastructure, 204, 209
New Zealand, 6, 8, 27, 58, 181–201, 255
Noise, 13, 33, 141, 151, 155, 288, 289
Notes, x, xi, 15, 33–35, 37, 40, 50, 73, 90, 145, 151, 153, 244, 273, 274, 277, 278, 280, 282–284, 286, 288, 290, 301, 345
Number, 358

O

Offline, 68, 71, 73, 135–139, 149, 150, 161, 163
Online, vin3, vii–ix, 2–7, 23–25, 36–41, 58, 58n1, 60, 61, 65, 85–107, 112–114, 117, 135–159, 167, 170, 172, 173, 350–353
Online Chinese, vii, ix, 6, 9, 13, 16, 17, 86, 90, 91, 158, 171, 181–201, 222, 253–267, 333, 334, 349–368
Online class, 13, 37–39, 45, 49, 66, 69, 70, 95, 104, 135–141, 143–145, 147, 149–153, 156, 157, 159, 160, 162, 164, 213, 215–218, 228, 255, 331, 333, 338, 343, 344, 365
Online course, viii, 11, 12, 14, 15, 18, 25, 27, 64, 66, 71, 74, 76, 78, 86–89, 92, 98–100, 102, 105, 106, 113, 151, 158, 182, 188, 199, 208, 210, 215, 216, 219, 256, 259, 270, 283, 286–291, 299, 317, 318, 332, 342, 349, 350, 352–354, 356, 357, 359, 361, 362, 365, 366
Online delivery, 13, 23, 150, 167, 170, 174, 176, 177, 179, 359

Online education, vii, viii, 25, 47, 66, 75, 77, 204, 209–210, 247, 255, 259, 350, 365, 368
Online learning, vii, 3, 10, 12, 13, 16–18, 24, 26, 28, 31, 37–43, 46, 48–50, 57, 58, 62, 64–76, 78, 88, 94, 113, 114, 139–141, 146–147, 149–151, 156–159, 181–183, 187–200, 211, 216, 256, 263, 266, 296, 312, 341, 350, 351, 353, 356, 359–365, 368
Online questionnaire, 63, 86, 98, 245
Online resources, 146, 148, 156, 273, 280, 292
Online teaching, vii, viii, 3, 9, 11, 12, 15–18, 25, 27, 30, 40, 43, 47, 48, 57–64, 67, 68, 72–74, 76, 86–96, 98, 99, 101, 103, 113, 122, 124, 125, 135–140, 144, 149–151, 157–159, 163, 172, 173, 174n4, 175–177, 182, 189, 199, 204, 208, 210, 213, 217, 219, 220, 236, 238, 240–248, 258, 259, 263, 266, 278, 281, 296, 298, 299, 318, 320, 322, 332, 335, 345, 346, 350–356, 362, 363, 365, 366, 368
Open e-books, 220
Opportunity/opportunities, v–vii, ix, xi, 18, 20, 24, 28, 36, 37, 41–43, 49, 65, 66, 71, 72, 76, 77, 87, 93, 102–106, 112, 123, 125, 127, 128, 139, 153, 154, 159, 169, 173, 174, 178, 179, 183, 184, 186, 187, 189–191, 193, 194, 196, 198, 200, 201, 204, 205, 208, 246, 248, 261, 265, 275, 277, 284, 287, 296–298, 302, 308, 310, 313, 317, 319, 320, 334, 338, 341–345, 351
Organized, 19n4, 40, 95, 96, 151, 154, 158, 177, 241, 242, 247, 261, 262, 308, 312, 313, 319, 321, 322
Outcomes, 7, 23, 27, 28, 31, 34, 40, 45–46, 58, 67, 71, 78, 87, 121, 126, 135, 169, 171, 183, 191, 197, 247, 255, 264, 296–298, 308–310, 318, 352–354, 356, 359, 364, 365, 367
Overview, vii, ix, 1–20, 26, 58, 168–169, 182–183, 204–207, 269

P

Pandemic, vi–ix, xi, 3, 6–11, 13, 14, 16–20, 19n2, 19n4, 23, 24, 27, 28, 30, 34, 45, 46, 57–59, 63, 65, 68–72, 75–77, 91–97, 111, 112, 124, 125, 135–159, 163, 167–179, 199–200, 203–223, 235, 236, 239–245, 247, 257, 261, 295, 296, 303, 305, 308, 309, 317, 318, 325–346, 350–352, 354, 355, 358, 360, 363, 365, 366
Participants, 11–13, 19, 19n4, 20, 28, 29, 33, 36, 44–46, 60, 62n3, 63–68, 70–73, 76, 86, 88, 92, 93, 96, 99, 100, 104, 211, 215, 222, 241, 299–322, 326, 328, 329, 331, 345, 356, 359, 363, 367

Part-time teacher, 205, 206, 210, 212, 213, 220
Pattern drills, 242
Pedagogical shift, 247, 248
Pedagogical skills, 207, 311, 320, 322
Pedagogy, 107, 182, 248, 267, 309, 318, 321, 322, 327
Peer-assistance, 244
Peer-learning, 244
People, vi, ix, 3, 9, 66, 68, 69, 138, 167, 184, 196, 236, 247, 262, 275, 283–285, 287, 291, 304, 305, 325–327, 329, 330, 336, 339–344
Perceptions, vii, 7, 10, 39–41, 46, 57–78, 236, 241, 245–248, 255, 351, 353, 360, 365, 368
Perspectives, v, 8, 27, 36, 58, 65, 92, 158, 179, 197, 213, 255, 287, 313, 315, 316, 318, 319, 321, 343, 349–368
Phonograph, 2, 4
Physical and human resources, 204, 209–210, 218
Pinyin, 26, 105, 125, 127, 135–139, 146, 152, 170, 272
Plagiarism, 352, 354, 358, 366
Platform and course deliver, 99–100, 104
Platform usability and access to materials, 99
Postsecondary, 364
PowerPoint, 44, 57, 59, 61, 135–139, 141, 145–147, 151, 153, 155, 156, 161, 272, 301, 309, 336
Practice, vii–ix, 7, 8, 10, 15–19, 29–31, 40, 42–44, 70–71, 73, 76, 91, 93, 98–106, 113, 126, 127, 151, 154, 169, 170, 177, 182, 184, 185, 188, 189, 191, 193, 194, 197–201, 206, 215, 219, 221, 235, 236, 240, 242, 245, 246, 248, 263, 270, 274, 276, 277, 279, 281, 283, 285, 287–290, 302, 305, 306, 308, 310, 313–315, 322, 336, 338–342, 344, 351–353, 361, 368
Precis writing, 125–127
Preference, 15, 17, 36, 37, 58, 62–64, 73–75, 79, 141, 176, 357, 359, 361
Presentation, 19n4, 25, 57, 61, 88, 127, 133, 145, 146, 151, 153, 197, 206, 244, 280, 292, 300, 317, 342
Problems, 12, 13, 24, 35, 36, 38, 40, 42, 43, 58, 66–68, 72, 73, 76–78, 86, 88, 89, 97, 101, 103–106, 111, 145, 152, 177, 218, 255, 264, 278, 284, 286, 297, 298, 307, 352
Productive skills, 270, 271
Professional development, 20, 266, 309, 310, 320–322
Proficiency level, 15, 46, 190, 302, 321, 355
Program/programs, vii, viii, 4, 7, 8, 12, 14, 17, 19, 26–29, 34, 58–60, 75, 94–96, 105, 113, 136–139, 168–170, 173, 181–187, 236, 240–242, 255, 270, 274, 300, 304, 313, 320, 335, 340, 350, 351, 356, 368

Pronunciation, 26, 30, 31, 35, 36, 39–41, 43, 48, 71, 72, 125, 135–139, 152, 154, 170, 186, 187, 191, 192, 194, 195, 197, 215, 240, 261, 274, 306, 342, 357
Pronunciation drills, 239, 242
Pronunciation practices, 238, 240
Putonghua, 237

Q

Quality of online teaching, 220
Question, x, 28, 31, 36–41, 37n1, 47–49, 62, 62n3, 63, 67, 71, 85, 90, 94, 96, 98–100, 104, 105, 113, 115–120, 125, 127, 135–141, 147, 148, 152, 154, 155, 171, 173–178, 188, 190, 192–195, 198, 211–213, 215, 238, 241, 242, 244, 246, 259, 264, 272–274, 278–280, 283, 284, 286, 288–290, 292, 297–300, 304, 307, 320, 321, 326, 328, 330, 336, 339, 340, 342, 351–354, 359, 360, 362, 367
Questionnaire surveys, 203, 204, 211, 212, 221–223, 245
Quiet place, 13, 40, 45, 69, 78, 286, 288, 289, 331
Quizlet, 61, 75, 76, 191, 198, 336, 337, 344, 358, 362

R

Raise Your Hand, 155, 156
Rapport, 12, 178, 291, 300, 302–304, 313

Reading, 16, 26, 33, 91, 94, 97, 102, 127, 135–139, 147, 148, 153, 158, 159, 163, 169, 183, 187, 193, 259, 261–264, 273–275, 289, 307, 338
Reading comprehension, 238, 240, 275, 290
Reading skills, 32, 240
Real-time, 133, 186, 199, 218, 306, 315, 336, 338, 344, 352–354, 358, 359, 362, 367
Receptive skills, 270, 271
Reconfiguration, 325–346
  See also Restructure; Reconfigure
Reconfigure, 167, 326, 329, 330, 342, 344, 345
Reflection, 17, 69, 74, 88, 124, 135, 140, 158, 167–179, 195, 203, 235–248, 255, 280, 298, 303, 305, 314, 315, 329, 345
Remote delivery, 333–337, 339, 342, 343, 345, 346
Remote instruction, *see* Remote delivery; Remote teaching
Remote synchronous teaching, 9
Remote teaching, 4, 8, 9, 12–16, 24, 25, 33, 58, 107, 168, 203, 204, 208, 215–217, 221, 320, 326, 332–334, 336, 337, 343, 345, 346
Remote teaching and learning, vii, 3, 4, 8, 12, 18, 211, 214, 218–221
Re-reporting, 6, 219, 258–260, 364
Research, vii, viii, 7, 16–18, 23–25, 27–28, 41–43, 45–47, 59, 62, 63, 86, 93, 98, 104–106, 126, 158, 159, 169, 183, 204, 211, 220–223, 248, 255, 274, 297,

Index

300, 310, 319–321, 328–330, 342, 345–346, 350, 351, 367–368
Residential, viii, 8, 10, 19, 29, 172, 179
Resources, 9, 11, 18, 25, 28, 32, 58, 85, 88, 89, 107, 114, 126, 138, 146, 148, 156, 159, 170–173, 177, 179, 185, 186, 190, 191, 204, 207, 209–210, 215, 216, 218, 220–222, 236, 237, 241, 255, 259, 260, 273, 274, 286, 291, 292, 296, 302, 325–346, 362, 366, 368
Restructure, 326
#RhodesMustFall, 112
Role of teachers, 263–267
Role playing, 17
Roma Tre, 7, 94–98, 100

S

Satisfaction, 12, 13, 39, 46, 73, 75, 99, 104, 105, 107, 140–144, 147, 150, 151, 174–176, 179, 190, 204, 213–216, 353, 359, 361, 363, 364, 367
Satisfaction level, 174, 175
Schemata, 245
Screen Share, 135–139, 146, 155, 156
Server systems, 209
Session, 5, 12, 13, 16, 17, 30, 32, 34, 35, 39, 42–44, 60, 65, 66, 70–72, 123, 139, 153, 154, 184, 187, 198, 210, 239, 242, 244, 247, 259, 274, 279, 281, 283, 285, 288, 289, 310,
311, 313, 329, 333, 336, 340, 365
Sharing of materials and PPT, 102, 103
Shift to remote teaching, 107
Short-answer questions, 238
Site, 114, 117, 170n3, 171, 177, 185, 206, 273, 320, 329
Situational speaking topics, 238
Skype, 28, 30, 31, 33, 34, 38, 39, 49, 50, 104, 238, 358, 362
Small group, 87–89, 105, 154, 178, 244, 274, 276, 289, 307, 316, 319, 336
Social distancing/social distance, vii, 6, 18, 70, 139, 167, 236, 351
Social networking, 18, 240
Social presence, 9, 12, 87, 88, 189, 190, 196, 297, 298, 302–305, 312–314, 316, 319
Socio-economic situations, 237
South Africa, 3, 6, 7, 111–134, 359
Speaking, 15, 24, 36, 37, 42, 67, 69, 71, 72, 79, 86, 97–105, 138, 151, 154, 169, 184, 185, 191, 193, 198, 199, 240, 246, 271, 274, 276, 278, 280–285, 287, 289, 290, 307, 314, 329, 337, 338, 340, 341, 362
Speaking ability, 240
Speaking and writing practice, 100–101
Speaking exercises, 101, 238, 239
Spoken, 106, 169–171, 174n4, 280, 284, 285, 340
Spontaneity, 296, 298, 306, 315
Stakeholders, vii, 16–18, 25, 217, 219–221, 345, 350

Strategy/strategies, 8, 9, 23, 34, 36, 68, 93, 107, 112, 114, 135, 140, 151, 152, 155, 156, 158, 167, 170, 177–179, 188, 190, 193, 195, 197, 200, 218–221, 248, 255, 269–292, 296, 299, 300, 303, 305, 306, 308, 310, 311, 313–315, 318–322, 352, 353, 367
Structure, 12, 44, 93, 96, 193, 194, 204, 209, 219–221, 245, 283, 286, 292, 296–299, 302, 307–310, 318, 319, 321, 353
Student perception, 57–77, 368
Students, vii, 1, 24, 57–77, 85, 111, 168, 182, 203, 235, 254, 269, 295, 325
Students protests, 112
Student-student interaction, 34, 66, 88, 187, 244, 314
Success, 13, 17, 27, 43, 47, 64, 76, 114, 121, 125, 132, 133, 186, 194, 222, 255, 292, 297, 299, 312, 319, 320, 331
Survey, 6–9, 13–15, 17, 28, 31, 36–41, 48–50, 58n1, 59, 62–64, 62n3, 68, 75, 77–79, 117, 119, 135, 139–155, 158, 159, 195–197, 203, 204, 211–218, 221–223, 228, 239–242, 245, 246, 340, 351–363, 367, 368
Survey results, 118, 224–228
Survive, 112, 121, 133
Sustainable development, 219
Synchronicity, 305, 306, 315, 316
Synchronous, 3, 9, 12, 14–17, 23, 24, 28–30, 32, 38, 42–44, 87, 88, 90, 94–97, 103, 106, 116, 117, 122, 126, 128, 133, 140, 173, 181, 184, 187, 189, 198–201, 207, 209, 214–218, 235, 236, 238–248, 276–278, 281, 283–289, 291, 298, 306, 309–311, 315, 322, 336, 340, 344, 350, 354, 357–358 interaction, 133
Synchronous and asynchronous teaching, 88, 241
Synchronous communication, 88, 181, 352, 353, 359, 362
Synchronous interaction, 43, 88, 133, 365
Synchronous online language teaching, 235–248
Synchronous online teaching platform, 238, 242, 244, 246, 248
Synchronously, 106, 214, 277, 286, 306, 308, 309, 312, 316, 317, 332, 344, 366

T

Talks, 66, 135–139, 158, 198, 246, 272, 273, 275, 277, 278, 280, 284, 285, 291, 336
Teacher education, 320, 322
Teachers' concerns, 241
Teacher-student communication patterns, 248
Teaching, v, vii–ix, 2–18, 20, 26–28, 30, 32–34, 42, 43, 45–46, 48, 57–64, 67, 68, 70–77, 79, 85–99, 101, 103, 104, 107, 111–159, 167–179, 181–201, 203–223, 235–248, 254–256, 258–261, 263–267, 270, 276,

Index   389

277, 284–285, 289, 291, 292, 295–302, 304–306, 308–322, 326, 329–338, 340, 342–346, 349–368
Teaching Chinese as a Foreign Language (TCFL), viii, 171, 172, 204–206, 219, 221–223
Teaching effectiveness, 157, 352, 354, 356–357, 365
Teaching experience, 14, 23–47, 135–140, 150–151, 218, 220, 296, 322, 352–355, 357, 363
Teaching method, 46, 135–140, 147, 159, 209, 254, 255, 265, 302
Teaching presence, 9, 11, 190, 196, 295–322
Teaching technique, 46, 135–139, 147–148, 153–154, 156–158
Team leaders, 264
Technical, 11, 12, 24, 27, 28, 30–32, 35, 40, 42, 43, 46, 67, 72–74, 91, 93, 133, 135–140, 144–145, 151–156, 161, 162, 190, 198, 199, 235, 238, 242, 247, 255, 264, 310, 315, 319, 346, 352, 357–358
Technical problem, 66–68, 72, 76, 97, 145, 177
Technological pedagogical content knowledge, 316, 318
Technology, viii, 2, 3, 5, 16–18, 23–27, 43, 112, 114, 138, 171–173, 181, 186, 187, 200, 201, 203, 207, 217, 235, 237, 246, 247, 270, 296, 300, 301, 304, 308–310, 315–322, 326, 327, 334, 340, 344, 345, 353, 361, 363, 368

Tencent, 337
Tencent Meeting, 139, 256, 358, 362
Tertiary, 136, 137
Tertiary institution, 236, 237
  See also Postsecondary
Textbook, 20, 37, 50, 95–97, 125, 127, 128, 137, 174n4, 185, 190, 204, 210, 257, 258n1, 270, 273, 286, 335, 345
Text material, 214, 224, 226
Theory of empathy, 253–256, 259, 265
Time management, 15, 35, 65, 255, 285, 357, 361
Togetherness, 133, 302
Tone/tones, 40, 90, 152, 154, 170, 194, 274, 292, 306
Tools, 2, 9, 11, 15, 18, 19, 30, 38, 42, 45, 57–61, 68, 75–77, 88–90, 97, 104, 105, 107, 114, 116–117, 133, 153, 156, 170, 181, 186–188, 190, 192, 196, 197, 276, 306, 308–310, 315, 316, 326, 327, 330, 332, 334–339, 342–345, 352–354, 357–359, 362, 363, 367
Topical presentation, 244
Traditional pedagogical methods, 206
Training, viii, 11, 12, 24–27, 43, 62, 67, 72, 73, 76, 86, 98, 105, 107, 135–139, 158, 204, 210, 217, 219, 237, 239, 241, 242, 247, 248, 263, 333, 345, 350, 353, 356–357, 363
Training regarding distance teaching, 92

Transition, 6, 7, 10–12, 16, 29, 58, 60, 95, 115, 124, 140, 150, 174, 176, 203, 254, 270, 275–283, 287, 291, 296, 301, 305, 310, 317, 330–333, 335–337, 340, 351, 352, 354, 355, 360, 365
Transitioned, 64, 75, 281, 291, 296
Types of remote teaching, 214–215, 222
Typing characters, 33, 105, 336

U
UCT, see University of Cape Town
Undergraduate programs, 169
University, 7–10, 12, 17, 25, 28–30, 44, 46, 57–77, 85–107, 111–114, 116, 117, 123, 135–159, 167–179, 181–201, 203–223, 237, 238, 240–242, 245, 253–267, 275, 281, 286, 299, 320, 321, 329–339, 341, 343–345, 359
University curriculum, 237
University of Cape Town (UCT), 3, 7, 13, 111–134
University of Milan, 7, 94, 96–98
Utilization of ICT, 206, 219

V
Venues of training, 353, 355
Videoconferencing, 26, 29, 33–36, 42, 43, 304, 306, 308, 315, 319, 322
Video material, 185, 214, 224, 226
Videos, 2, 18, 19, 25, 34, 60, 61, 67, 87, 89, 91, 97, 102, 104, 115, 116, 138, 146, 156, 183, 187, 190, 191, 193, 195, 198, 207, 209, 256, 259, 260, 272–275, 277, 278, 280, 283, 286–288, 290, 300, 301, 305, 335–338
Virtual
  campus, 116
  classroom, 13, 58, 115, 121, 122, 124, 177, 244, 315, 317, 334–337, 343
  lectures, 126
Visualization, 5, 189, 220
Vocabulary, 26, 29, 30, 32, 33, 42, 60, 73, 75, 79, 95, 135–139, 151, 153, 174n4, 188, 191, 192, 194, 195, 197, 206, 239, 257–258, 272–275, 282, 287, 290, 292, 311, 336, 342
Vocabulary exercises, 238, 239
Voices of students, 239–241
VoiceThread, 274, 289, 358, 362
Vula, 114–117, 124, 126–128

W
WeChat, 18, 28, 135–139, 146, 158, 171, 172, 189, 190, 256, 354, 358, 362, 363, 367
WhatsApp, 39, 117, 135–139, 146, 152, 155, 156, 161, 362
Whiteboard, 61, 135–139, 146, 152, 153, 162, 187, 274, 278, 283, 315, 336
Willingness, 14, 99, 100, 159, 352–354, 356–357, 359, 361, 366

Workload, 69, 126, 135–139, 150, 151, 197, 199, 200, 310, 311, 319, 320
Workshop/workshops, 11, 19, 19n4, 138, 177, 206, 210, 241, 242, 331, 332, 355
World Health Organization (WHO), vin4, 236, 351
Writing
  character writing, 61, 70, 72, 76
  handwriting, 70–72, 76
Written, v, 7, 26, 33, 61, 63, 71, 88–90, 96, 97, 103, 105, 106, 125, 128, 132, 138, 148, 152, 158, 169, 179, 193–196, 209, 212, 273–275, 280, 289, 290, 298, 311, 336, 340, 352

Z

Zero-rated
  internet access, 117
  site, 117
Zhejiang Sci-Tech University (ZSTU), 9, 135–139
Zoom, 2, 5, 18, 28, 60, 61, 65, 66, 92, 105, 117, 124, 135–139, 143, 144, 146, 147, 150, 151, 154, 156–158, 173, 178, 191, 195, 199, 200, 209, 218, 238, 241, 244–247, 270, 276–278, 284, 307, 309–311, 317, 318, 336, 337, 339, 340, 344, 358, 362, 367

Printed in the United States
by Baker & Taylor Publisher Services